Traces of God In A Secular Culture

Traces of God In A Secular Culture

George F. McLean, O.M.I.

alba house

DIVISION OF THE SOCIETY OF ST. PAUL
STATEN ISLAND, N.Y. 10314

154979

Current Printing (*last digit*):

9 8 7 6 5 4 3 2 1

LIBRARY OF CONGRESS
CATALOGING IN PUBLICATION DATA

McLean, George F
Traces of God in a secular culture.

Includes bibliographical references.
1. God.   2. Religion—Philosophy.   I. Title.
BT102.M25   211   73-3141
ISBN   0-8189-0268-X

DESIGNED, PRINTED AND BOUND IN THE UNITED STATES
OF AMERICA BY THE FATHERS AND BROTHERS OF THE
SOCIETY OF ST. PAUL, 2187 VICTORY BOULEVARD,
STATEN ISLAND, NEW YORK 10314 AS PART OF
THEIR COMMUNICATIONS APOSTOLATE.

Foreword

IN THE KALEIDOSCOPE variations of our culture there appear in startling contrast not only an affirmation of man but a search somehow to proceed beyond him. Thus, the fascination with human consciousness becomes a drive to enter into psychological dimensions as yet unexperienced; the focus upon community begins to burst the bonds of the established structure; and the passion for peace flows over into an ideal that has always surpassed human realization. In a dialectical manner, there seems to have arisen from the denial of all except man a search beyond oneself for the key to truly human meaning. In the heart of contemporary culture there appears to be developing a new search for God.

The roots both of this denial of the divine and of the initial renewal of the search for a transcendent which has followed were studied extensively in *Religion and Contemporary Thought*. What is needed now is an application of the means which contemporary man has at his disposal for philosophical reflection in order to carry forward the new appreciation which man has of himself and fully evaluate any new indices of the divine which that might imply. In fact, if, as has been suggested, at this stage of the evolution process in which he has become conscious of himself, man must assume responsibility for the direction of his future development, then it is in this radical search for his own meaning that he is preeminently human.

In his "The Problem of God—A Programmatic Essay," Langdon Gilkey examines the nature of this project in some detail. One cannot now turn away from the secular, but must find there the point of departure for any future religious discussions. Dr. Gilkey finds this point of departure in the contingency, relativity, temporality, and autonomy of man. The resulting search for religious meaning will require new modes of discourse concerning God, the sacred will need to be seen differently in future cultures, and philosophy as well as theology will need to take new account of the person. This essay is programmatic rather than definitive;

it suggests the point of departure, but leaves to others the immediate task of actually carrying out this search.

It is the purpose of the three parts of this work to carry this project forward using the contributions of what might be loosely categorized as the three major orders of modern philosophic thought: process and pragmatic philosophy, the philosophy of the person, and linguistic studies.

It would not be incorrect to say, though they seldom use the terms, that the search of the pragmatists is for the authentic dimensions and possibilities of human progress. This concentration upon progress is at the center of the pattern of Anglo-American thought; in fact, its roots are deep within the thought of William James and John Dewey and go to the heart of what is called the Golden Age of American Philosophy. Working essentially with an ethical orientation, pragmatism has concentrated on the processive character of human existence. Future discussions concerning the problem of God, understood as fundamentally concerned with the character of human progress, will need to take account of these pragmatic insights concerning progress, after the manner of the article by E. Fontinell. For its part, recent questions concerning the adequacy of progress as the human goal have renewed the awareness that a broader, religious context is needed in order for progress to be truly human.

What is more, the clarification of the significance of progress for the identification of the existence or nature of God will be quite notably aided by work in metaphysics and aesthetics after the manner of the process philosophy of Alfred North Whitehead. Such work is done in the articles of Walter Stokes, Charles Hartshorne, and Lewis Ford. Once again the search is not simply for an additional being but for the significance of human progress itself. It is argued that if human progress is ultimately founded in a divine for whom it has no meaning, then it is ultimately meaningless. The issue remains a delicate one; the present attempt to realize an autonomy for man that is independent without being either meaningless or exclusive is largely at stake. It is no solution to develop on this basis a notion of the divine which is neither ultimate nor transcendent, for this would be but man himself. The work of the above authors and that of Eulalio Baltazar, concerning the meaning of eternity in view of the significance of process, are all attempts to develop the notion of God in such a way that it not only frees man to be himself but inspires his efforts and crowns his every act.

What can an overall study of the dynamics and dynamism in the mystery of God accomplish? If the distinction of Marcel between problem and mystery has validity, it would be not only too much, but in principle impossible, to speak of achieving a solution. But if, as seems true, this issue is central to man's continual probing for insight concerning himself, then reflection upon the implications of the notion of progress itself should be a first step in the development of the amplitude of man's religious meaning.

In order further to deepen this evolving understanding of oneself and of God it is necessary to combine two elements. The first is a new study of these questions in the light of those contemporary insights concerning the person developed by the various personalist philosophies and existential phenomenologies. The second is a linguistic analysis of the meaningfulness of the language in which philosophers and theologians have carried on their investigations of the notion of God.

It would, of course, be overly simple merely to contrast the work of the existential phenomenologies on the continent with that of the more critically oriented positivistic and analytic philosophers in the Anglo-American countries. On the one hand, the phenomenologies do constitute a critical attempt to recommence the work of philosophy upon a reflectively evaluated basis, and in recent years the phenomenologists have often extended their work to hermeneutics. On the other hand, linguistic analysts have opened a new road to the study of intentional factors. It remains true, nevertheless, that the two approaches stem largely from different roots and that the personalists develop their work on the notion of God in a manner which is predominantly positive while the manner of the analysts is especially critical. Hence, Part II of this volume will be concerned with the study of the person and Part III with linguistic analysis.

Attention to person is central because the key to man's expanded responsibility is his self-awareness. Hence, approaches to philosophizing which concentrate upon reality as found in and through this personal self-consciousness have become increasingly central for the question of God to the degree that this problem began to appear as an authentically human problem—perhaps even *the* authentically human problem. As what previously had been hidden depths of human meaning were brought to light it was also seen that personal meaning must somehow surpass its individual realizations in men. Hence, the question concerning the existence of God was no longer that of the existence of another, even if supreme, being; instead it had become identical with man's search for his own meaning. In this the future of both man and religion were entwined.

Although Martin Heidegger does not directly confront the religious issue, it has seemed necessary to begin the study of the person and of God with an investigation of Heidegger's position concerning the nature and extent of a metaphysics developed upon a phenomenological basis. At present and for the proximate future it would seem that his approach will constitute one of the most important influences upon philosophical and theological thought in the religious field. Hence, it is essential to determine whether this position conceives man by his own powers to be impervious or merely neutral with regard to any knowledge of God. Or should it be said, as does Professor Langan, that within the confines of the phenomenological method, and even in the work of Heidegger as its prime realization, there are as yet undeveloped areas which must be explicitly concerned with the divine.

That such areas do exist in man is, of course, the position of many. It is the direct concern of Maurice Nédoncelle to investigate these areas in detail. In particular he is concerned with identifying the distinctive contribution made by the appreciation of man as authentically personal to the discovery of God, not only as divine, but as a person. Only this summons up in man the fully personal response that constitutes at the same time both man's higher religious life and the achievement of his own most fully personal self-possession.

Gabriel Marcel and Martin Buber are also prime exponents of the development of religious thought upon this basis. The comparison of their work in the paper of Dr. Schwarcz underlines the contrast between the personal response as found in the more simply biblical and intentionally a-philosophical position of Buber, on the one hand, and in the non-systematic but more elaborate Western philosophy of Marcel, on the other.

Common to all these positions on the meaning of the notion of God is an important critique of the classical tradition of Western philosophy and a desire to respond to present human problems. The work of discovering the way in which elements of past thought must be transformed in this new light is begun in the article of Augustin Leonard and strikingly implemented in that of L.-B. Geiger. If the rejection of God in all traditional senses has been considered a prerequisite for an adequate realization of man's freedom, then there is need for this direct confrontation of the many meanings of human freedom, the identification of their order and existential root, and the re-evaluation in this light of their religious dimension.

Though, as mentioned above, there has been an extraordinary cleavage between the approaches to philosophy through language and through person, at no point does this cleavage break down more dramatically than in the investigation of the religious issue. The analytic approach has been significantly influenced by the position of Flew which requires that all meaningful propositions, at least in principle, be able to be falsified, that is, that there be able to be some observable situation from which it could be known that a religious statement is false. This general position has been used by many in the English speaking world to show that contemporary man can make little significant meaning out of religious language. The paper of Kai Nielsen not only sharpens this position, but responds to the attempts of various of its opponents to establish a critical basis for valid religious meaning and language. Notably, it addresses itself critically to the position of Charles Hartshorne, and to that of W. Norris Clarke whose major article on the subject follows.

With the paper of Clarke there begins a three part search for an authentic source of meaning for religious language. It first surveys the objections and then, with special attention to the person as the source of metaphysical meaning, proceeds systematically to elaborate the basis and growth of substantive religious insight. The article of Peter Slater carries this investigation more directly to the usage of language in the religious and especially in the Christian context in view of the critique this language has undergone among the so-called 'Christian atheists.'

There is, however, in the work of demythologisation carried out by Rudolf Bultmann an additional foundation for recent rejection of the significance for religious language. It is to this in particular that the article of Ralph Sleeper addresses itself, with the intent of restating the character of religious language on the basis of a more precise identification of the character of man's experience of transcendence.

It will be noted that the above approaches, in their concern with more adequately redeveloping the basis and character of religious language, agree in underlining the uniquely personal character of the religious fact. Now so generally diffused in all branches of contemporary philosophy, this dimension will constitute the terms of future development in the religious field. Indeed, the very transition from language concerning God to religious language in which man as well as God is present may be taken as a first manifestation of this development.

In each of the three areas signaled above a fairly limitless, but richly rewarding field of work lies ahead. The days in which people speak of the death of God seem, for the present, to be past, but they have left an important legacy. From that death has come new life for it is now more manifest that it is in God that man is born.

Acknowledgments

THE EDITOR ESPECIALLY wishes to express his appreciation to the many distinguished scholars who have contributed to this volume. Acknowledgment is made also to the following publishers: to the The Catholic University of America Press for permission to quote from: W. Norris Clarke, "Analytic philosophy and Language About God." **Christian Philosophy and Religious Renewal**, ed. George F. McLean (Washington, D.C.: The Catholic University of America Press, 1966): and Louis B. Geiger, "Freedom and Christian Philosophy," **Christian Philosophy and Religious Renewal**, ed. George F. McLean (Washington, D.C.: The Catholic University of America Press, 1966); to the Clarendon Press for permission to quote from **The Oxford Translation of Aristotle**, Vols. II, VIII, IX, ed. W. D. Ross (Oxford: The Clarendon Press, 1908-1952); to Editions De L'Epi for permission to quote from M. Nédoncelle, **Conscience et logos** (Paris: Editions De L'Epi, 1961); to Farrar, Straus and Giroux, Inc, and Editions Gallimard for permission to quote from G. Marcel, **Creative Fidelity** (New York: Farrar, Straus, 1964; Paris: Gallimard, 1940), © Editions Gallimard; to Editions Gallimard and Henry Regnery Company for permission to quote from G. Marcel, **Journal Metaphysique** (Paris: Gallimard, 1927; Chicago: Regnery, 1967), © Editions Gallimard; to Editions Gallimard and Northwestern University Press for permission to quote from M. Merleau-Ponty, **Le visible et l'invisible** (Paris: Gallimard, 1964; Evanston, Ill.: Northwestern University Press, 1964), © Editions Gallimard; to Harper and Row, Inc. for permission to quote from: M. Buber, **Eclipse of God** (New York: Harper, 1952); M. Heidegger, **The Later Heidegger and Theology**, trans. James M. Robinson (New York: Harper and Row, 1963); and G. Marcel, **Being and Having** (New York: Harper and Row, 1965); to the International Philosophical Quarterly for permission to quote from M. J. Charlesworth, "Linguistic Analysis and Language About God," **International Philosophical Quarterly** I (1961), 163-65; to V. Klostermann for permission to quote from M. Heidegger, **Holzwege** (Frankfurt: V. Klostermann, 1950); to The Open Court Publishing Company for permission to quote from: Charles Hartshorne, "Introduction to St. Anselm," **Basic Writings of St. Anselm** (2nd ed.; La Salle, Ill.: Open Court Publishing Co., 1962); and G. Marcel, "I and Thou," **Library of Living Philosophers—The Philosophy of Martin Buber**, ed. P. A. Schilpp (LaSalle, III.: Open Court Publishing Co., 1967); to the Philosophical Library, Inc. for permission to quote from: M. Heidegger, **Essays in Metaphysics** (New York: Philosophical Library, 1960); and G. Marcel, **The Philosophy of Existentialism** (New York: Philosophical Library, 1961); to **Philosophical Studies** for permission to quote from C. B. Daly, "The Knowableness of God," **Philosophical Studies**, IX (1959), 103-105; to Henry Regnery Company and Harvill Press Ltd. for permission to quote from G. Marcel, **The Mystery of Being**, Vols. I and II (Chicago: Regnery, 1960; London: Harvill Press, 1951); to the Aristotelian Society for permission to quote from H. W. Carr, "The Interaction of Mind and Body," **Proceedings of the Aristotelian Society,** XVIII (1917-1918), 32; to W. A. Bradley for permission to quote from Jean-Paul Sartre, **Le diable et le bon Dieu,** © Editions Gallimard, 1951, in the translation published by Alfred A. Knopf, New York, in 1963; to The Clarendon Press for permission to quote from **The Oxford Translation of Aristotle,** Vols. II, VIII, IX, ed. W. D. Ross (Oxford: The Clarendon Press, 1908-1952); to Cross Currents Corporation for permission to quote from Eugene Fontinell, "Religious Truth in a Relational and Processive World," **Cross Currents,** XVII (1967), 304-14, © 1968 by Cross Currents Corporation; to Harper and Row, Inc. for permission to quote from: Schubert Ogden, **The Reality of God** (New York: Harper and Row, 1963); to Holt, Rinehart and Winston, Inc. for permission to quote from John Dewey, **Ethics** (New York: Henry Holt and Co., 1959); to International Publishers for permission to quote from Karl Marx, **Theses on Feuerbach,** appendix to Fredrich Engels, **Ludwig Feuerbach and the Outcome of Classical German Philosophy,** ed. C. P. Dutt (New York: International Publishers, 1941); to the Macmillan Company for permission to quote from: Harvey Cox, **The Secular City** (New York: Macmillan, 1965), © Harvey Cox, 1965; and John Hick and Arthur C. McGill, "What Did Anselm Discover?", **The Many Faced Argument** (New York: Macmillan, 1967), © John Hick and Arthur C. McGill, 1967; to the Macmillan Company and Ernest Benn, Ltd. for permission to quote from Alfred North Whitehead, **The Aims of Education** (New York: Macmillan, 1929; London: Ernest Benn, Ltd., 1966), © 1929 by the Macmillan Company, renewed 1957 by T. North Whitehead; to the Macmillan Company and Cambridge University Press for permission to quote from: Alfred North Whitehead, **Adventures of Ideas** (New York: Macmillan, 1933; Cambridge, England: University Press, 1933), © 1933 by the Macmillan Company, renewed 1961 by Evelyn Whitehead; Alfred North Whitehead, **Process and Reality** (New York: Macmillan, 1929; Cambridge, England: University Press, 1929), © 1929 by the Macmillan Company, renewed 1957 by Evelyn Whitehead; Alfred North Whitehead, **Religion in the Making** (New York: Macmillan, 1956; Cambridge, England: University Press, 1926); and Alfred North Whitehead, **Science and the Modern World** (New York: Macmillan, 1929; Cambridge, England: University Press, 1927), © 1929 by The Macmillan Company, renewed 1957 by Evelyn Whitehead; to **The Monist** for permission to quote from C. Hartshorne, "Present Prospects for Metaphysics," **The Monist,** XLVII (1963), 207-208; to The Open Court Publishing Co., for permission to quote from: Anselm, **Monologion,** in **Basic Writings of St. Anselm** (LaSalle, Ill.: Open Court Publishing Co., 1962) and C. Hartshorne, **The Logic of Perfection** (LaSalle, Ill.: Open Court Publishing Company, 1962); to Penguin Books, Inc. for permission to quote from Dante's **The Divine Comedy,** trans. Dorothy Sayers (Middlesex: Penguin, 1949); to Princeton University Press for permission to quote from: Ernst Cassirer, **Philosophy of Enlightenment** (Princeton, N.J.: Princeton Press, 1951); to the Review of Metaphysics for permission to quote from K. Schmitz, "Weiss and Creation," **Review of Metaphysics,** XVIII (1964), 162; to the Viking Press, Inc. for permission to quote from Friedrich Nietzsche, **The Portable**

Nietzsche (New York: Viking, 1954); to The Westminster Press for permission to quote from **Christ and Time,** rev. ed. by Oscar Cullmann, trans. by Floyd V. Filson (Philadelphia, Pa.: Westminster Press, 1950), © 1964; to the Westminister Press and William Collins Sons and Co. for permission to quote from Thomas J. J. Altizer, **The Gospel of Christian Atheism** (Philadelphia, Pa.: Westminster Press, 1966; London William Collins Sons and Co., 1967), © 1966, W. L. Jenkins.

CONTENTS

Introduction

The Problem of God:
A Programmatic Essay

◊

by
Langdon Gilkey

THIS IS A progmmatic essay regarding the problem of God. As
such the scope of its concern is restricted in two important ways.
First, it will outline only a proposal for a method of dealing
with the problem of God, or of talking about God; it will not
embark upon a systematic or constructive elaboration of a doctrine or view of God. Secondly, it will not argue for this proposal, except incidentally; it will merely state what the proposal
is. Essentially, the essay is an outline and not a defense of a
possible theological methodology.[1] We shall begin with some
brief remarks about the central importance of the problem of
God for theology, and about the causes in the contemporary scene
that make this such a serious problem.

THE IMPORTANCE OF THE PROBLEM OF GOD TODAY

It is generally agreed that the major theological crisis of our
age centers about the problem of God. This does not mean merely
that we do not know what we should think or believe about God,
that is, that we do not know what "doctrines" or symbols to
apply to Him. Rather the focus of the "problem-character" of
the symbol God is whether as modern men we can think of him
at all, that is whether any doctrine of God is possible in a secular

[3]

time. If this be so, it is the central theological problem, and that to which all others are subsidiary. Logically, if this problem be answered in the negative, there are no other theological problems whether of revelation, christology, eschatology, anthropology, or ecclesiology, for in that case it would be impossible for modern man to speak meaningfully of the divine, of "God." Moreover, this is not just a theologian's problem, of interest merely to sophisticated seminarians; it is also a church problem. The sense of the meaninglessness, irrelevance, and emptiness of theological language permeates church life and is the ground in Christian communal existence for the appearance of the problem within theological reflection.

Finally, though a revision of traditional views of God may also be called for,[2] the problem is not with a particular view of God, as if a new or modern view would resolve the crisis. The problem is serious precisely because in the present situation any view of God, the sacred, or the divine is in difficulty. All relevant alternatives, whether Biblical, neo-Reformation, Thomistic, process, or Tillichian, are faced with the same issues. A mere transition from metaphysical to Biblical categories, or the reverse; from a transcendent to an immanent view, or the reverse; from Epiphany to eschatological theologies, or the reverse; from Thomistic to Hegelian to process, or the reverse, will not answer the secular challenge which finds all these views of the divine almost equally unintelligible and empty. As has been aptly stated, the problem concerns the death of God, not of this or that view of God. To put the point in modern linguistic terms, the problem is one of the death of the word "God" and hence of any view of God whatsoever.

As this indicates, we agree with many commentators that the basic cause of the problem is the character of the modern spirit, or *geist*, whence is drawn the most fundamental definition for the word "secular." It is risky to characterize this secular spirit of contemporaneity, but it is a risk that must be taken in order to unravel the present theological difficulties. We assume that contemporary philosophy, while not the only clue to what contemporary men feel about their world and themselves, is as good an entré into the modern *geist* as any. Our own interpretation of this spirit is stated as follows and without adequate defense.

THE MODERN SECULAR SPIRIT

Epistemologically, the "secular" is characterized by a concentration on immediacy as the sole grounds for meaningful, valid speech or thought. From this flows the concern of present linguistic and phenomenological philosophy with the two aspects of immediacy, namely, speech and direct experience or essences. Ontologically, this secular confinement of reflection to immediacy implies an emphasis upon the radical, blind, or arbitrary contingency of all that is, as well as upon its relativity and upon the transience of all things as the essential and exhaustive structures of the real. Consequently, there is denied any non-contingent absolute, or permanent "ground," "reason," or structure to process.

The categories of self-sufficient being, of logos, and of eternity are alien to contemporary ontology, if ontology is at all possible in such an epistemological and ontological situation. The only reality is contingent and relative change. From this implicit ontology or radical contingency, relativism, and transience, which excludes the possibility of a universal or rational structure known by speculative reason, there results the radically empiricist epistemology of modern thought. Thus, while scientific inquiry deals with the immanent structures of sensory experience, philosophy can deal only with an analysis of language or with an analysis of the essential phenomena that appear in direct experience. Thought and being, man and the ultimate structure of things, are radically disjoined.

"God is dead" and man has "come of age," but he has done so in a world that is devoid of sacrality, that is in itself blind and purposeless, and so is merely something to be understood and manipulated for man's own moral and social purpose. Thus, modern myths, which by embodying our fundamental sense of reality and of value structure our hopes, concern neither God, the universe as a whole, the cosmic process, or even the progress of history as did those of the classical Christian tradition, of liberal progressivism, and of Marxism. Rather, modern myths are based upon the other major category of secularity: human autonomy.

What we tend to believe in is not the divine, the rational, or the progressive structure of existence as a whole, but solely our own intellectual and moral powers. The universe outside is mere "nature," and provides no help or meaning. If only we know enough, are sufficiently aware, and sufficiently moral, we believe that we can control our world, ourselves, and ultimately our destiny. A metaphysical or natural theological solution to the problem of God must presuppose the power of philosophical reason to know reality's ultimate structure. The disappearance of any sense of objective rationality or moral meaning in the cosmos, in history, or in universal process, when combined with the epistemological "shrinking" referred to above, make such a solution as elusive and difficult in our time as is a revealed solution.

This secular confinement of reality, and of meaningful and true statements, to the immediate and contingent, to the relative and transient, to the things and people around us, has had a vast influence on contemporary religious life. There, it has manifested itself as a sense of the absence or elusiveness of God. Our religious and church life is barren beyond any other age of self-authenticating experiences of the divine, whether we refer to hearing the Word, to prayer, or to sacramental life. Direct experiences of "encounter" with God are talked about theologically, but they are rarely experienced. Thus, a theological method which begins with "faith's knowledge of God" or "acknowledgment of the Word of God addressed to me," that is, theologies based upon the assumptions of revelation of the Word and of the reception of these by faith, presuppose precisely what is currently being questioned. Have we, in fact, heard a divine Word? Is faith, though desired, a real possibility or an illusory hope? If faith is vividly experienced, certainly for the believer the reality of God follows directly from this experience. But if one's possession of faith is doubted or if one only hopes for faith, then in faith alone there is no basis for certainty about God, nor is there in faith any ground for meaningful language about Him. In such a situation the repetition of a theology which presupposes our possession of faith and our certainty of the reality of God will not help.

In church life the result has been that both experiences of God and speaking about him have been weakened. Because no specifically religious experiences seem easily possible, church language appears unreal and meaningless. Several important problems for theological method are implied here if church language is apt to be meaningless to the people who hear it. Linguistic analysis of church language must assume at the outset that the language game it analyzes is actually "played," that is, that it communicates in a community and is in fact used. Yet, it is precisely this that cannot be assumed about religious language in our churches. Correspondingly, phenomenological analysis of religious experience or "feeling" presupposes the existence of such experiences or "feelings" as a basis for theology. Yet, these cannot be assumed at the outset, any more than can the meaningful usage of religious discourse. The secular spirit has been a powerful dissolvent. It has eaten away not only the traditional concepts and experiences of the faith and its traditional methodologies—metaphysical or philosophical, and revelational, fideistic or biblical; even more uncomfortably, it has also dissolved those new methods centered upon an analysis of language or of religious experience with which a new answer to the problem might be devised.

THE POINT OF DEPARTURE FOR WORK UPON THE QUESTION OF GOD

Ordinary Experience and Religious Symbolism

How, then, do we begin? It is apparent that, unless we are to presuppose precisely that which is doubted, that is, a faith knowledge of God or the possibility of rational speculation in philosophy, we must begin with immediacy. This cannot be a "religious" immediacy, as it was for Rudolf Otto, for religious feeling or experience is elusive and our words about it are not firmly founded. Therefore, we must start with the immediacy of secular experience. But what can be known about God-language there? On the one hand, as secular experience is not "faith experience," it cannot be assumed to know either a revelation or a divine Word that could establish biblical God-language. If we begin neither with faith nor with philosophical ontology, language about God seems to be precluded from the start. Thus beginning in secular immediacy can provide us only with a *prolegomenon* to discourse about God. Secular experience taken "as is," with all its ambiguity and variety, cannot by itself produce any positive theological language.

Although it cannot "prove God," such a prolegomenon is by no means useless. It can show that religious discourse is meaningful because related to important and pervasive aspects of ordinary secular experience. This meaningfulness of religious language is not established by pointing to its ordinary "use," for this is a secular culture. Rather, it is established by showing that there are ranges or regions of experience which, because of their particular and unique character, call for religious symbolization. A language game can be said to be meaningful if there are areas of experience which it alone thematizes and brings to clarity, for meaning is basically an interaction of linguistic symbols and shared experiences that makes communication through language possible. If such areas of common experience relevant to religious discourse can be shown to exist in secular life, then religious language is established as a meaningful part of human culture. Correspondingly, a secular self-understanding that blocks out such areas of secular experience and such forms of language is shown to impoverish, if not endanger, the full life of man.

The prolegomenon we propose seeks to establish the meaningfulness of the general language game of religious discourse by unveiling aspects of ordinary experience to which religious symbolization is appropriate and essential, because in them, so to speak, something "appears" which requires the thematization of religious language. Investigation of the reality or the ontological nature of what it is that appears is not a part of such a prolegomenon; such ontological questions are "bracketed out." Speaking linguistically, the question of the validity of particular statements or claims about the sacred is not investigated. This is an analysis of the secular "situations" to which religious usages of words might apply; it is not a test of the truth of particular religious propositions. It is a prolegomenon rather than an example of theological discourse. Nevertheless, the prolegomenon is essential to the renewal of theological language, for religious discourse must be related to ordinary, secular, day-to-day experience in order that its symbols might regain their life and meaning. To paraphrase Kant,[3] the main thesis of our prolegomenon is that secular experience without religious symbols is blind, unarticulated, and terrifying; religious symbols without the content of secular experience are empty and meaningless.

Secular Experience and the Presence of the Non Secular

One presupposition of this proposal is that there is a split or disjunction between the secular self-understanding as outlined above and secular experience as actually lived. That is, it is assumed that cultures can apprehend and thematize their experience in ways which at certain crucial points do not fit the felt tonalities, real dimensions, and actual characteristics of their experience. Such an assumption, we take it, is necessarily implied in any historical relativist view which recognizes the variety of cultural self-understanding amid a basic and universal mode of human being in the world. For this reason it must be a second point of the prolegomenon to show that at certain definite points secular experience belies secular self-understanding. It must be shown that elements or dimensions appear in actual secular experience which the symbolic accounts of that experience, being merely contingent, relative, transient, and autonomous, do not in fact successfully thematize. The appeal here is to the characteristics of secular experience itself, not to religious norms. Nevertheless, the content of the appeal is the assertion that secular experience manifests a religious dimension, one of ultimacy and sacrality which only religious symbolization can express and clarify.

Put in terms of religious language, the essence of secularity was that the cosmos was drained of ultimacy and sacrality: the gods have long since fled from field and stream. The biblical and the philosophical Gods are now dead, and only flux is king. Further, we said that for secularity the ground of our hopes and the source of our norms resides only in man's own autonomous capacities. If this be so, a prolegomenon which aims to show the error of this restrictive self-understanding and of its myths of autonomy will seek to establish that in and through both our autonomy and the cosmos which is our setting a dimension of ultimacy and sacrality reveals itself. Our autonomy is experienced in secular life as essentially ambiguous and often helpless. It is therefore not the resource for our norms and hopes which modern myths believe.

Correspondingly, the values and meanings of our existence find their roots in what is "given" rather than in our own powers. What in various ways grounds and establishes our capacities, and which we can neither create nor control, is the basis of whatever value our autonomy itself can muster; it is, therefore, something on which we absolutely depend. Thus a secular self-understanding that locates meaning solely in autonomy, and finds the "given" devoid of grounds for hope, is at variance with our actual experience of life.

It is, then, central to the prolegomenon to show that both within our secular experience of the "given" in life, and in our experiences of our own autonomy, a non-secular dimension appears. This is a dimension of ultimacy and of sacrality with which religious language peculiarly deals and which can be thematized in no other terms. What is shown is that man is a religious being whose experience of the sacred, both positively as the ground, limit, norm, and resource of his life and negatively as the infinite and uncontrollable threat to his life, characterizes his humanity. It provides the only way of understanding rationally the positive characteristics of man's autonomy, his creative powers, and the negative uses he makes of those powers. In all human experience, including the secular, such a dimension reveals itself negatively and positively; it alone accounts for the unique structures of human experience. Consequently, religious language, as the form of language appropriate to this dimension of experience, is both meaningful and essential to man's life. We bracket out what the mode of reality or the "nature" of the sacred may be. Instead, we seek to show both that the sacred appears and thus, in terms of their referents in ordinary experience, the meaning of religious language.

As a methodological consideration, therefore, we propose a phenomenological hermeneutic of secular experience to uncover the latent, but very significant, religious dimension there. It is the dimension with which all religious language, including Christian theological discourse, is concerned. It is our thesis that a dimension of ultimacy does in fact appear at the center of each significant facet of man's being in the world. It is this dimension which grounds man's powers, possibilities, and joys, and which man experiences as a threat to his being and value. Not directly, but indirectly it appears therefore as the basis of our dealings with the world, with ourselves, and with our history, both as the threat to these dealings and as the resource for our confidence and hope. Our deepest joys and anxieties alike, our most significant norms and our most important hopes find their roots and thus their comprehensible symbolic thematization in this region of ultimacy. To show this, the religious character of man as being in the world in relation to our horizon or dimension of ultimacy, is the fundamental purpose of the proposed prolegomenon. Here is the ground in ordinary secular experience of the language we call "God language." It is to these experiences of ultimacy within ordinary experience that the symbolic forms of Christian discourse refer and which, in part, they mean when Christians talk about God and his activities.

Contingency, Relativity, Temporality, and Autonomy

As this dimension of ultimacy or sacrality does not appear directly in secular experience, how does one look for it there? We suggest that it appears in dim awareness, not explicit consciousness, in four areas of ordinary experience: (1) when we experience the grounds or the bases of our being or our powers: (2) when we experience the limits of our powers, and thus that they are unconditionally threatened; (3) when we experience the ambiguity of our destiny and freedom, and both the possibility and the threats in that apprehension; and (4) when we experience a basis for our hopes and confidence.

In each of these cases there is present an experience of ultimacy, of unconditionedness, and of sacrality. Any discourse about these regions of experience has the character of religiously symbolic discourse. That is, such discourse is multivalent or symbolic in a special sense in that it speaks of the finite, but only in so far as this is related to an ultimacy or a sacrality which appears within and to it.

This experience of ultimacy and sacrality—as ground and limit, and in ambiguity and hope—appears in relation to every significant aspect of man's being. On all his levels man is man in relation to this dimension. He must be understood in this way if he is to be comprehended, and only if lived in this light can his life manifest its fullest possibilities. Thus, ultimacy appears with regard to man's being, to his knowing, to his meanings, to his valuing, to his decision-making, to his experience of isolation, guilt, and stain, and to their resolution in self-acceptance and reconciliation, and finally to his temporality or death. In each of these "areas" the unconditioned appears as the ground, limit, threat, and resource to all man is and does.

In essence, therefore, our prolegomenon considers contingency, relativity, temporality, and autonomy because they are the categories of the secular spirit. In each case it is the intent of the prologomenon to show how these fundamental "ontological" categories of our being, as viewed by modern man, imply a religious dimension for modern existence. Each of these categories in the self-understanding of modern man has led to a secular view of the world as merely contingent, relative, transient, and autonomous. Nevertheless, each of them, when lived and experienced by modern man, as by his predecessors leads inescapably to an apprehension of an ultimate threat, an ultimate ground, and an ultimate hope which provide the real horizon within which even modern man lives. He too is threatened by the deepest anxieties. by the possibility of despair and meaninglessness by his own demonic reactions, and by the fear of isolation and death felt by other ages, and these threats can be understood only in terms of the category of ultimacy and unconditionedness.

Correspondingly, modern man lives by "myths": he models his life on sacral images and by religious hopes, he directs himself and his history beyond the evidence even presupposing this dimension. Thus the phenomenological evidence centered around the fundamental categories of the secular spirit refutes its own self-understanding and drives to the recognition of a religious dimension in human existence. By implication, if this religious dimension is there, religious language is necessary and meaningful if man is to be fully man.

Through this prologomenon, therefore, the place and essential character of religious discourse are established and the possibility of its meaningfulness in a secular age is assured. The place of religious language is the experience of ultimacy and sacrality as it appears in each facet of human life. Its character is correspondingly defined as fundamentally symbolic, multivalent, or polysemic in form. It refers to the infinite and the sacred that appears within the finite and the profane. In turn, the sacred grounds, limits, and threatens the profane, whose structure it provides with meaning and hope. Thus, religious discourse forms the basis of every creative activity, as well as of every demonic propensity of man. This language always implies man's total self-involvement, because it refers to that which grounds both his being and his value and which, therefore, can threaten all that he is and does. It is also a type of language that is productive of ethical norms and models for man's life, since all his important relations to the world and to others are determined at this level. Finally, this language is related to his questions of identity and of hope, for which reason it is the language in which his "faiths" are always couched. Hence, as always, religious language: a) refers to the ultimate or the sacred; b) involves existential or ultimate issues; and c) is productive of models and standards by which a community lives its life. Such symbolic forms and myths which deal with this area of experience and discourse are communally borne and transmitted over historical time. Each man relates himself to answers at this level by subsisting within some community which bears symbolic forms that give him relevant and valid answers to life's ultimate issues.

If this analysis of secular experience is successful in uncovering its religious dimension, and thus its usage, if only in surreptitious forms, of religious language, we will have established the meaningfulness of this realm of discourse. We will also have established the "referent" in ordinary experience for the particular symbolic forms of any given religious tradition. It is our ordinary secular experience of contingency that the symbol of creation is talking about, our search for meaning that providence is about, and so on. These theological symbols have potential meaning, that is, reference to actual experience, because they refer to real aspects of ordinary experience. In locating those referents, we have at least potentially delineated part of the meaning of theological symbols.

As we have noted, such a prologomenon is not yet theology; it can make no more positive assertion than that a sacred dimension appears in phenomenal experience. To determine what that ultimacy and sacrality is or is like would involve more than an analysis of general experience, for in an analysis of general experience all imaginable possible characterizations of the sacred appear, as Being or as Void, as meaning or as the negation of meaning, or as love or as condemnation. Thus, just as linguistic analysis cannot test particular assertions with regard to their validity, and as phenomenology brackets all questions of reality or ontological structure, so our prologomenon provides the grounds for theological or religious language, but is not itself an example of it.

RELIGIOUS LANGUAGE IN A SECULAR AGE

The Sacred in Culture

How then is God talked about in our age; is a theology possible that is secular and yet Christian? In a secular culture an analysis of our general usage of language or of general experience will not of itself provide the basis for positive theological assertions. It is precisely the linguistic effect of the secularization of our cultural life that religious language is no longer an essential part of ordinary usage, of common sense language, of political or moral speech, or of scientific discourse. Accordingly religious language, in so far as it remains in cultural life, is driven "underground" and reappears as the tacit or unacknowledged scientific, political, and social mythologies by which we live. Even a careful phenomenological hermeneutic that might uncover a "re'-ligious" dimension in experience, uncovers too broad a variety of religious possibilities for theological assertions: the experience of an ultimate Void, the appearance of demonic absolutes, as well as the creative presence of the sacred. Positive theological assertions must be grounded not in this sort of generality, but in some deep but particular apprehension of the nature of things which excludes alternatives and thus makes a claim about what is real and of value.

Thus, a "break" or "new" departure, based on some definite special stance taken, necessarily appears in the movement from prologomenon to theology. Such stances are universal in human experience and found in each cultural world view (weltanschauung). Within that wider matrix in philosophy they are the implicit and often unacknowledged ground for each "point of view" in philosophy, and provide the explicit and celebrated basis for each religious community. Human thinking, valuing, and thus man's total existence rests on such presuppositional attitudes with regard to what is real, how the truth is to be known, and what is of value—what Stephen Toulmin calls answers to "limiting questions."[4] The origin of these particular attitudes or perspectives is difficult to determine, though generally they come from our cultural or communal surroundings. Ultimately they arise from some apprehension of the ultimate nature, structure, and purpose of things which gives illumination, clarity, direction and healing to a man's existence. This apprehension, set within communal symbols, is then passed on in a tradition.

Thus, even in secular life we can, I believe, speak legitimately of "hierophanies" or "revelation" of the sacred as manifestations of the ultimate sacral structures or horizons of our ordinary common life. Every positive point of view in secular or religious life reflects a particular, but fundamental perspective of this type. It originates in an existential apprehension and is borne communally, whether it be mediated through culture as a whole and centered upon the scientific, the political, or the social communities of secular life, or mediated through a religious tradition. As we have argued, since the dimension of ultimacy and sacrality lies back of all thinking and doing, religious language is necessary to express the foundation of every human point of view.

More concretely, an apprehension of this dimension lies back of each positive point of view. This apprehension can be called a "revelation" because we do not "discover" it or "think to" it, since it founds our powers of discovery and of thought. In unraveling the philosophies and stances of men, we ultimately arrive at a specific religious symbolization based upon a particular hierophany of the sacred. Our modes of apprehending the world, of thinking about it and valuing within it are, therefore, given to us historically and communally by the community in which we spiritually exist, be it the scientific community, the democratic community, *das Volk*, or the church. These modes are mediated to us by the often tacit symbols and norms of that community's life. Revelation of the sacral ground of life is thus universal and general; without it there would be no life, no meaning, no thought, no valuing, and no hope in human experience. Each example or illustration of this universal apprehension of the sacred is, however, special and historical. It originates in some particular hierophany of the sacred through definite media; it is passed on historically in a particular communal tradition by means of its quite particular symbolic structures appropriate to that original apprehension.

Christian Theology

Christian theology is reflection upon one of these many stances in life from the point of view of one within that stance. For this reason, in terms of reflective thought, it represents a commitment to one mode of apprehension of the sacred, one set of symbolic forms, one set of definite norms for truth and for value, and one form of hope. Faith means standing within this perspective. This, in turn, means viewing the sacred, and therefore our own life and destiny, in the light of this community's history and hence, in terms of these symbolic structures. The reason one does this is that in this community and through these symbolic forms, illumination, clarity, direction, and hope have been experienced. Here the ultimate and sacred ground of our life, our meaning, our truth, our freedom in community, and our destiny has manifested itself to us.

This is not a "queer" thing to do. Each human lives in some historical and spiritual community. He looks at things from the point of view of the symbolic structures and norms of this community because it is within it that illumination, direction, and hope have been experienced. There are no universal positions or universal symbolic forms—though most of us like to think of ours in that way. In the next valley even the most objective philosophy seems alien. In this sense traditional symbols, norms, and something like "faith" are prerequisites for any assertion or testing of validity. They may be the tacit acceptance of communal values, norms, and attitudes by the scientific community, or the more explicit acceptance of such a symbolic structure by political and social communities, or the quite open acknowledgment of all of this in traditional religious communities. Formally, therefore, there is no vast difference between theology and other types of thinking although theology is unique as regards both the particular type of community in which it occurs and whose ethos it explicitly represents, and the particular symbols with which it reflects. In any case, in order for any positive assertions to be made about what is real, how truth is to be known or verified, what in life is of value, and what are our grounds for hope, some stance is required, some community must be inhabited, and some set of symbolic structures and norms affirmed. Speaking about God in a Christian way, then, implies "faith," subsistence in the historic community, and the utilization of the symbols of the Christian apprehension of the sacred.

Theology, however, cannot be merely the repetition or even the expression of traditional symbols, as is often the case in biblical or traditional theologies. As was pointed out above, religious discourse, of which Christian theological assertions form one variety, has meaning only insofar as it thematizes ordinary, secular experience, namely the range of experience where ultimacy and sacrality are apprehended. Thus theological symbols, explicated without reference to ordinary experience, have meaning only "eidetically" in terms of their inherent structures or intentional meaning. They do not have *religious* meaning for us, though we who study them may realize emphatically that they have had some such meaning for others. Consequently, they will have no religious usage among ourselves and in our situation. The meanings of religious symbols for others are available to us through a careful study of religious, Biblical or otherwise, but we must not confuse an understanding of their eidetic meanings with the religious meaning for us of these symbols in our contemporary situation. That meaning is possible only when these symbols are united to the experiences in our actual, contemporary life which they symbolize, only when they are conceived and understood as answers to the questions raised by the ordinary life we lead. The union of the two is the task of theology and of preaching.

This means, in turn, that religious, or in this case Christian, symbols are not to be understood as answers to "religious" problems. Consequently, they do not find their "meanings" solely or even mainly in church, in faith, or in the area of religion. They are symbols expressing experienced answers to the problems of ordinary, secular life. Thus the task of systematic theology is to conceive of the symbols of its tradition in terms of the experiences of ultimacy within secular life; alternatively, it is to understand the dimension of ultimacy and sacrality as it is apprehended in ordinary life through the symbols of the Christian tradition. A Christian is one who names "Christianly" and so apprehends "Christianly" the sacred, which is experienced in and through his contingency, his search for meaning, his knowing, and his experiences of valuing, of renewal, and of hope. That is, he "names" the sacred "God," the father of Jesus Christ as that symbol ("God") has been expressed in what theology calls the "Word" and thence in the wider system of symbols inherent in Christian history. A Christian theologian is one who understands reflectively the symbol "God" and its whole correlate system of symbols by comprehending it solely: a) as an answer to the experiences of ultimacy in ordinary life; and b) in terms of Christian symbolic structures.

Systematic theology as Christian speaking of God, then, has three essential elements or stages. First, the prologomenon which is a phenomenological hermeneutic of secular experience. This is achieved by an analysis of the way in which modern man experiences his being in the world as characterized by contingency, relativity, transience, and autonomy, which analysis manifests the positive and the negative appearance of the ultimate and the sacred within these aspects of our being in the world. For theology, this prologomenon functions in two ways: a) by establishing the meaning of religious discourse by showing the experiences which religious symbols thematize; and b) by passing on to theology these "potentialities for meaning" through its delineation of the experiences which religious symbols mean and in terms of which these symbols are to be comprehended. For example, our experiences of our own contingency provide the experimental situations to which the symbol of creation potentially refers and which it might in its own way "mean."

Second, there is the eidetic analysis or, in another sense of that oft used word, a hermeneutical analysis[5] of community symbols, both biblical and traditional. Here the objects of analysis are the eidetic or intentional meanings of these symbolic forms. Every such form and system of symbolic forms has a definite, unique meaning. This uniqueness of its meaning gives to each religious tradition the possibility of mediating to communal experience a definite and unique apprehension of the sacred. Though the sacred is universal, it is experienced differently in each tradition because of the unique *gestalten* of the community's symbolic structures. Thus, the theologian analyzes the symbols of his community and its tradition to see the unique meaning which they each possess, both alone and as a system of symbols. From this analysis there appears the unique apprehension of the sacred which that community mediates to us.

Finally, systematic theology is the mutual interpenetration ("correlation" was Tillich's term) of experienced questions and symbolic answers, the one being a means for understanding the other. This is not an understanding of the symbol by and through itself, and thus of "God" by himself. Meaning is an interaction of symbol and experience. Religious meaning is an interaction of the experience of the sacred with religious symbols which mediate and thematize that experience. Thus, theology is an understanding of the biblical symbols in terms of the secular experiences of ultimacy, and of these experiences in terms of the symbols; together they form "Christian" meanings. Correspondingly, it is an understanding and speaking of God in terms of his relations to, his activity in, and his appearance through creaturely life. If "creaturely symbols" are, as Eliade and Tillich insisted, the finite media through and in which the sacred appears, a symbolic understanding of God is an understanding of this appearance in and to ourselves as finite creatures: contingent, relative, transient, autonomous, and guilty. This apprehension is comprehended in terms of the whole structure of Christian symbolism. This is based on the originating creaturely symbols of Israel's history and the person of Jesus through which, for this community, the sacred has manifested itself normatively. Through this mutual interaction of contemporary experience and traditional symbols theology is properly "demythologized" and rendered "existential." Nevertheless, it does not thereby become mere anthropology, but remains Christian discourse about the sacred as it appears in and to human existence. It speaks of "God" as the "father of Jesus Christ" as he manifests himself in the total range of our ordinary secular contemporary existence.

Criteria for Christian Discourse

The criteria or modes of validation of Christian discourse about God follow from its characteristics as speech which is within this community, based on these symbols, and concerned with the ultimate or foundational issues in secular human existence. 1) This speech originates in an experience of illumination and renewal which takes place in the community and is mediated through these symbols. As expressive of the ethos of this community, it is, therefore, "valid" only if it faithfully reflects the meanings of these symbols as they have functioned in that community's life. A theology is validated first by showing the legitimacy of its use and interpretation of the Biblical and traditional symbols. 2) This speech has meaning only as it celebrates felt joys and expresses felt answers to real problems, issues, and crises. Thus, a theology is valid if it illumines the existential or ultimate questions of ordinary life, and if it provides useful models and directions for contemporary decisions and creditable grounds for hope. The second validation of a theology is in its relevance to contemporary ordinary experience as a symbolic structure making that secular experience intelligible, bearable, and hopeful. 3) This speech purports to give symbolic expression to the foundations of human being in the world, and hence to all the various elements of human culture. It is validated, therefore, in so far as it is able to elaborate its symbols into intellectual categories that express the foundations of inquiry, of art, of social structures, of psychology, and of ethics.

As with any total viewpoint in philosophy, a theology can claim to be "true" only if it can provide on its own terms a secure intellectual foundation for our whole creative life in the world. In so far as it purports to be dealing with ultimacy, this claim of universal applicability is, of course, inescapable. Inevitably, this requirement leads theological speech toward ontological elaboration, toward becoming a "Christian philosophy" and so capable of mediating between what is ultimate and what is proximate, between religious speech about sacrality and cultural speech about science, art, literature, politics, and the supermarket. Thus the fidelity of its interpretation of traditional symbols, its relevance to contemporary and secular experience, and its width of cultural scope are the three "objective" criteria of theology in terms of which it finds warrants for its arguments.

The character of religious discourse, as speech in response to an involved apprehension of the sacred within the finite, means that the most important "criterion" is existentially subjective, not objective. This criterion is the involvement implied in any apprehension of sacrality. Without an existential reception of the hierophany, without an apprehension of the sacred in and through the symbols, there is no multivalence, no religious use of language, no positive or assertive religious speech at all, and thus neither a valid use of symbols nor any relevance to ordinary experience.

Ordinary experience does reveal the presence as well as the absence of ultimacy and sacrality. For this reason, it cannot be understood or dealt with on a purely secular basis, separated from the symbolization that makes this apprehension possible. In the past, theological symbols, whose task it is to thematize this dimension of life in the world, have removed themselves into the cloister or the chapel; they have existed apart and self-sufficiently, confined in their inherent rather than their experienced meanings. Thus they became empty and finally expendable for a life that is lived in the world. Secular Christian theology understands ordinary experience in terms of Christian symbols, and its symbols in terms of ordinary life. The first provides the "matter," that is the experience of our being in the world, for which the second provides the "form" or the symbolic thematization. This is, I am convinced, what religious discourse and hence theological language is "for," what the usage of this language is, and hence where its meanings lie. The proper usage of Christian symbolic language is to articulate, clarify, and bring to stronger and so controllable expression the dimension of sacrality dimly experienced in ordinary life. Correspondingly, it is this alone which can add celebration and serenity to secular existence, which at present is both unaware of the sacral glories that ground its being and meanings, and unable to cope with the ultimate anxieties of which it is not symbolically conscious.

◇

1. A much more complete defense of this proposal is to be found in my book **Naming the Whirlwinds: The Renewal of God-Language** (Indianapolis, Ind.: Bobbs-Merrill, 1969).

2. For example, see the views of Leslie Dewart and Schubert Ogden that the main cause of the present problem of God lies in the character of traditional theism. Leslie Dewart, **The Future of Belief** (New York: Herder and Herder, 1968), chaps. I, II, and VI; Schubert Ogden, **The Reality of God** (New York: Harper, 1967), esp. pp. 16 ff. and 46 ff.

3. The author owes this "re-usage" of Kant to his phenomenological colleague Eugene T. Gendlin, whose excellent **Experiencing and the Creation of Meaning** (New York: Free Press, 1962) provided the source for many of the fundamental ideas of this proposal.

4. Stephen Toulmin, **Reason in Ethics** (New York: Cambridge Univ. Press, 1964), esp. chap. 14.

5. This latter is the meaning of this elusive word in the "hermeneutical" theologians, and the way in which Paul Ricoeur uses it in his **Symbolism of Evil** (New York: Harper, 1967), pp. 347 ff. For our own use of this word to describe our prolegomenon as a "phenomenological hermeneutic," cf. Herbert Spiegelberg, **The Phenomenological Movement** (The Hague: Nijhoff, 1965), esp. pp. 318 ff. and 694 ff.

Part I

Process

Toward A Pragmatic
Reconstruction of Religion

◇

by
Eugene Fontinell

THAT INSTITUTIONAL RELIGION is in deep crisis is beyond dispute, though the nature of and reason for that crisis may be expressed in diametrically opposed language. For some, the term "crisis" is too mild to do justice to the reality of the situation in which religion finds itself. They would consider "collapse," understood as a functional breakdown or an existential irrelevance, to be a more accurate description. Nor is there universal agreement on the degree and permanence of this collapse, though there is a significant convergence in the descriptions of it by psychologists, sociologists, philosophers and theologians of every major religious tradition.

I agree with those who see religion to be in a state of collapse.[1] The necessity for the effort which I urge in this paper can be understood only against such a background. Despite my negative evaluation of the present state of religion, this undertaking is intended as a positive effort.[2] My hypothesis, stated starkly and simply, is that only a radically reconstructed religion can enable religion both to survive and to serve man. In fact, there can be no significant survival that is not also a human service.

The kind of reconstruction I envision is not an esoteric religious project, since, in my judgment, the collapse of religion is but a heightened manifestation of a broader cultural collapse. The western world, understood as a stable world-order providing

[27]

a fundamental value-structure within which men located and identified themselves, has been collapsing for several centuries. A century ago only a prophet such as Nietzsche perceived this; but in the second half of the twentieth century it is as well known as is the daily newspaper. Due to the industrial, technological and communications revolutions, this collapse can now be said to be world-wide. It is, then, man and his world which stand in need of reconstruction, and I am not interested in any reconstruction of religion that is not simultaneously a reconstruction of these.[3]

Corresponding to the range of evaluations of the bleakness of our present situation will be a variety of curative responses to it. We can assume that every respectable response will endeavor to better the situation by conserving certain values, insights, and visions previously achieved, and by creating and assimilating new values, insights, and visions. Despite diversity in detail, approaches to reconstruction will fall into either of two groups. The first will be comprised of those who will operate within a framework of ideas which, in its fundamental principles, has been constructed at an earlier time. It is the task of those making this approach to modify their framework in order to be able to account for new experiences, ideas and values. The second group will be made up of those who desire to radically reconstruct the traditional framework of thought. From within this reconstructed framework, they will attempt to account for previous intellectual and other achievements which are of enduring worth.[4]

My approach falls into the second of the two groups, a fact that describes it rather than supports or rejects it. All communication is difficult; it becomes still more difficult when its subject is religion. Success is unlikely without deliberate effort to clarify one's assumptions. Because we use the same language and are wrestling with somewhat the same problem, we tend to ignore the fact that we often use that language quite differently. For example, most of those concerned with doing something about religion—whether they label their doing renewal, reform or reconstruction—would probably agree on the following needs:

to remove the opposition between "sacred" and "secular"; to overcome stultifying religious passivity; to relate religion to concrete human problems; to avoid reducing religion to abstract formulas; and to have religion lead us more deeply into the world rather than to escape from it. Despite widespread agreement on these needs, attempts to fulfill them will differ sharply because of the diverse assumptions which undergird these attempts. In their most basic form these assumptions constitute what I shall call a metaphysics or world-view. I do not intend that metaphysics be understood in a narrow, technical fashion but rather as combining fundamental perspective and a number of key principles or ideas within which we think and act.

For this reason I will describe briefly the world-view which is the framework for my reflections on the reconstruction of religion. This world-view is fundamentally that which emerged from the classical period of American philosophy, particularly in the work of William James and John Dewey. I contend that this tradition has rich resources for a reconstruction of religion and of all human experiences.

However, two cautions must be urged. First, I am not advancing this tradition as the only worthwhile approach to the problems under consideration. I subscribe to a kind of metaphysical pluralism in that I do not believe any one metaphysics can be fully adequate to the depth and richness of human experience and to the world in which it operates.[5] Secondly, I intend neither to appropriate James and Dewey in the cause of religion nor to show that they were basically Christians. I merely claim that their thought provides possibilities for an enriched development and transformation of religion and Christianity. On my hypothesis, however, the result of a dynamic transaction between the philosophies of these men and Christianity would be something different from what either were or are when considered independently.[6]

Since I will make repeated use of the terms pragmatism, reconstruction, and religion, I will attempt to clarify something of what I mean by each. William James and Charles Sanders Peirce, the "founder" of pragmatism, insisted that pragmatism was a method, not a metaphysics. This distinction is acceptable and even necessary only so long as no dichotomy is introduced between method and metaphysics. Even taking Peirce's restricted definition of pragmatism as a method whereby we render ideas clear in terms of their consequences, do we not thereby imply a different world from that in which ideas are made clear by an analysis of their internal consistency? The matter becomes more complicated when James describes pragmatism as a method whereby we make the truth. Consider the difference between a world in which we "invent" the truth through acting upon ideas and a world in which we "discover" the truth by abstracting ideas corresponding to an already permanently structured reality. If pragmatism does not necessarily involve a processive world, it is eminently congenial to and congruent with such a world. Regardless of its meaning for James and Dewey, I will understand pragmatism as combining a methodological dimension with the metaphysics or world-view within which they reflected.

I use the term reconstruction in order to take cognizance of both continuity and development, and to avoid the polarities of mere repetition and total revolution. Since I will urge radical development and change, I wish to stress that not all change is destructive. On the contrary, I would argue that change through reconstruction enables us to avoid change through revolution. I further maintain that such change is actually constructive because it retains earlier insights and values, though in a transformed manner. This premise is crucial, as we shall see, for reconstruction accounts for continuity through fuller inclusion of these values in the world-process, rather than continuity through exclusion or exception from this process. Another important connotation of reconstruction is that it is existential as well as theoretic. An effort of reconstruction cannot be restricted to or terminate in a system of ideas.

An attempt to define religion even at the end of this paper would be inconsistent with my approach. However, one could hardly call for a reconstruction unless there were some reality in need of reconstructing. I will assume, therefore, that we are aware of a phenomenon called religion which involves ideas, symbols, practices, and institutions distinguishable from other phenomena, such as art, science, or politics. Though I refer to it as a phenomenon, I agree with James that "the word 'religion' cannot stand for any single principle or essence, but is rather a collective name."[7] Dewey is correct in stating "that concretely there is no such thing as religion in the singular. There is only a multitude of religions."[8] I am aware that I am straddling "phenomenology" and "nominalism," but James and Dewey have done the same. They affirmed that terms might have a universal thrust without their corresponding to a universal essence.

Such a combination of concrete locus and universal thrust is most relevant to a reconstruction of religion. Any reconstruction of religion must, in the first instance, be a reconstruction of that religion in which the reconstructor is involved. Otherwise, one will fall into the trap of abstract and empty theorizing. Nevertheless, there can be no significant reconstruction which is parochial and without some aspect of universality. Hence, I have decided to speak of reconstruction of religion, despite the fact that my primary locus or context is Christianity or, more specifically, Roman Catholicism.[9]

PRAGMATISM'S WORLD-VIEW—A GLOSS[10]
Processive and Experimental

The world[11] is in process; it is unfinished. Man has a crucial role to play in the development of the world since he is continuous with, constitutive of, and constituted by it. The process which pragmatism attributes to reality cannot be restricted to a superficial or accidental dimension of the world. Hence, any dualism dividing reality into a substantial unchanging part and an accidental changing part is unacceptable. The key to this open and developing world is the possibility of real novelty; the "new" always emerges from what is already in existence. However, it cannot be understod as simply a particularization of an essence that is eternal or absolutely permanent. It is the possibility of real novelty in all spheres of reality that gives life its excitement and zest, its risk and uncertainty.

In affirming that novelty is a real characteristic of the world, pragmatism does not deny that there are also regularities and a kind of permanence. The world we inhabit is both precarious and stable. It is pervaded by constancy and regularity intertwined with uncertainty, unpredictability and uncontrollability. Hence, it is neither a world of chaotic flux nor of perfect and complete order. Though the world does not meet all our demands and satisfy all our desires, it is not an essentially hostile world, but is to some degree responsive to our need for order. Man's task is to contribute to the ordering of the world; he must not simply mirror it. Not a mere spectator, man participates in the ongoing task of the world. This is most important in the sphere of knowledge, for it means that any "correspondence" which might characterize knowledge is subordinated to its primary role as a means by which man actually transforms reality.

Nothing is more central to the world-view of James and Dewey than their theory of experience. Though both might be called empiricists, the label is misleading unless one takes into account the radical difference between experience as understood by James and Dewey and experience in the classical empirical tradition from Locke to Mill.[12] Experience is a flow; it is organic and dynamic rather than atomistic and passive. Dewey finds that experience is simply any interaction or transaction between an organism and its environment, whether that environment is a tree, a book, or another person.[13] It must be stressed, however, that neither the organism nor the environment is constituted in itself, independently of the other. I will return to this exceptionally important point when I discuss Dewey's category of "the social."

Pragmatism rejects the view that experience is "subjective," that it is a subject reacting to an "objective" world composed of independently structured objects. Assuredly there are subjects and objects; but they are derivative and functional, and do not represent essentially different kinds of reality. In its primordial concreteness experience is neither subjective nor objective, for this is a functional distinction which takes place within experience.

This view of experience rules out assigning faith to a realm called subjective and knowledge to a realm called objective.[14] Knowledge itself is one mode of experience, and only a "vicious intellectualism" would insist that knowledge is man's only access to reality. There are as many different experiences, each with its subjective and objective dimensions, as there are different ways of interacting with the world.

Dewey on "The Social"

Dewey concedes that by "the social as a distinctive mode of association is denoted specifically human forms of groupings," but he denies that the social can "be placed in contrast with association in general."[15] Hence, the assertion that "all human experience is ultimately social"[16] must be seen as a specific manifestation of the broader metaphysical principle "that associated or conjoint behavior is a universal trait of all existences."[17] It is important to realize that reality is made up not of independently existing substantial things, but of individual existents constituted by their relations. The social is not added on to a world ultimately composed of atomistic or radically independent entities. It is instead the most inclusive experienced mode of relationship in a world that is essentially or "through and through" relational.[18]

Pragmatism rejects the notion of any isolated individual, but it does not affirm some all-encompassing collective. The traditional opposition between the social and the individual is artificial and unnecessary, for the individual and society are interrelated and interdependent. They are co-constitutors inasmuch as each makes a necessary, indispensable contribution to the constitution of the other. Since we live in an ever-changing world, it is imperative that we develop an "individualism" suitable to such a world. We must not base this individualism on the assumption of the existence of absolutely unchanging essences. Of this Dewey would say that it "treats individualism as if it were something static, having a uniform content. It ignores the fact that the mental and moral structure of individuals, the pattern of their desires and purposes, *change with every great change in in social constitution.*"[19]

Any attempt at reconstituting religion should be a continuation of Dewey's great effort to intensify both individuality and sociality by viewing them as inseparable and organically interwoven. Today more than ever we need to be reminded of the pitfalls of a simplistic, abstract either-or concerning individuality and community. The view that we can achieve our identity and individuality only through a negative and destructive relation to the communities in which we exist is just as self-defeating as the view that we can achieve order and personal security only by a passive submission to those communities.

James on the Role of Faith

Faith or belief plays an important role in the thought of all the pragmatists, but it is James who gave it the most explicit emphasis. It is not simply that James grasps the existential fact that everyone is "personally all the time chock-full of some faith or other,"[20] or that "we cannot live or think without some degree of faith."[21] More important, he states that the only alternative to faith is a destructive nihilism—"the only escape from faith is mental nullity."[22] James insisted upon the necessity and universality of belief. Contrary to numerous critics, he did not encourage willfulness or wantonness of belief, nor did he advocate belief for belief's sake, since "his whole purpose had been to *justify* belief."[23] What should be noted is that his attempt to justify belief or faith does not mean that he held that every belief or faith is justifiable.

The most important and criticized dimension of Jamesian faith is its creativity. The full scope and importance of the creativity of faith has been missed by most commentators because they have concentrated on what appears to be a "wishing will make it so" attitude on the part of James. They have restricted their analysis to those parts of *The Will to Believe*[24] in which

James argues that belief is a necessary factor in some truths—that in some instances faith creates truth.[25] Properly qualified, I think that James' position here is quite defensible, but it is not the most significant aspect of the creativity of faith.

The more ample reality of faith can be appreciated only when it is viewed as operating within the unfinished and processive universe to which I have earlier referred. James believes "that work is still doing in the world-process, and that in that work we are called to bear our share."[26] From his standpoint "our acts redetermine the previous nature of the world." This is why faith has an indispensable role to play. "It (faith) may be regarded as a formative factor in the universe, if we be integral parts thereof and co-determinants by our behavior, of what its total character may be."[27]

For the man of faith there is no escape from continual risk, doubt, and uncertainty. He must decide whether he wishes to risk all by placing his faith, and thereby his life, in the service of the positive possibilities of the universe, or whether he wishes to stand pat and await more conclusive evidence. James' pragmatic faith allows him to escape the pitfalls of both absolutism and scepticism, while retaining the strength and insights of both. Negatively, absolutism is characterized by a closed, *a prori*, "once and for all," and absolutely certain affirmation of specific values and truths. Positively, absolutism is characterized by a fervent and full commitment to what it claims to be of value or true. Negatively considered, scepticism is a lack of courage and a cynical refusal to commit oneself to anything. Positively, it stresses the incompleteness, inadequacy, and uncertainty which belongs to all human endeavors.

James would insist that even we can never be absolutely certain that we possess truth, "we do not thereby give up the quest or hope of truth itself." Hence the creative potential of man, individually and collectively, is capable of being realized on James' terms since it does not demand absolute certitude or absolute rationality before acting. "I find myself," James tells us, "willing to take the universe to be really dangerous and adventurous without therefore backing-out and crying 'no play.'"[28] The service which such a philosophy of faith might render to a reconstruction of religion is obvious.

GENERAL CONDITIONS AND POSSIBILITIES FOR A PRAGMATIC RECONSTRUCTION OF RELIGION

It is beyond dispute that religion is a phenomenon. What is disputable is whether religion ought to exist and, if so, in what form. A pragmatic reconstruction must begin with the phenomenon, but, being more than a mere description or analysis, it must be an effort to transform the phenomenon. Of course, this effort presupposes the prior value judgment that religion is both worthwhile and in need of transformation. The first moment of any reconstruction will of necessity be theoretic. If successful, however, it must issue in positive consequences. A philosophical effort such as this cannot, in itself, bring forth these consequences. At best, it can present an hypothesis or string of hypotheses which are congenial to present and past experience and suggestive of possibilities for future experience. However, if these hypotheses are in any way worthwhile, they should serve as guidelines for action. Though by its very nature a pragmatic reconstruction will not result in an eternal blueprint for religious or any other kind of activity, it must render some service to the concrete ongoing religious life. In general, then, a pragmatic reconstruction of religion must enable a richer religious life to emerge, or at least show the possibility of such an emergence. It must present criteria for a progressive realization of this life. The key feature of this approach is that the worth of any hypothesis, guideline or criterion is ultimately determined by the consequences to which it gives issue.

Theory and Consistency

By definition, a pragmatic approach must be tentative, hypothetical, and experimental. However, this does not excuse it from rendering concrete judgments. The fear that pragmatism means "anything goes" is misplaced and perdures only by unwillingness to move beyond the popular understanding that reduced pragmatism to a few statements taken out of context and transformed into utilitarian slogans. Pragmatism avoids both affirming and ruling-out, *a priori*, any particular values. It allows and indeed insists upon the need for values, even universal and enduring ones.

It requires, however, that these values must continually be evaluated in terms of the changing experience of the community. From the pragmatic point of view, the value of religion can be neither affirmed nor denied on the basis of a non-experiential criterion, whether this be a metaphysical system, a psychological theory, an "other world" derivation, or a "future world" confirmation. A pragmatic approach insists that religion must yield concrete fruits for individual and communal human life. Hence, pragmatism avoids a sentimental subjectivism and a closed-minded objectivism. It further attempts to show the possibility of having an approach to life in general and to problem situations in particular which is at once rigorous and sensitive, committed and open.

Pragmatism has been accused of giving such an important and necessary role to experience, action, and the lived consequences of ideas that it diminishes the role and importance of thought or intelligence. No criticism could be farther from the mark. "It is not the abandonment of thinking and inquiry that is asked for," Dewey remarks, "but more thinking and more significant inquiry."[29] My emphasis upon "lived consequences" in any pragmatic reconstruction of religion is not meant to belittle the intellect, but to affirm it. The fact that the theoretic element cannot be evaluated "in itself" or in isolation from the life of the community does not mean that this element is expendable. On the contrary, action can no more be separated from thought than thought from action.

Any pragmatic reconstruction of religion which excludes the theoretical or speculative will be thin and superficial indeed.[30] For this reason, I would insist that any attempt to reconstruct religion will need to develop a rational or philosophical theology. This is to be understood as the bringing of "religious beliefs into ac-

cord with philosophic truth." John Herman Randall describes
rational theology in this way and goes on to say that it is an
enterprise whose value "is not only intellectual but genuinely
religious. Its worth lies not in the formulations of the moment—
they will soon give way to others. It lies rather in the conviction
that it is supremely important to make the never ending effort
to understand."[31]

The test of the worth of a rational theology will be "the test of
the value of any philosophy which is offered us: Does it end in
conclusions which, when they are referred back to ordinary life-
experiences and their predicaments, render them more significant,
more luminous to us, and make our dealings with them more
fruitful?"[32] This test gives priority to experience by assigning
it the role of "ultimate" arbiter, but it also requires a certain
rational consistency or coherence.

In "The Sentiment of Rationality," James states that "of
two conceptions equally fit to satisfy the logical demand, that
one which awakens that active impulses, or satisfies other aesthetic demands better than the other, will be accounted the more
rational conception, and will deservedly prevail."[33] Two things
must be noted here. First, James understands "rational" as combining "logical" and "active" dimensions. Second, while satisfaction of these "active impulses" is the ultimate determinant
of the worth of any rational system, such satisfaction cannot
stand alone or act as a substitute for the "logical demand."

In general, individual men seem to prize either rational consistency or personal fulfillment. The entire effort of James and
Dewey and of the pragmatic tradition is to expose this as a
false "either-or." From their perspective, rational consistency is
a necessary factor in any personal fulfillment which goes beyond
that of a narrow and whimsical emotionalism or individualism.
The approval of rational consistency as an indispensable factor
in a mature human life in no way jeopardizes pragmatism. Such
consistency is valued precisely because "it works" and has proven
itself fruitful in man's undertakings. Of course, since experience
is the primary and ultimate referent, any rational consistency
must be, at best, relative and tentative. Ongoing experience is

always seeping-in and creating deficiencies in the greatest of rational systems.

One further observation concerning the term consistency is relevant to any concern with religion. It is crucial to distinguish that consistency which is characterized by an abstract conceptual scheme from that which is manifest in a personal life. The concrete living person possesses consistency when there is manifest a "holding together" of a set of abstract ideas and such other modes of experience as the affective, esthetic, and religious. Hence, the person has an integrating power quite beyond that of any system of ideas.

At times, the person can embrace concepts which in the abstract are inconsistent and contradictory. This cannot be a permanent state, however, since significant inconsistency gradually becomes a debilitating conflict. At this point the person will surrender one or the other of his conflicting ideas (usually sets of ideas) or he will bring them together in some synthesis. This, I believe, is the precise service that can be rendered to religion by a pragmatic reconstruction. James stresses the directing, integrating, and reconciling functions of pragmatism. Its "only test of probable truth is what works best in the way of leading us, *what fits every part of life best and combines with the collectivity of experience's demands, nothing being omitted.*"[34]

This "fitting together" into a reasonably consistent whole is unending; it is never absolutely achieved. The relativeness of any personal or cultural consistency springs from the processive reality in which man finds himself. For many, a radically developmental man and world is the most serious threat to religion. A pragmatic reconstruction of religion would endeavor to neutralize the threat of a processive world and to "hook into" its profound possibilities. This is obviously a formidable task. It will not be achieved by mouthing praiseworthy words about a dynamic world, while insisting that there are values, truths, or doctrines that remain fundamentally untouched by process. As the development which is presupposed by pragmatism does not admit of exceptions, religion itself is not exempt from development. Its efforts to excuse itself from the risk and struggle that go with change has done much to render it irrelevant to man's contemporary situation.

Development and Continuity

There is a great need, therefore, to reconstruct religion so as to enable it to acknowledge its radically developmental nature. Without presuming to do this in a few words, I would offer a few suggestions. In keeping with the kind of development earlier described, no theory of the development of religion would be adequate which restricts change to "accidentals." Development by transformation is radically different from development by extrinsic addition.[35] The first acknowledges change "through and through," while the second admits only of change along the edges.

To stress such a radical development is not to deny the continuity which also characterizes man and the world. This question of great subtlety awaits philosophical refinement. Still, it is the same man, the same world, and the same church which are now different from what they were. The sameness, however, is due to the fact that the "new" has grown out of the "old" and must not be attributed to some principle or core reality which remains always the same. Thus, a church which was truly developing would grow as a whole; its entire life would be involved in the development, rather than having a part of its reality which would stand outside change.

Having acknowledged the radicalness and depth of the change which belongs to the world, I must quickly add that such change does not imply that man or the world are changing in their entirety at every moment. It would be the sheerest folly to attempt any total change of man or the world, or even of a particular human community. The "radicalness" affirmed by pragmatism does not assert that every value is open to doubt all the time and in every institution of a society. It is necessary that there be a conserving function in any society.[36]

Pragmatism does not prohibit us from affirming that certain values and truths have emerged which ought to endure as long as man endures. According to Dewey:

"The fundamental conceptions of morals are neither arbitrary nor artificial. They are not imposed upon human nature from without but develop out of its own operations and needs. Particular aspects of morals are transient; they are often, in their actual manifestation, defective and perverted. But the framework of moral conceptions is as permanent as human life itself."[37]

Pragmatism would insist, of course, that only those values can endure which continue to grow, and in their growth are transformed.[38] Hence, any pragmatic reconstruction of religion is not obliged immediately to transform its entire reality. On the contrary, it must discriminate among those features of religion which should be jettisoned, those which should be allowed to die quietly, and those which should be continued and developed. Any serious concern with the development of the new must have greater, not less, concern with the past.[39]

Understanding that "to develop" is not simply "to repeat," I would contend that in an adequate reconstruction of religion, the deepest and richest strains of the historical Christian community and the great Christian thinkers would be continued, developed, and enriched. Of course, we cannot avoid picking and choosing that which is to be developed and that which is to be discarded. Such activity, however, seems to have been present from the first moment of Christianity. The early Christians had to decide which features of Judaism to retain, which writings were "sacred," and which laws of the state to obey. Today we continue this sifting-out process when we honor and praise a St. Francis of Assisi rather than a Cardinal Ximenes or a John XXIII rather than a Pius IX, and when we hail Vatican II rather than Vatican I. In the long-run, the kind of religion we have will depend upon how well we pick and choose. Pragmatism does not pretend to present a method which will always guarantee a correct choice. However, it does maintain that we might create a viable religion by surrendering the illusion of an infallible, absolute standard for guidance and concern ourselves instead with the observable consequences of our decisions.

Commitment and Openness

A pragmatic reconstruction of religion is a call to members of religious communities to move themselves into the center of the struggle in which man is engaged. It asks religion to surrender its defensiveness and protectiveness and to tap its great resources of creativity and dynamism. A dynamic religion cannot survive simply because science and philosophy cannot absolutely disprove its claims. Against a militant scientism, it is important for religion to insist upon aspects and dimensions of human experience which cannot be accounted for by science. In doing this, religion keeps man aware of that mystery which engulfs him and in which he shares. This sense of mystery is one of religion's most distinctive and richest features; but it is also its greatest temptation.

Mystery can be a trap, an escape, and an obfuscation unless it is continually feeding and being fed by the diverse particulars of human experience. Though it is often on their lips, most Christians have long-since ceased to have any personal or communal vital awareness of mystery. Their faith has been rationalized to the point of rendering it almost completely flat. The paradox highlighted by contemporary experience is that mystery cannot be approached directly; it cannot be sought and encountered as if it were an object among other objects. Mystery is lessened not deepened, it becomes mystification of the driest sort, when the organic interaction between the science or philosophy of the culture and religion is diminished. It is ironic that those who have affirmed most strongly the "rationality" of faith either have isolated themselves from the rationality of their culture or have juxtaposed their faith to it. A faith which was intimately bound-up with the developments of science, art, literature, and technology could not help but develop both its sense of mystery and its relevance to human life.

A more serious charge against religion is that it involves commitment and therefore cannot possess the openness so prized by contemporary man. Pragmatism rejects the mutual exclusion of openness and commitment. Ralph Barton Perry summarizes James' attitude on this matter as follows:

> Who shall say that it is not humanly possible both to believe, and also to harbor saving doubts; both to cast in your lot with one party, and also respect your opponents; both to feel a passionate devotion to your own cause and yet desire to give every cause a hearing; both to believe yourself right, and yet acknowledge the possibility that you may be wrong?[40]

Openness, then, is the willingness to acknowledge the limited and inadequate aspect of one's most cherished beliefs. Commitment is not fanatical closed-minded adherence to a belief; instead it is a willingness to place oneself in the service of an ideal or a person.

I would suggest that there is no authentic commitment without openness and no productive openness without commitment. As evidence, I would cite modern science which, more than any other human achievement, has made man aware of the value and necessity of "openness." In doing this, however, scientists did not destroy the older ideal of giving oneself totally to that which one believes. Rather, they transformed it by existentially demonstrating that they could be faithful to the ideal of science only by a willingness to call into question and acknowledge evidence against even their most basic scientific principles.[41]

This experience of science suggests to pragmatism that we can surrender the notion of absolutely certain knowledge without becoming sceptics. In a variation on Kant's doctrine of "regulative ideas," pragmatism acknowledges that there is no significant experimentation which is not related to a broader and more inclusive ideal or vision. For this reason, it does not seem excessive to suggest that a religion characterized by the broadest and most inclusive vision must also be characterized by openness, experimentation, and a plurality of expressions. Only in this way can such a religion progressively incarnate its vision and ideals, and keep them from being frozen in the mode of a particular culture or moment in history.[42]

ROLE OF FAITH

It is evident that no reconstruction of religion will progress unless the nature and role of faith in religion and the world is clarified. For this, it will not be sufficient to call upon either the traditional Protestant emphasis upon faith as individual, with its temptation toward subjectivism, or upon the traditional Roman Catholic emphasis upon faith as communal, with its temptation toward objectivism. Nor will it be sufficient to affirm both aspects of faith in some form of juxtaposition. There is needed a re-thinking of faith within a metaphysics which can allow maximum play, interaction, and development to both the individual and communal features of faith: Pragmatism has rich possibilities for just such reconstruction.[43] I have previously described James' view on faith and Dewey's doctrine of the social; together they offer a resource for the reconstruction of faith. Here I would like to make a few observations and suggestions to this end.

Belief

A pragmatic view of man and the world gives a central role to belief and faith. The effort to divide men into believers and non-believers is misleading. All men are believers when belief is understood as an affair of leading, as a pointing ahead; it is a movement beyond that for which there is evidence or at least for which evidence is not present or consciously attended to. From daily routine to the most sophisticated scientific endeavor, every moment of one's life is permeated by such beliefs. Belief, then, is rooted in the human condition; to be a man is to believe.

Just as evident as the fact that all men are believers is the fact that all men do not share the same beliefs. The human community embodies a variety of beliefs, not all of which are of equal importance or worth. Beliefs can and have energized men in the face of the tasks which confront them, but they have also de-energized them and served as obstacles to their development. Hence, we are not excused from evaluating the beliefs of others as well as our own. In the final analysis, the basic criterion of the worth of a belief is the quality of life that it brings forth.

Among the many beliefs which permeate our lives some are more fundamental and have a more immediate bearing on those values which give our lives their specific characteristic and basic meaning. For example, it is one thing to believe that the Yankees will win the pennant, or that the airplane in which I am flying will arrive at its destination, or that the food which I purchase is not poisoned. But it is quite another matter to believe that there are deterministic laws which completely control man's life, or that democracy is the means of human fulfillment, or that Jesus is the incarnate Son of God. The latter beliefs are each characterized by their comprehensiveness, by the fact that they influence every aspect of a person's life. I will call such comprehensive belief faith, which

> "as I will now employ it will refer to a belief or set of beliefs which bear upon human life in its comprehensive effort. Faith plays the role of holding together the diverse aspects or modes of human life or experience. It might be described as an integrating experience whereby knowing-experience, affective-experience, esthetic-experience—in short, all forms of experience—are brought into a relatively cohesive whole which is expressed in the life of the person. Faith thereby serves to order, direct, illuminate and render meaningful human life."[44]

A pragmatic reconstruction of faith will inevitably involve the loss of what seemed to be some of its most distinctive features. Faith cannot be a refuge or a secure haven that protects believers from the anguish and terrors of the world. The Christian has been accused of a "failure of nerve." Too often the charge has been true, not because he believed, but because he did not really believe. When faith is used to avoid responsibility, when it is employed as an excuse for not joining in the common human struggle, then it is being misused and deserves condemnation.

Answers and Certitude

Another misconception is that faith answers the questions

confronting mankind. It is now evident, I believe, that a God who fills in the black spaces—the so-called "God of gaps"—is dead. It is not permissible to believe in God in order to buttress our scientific, philosophical, or even theological systems. The effort of religion to use God in this way has brought both religion and God into disrepute among reflective men.[45] One simple example will suffice. If one maintains that we must believe in God in order to explain motion in the world, what happens to God when a Newton comes along to explain motion without God? The history of science and philosophy in the modern era is the record of the collapse of one argument after another as sufficient reason for affirming God.

For many this has meant the end of Christianity, the undermining of its very reason for being. For others, however, it is seen as a purification of Christian faith and the pathway to a rich renewal and development of this faith. Thus, to Protestant theologian, Carl Michalson, it signifies "not the end of dependence upon God, but the beginning of an existence in which everything is received from God, hence under responsibility to him. Therefore, not the end of God in the world but the end of God as the explanation of the world and the beginning of God as the source of the world's meaning."[46] If we are to continue to believe in God, therefore, it cannot be because he solves our problems or gets us out of difficult situations. It can only be because he has called us as free men to be responsible before him.

The Christian faith has attracted some and repelled others because it has appeared to be a kind of insurance policy or no risk guarantee concerning the meaning of human existence. Such a faith supposedly provides certitude and frees us from all doubts. I would suggest that this faith of easy security and of superficial consolation which pretends to involve no risk or doubt is destructive of authentic faith. Such a view leads many men to surrender their Christian faith because they cannot honestly deny their doubts, their insecurities, and their anguish. Nothing is more necessary, therefore, than to understand that while faith enables us to live with risk, doubt, anguish and uncertainty, it does not remove them. It is perhaps this very lack of certitude which characterizes faith, for in the final analysis the believer must be willing to live his faith with no external assurance of its truth and authenticity.[47] If he had such assurances, he would have no need of faith.

This does not mean that faith is totally without evidence. The believer has the lived evidence of his personal life and of the life of the community within which he believes. There must also be some relative fulfillments accruing to the human community if any reflective believer is to maintain his faith. Such evidence, however, is never absolutely compelling; it can never be such that every right thinking person will be forced to believe in this way. If it were, there would be no freedom and no faith.

Faith and the Future

So far I have said that faith is no refuge, no risk-free, doubt-free answer to our problems. Let me now suggest something of what faith is or ought to be in more positive terms. Many contemporary philosophers and psychologists maintain that man is distinguished from other beings because of the role of the "future" in his life. Because man is not a completed or finished being, what he will become cannot be separated from how he relates to the future. Because man has a future he is not chained to what he now knows or is; nor is he bound to the kind of society or world in which he now finds himself. Man is the being who can play a decisive role in the transformation of himself and his world. In order to do so, however, he must believe that he is able to do this. Were man to fully and completely stop believing, whether consciously or unconsciously, explicitly or implicitly, human development would come to a halt and man would be dead.[48]

Faith is the energy which spurs man to transcend himself, to move beyond the inadequacies of the present, or, as a minimum, to affirm a relationship which turns him outward and is non-isolating. Such faith, of course, cannot be the preserve of Christians alone as is shown by the following text from Roger Garaudy, Marxist and atheist.

As far as faith is concerned, whether faith in God or faith in our task, and whatever our difference regarding its source— for some, assent to a call from God; for others, purely human creation—faith imposes on us the duty of seeing to it that every man becomes a man, a flaming hearth of initiative, a poet in the deepest sense of the word: one who has experienced, day by day, the creative surpassing of himself—what Christians call his transcendence and we call his authentic humanity. This ideal is exalted enough and difficult enough of achievement to demand the combined efforts of all of us.[49]

A faith which keeps man turned to the future must never become closed. It must be ever open and responsive to new insights, new discoveries and, most of all, to new possibilities. Such a faith will welcome the fullest reflective criticism even of itself. A faith which asks for a privileged sanctuary protected from the cumulative insights of human experience is a faith which is weak at the core. We might even suggest that it is deficient as faith since it can continue to exist only by closing itself off from the creations progressively achieved by man.

In stressing the openness and future-oriented aspects of man, it is crucial to avoid any interpretation which sees human fulfillment or the fruits of faith as located only in the future. The "future" is a denigration of lives lived and lives being lived, unless it is at once reconstruction of the past and an enhancement of the present. There can be no worthwhile future or faith in the future, therefore, which denies the past or which can be affirmed only at the expense of the present.[50] This concern for the future which avoids betraying the present is, according to John McDermott, characteristic of American experience.

Over against the doctrine of obsolescence in which the history of man waits patiently for a paradisiacal *Deus ex machina,* the

American temper points to a temporalized eschatology in which the Spirit manifests itself generation by generation and all counts to the end.[51]

GOD IN PRAGMATISM

Any pragmatic reconstruction of religion will require the development of an appropriate "philosophy of God." To suggest that the God of traditional Christianity could remain existentially or conceptually untouched by such a reconstruction would gravely compromise and emasculate it at the outset. Without presuming to present anything approaching an adequate pragmatic philosophy of God, I wish to advance a few tentative and hypothetical suggestions. They are presented without argument or pretense of "proof," though each of them is most controversial.

There is no theology, rational or other, which emerges independently of an historical-cultural context or of the metaphysics or world-view by which the context is articulated. That is why any pragmatic reconstruction of religion must proceed from and develop within the metaphysics I have briefly outlined. To the extent that pragmatism really expresses a world-view radically, though not totally, different from classical metaphysics, the God of pragmatism will be different from the God of classical philosophy. As an example drawn from the most sensitive dimension of the question, it is not possible to reconcile a God who is immutable, omnipotent, and omniscient with a world which is unfinished, in process, and which manifests real chance and novelty. I will not argue this point here nor will I rule out the possibility of some reconciliation. However, I would insist that any attempted reconciliation must not begin with an unquestionable assumption that God is immutable, omnipotent, and omniscient. Anyone making such an approach today is open to the charge of "bad faith."

Knowledge

One of the formidable obstacles in the way of rethinking God is the refusal of most "religionists" to surrender their "spectator" or correspondence theory of knowledge. A corollary of this is the inability to credit any religion or faith which does not give some kind of knowledge. I have argued elsewhere[52] that while faith is a mode of experience, it is not a mode of knowledge. Such an expression is open to great misunderstanding; no doubt it is not the happiest of phrasings. However, the objections give evidence of the cultural bias that only knowledge, in some form or other, is really worthwhile—and this despite the many protestations concerning the priority of love or religious experience. The scriptures, creeds, and dogmas are all viewed as giving us some kind of "information" about God; religious symbols are viewed as representing in some way a dimension of God's reality. Against a view which maintains that all of these are nothing more than psychological projections, mere subjectivistic expressions of man's inner life, the emphasis upon the "objectivity" of faith and religion is understandable. The question, of course, is whether the alternatives of subjectivism or objectivism are exhaustive. The primary thrust of any pragmatic reconstruction of religion would be to show that they are not.

I would contend that religion and faith have distinct and indispensable roles to play. Although they will always involve knowledge, they are neither identical with nor inseparable from this knowledge.[53] In general, religion and faith can be defended in virtue of their contribution to the illumination, expansion, enrichment, and progressive development of man's life. Religious symbols cannot be understood as giving knowledge; they are

"not representative but functional and participational.[54] Thus, they should serve to order, direct and intensify the developing life of the community and those persons who are expressions of the community. Symbols, then, are always constructions of some human community and must continually be evaluated in terms of their service to the life of the community. While they are constructions of the community, it is not legitimate to rule out, *a priori,* the possibility that the constructing is done in the *presence* of or in an experience with this *Other* whom we traditionally call God."[55]

Any reflective approach to God is to be evaluated by the same criteria used for evaluating any rational theology. Initially it must have a reasonable consistency so that it will conceptually hold together diverse modes of experience. But the decisive criterion must be whether it enables the person and the community to live their faith more fruitfully. It would be foolish to imagine that one could work out a fully-formed rational theology which would then be "tested" by the community. On the contrary, there must be continual interaction between the theologian or philosopher and the existential life of the community (and not only his immediate religious community). As I have earlier indicated, there is no sudden and entire change (*in toto*); communities change in bits and pieces, in fits and starts.

A worthwhile rational theology will be responsible to this and not try to achieve any definitive "philosophy of God." Such an approach should minimize the errors and excesses of both rationalism and sceptical empiricism. A pragmatic rational theology will acknowledge the "rationalistic" insight that man has a continuing need to "know" God or at least in some way to grasp or envision "the whole." But pragmatism also concedes to empiricism its insight that we do not and cannot "experience" the whole, and hence that any ideas or concepts of God are inevitably human constructs.[56]

Pragmatism and God

Though pragmatism is itself a form of empiricism, it differs from any empiricism which would view such constructs as nonsense or subjectivistic psychological projections. Having rejected any subjective-objective metaphysical dualism, it asks only that such constructs prove fruitful in their "leading" function within the community. Hence, pragmatism can allow the fullest expression to speculative or imaginative forays, so long as these are not considered to be eternal mirrorings of God. Instead, they must be recognized as distinct and necessary ways in which man contributes to the development of himself, of the world, and perhaps even of God.

The God who emerges from pragmatism would probably lose some of his sovereignty. However, he may gain as a God of love who desires to share his life with an autonomous being and is willing to risk something of himself in order to help this being come into existence. By the same token, man may lose some of the security and superficial help which he received or believed he received from God. This may be a small price to pay for the privilege of sharing with God the task of "building the earth." Such a cooperative endeavor avoids presenting man as either an isolated and tragic demi-god, free to do anything he desires, or as a divine "rubber-stamp," whose freedom is limited to approving what God already is or has done.

I would submit that responsibility *before* God is a richer value and symbol than responsibility *to* God, when the latter is understood as simply carrying out divine commands. The first, responsibility before God, seems most congenial to the incarnation, understood as the call of God to join with him in the task of redemptive creativity. The second, responsibility to God, still manifests an image of God as an oriental potentate giving orders which we are to follow blindly and unquestioningly. From the pragmatic perspective, both God and man are responsible for the world, since it is his world and ours.

CONCLUSION

It would be grossly misleading to offer a pragmatic reconstruction of religion as some magic solution to the ills of religion, to say nothing of those of mankind. I do believe, of course, that such a reconstruction would give some direction. It suggests possibilities for breaking beyond some of the dead-end situations in which religion finds itself. At the same time, it involves a sizable risk and will undoubtedly lead to the surrender of many ideas, institutions, and practices which now seem indispensable.[57] None of these, however, is excluded *a priori*. In all likelihood, many of them can survive and benefit from reconstruction; those that cannot ought to be surrendered willingly, if not happily.

In some sense it is rather ridiculous to discuss the advisability of religion's willingness to surrender some of its claims. Such matters are not resolved by abstract debate or deliberate *fiat*. Consider, for example, the claims of religion in the realm of knowledge. For the past four hundred years there has been a succession of one reduction after another in the knowledge-claims of Christianity. The increasing isolation and irrelevance of religion with regard to the ongoing problems of mankind has happened. The isolation and irrelevance is not yet total, but it seems a reasonable conjecture that if religion continues as it has it cannot avoid becoming a relic—precious to a few, but in no way at the center of the world and human formation. My hypothesis is that this is not good for man and most certainly not for religion. But religion as such is not important; only if it plays a distinctive and indispensable role in human life is the effort I suggest worthwhile. By the very criteria which I have accepted, however, I can have no advance certainty that such an undertaking can or ought to succeed. This is both the strength and limitation of a pragmatic approach. It is willing to entertain any hypothesis, but it insists that even religious hypotheses are not exempt from "making their way," from bearing observable fruit.

Throughout I have stressed this point of testing by observing the consequences of an idea or practice. I do not think that we already have some litmus-paper test whereby we can discover those religious institutions, symbols, and practices which are worthwhile and those which are not. No such test now exists, except in the broad and admittedly vague form which I have described. It has been a common misunderstanding of Dewey's call for the extension of the scientific or experimental method to all spheres of human life that he desired some mechanical application of a specialized method to every mode of experience.[58] The possibility of devising an experimental method which can be employed in religion is presented here as an hypothesis.

The call for experimentation, whether in ethics, or politics, or religion, is not a call to destroy every existing aspect of these institutions and then miraculously to create, *ab ovo,* better ones.

It suggests instead that we not hesitate to construct hypotheses on the basis of the already significant accumulation of human experience. Further, it contends that experimentation, in the sense of choosing those ways which have proved fruitful and borne the test of time, has always been the unarticulated method of man and of the evolutionary cosmos itself. Modern science has refined this method and brought it to fuller consciousness. Pragmatism suggests that this method awaits further development and refinement by being adapted to such areas as morality and religion.

The question is whether the change will be programmed and proceed with some degree of order and awareness, however incomplete and tentative, as to where we are going or want to go. Or will we continue to drift aimlessly, changing only when that which we desired to preserve has been lost, thereby courting the destructiveness of violent change? This, of course, is not a question for religion alone. It is the most pressing question confronting man and all of his institutions. Religion could render mankind a great service were it to discover some ways of bringing about continual but orderly institutional change. It would seem that a religious community, more than any other, should be most fit for just an undertaking, for it should be moved by the deepest, richest, and least enclosed vision and ideals. Should it not be most aware of the impossibility of any permanent articulation of this vision, and should not the mystery which is awakened by the faith in a revealing and self-communicating God suggest the widest range of possibilities which man through his efforts is to realize and incarnate?

Yet, as history too painfully attests, "religion" has become labeled and indeed often labels itself as the most conservative of institutions, jealously guarding its treasure and fearful of any activity which appears to threaten it. The most damning irony, of course, is that this treasure, which really should be preserved, has turned into a "handful of dust," desired for the most part only by lifeless, unimaginative, and fearful people. Perhaps this is an overstatement, but it comes much too close to reality to give comfort to anyone desirous of once again seeing religion do its share. The pragmatic moral is that unless the vision of a religion touches and is touched by every aspect of developing experience, it can neither make its contribution nor realize its potential.

Christianity is a case in point. At one time it was the formulator and the center of all spheres of the culture which it engendered. Gradually it withdrew to a territory called "the sacred." In our time, even those who are believing Christians are dissatisfied with such a partitioning of territories and are seeking a way of once again being present to every sphere of human life. The fact that Christianity can never again be present in the way she was in an earlier age raises the question of the new way or ways which can be discovered or created that will lead to a new and perhaps more intimate presence. No one knows what they are. It is my belief that a pragmatic reconstruction of Christianity may at least start us in the direction of such a presence.

◇

1. Whatever disagreements one might have with Thomas Altizer and William Hamilton, we are all in their debt for having pointed out this collapse and forcing to the surface what many were playing down by emphasizing signs of hope.

2. Criticism of religion is a necessary prelude to any reconstruction. Cf. Paul Tillich, **The Protestant Era** (Chicago: Univ. of Chicago Press, 1957), p. 185. Abridged edition. "The first word, therefore, to be spoken by religion to the people of our time must be a word spoken against religion."

3. I do not mean to give the impression either that there were no positive values involved in the collapse of the western world or that there are not already underway efforts at reconstruction. Paradoxically, the very movements which contributed to the collapse, such as the political, industrial and scientific revolutions, were themselves reconstructions and

provide the resources for further and more conscious reconstructions. Hence, I do not subscribe to any reading of history which would see the modern era as a decline, absolutely or relatively. Though there have been losses, the positive possibilities which have emerged are tremendous. The potential for reconstruction is proportionate to those possibilities.

4. These are general tendencies; neither does, could, or should exist in some pure form. For example, any vital thought, however continuous it endeavors to be with earlier ideas, principles, or categories, cannot help but realize some degree of reconstruction even of its most basic and ultimate principles. On the other hand, the most radical reconstruction begins from an inherited intellectual framework which is the result of earlier efforts at coping with the human situation.

5. Cf. William James, "The Dilemma of Determinism," **The Writings of William James—A Comprehensive Edition**, edited with an "Introduction" and "Annotated Bibliography" by John McDermott(New York: Random House, 1967), p. 606. Referred to hereafter as **Writings**. In discussing his theory of indeterminacy, James states: "It gives us a pluralistic, restless universe, in which no single point of view can ever take in the whole scene."

6. I am treating the thought of James and Dewey as expressing a similar if not unified viewpoint. In a more extensive treatment, it would be necessary to call attention to a number of differences of content, style, and concern between the two thinkers. For example, James is characterized by a kind of Augustinian "metaphysical restlessness" which is apparently absent in Dewey. Also, James seems willing to say almost anything about God if it gives satisfaction and consolation to anyone, while Dewey is much more suspicious of the entire tradition and enterprise of religion. Notice that I qualify this by saying "seems" and "apparently" because I would argue that, despite their differences, James does not condone indiscriminate religious emoting nor justify every kind of satisfaction. On the other hand, Dewey has a sensitivity to the religious dimension of man and the world which does not suffer comparison with James.

7. James, **Writings**, p. 741.

8. John Dewey, **A Common Faith** (New Haven: Yale Univ. Press, 1960), p. 7.

9. For a fine statement on the necessity of recognizing and accepting one's immediate religious context while continually working to bring forth a richer and more universal context, see Rosemary Ruether, "Post-Ecumenical Christianity," **The Ecumenist**, V (1966), 3-7. For a fuller statement of her position see **The Church Against Itself** (New York: Herder and Herder, 1967).

10. What follows, as I have already indicated, is but a brief statement of the subtle and complex world-view which permeates the efforts of James and Dewey. I am here giving only the barest hint of what is involved. For a somewhat fuller "hint," see my "Religious Truth in a Relational and Processive World," **Cross Currents**, XVII (1967), 287-301. Originally written for the Workshop on the Problem of God, it will also appear in the **Proceedings** of that Workshop, to be edited by George F.

McLean and published by The Catholic University of America Press.

11. To avoid giving the impression that there is some "reality as such" which undergirds the world, I am using "world" and "reality" interchangeably. Actually there are many worlds, all of them real in the Jamesian or Deweyean sense. "Anything is real," James tells us, "of which we find ourselves obliged to take account of in any way." **Writings,** pp. 253-54. See also, John Dewey, **On Experience, Nature, and Freedom,** edited and introduced by Richard J. Bernstein (New York: Liberal Arts Press, 1960), p. 59, where Dewey says that "reality" is "a denotative term, a word used to designate indifferently everything that happens." John Herman Randall, Jr. puts the issue as follows: "Everything encountered in any way is somehow real. The significant question is, not whether anything is 'real' or not, but how and in what sense it is real, and how it is related to and functions among other reals." **Nature and Historical Experience** (New York: Columbia Univ. Press, 1958), p. 131.

12. For a succinct contrast between these two meanings of experience, see Dewey, "The Need for a Recovery of Philosophy," in **On Experience, Nature, and Freedom,** p. 23.

13. John Dewey, **Experience and Education** (New York: Macmillan, 1956), pp. 41-42.

14. Cf. John Dewey, **Experience and Nature** (New York: Dover, 1958), p. 424. "The habitual avoidance in theories of knowledge of any reference to the fact that knowledge is a case of belief, operates as a device for ignoring the monstrous consequences of regarding the latter as existentially subjective, personal and private."

15. John Dewey, **Philosophy and Civilization** (New York: Minton, Balch & Company, 1931), pp. 79-80.

16. Dewey, **Experience and Education,** p. 32.

17. Dewey, **Philosophy and Civilization,** p. 77.

18. Cf. John J. McDermott, "Introduction," **Writings,** pp. xxv-xxvi. "For James, it is precisely the ability of man to enter into the relational fabric of the world, in a participative and liberating way, which enables him to become human."

19. John Dewey, **Individualism Old and New** (New York: Capricorn, 1962), p. 81. Italics added.

20. James, "The Will to Believe," **Writings,** p. 717.

21. James, "The Sentiment of Rationality," **Writings,** p. 336.

22. **Ibid.,** p. 335.

23. Ralph Barton Perry, **The Thought and Character of William James** (Boston: Little Brown and Co., 1935), II, 248. For a series of letters in which James expresses his dismay at the misunderstanding of his position, see **Ibid.,** pp. 240-49.

24. William James, **The Will to Believe** (New York: Dover, 1960). For a fresh and insightful reconsideration of the central problem of this essay see Walter Arnold, "Is There an Ethics of Belief?," **Cross Currents,** XVII (1967), 333-42.

25. Cf. James, **Writings,** pp. 337, 730-31.

26. **Ibid.,** p. 736.

27. **Ibid.**, p. 737.

28. **Ibid.**, p. 470.

29. Dewey, **Individualism Old and New,** p. 140.

30. A special word of warning should be given to those Roman Catholics who may suddenly find themselves attracted to pragmatism as a result of their dissatisfaction with certain rationalistic excesses in their own tradition. I would contend that properly developed pragmatic religion would be more, not less, intellectually demanding—but, of course, in a radically different way.

31. John Herman Randall, Jr., **The Role of Knowledge in Western Religion** (Boston: Starr King Press, 1958), p. 140.

32. Dewey, **Experience and Nature,** p. 7.

33. James, **Writings,** p. 325.

34. **Ibid.**, p. 390. Italics added.

35. Cf. Thomas J. J. Altizer, "Catholic Theology and the Death of God." **Religion in Contemporary Thought** (New York: Alba House, 1973), pp. 187-202. "Among others things to think historically is to recognize a transformation in consciousness in accordance with the movements of history, and such thinking leaves no room for the naive supposition that historical or organic development is simply the progressive enlargement of an original and never changing form."

36. Developmentalist though he was, Dewey nevertheless asserts the need for such a function. Cf. John Dewey and James H. Tufts, **Ethics** (New York: Henry Holt and Company, 1959), pp. 374-75; also, John Dewey, **The Quest for Certainty** (New York: Minton, Balch & Company, 1929), pp. 272-73.

37. Dewey, **Ethics,** p. 344.

38. In the dispute concerning the existence of "absolutes," it is significant that the values, such as justice, love, and truth, which are cited as evidence in favor of absolutism, defy any universally accepted abstract definition and seem capable of multiple expressions and unlimited development.

39. Cf. Dewey, **Philosophy and Civilization,** p. 7. "The life of all thought is to effect a junction at some point of the new and the old, of deep-sunk customs and unconscious dispositions, that are brought to light of attention by some conflict with newly emerging directions and activity." Also, James, **Writings,** p. 450. "Truth grafts itself on previous truth, modifying it in the process, just as idiom grafts itself on previous idiom, and law on previous law."

40. Ralph Barton Perry, **In the Spirit of William James** (New Haven: Yale Univ. Press, 1938), p. 206.

41. I do not wish to unduly romanticize scientists. I am not contending that any one scientist has ever been fully faithful to this ideal of commitment and openness. One finds in the scientific community, as in any religious community, a formidable gap between the existential life of its members and the vision or ideal which they affirm. Scientific "saints" are just as rare as religious ones. All I am claiming, therefore, is that "science" as a distinctive mode of human experience expressed in a

community of scholars manifests at least as ideals the features which I have described.

42. Cf. Robert Pollock, "Freedom and History," **Thought**, IV (1952), 411. "Truth and value must be given actuality, they must be progressively inserted into history if the tendency to rationality is to remain vital. Hence the need for an unending reconstruction of personal-social life in the image of truths and values as they are apprehended." Also, p. 413. "Static truths and values become unendurable, for they have to be brought into life if there is to be growth toward infinity."

43. Robert Pollock would contend that the effort of pragmatism to overcome the opposition between the individual and the community is a continuation of a process initiated by Christianity. Cf. "Freedom and History," p. 416. "In linking the personal and the social together Christianity thus initiated a process in which, more than ever, society has become the medium of human unfolding.

44. Fontinell, "Religious Truth," p. 304.

45. It is just such **religion** which William Hamilton, following Dietrich Bonhoeffer, rejects. Cf. Thomas J. J. Altizer and William Hamilton, **Radical Theology and the Death of God** (New York: Bobbs- Merrill Co., 1966), p. 40. "I take religion to mean," Hamilton asserts, ". . . any system of thought or action in which God or the gods serve as fulfiller of needs or solver of problems."

46. Carl Michalson, **The Rationality of Faith** (New York: Charles Scribner's Sons, 1963), p. 135.

47. It has been frequently noted that there is a vicious circle involved in any attempt to "ground" faith upon some authority, whether that authority be the scriptures, the Church, or science, inasmuch as any such authority can be affirmed as an authority only by what is itself an act of faith.

48. Cf. Teilhard de Chardin, "Building the Earth," **Cross Currents**, IX (1959), 325. "Religion has sometimes been understood as a mere antidote to our evils, an 'opiate.' **Its true purpose is to sustain and spur on the progress of life.**"

49. Roger Garaudy, **From Anathema to Dialogue** (New York: Herder and Herder, 1966), p. 123.

50. Dewey, with all his stress upon the future, avoids any futurist trap. In his later writings in particular he went to great pains to stress that experience is not only instrumental—a means for future experience, but also consummatory—a fulfillment realized and terminated in the present. This theme runs throughout his **Experience and Nature** and **Art as Experience** (New York: Capricorn, 1958). See also **Experience and Education**, p. 51: "The ideal of using the present simply to get ready for the future contradicts itself;" and, **Ibid.**, p. 93: "It (experience) can expand into the future only as it is enlarged to take in the past."

51. John J. McDermott, **The American Angle of Vision** (New York: Cross Currents, 1966), p. 86.

52. Eugene Fontinell, "Reflections on Faith and Metaphysics," **Cross Currents**, XVI (1966), 35 ff.

53. Cf. Randall, **Role of Knowledge in Western Religion**, p. 6.

54. **Ibid.**, pp. 113-14; also, Randall, **Nature and Historical Experience**, pp. 263 ff. Randall has noted the similarity of his position on symbols to that of Paul Tillich with whom he taught a number of courses on myths and symbols. Cf. **The Journal of Philosophy**, II (March 4, 1954), 159. Tillich has presented his theory of symbols as participational in a number of works. See, e.g., **The Dynamics of Faith** (New York: Harper & Brothers, 1957), Chap. III, "Symbols of Faith," also, "Religious Symbols and Our Knowledge of God," **The Christian Scholar** (September, 1955).

55. Fontinell, "Religious Truth," pp. 313-14.

56. Cf. Randall, **Nature and Historical Experience**, p. 198. "We never encounter 'the Universe': we never act toward, experience, or feel being or existence as 'a whole.'" Nevertheless, "existence can of course **become unified** . . . But this unification always involves the element of 'myth.'" (**Ibid.**, p. 130) It is necessary to stress that "myth" is by no means a pejorative word for Randall. He would hold that such notions as the "Unmoved Mover," the "Unconditioned Conditioner," and the "First Cause" are all "metaphysical myths," and "such myths are very far from being 'meaningless.'" (**Ibid.**, p. 200).

57. Cf. Dewey, **Experience and Nature**, p. 222. "If we once start thinking no one can guarantee where we shall come out, except that many objects, ends and institutions are surely doomed. Every thinker puts some portion of an apparently stable world in peril and no one can wholly predict what will emerge in its place."

58. Cf. Dewey, **Individualism Old and New**, p. 156. "Experimental method is something other than the use of blowpipes, retorts and reagents. It is the foe of every belief that permits habit and wont to dominate invention and discovery, and ready-made system to override verifiable fact."

A Whiteheadean Approach
To the Problem of God

◇

by
Walter E. Stokes, S.J.

YEARS BEFORE the "death of God theology," in the Lowell
Lectures of 1926, Alfred North Whitehead remarked: "The modern world has lost God and is seeking him."[1] It may be worthwhile to explore a Whiteheadean approach to the problem of God
for today. Many philosophical voices in a variety of idioms have
converged on a series of related questions. Can God's existence
be reconciled with man's deepened experience of himself as a free
creator of the world? Can God's existence be accepted without
destroying man's dignity in his free creative role in the universe?
Can God's existence be affirmed as transcendent without making
God a functional element in an abstract scheme? All these questions are concerned with reconciling God's presence in experience with his transcendence; with preserving as unique both
God's actuality and man's freedom.

In a widely read expression of this concern, John A. T. Robinson questioned the relevance of a theism that would think of
God as a heavenly, completely perfect person who resides above
the world and mankind.[2] In an equally popular work, Harvey Cox
strikes the same note: "The willingness of the classical philosophers to allow the God of the Bible to be blurred into Plato's
Idea of the Good or Aristotle's Prime Mover was fatal. It has

[61]

resulted in a doctrine of God which in the era of the secular city forces men like Camus to choose *between* God and human freedom, between Christian faith and human creativity."[3] This tension appears again in Gabriel Vahanian's reflection on the theme in Archibald Macleish's *J. B.* that a God of justice has nothing to do with life because life is moved by love: "Why try to prove God, if all that man needs is to be himself? Why seek God, if all that man wants is love?"[4]

In still another idiom, this is dramatized by Jean-Paul Sartre in *The Devil and the Good Lord:* "Silence is God. Absence is God. God is the loneliness of man. There was no one but myself. I alone decided on evil, I alone invented Good. It was I who cheated, I who worked miracles, I who accused myself today, I alone can absolve myself; I, man. If God exists, man is nothing; if man exists. . . ."[5] Maurice Merleau-Ponty recalls Jacques Maritain's rejection of a God conceived as "the absurd Emperor of the world" who would finally sacrifice man to the cosmos. But Merleau-Ponty goes on to ask whether or not the notion of God as necessary being is not so bound up with this notion that without it God would cease to be the God of Theism: "Yes, *where* will one stop the criticism of idols, and *where* will one ever be able to say the true God actually resides if, as Maritain writes, we pay tribute to false gods 'every time we bow before the world.' "[6]

In a contemporary form of Marxism, Roger Garaudy stresses the two essential dimensions of man: subjectivity and transcendence. In this view, to exist is to create. Man's basic task is to stretch his creative energies to the maximum for the sake of realizing man's dynamic totality. In the area of knowledge, the weakness of religion is not in the questions it raises but in its attempt to give dogmatic answers: "Beyond the myths about the origin, and meaning of life, beyond the alienated notions of transcendence and death, there exists the concrete dialectic of finite and infinite, and this remains a living reality as long as we remain aware *that it is not in the order of answers but in the order of question.*"[7] In the realm of action, this creation will be the fulfillment of the specifically human need to create and to create oneself so that the infinite is absence and exigency rather than promise and presence. Accordingly, Garaudy asks:

"Is it to impoverish man, to tell him that he lives as an incomplete being, that everything depends upon him, that the whole of our history and its significance is played out within man's intelligence, heart and will, and nowhere else, that we bear full responsibility for this; that we must assume the risk, every step of the way, since, for us atheists, nothing is promised and no one is waiting?"[8]

In still another idiom, Thomas Altizer expresses this tension between man's creative subjectivity and a transcendent reality:

"Once the Christian has been liberated from all attachment to a celestial and transcendent Lord, and has died in Christ to the primordial reality of God, then he can say triumphantly: God is dead! Only the Christian can speak the liberating word of the death of God because only the Christian has died in Christ to the transcendent realm of the sacred and can realize in his own participation in the forward-moving body of Christ the victory of the self-negation of Spirit."[9]

Varied though they be, these thinkers converged in their preoccupation with the dignity intrinsic to man's creative freedom and their rejection of a God, wholly other or totally transcendent Being, whose very existence threatens man's creative freedom.

A Whiteheadean approach to the problem of God starts with a basis in experience which begins a cycle process of rhythmic growth in the knowledge and experience of God. In the order of discovery, there is a process. This growth process begins with the stage of romance wherein experience of God has the freshness of novelty, combining realizations not yet explored with "possibilities half-disclosed by glimpses and half-concealed by the wealth of possibilities."[10] This naturally leads on to the stage of precision, which adds to man's experience the coherence and

adequacy of a scheme of interrelated notions. Since no determinate meaning can be given to expressions of our notion of God
as personal, individual, and actual apart from the framework
provided by such a scheme, this stage in man's knowledge of
God depends on the previous stage of romance. "It is evident
that a stage of precision is barren without a previous stage of
romance: unless there are facts which have already been vaguely
apprehended in their broad generality, the previous analysis is
an analysis of nothing."[11]

Still lest God become a counter in an abstract scheme, another
stage is required: the stage of synthesis. This final stage is "nothing else than the satisfactory way in which the mind will
function when it is poked up into activity." [12] Though this
represents momentary final success, each of the stages must be
continually revivified, recreated, and developed in an unending
process if man is to know the living God, If man's knowledge of
God is to be real, it must grow in unending cyclic process, even
though attention may focus now on precision, now on synthesis,
and once more on romance. Man must continuously press on
toward knowledge and experience in the indeterminate future;
he must not rest with the notion of a God caught somehow in
the net of concepts at some moment in his past life.

THE STAGE OF ROMANCE

In this stage of man's growth in the experience and knowledge
of God, man's situation in the world raises for him the question of
"what in the way of value, is the attainment of life?"[13] This
begins in one moment of self-consicousness with three fundamental concepts:

1. that of the value of an individual for itself;
2. that of the value of the diverse individuals of the world
   for each other; and
3. that of the value of the objective world which is a community derivative from the interrelations of its component
   individuals, and also necessary for the existence of each
   of these individuals.[14]

Man's grasp of the character of the universe is like the intuition of the character of a friend in which the permanent character of the universe is brought into a unity. Man's consciousness of God begins with self-valuation, and broadens into the intuition of the character of the universe as a realm of interrelated values and, finally, of adjusted values. Drawing on experience set down in the philosophy of Berkeley and Bacon, concretized in literature, especially the Romantic poets, and abstracted in the formalized viewpoints of science, especially quantum phyiscs, relativity, and evolution, Whitehead gives the experiential base for his intuition into the character of the universe. One principle source is poetic expression in Shelley who concretizes the flux of things, and in Wordsworth who captures the intuition of enduring permanence. Together they express the solidarity of the universe of real novelty with enduring permanences. "Both Shelley and Wordsworth emphatically bear witness that nature cannot be divorced from its aesthetic values; and that these values arise from the cumulation, in some sense, of the brooding presence of the whole unto its various parts."[15] Here Whitehead discovers first of all the value of the individual: "Remembering the poetic rendering of our concrete experience, we see at once that the element of value, of being valuable, of having value, of being an end in itself, of being something which is for its own sake, must not be omitted in any account of any event as the most concrete actual something."[16] This value is not self-sufficient, but draws together into its self-valuation the larger universe in which it finds itself because the poet grasps nature as a unity *(in solido)*. Poetry leads to the question: "What is the status of the enduring stability of the order of nature?"[17] Because stable order implies limitation, there must be a source of limitation which cannot in turn have a further explanation of its definiteness. In this sense, God is the ultimate irrationality: both the principle of limitation and the ground of rationality. However, this is but a stage in man's rhythmic growth in the knowledge of God; this unsystematic affirmation must find a systematic context lest its meaning remain thoroughly indeterminate.

THE STAGE OF PRECISION

This stage of romance finds its completion in the stage of precision, since the half-glimpsed and half-concealed possibilities require as adequate and coherent a formulation as is humanly possible. On this level the religious problem is "the question whether the process of the temporal world passes into the actualities, bound together in an order in which novelty does not mean loss."[18] Here man strives to give adequate and coherent schematization to romantic experience. In fact, the notion of God requires metaphysics, because there are no "floating statements" but only answers to questions.

Solidarity

For Whitehead the central problem of philosophy is "to conceive a complete *(panteles)* fact."[19] In the tradition of Plato and Aristotle, Whitehead asks: What is ultimately most real and valuable?[20] Rather than being a ferocious debate between irritable professors, philosophy must try to clarify the fundamental beliefs which finally determine the emphasis of attention that lies at the base of character.[21] It seeks the general ideas that are indispensably relevant to everything that happens. Each aspect of experience is judged in terms of its place in and contribution to these general ideas and fundamental beliefs that we find credible, reliable, and humanly important. Philosophy is concerned with what really matters; it is orientated toward the complete fact in its complexity and concreteness.

For this reason "solidarity" is the key to Whitehead's metaphysics. This notion, borrowed from the legal notion *in solido,* has as its direct source H. W. Carr who used it to describe the interrelation of soul and body in man.

"The term which seems best adapted to express the interaction of the mind and body is solidarity. The old legal meaning of this term fits the notion. It was originally a term of Roman and Civil law to express the character of a contract which in a single matter involved several obligations on the part of the debtors, with corresponding rights to the creditors. . . . The term solidarity means that diverse, even divergent, activities together bring to pass a single common result to which all the activities contribute without sacrificing their individual integrity."[22]

In Whitehead's metaphysics, "solidarity" means that the universe is an organic whole, a plurality of individual entities which produce the one single result which is the complete fact. In so doing, the divergent and diverse activities produce the single result without losing their individuality. The unity of the universe is constituted by the interaction of a plurality of interrelated individual entities—each individual is essentially what it is by its relation to the universe.

This is Whitehead's metaphysical formulation of Wordsworth's nature *in solido*. Its technical formulation is Whitehead's Ontological Principle "that apart from things that are actual, there is nothing—nothing either in fact or efficacy. . . . It is the principle that everything is positively somewhere in actuality, and potency everywhere."[23] This principle expresses Wordsworth's experience of "that mysterious presence of surrounding things, which imposes itself on any separate element that we set up as individual for its own sake."[24] It involves the discovery that the universe is made up of interconnected unities that are suffused with the modal presence of others. In this way Whitehead restores the interconnectedness of things to a universe shattered by the abstractions of Cartesian substance. He takes seriously Wordsworth's warning that:

Our meddling intellect
Misshapes the beauteous forms of things .
We murder to dissect.

In this movement away from disconnected abstractions to the
and end in itself, of being something which is for its own sake,

interrelatedness of concrete fact, he goes along with Bergson. But Whitehead does not think that "spatialisation" of things is an error bound up with man's intellectual grasp of reality, since by using his intellect properly man can overcome the tendency to misunderstand abstractions for concrete reality and so avoid the fallacy of misplaced concreteness.

Reasoning to God

Whitehead holds that each element within his metaphysical scheme requires each of the others for its own intelligibility. They are meaningless in isolation from one another. These coherent notions are: the actual entities of the temporal world, together with their formative elements—eternal objects, God, and Creativity. Together they interpret every element of human experience. This means that metaphysics grasps the concrete existents of the universe in their solidarity. In this scheme, God is not a mere function of experience but His transcendence is encountered within experience.

Whitehead believes that Plato discovered those general ideas which are relevant to everything that happens: the Ideas, Physical Elements, Psyche, Eros, Harmony. Mathematical Relations and the Receptacle.[25] In adapting Plato's seven basic notions Whitehead takes as his starting point "the notion of actuality as in its essence process."[26] He adopts Plato's Receptacle: "The community of the world, which is the matrix for all begetting, and whose essence is process with retention of connectedness—this community is what Plato terms the Receptacle."[27] More precisely, Creativity is that "ultimate principle by which the many which are the universe disjunctively, becomes the one actual occasion, which is the universe conjunctively."[28] Creativity is conditioned by the actual world as related to each novel coming-to-be of individual actual entities in the temporal world. Because each actual occasion is a unique synthesis of the actual world relative to its becoming, there is no completed set of actual things that make up the universe. Because the set of all occasions is the initial situation for the novel actual occasion, "actual world" is always a relative term. This actual world provides the "data" for each novel actual entity in process. But this data is active, not passive, precisely because Creativity is with the actual world. This initial datum with Creativity is the "real potentiality" of the novel actual occasions. It is real in the sense that Plato affirms the reality of non-being in the *Sophist*.

The counterparts of Plato's Ideas are Whitehead's Eternal Objects. In abstraction from actual entities, including God, the eternal objects together with Creativity constitute unlimited, abstract possibility. Accordingly, the very meaning of actuality is "decision" whereby unlimited possibility is limited and so attains actuality. Just as potentiality for process is the meaning of the more general term "entity" or "thing," so "decision" is the added meaning of the word "actual" in the term "actual entity." This means that all forms of realization involve limitation. Each actuality is this, and not that. Each involved negation and exclusion, because mere omission is characteristic of confusion. To be is to be finite; only the finite can be actual and intelligible. Infinity has the character of undetermined, abstract possibility. The primordial limitation of Creativity is God in his contemplation of the eternal objects in a harmony of conceptual valuation. The order and harmony of the universe indicates that there is a "givenness" or relevant eternal objects for each actual occasion in the temporal process. For this reason, there must be a non-temporal actual entity to account for this graded relevance of eternal objects: "The limitation whereby there is perspective relevance of eternal objects to the background is characteristic of decision. Transcendent decision includes God's decision."[29]

There is a circular movement from the world to God and from God to the world. Since the powers of human knowledge are limited, while God is without limit, this process has no end. The notions of God and the world require one another for their own intelligibility, so that it is equally true to say that the world creates God as it is to say that God creates the world. This means that there is mutual immanence between God and the world. Instead of regarding this as anti-theistic, Whitehead's claim is that it is very much in accord with "the Galilean origins of Christianity."[30] This opposes several strains of thought combined in traditional theism: the divine Caesars that led to fashioning God in the image of an imperial ruler; the Hebrew prophets that led to fashioning God in the image of moral energy; and "unmoved mover" of Aristotle that led to fashioning God in the image of an ultimate metaphysical principle. Together these strains produce the idea that God is "an aboriginal, eminently real, transcendent creator, at whose *fiat* the world came into being, and whose imposed will it obeys."[31] Over against this, Whitehead's natural theology "dwells on the tender elements in the world, which slowly and in quietness operates by love; and finds purpose in the present immediacy of a kingdom not of this world."[32] In Whitehead's metaphysics God by his very nature enjoys maximum freedom[33]—to be is to be free—but his freedom is of this degree because it is totally unconditioned and has the total initiative.

God Related to World

Essential to Whitehead's view is that God is not an exception to the requirements of metaphysics. To be is not only to be free but also to be related. Religious intuition tells us that God loves all beings and is related to them by a sympathetic union surpassing any human sympathy. All our experience supports the view that knowing and loving constitute the knower or lover, not what is known or loved. But according to the traditional theism, God's knowledge and love of this world are an enormous exception to the rule, for divine knowledge and love make a real difference in the creature, but cannot make any difference to an immutable and necessary God.

The traditional view maintains that God is not really related to the world but that God in knowing and loving himself knows himself as Creator of the world. Because God is not really related to this world in knowledge and love, ". . . it follows that God does not know or love or will us, his creatures. At most, we can say only that we are known, loved and willed by Him."[34] Classical formulation of this view is given by St. Thomas: "God's temporal relations to creatures are in Him only because of our way of thinking of Him; but the opposite relation of creatures to Him are realities in creatures."[35] St. Thomas' reasoning is equally clear and sound.[36] A real relation in God to the world would have to be either predicamental or transcendental. However, a predicamental relation would mean that God acquired a new accidental relation;[37] and a transcendental relation would mean that God depended on creatures. Rejection of accidental perfection is deeply rooted in St. Thomas' metaphysics of God as subsistent being *(esse subsistens)* and suggests no new path for exploring ways to make more precise the relation of God to the world.

However, even St. Thomas' own argument against a real transcendental relation of God to the world indicates that not all possibilities have been considered. Basic to his view is that whatever by its very nature is referred to something else depends on it, at least as a condition of its being, since without it this being can neither be nor be thought of. Accordingly, God could not be transcendentally related to creatures in or by a real relationship without God being essentially dependent on this world. In such a case, God's nature could neither be nor be thought of apart from this world, and such dependence would make Him a radically contingent being.[38] In a discussion of Paul Weiss' Whiteheadean approach to God's relation to the world, Kenneth L. Schmitz[39] rightly sees that in this question the nature of relation is the central philosophical question. "The modal philosophy sees the margin of being of Actualities to be in their standing over against an imperfect God, whereas the philosophy of creative act sees the margin of being of creatures to lie within their being a non-reciprocal relation to a perfect God. The philosophical issue, then is between conceptions of relation."[40] However, a development of the philosophy of relation within Whiteheadean metaphysics would make it possible to move between the alternatives set down by Schmitz.

Concern with categories proper to "things" also led theists to stress God's liberty of indifference. This stressed God's perfection as an incommunicable supposit instead of his perfection as person in out-going self-relating. St. Augustine's theology of the Trinity has enabled modern man to think of person as communicable as well as incommunicable.[41] For Augustine, person is at once absolute and essentially toward another *(ad alium)*, so that the person constitutes self in a relation of opposition to the other. To understand the Persons in the Trinity, Augustine used the analogy of man, mind, and soul rather than the analogy of the cosmos. The analogy that enables Augustine to develop his theology of the Trinity is that of memory, intellection and the love of self which is identical with the ecstatic love of God, that is, man seen as related to God, proceeding from God, and constituted in his personality by a pre-awareness of God as the source of his being.

The Augustinian notion of liberty contrasts the personal autonomy of the free man with the bondage of a slave. What it excludes is not necessity but coercion from without. A being who enjoys this liberty acts for its own good without being coerced. This contrasts the unique personal value of an individual's power of self-determination or auto finality whereby he has dominion over himself to the slave who is merely a means for obtaining goals set by others. It is in this sense that God, although He loves Himself necessarily, loves Himself freely. If God wills to extend His love to creatures, He is free to do so. From this perspective, in His creation of the world liberty of indifference is necessarily involved, but the more significant aspect is the personal one by which in self-giving and self-relating to the world God placed Himself in a state of gift. Thomas, similarly, in his theology of the Trinity insists that within the Trinitarian life of God and in the very notion of person there enters the idea of relation: the Persons are subsistent relations. Within the trinity the persons are constituted as distinct subsistent relations: subsistent because of their identity with God's absolute essence, and distinct because of their relative opposition.

This notion in Augustine's and Thomas' theology of the Trinity, that persons are constituted in relation of opposition or mutual immanence, is taken over and broadened to all reality in the Whiteheadean approach. First, God's freedom may be understood as self-determination, self-relation, or self-giving without coercion from without, and this may extend itself to self-giving in creation. Second, person is understood to have two aspects, the incommunicability of a rational supposit and the communicability of the relation of opposition which constitutes persons. Both together provide as a new dimension to the doctrine of relations a dynamic, self-relating, and outgoing personal relation.[42]

From this perspective, God's relation to the world is real but God is not a "thing" which essentially depends on another. Because he is a personal, self-relating being, God can be understood to be Creator by an everlasting, free decision which is contingent, not necessary. It is true that God's nature and personal being as infinite actuality also determine him to be what he is. But creation reveals that God is also what he is everlastingly by a free decision to create the world, so that not everything that is true about God is due to the necessity of his nature. By deciding to create, God becomes a being in a way which could not be realized apart from that historical situation with this particular relation of opposition.

This relation of opposition does not imply imperfection in God, any more than the relations of opposition in the theology of the Trinity of the Fathers of the Church or the mutual immanence of the Divine Persons implied any imperfection in the Father, Son, and Holy Spirit. This real relation is identified with God's personal being as he freely chooses time, history, and human freedom. God's free-self-giving or self-relating adds no perfection to Him; rather it gives rise to a real distinction based on the reality of a new relation of opposition. If relation can be active-self-relating, it can be identical with directing one's powers in love. Such a relation based on the relative opposition of God and this world is God's actuality loving this world rather than another or no world at all. This does not involve accidental perfections, since love is the sharing of gifts possessed.

Consequences

If God is really related to this world, God is in history.

Through this relation he reveals himself to us through time and history as other than he could have been. This means that God is not the perfect Being of the Greek world wherein immutability and eternality are associated with perfection. This Greek notion of perfection has its roots in considering man's mind as the measure of intelligibility. Without doubt man has a tendency to associate intelligibility with necessity. However, once the Supreme Reality is discovered to be a personal being, the human mind, with its imperious demand for the intelligible to be the one same thing, can no longer be the measure of what is ultimately real and valuable.

We read the contingent aspects of God's living reality in time and history; the evolving universe gives testimony to the totality of that gift. So that God's gift may achieve its fullness in free beings who are themselves capable of placing themselves in return in a state of gift, the universe is ordered to become a universe-with-man. To bring about a universe in which God's love can attain its fullness in man's free response, all the forces of nature interact. Time, history, and freedom make a difference because through them God reveals that He is a living God in man's future waiting for man's free return of self. God wills to be a lover responding to man's free return of love.

The paradox is that the autonomy of man's free response is God's gift of Self to man. That gift increases as man's return gift of self increases, for man's life is a project to be achieved in time and through history. In this way, God through his own act of self-giving constitutes man whose genuine free response completes God's gift. Without freedom, man could not place self in state of gift in return and God's love of the world would be without the fullness that freedom makes possible. In community, man can strive for those social conditions which can make man's free response to God possible. Aware of God's call to a share in His creative activity, man grows in the consciousness of his responsibility to make that response possible. Since God wills to give Himself in personal love, risk becomes a necessary element in creation, for only free self-giving creatures can give personal love in return.

To be free and responsive and yet be time oriented, man has to be spirit-matter, capable of assimilating the past and appropriating it for the future. When we look at man we see that he is spirit essentially ordered to fulfilling his creative responsibility in time. *To be* a man is *to be creating self* in personal history. For man as spirit-ordered-to-time, time becomes a necessity for placing self in state of gift in return of God's love. Time does make a difference, for it is only in time that man completes God's love. In choosing to give self in love to a spirit-in-flesh, God makes time valuable.

Since Whitehead himself holds that God has no temporal priority over the world, so that God is not before all creation but with all creation, many have concluded that in the Whiteheadean approach God cannot be creator of this world. However, because the notion of creation is not necessarily linked to the notion of the world having a beginning in time, Whiteheadean metaphysics need not reject the notion that God creates the world. Certainly, the traditional phrase "creation out of nothing" seems to imply that the created world has a beginning in time. But the phrase, "out of nothing" means only that the creator makes the world neither from pre-existing material nor from his own being. Therefore, the notion of creation is indifferent to the world being eternal or having a beginning in time. Creation means that God has a radical and fundamental initiative in the coming-to-be of each temporal process. The essential point is that God has the total initiative in the coming-to-be of the world.

Again, once causality is thought of in personal terms, this radical initiative need not threaten the creature's own autonomy. In fact, in interpersonal relations the causal activity of one person on another does not diminish one's autonomy but can actually enhance it. One person can act on another without reducing his autonomy as a person because his action calls the other to create himself. God's initiative is a call to man to create himself freely; it is not a threat to man's freedom. From this point of view, there is nothing about man or any other creature that does not radically depend on God's initial causal activity; but at the same time almost everything of importance to man depends on man's creative response. There is lawfulness because each creature has real potentialities limited by its historical situation; but there is room for spontaneity because each creature freely responds to God's call. Once this creative activity is thought of in the analogy of person rather than the analogy of things, it is possible to understand that God's creative activity is a call to the creature to co-create itself. Since this involves interpersonal activity, the intensity of God's activity does not diminish but enhances the freedom of the creature. Certainly it is true that the more a mechanical force acts on something in a purely mechanical way, the independence of the thing acted upon is diminished. But a person acting on another need not lessen the freedom of the person acted upon, and can even intensify the creative freedom of that person. Furthermore, since the creature depends totally on the creator for its creative aim, the creature's autonomy is in direct, not inverse, proportion to God's creative activity.

Man's free decisions are seen to share truly in God's creative activity and to produce novelty that really matters. Further developments of the implications of this view which suggest themselves are: God's really waiting upon man's free decisions; His concurrence with man's self-creativity and with the real novelty in man's free decisions; a doctrine of Soul conceived in terms of "self-relating" rather than "unmoved mover" or "self-moving mover"; a morality built around man's call to responsible creative activity. Moreover, God's real relation to the world seems most compatible with developments in theology, especially in that of the Incarnation and of the indwelling of the Holy Spirit. For these reasons a recasting of the traditional view is worth exploring. Between a philosophy of creative act which excludes the possibility of the real relation of God to the world and a modal philosophy which demands reciprocal relations between God and the world, it is possible to posit as a "third position" a philosophy of creative act with real but asymmetrical relations between God and the world.

In this stage of precision, the metaphysical scheme in an important but reformable way has interpreted the final opposites of experience in terms of God and the World.

"In our cosmological construction we are left with the final opposites, joy and sorrow, good and evil, disjunction and conjunction—that is to say, the many in one—flux and permanence, greatness and triviality, freedom and necessity, God and the World. . . . God and the World introduce the note of interpretation."[43]

However, now that experience has been enriched by philosophical reflection, schematization presents man with the danger of being guilty of the fallacy of misplaced concreteness, even in the case of knowledge of God.

THE STAGE OF SYNTHESIS

Not only is this interpretation of experience in terms of God and the World itself capable of reformulation, the rhythmic process demands completion in the further stage of synthesis. The work of precision leads back to the concrete historical experience of mankind as he moves to build civilization through art, its sublimation in the pursuits of truth and beauty, the impetus towards Adventure beyond perfection realized, and, finally, the sense of Peace. Only a return to life and activity can mediate the empirical dimensions of the stage of romance and the schematic formulations of the stage of precision.

In the study of the creating of civilization, the four interrelated factors of art, truth, beauty and adventure are involved:

"We have found the growth of Art: its gradual sublimation into the pursuit of Truth and Beauty: the sublimation of the egotistic aim by its inclusion in a transcendent whole: the youthful zest in the transcendent aim: the sense of tragedy: the sense of evil: the persuasion towards Adventure beyond achieved perfection: the sense of Peace."[44]

The Whiteheadean reflection moves to the level of life and action and now calls on "those exceptional elements in our consciousness"[45] as we build a civilization of art, truth, beauty, and adventure. Art sublimates man's drive to enjoy the vividness of life

4

which first springs from sheer necessity, yet points beyond itself. "It exhibits for consciousness a finite fragment of human effort achieving its own perfection within its own limits."[46] This embodiment of Beauty tends toward shallowness because it concentrates on adapting immediate Appearance for immediate Beauty. In both science and art man seeks Beauty and Truth so that "the finite consciousness of mankind is appropriating as its own the infinite fecundity of nature."[47] Both exercise a healing role as they reveal absolute truth about the nature of things: "Churches and Rituals, Monasteries with their dedicated lives, Universities with their search for knowledge, Medicine, Lay, methods of Trade—they represent that aim at civilization, whereby the conscious experience of mankind preserves for its use the source of Harmony."[48] In this way art, truth and beauty beget civilization which is the relentless pursuit of the major perfections of harmony.

Because the very essence of real actuality is process, it is impossible to maintain perfection statically; actualities of civilization must be understood to be becoming and perishing. Moreover, to be is to be finite in the sense that all actualization excludes other possibilities which might have been and are not. Art must create individuals which are immortal in their appearance of immortality by their contribution to the whole: "Thus civilization in its aim at fineness of feeling should so arrange its social relations and the relations of its members to its natural environment, as to evoke into the experiences of its members Appearances dominated by the harmonies of forceful enduring things."[49] Art, truth, beauty, and adventure each point beyond themselves to a permanence which transcends them.

This transcendent element is the Harmony of Harmonies, Peace. Although it is difficult to put into words, this is ever at the fringe of man's consciousness: "It is a broadening of feeling due to emergence of some deep metaphysical insight, unverbalized and yet momentous in its coordination of values. Its first effect is the removal of the stress of acquisitive feeling arising from the soul's preoccupation with itself."[50] This excludes the pursuit of beauty and truth, art and adventure in hungry egotism and this involves the transcendence of the self. This experience of Peace is ". . . primarily trust in the efficacy of Beauty. It is a sense that fineness of achievement is, as it were, a key unlocking treasures that the narrow nature of things would keep remote. There is thus involved a grasp of infinitude, an appeal beyond boundaries."[51] Peace is at once the understanding and the preservation of tragedy since it is the intuition of the permanence of things in the face of fading beauty, pain, and sudden death. Peace ". . . keeps vivid the sensitiveness to the tragedy; and it sees the tragedy as a living agent persuading the world to aim at fineness beyond the faded level of surrounding fact. Each tragedy is the disclosure of an ideal:—What might have been, and was not: What can be."[52] As yet untouched by tragedy, youth is especially sensitive to the harmony of the soul's dynamism with ideals which transcend self-gratification.

This sense of Peace habitually at the fringe of consciousness implies something more than itself. No argument could possibly prove that this gap exists because all such demonstrations are only helps for man to bring to reflective consciousness what is intuitively present within man's consciousness. At this point he "is seeking, amid the dim recesses of his ape-like consciousness and beyond the reach of dictionary language for the premises implicit in all reasoning."[53] In this reflection, the incompleteness is in the area of transcendence which is essential for adventure and peace. This requires that the notion of God as Eros, the persuading force in the world, be complemented by the notion of God as final Beauty: "This Beauty has always within it the renewal derived from the Advance of the Temporal World. *It is the immanence of the Great Fact* including the initial Eros and this final beauty which constitutes the zest of self-forgetful transcendence belonging to Civilization at its height."[54] Immanence is the key to understanding how the World is lured toward perfection that is really possible for its individual occasions: "This is the secret of the union of Zest with Peace:—That the suffering attains its end in a Harmony of Harmonies. The immediate experience of this Final Fact, with its union of Youth and Tragedy, is the sense of Peace."[55] The same insight is expressed in other terms in *Religion in the Making*:

> The order of the world is no accident. There is nothing actual which could be actual without some measure of order. The religious insight is the grasp of truth: that the order of the world, the value of the world in its whole and in its parts, the beauty of the world, the zest of life, and the mastery of evil, are all bound up together—not accidentally, but by reason of this truth: that the universe exhibits a creativity with infinite freedom, and a realm of forms with infinite possibilities; but that this creativity and these forms together are important to achieve actuality apart from the complete ideal harmony, which is God.[56]

In this last stage of synthesis, Whitehead returns to the history of man's effort to create civilization and shows God as Eros and Beauty present within man's consciousness, and effectively directing man's pursuit of civilization even in the face of tragedy.[57]

The experience central to the human situation is value-affirmation. In this reflection, man knows himself as situated in the world faced by a variety of values-to-be-realized in time. He recognizes that some values are real possibilities and others are not. He also realizes that some values are compatible with his historical situation and some are not, and that some are compatible with each other and others are not. In the project of self-creation throughout his life, man must strive to bring these values into aesthetic harmony, aiming at intensity of feeling both in its subjective immediacy and in the occasions beyond itself to achieve objective immortality.[58] Man realizes that to achieve his individual destiny he must create civilizations which embody truth and beauty. At any moment of his life-project a man can know that he must choose among values which aim at intensity of feeling; and choose he must because not to choose would itself be activity. To achieve some of these values, one must freely enter into communities of knowledge and love.

In entering such a community, a man implicitly affirms that he knows and loves Beauty and Truth. He affirms that he knows and loves something as true, or as good, or as beautiful, and at the same time knows and loves truth, goodness, and beauty to-be-realized. What is actually known and loved is limited and recognized as limited compared to what is as yet unrealized and remains to be realized. Furthermore, the drive for truth, goodness and beauty which led to joining the community can be recognized to be beyond the goals already achieved. This means that there is a dynamism in the valuing process that cannot be satisfied with any succession of temporal values or any intensification of these temporal values. Man discovers within his life-process a non-temporal factor which transcends all temporal realization and yet is immanent to each temporal process. For example, a man's drive for truth and beauty can be satisfied by no limited truth whatsoever. To recognize limited truth as limited is to be already beyond limited truth in one's dynamism of knowledge and love for unlimited truth. Each new discovery of truth and beauty is recognized for what it is—limited truth and beauty unable to stifle man's drive for unlimited truth.

This recognition of truth as limited implies that the drive for truth transcends its temporal embodiment. No temporal truth added to temporal truth could satisfy this drive. In fact, man's self-creative process reveals the presence yet absence of an unconditioned non-temporal source of value which man can value without reservation or qualification. Since this answers to man's finer religious instincts, it can be called God, the source of all value in the temporal world.

CONCLUSION

A Whiteheadean approach has rich resources with which to meet the contemporary problem of God. If man today is asking if God's existence can be reconciled with man's deepened experience of himself as free creator of the world, the Whitehead-ean approach with its notion of God's persuasive personal action in the world, with its discovery of God's presence yet absence in man's creative activity, and with its stress on the mutual immanence of God and the World, offers pathways for further development. If man today is asking if God's existence can be accepted without destroying man's dignity in his free creative role in the universe, the Whiteheadean approach with its unwillingness to make God an exception to metaphysics, with its rejection of God as an eminently real despotic ruler of the universe, and with its view that God and man are the responsible co-creators of the universe, shows that man is not forced to choose between man's dignity and God's existence. If man today is asking if God's existence can be affirmed as transcendent without making God a functional element in an abstract scheme, it may be fruitful to realize that knowledge and experience of God involves a cyclic growth process from experience to schematization, from formulation to God present in the dynamism of man's life and activity. Finally, if man today is searching for a living God of the future rather than an anthropomorphic God of frozen history, a Whiteheadean approach offers man a living God for today and tomorrow—the growth process has only begun.

◇

1. Alfred North Whitehead, **Religion in the Making** (Cambridge: University Press, 1927), p. 62. Hereafter this work is referred to as **RM.**

2. John T. Robinson, **Honest to God** (Philadelphia: Westminster Press, 1963), p. 39.

3. Harvey Cox, **The Secular City** (New York: Macmillan, 1965), p. 77.

4. Gabriel Vahanian, **The Death of God** (New York: Braziller, 1957), p. 127.

5. Jean Paul Sartre, **The Devil and the Good Lord** (New York: Vintage, 1962), p. 141.

6. Maurice Merleau-Ponty, **In Praise of Philosophy**, trans. John Wild and James M. Edie (Evanston: Northwestern Univ. Press, 1963), p. 47.

7. Roger Garaudy, **From Anathema to Dialogue**, trans. Luke O'Neill (New York: Herder & Herder, 1966), p. 89.

8. **Ibid.,** p. 95.

9. Thomas J. J. Altizer, **The Gospel of Christian Atheism** (Philadelphia: Westminster Press, 1966), p. 102.

10. Alfred North Whitehead, **The Aims of Education** (New York: Macmillan, 1939), pp. 28-29. Hereafter this work is referred to as **AE.**

11. **Ibid.,** p. 29.

12. **Ibid.,** p. 37.

13. Whitehead, **RM,** p. 49.

14. **Ibid.,** p. 48.

15. Alfred North Whitehead, **Science and the Modern World** (New York: Macmillan, 1926), p. 127. Hereafter this work is referred to as **SMW.**

16. **Ibid.,** p. 136.

17. **Ibid.,** p. 134.

18. Alfred North Whitehead, **Process and Reality** (New York: Macmillan, 1929), p. 315. Hereafter this work is referred to as **PR.**

19. Alfred North Whitehead, **Adventures of Ideas** (New York: Macmillan, 1933), p. 203. Hereafter this work is referred to a **AI.**

20. See Ivor Leclerc, **Whitehead's Metaphysics** (New York: Macmillan, 1958).

21. Whitehead, **AI,** p. 125.

22. H. W. Carr, "The Interaction of Mind and Body," **Proceedings of the Aristotelian Society,** XVIII (1917-18), 32.

23. Whitehead, **PR,** p. 64.

24. Whitehead, **SMW,** p. 121.

25. Whitehead, **AI,** p. 203.

26. **Ibid.,** p. 355.

27. **Ibid.**

28. Whitehead, **PR,** p. 31.

29. **Ibid.,** p. 248.

30. **Ibid.,** p. 520.

31. **Ibid.,** p. 519.

32. **Ibid.,** p. 520.

33. This is developed by William A. Christian, **An Interpretation of Whitehead's Metaphysics** (New Haven: Yale Univ. Press, 1959), pp. 371-72.

34. C. Hartshorne, **The Divine Relativity** (2d ed.; New Haven: Yale Univ. Press, 1964), p. 16. The question is discussed thoroughly, **ibid.,** p. 1-59.

35. Thomas Aquinas, **Summa Theologica** (New York: Benziger Brothers, 1947), I, q. 13, a. 7 ad 4. See also **On the Truth of the Catholic Faith (Summa Contra Gentiles)** (New York: Doubleday, 1955), Part II, chaps. 11-14; **De Potentia** (Westminster, Md.: Newman Press, 1952), q. 7, a. 8-11.

36. The basic argument is given in **S. C. G.,** II, 12.

37. **S. C. G.** I, 23; **S. T.,** 1, 3, 6 resp.

38. **S. C. G.,** I, 13.

39. K. Schmitz, "Weiss and Creation," **Review of Metaphysics,** XVIII (1964), 147-69.

40. **Ibid.,** p. 162.

41. For an excellent summary of this point, see P. Henry, **St. Augustine on Personality** (New York: Macmillan, 1960).

42. Whitehead, **AI**, "The New Reformation," pp. 205-25.

43. Whitehead, **PR.**, p. 518.

44. Whitehead, **AI**, p. 386.

45. Ibid., p. 379.

46. Ibid., p. 348.

47. Ibid., p. 350.

48. Ibid., p. 351.

49. Ibid., p. 363.

50. Ibid., p. 367.

51. Ibid.

52. Ibid., p. 369.

53. Ibid., p. 380.

54. Ibid., p. 381.

55. Ibid.

56. Whitehead, **RM**, p. 105.

57. Cf. Aimé Forest, "St. Anselm's Argument in Reflexive Philosophy," **The Many-faced Argument,** eds. John Hick and Arthur C. McGull (New York: Macmillan, 1967) for an informative exposition of this type of approach in recent philosophy. He says of Blondel: "In the very depths of the act in which we become conscious of what we are, we recognize an interior beyond, since this is constitutive of the dynamism of our souls." **Op. cit.,** p. 281. A comparison between Blondel and Whitehead in this area remains to be done.

58. Whitehead, **PR**, p. 41.

Process Philosophy and
Our Knowledge of God

◊

by
Lewis S. Ford

IN PAUL TILLICH'S words, God is that which ultimately
concerns us. We might equally well define him as that being
which is supremely worthy of worship. In either case philosophical
inquiry can profitably explore what is entailed by these concepts.
Whatever God is, he must be perfect, even if we differ as to
whether he exists. In the final analysis it is the notion of divine
perfection that makes the theist's affirmation and the atheist's
denial significant.

Among process philosophers, Charles Hartshorne has characteristically championed arguments for the existence and nature
of God which derive their force and validity from the logic of
divine perfection. His contribution to this volume is no exception. That God is the best conceivable being is not a new notion,
having acquired a considerable degree of philosophical maturity
at the hands of Plato and Aristotle. What may be new, or at
least deserving of further exploration, is our concept as to what
is best. As Frederick Sontag discerns at least seven types of
divine perfection exhibited in the history of philosophy from
Plato to Hegel,[1] one cannot easily assume that perfection "obviously" entails self-sufficiency or whatever. In fact, what gives
process thinking its impetus and its urge to explore the logic of
perfection is its conviction that the perfect is not self-sufficient,

and that traditional thinking about God has been side-tracked too long by this characteristically Greek notion.

PERFECTION AND SELF-SUFFICIENCY

Let me simply pick up one thread of this argument. Since Jewish, Christian, and Muslim theisms overwhelmingly ascribe subjectivity to God, there is at least a *prima facie* case that subjectivity belongs to divine perfection. If, however, that which is subjective cannot be self-sufficient, we must either abandon the identification of perfection with self-sufficiency, or recognize that the God of religious faith is imperfect. Plotinus, Tillich and the tradition of negative theology could well have chosen the latter alternative, but they have usually conceived of God as beyond both subjectivity and objectivity, rather than as purely objective and devoid of all subjectivity.

Any self-sufficient subjectivity must be non-corporeal, for it will have no need of a body to sustain it in being and activity. Here we must postulate the existence of something for which we have no ordinary finite analogue, unless we wish to permit the introduction of disembodied souls after death. Even assuming that incorporeal subjectivity is perfectly intelligible, we find that the self requires or can be enriched by three things having reference beyond itself: (a) other selves, (b) the experience of other beings, and (c) the referents for thinking, willing, deciding.

If we are of any value to God, we can enrich his life through social interaction. By himself God can enjoy no social intercourse, unless we adopt Augustine's social conception of the Trinity. Yet if the sociability of the Trinitarian relationships is beneficial to God, why would not God's social life be further enriched by interaction with all subjects? Aristotle clearly recognized, however, that self-sufficiency precludes sociability: "One who is self-sufficient can have no need of the service of others, nor of their affections, nor of social life, since he is capable of living alone. This is especially evident in the case of God. Clearly, since he is in need of nothing, God cannot have need of friends, nor will he have any."[2]

Such a solitary being could exist, bereft of companionship, and experiencing and interacting with no other subjective beings. Yet its experience would still be dependent upon that which is experienced. What we experience is derived from beings beyond ourselves, and it is their existence and activity which enriches our experience and provides it with novel content. Apart from other beings we have no experience at all; at least we have no way of distinguishing between experiencing and thinking. Again Aristotle is sensitive to the requirements of self-sufficiency, and is prepared to deny experience to God: "And are there not even some things which it would be absurd that it should know? Clearly it knows what is most divine and most honorable; and it does not change, for any change would be for the worse and would imply some kind of process . . . Accordingly, a divine mind knows itself, since it is the supreme excellence."[3]

Here we are left with either Aristotle's Unmoved Mover, "thinking on thinking," or the God of classical theism who knows all things, including future contingents. Boethius noted that such future contingents must already be necessitated even if it is not God's knowledge which causes them to be what they are. But, ignoring such puzzles about human freedom, we must inquire into the sort of knowing this might be. It must be radically different from our own, for we are not consciously aware of all that we know at any one time. Divine contemplation cannot be a process of remembering or calling into consciousness what God already knows, for this would imply that he is somewhat deficient in awareness. Nor can it consist in drawing new inferences from known premises, for these inferences must already be known. Nor can it be a process of willing a decision, for no decisions can be made in the realm of pure possibility since no possibility excludes another. Decisions are made with respect to actuality by "cutting off" possible alternatives for this rather than for that. Divine decision must terminate either in the creation of some finite actuality or in some definite influence upon finite actuality; and in either case, some being beyond God is required.

In short, an entirely self-sufficient deity would have nothing to do. One could merely respond that this is just as it should be, for God ought not have need to do anything. But subjectivity is not easily bought off, for it seems to have an innate tendency to go beyond itself, to terminate in something other than itself. Since Husserl phenomenology has insisted upon the intentionality of subjectivity: consciousness is always conscious of something other than itself. Can it not also be that consciousness is always a process whereby one thought or experience is always being superceded by another?

If subjectivity were devoid of this conatus or drive toward the other, what would distinguish it from objectivity? That which is purely objective can be wholly self-sufficient, for its satisfaction or completion need not depend upon anything toward which it is directed. Precisely because it is objective, it lacks the directedness which is inherent in subjectivity. The intentionality of subjectivity renders it necessarily dependent upon some object for its completion.

Therefore, if Plato were correct in identifying the best with that which is wholly self-sufficient, then he would be completely consistent in affirming the transcendent and supreme worth and dignity of the Form of the Good. This Good would be supremely worthy of worship. Clearly it articulated the ultimate concern of a Socrates. It is identical with the God of classical western theism —except that it lacks subjectivity. This lack is clearly not a defect if our criterion for perfection is self-sufficiency.

In its vision of perfection, process theism does not deny the value of self-sufficiency as much as it questions its application to particular beings. What is finally self-sufficient is neither God nor the world, but both in reciprocal interaction. The unity and value of the whole is preserved by each being requiring and being enriched by every other being.

THE ONTOLOGICAL ARGUMENT

The logic of perfection quite naturally culminates in the ontological argument which explores the mode of existence appropriate to divine perfection. Within the tradition of classical theism, that logic found its most thorough-going explication in Anselm's *Proslogion*,[4] the themes of which have been appropriated by process theism. Anselm's criterion for perfection, "that than which a greater cannot be conceived," has been adopted by Hartshorne in terms of "unsurpassability." In view of God's real interaction with the world (which had been denied only on the basis of the false criterion of self-sufficiency), Hartshorne argues that God's concrete actuality is contingent upon this continuing interaction. Through God's constantly enriching experience of temporal process, that which God concretely was will be surpassed by what God concretely will become, even though he cannot be surpassed by any other being. Anselm failed to distinguish between the abstract nature and the concrete actuality of God. If we construe him as referring only to the abstract divine nature, there is a large measure of agreement with Hartshorne. Both assert that the divine nature is absolutely unsurpassable and necessarily exists.

The renewed interest in the ontological argument initiated by Hartshorne and Norman Malcolm has centered on the "second argument," found in chapter 3 of the *Proslogion*. The first argument, traditionally assumed to be *the* ontological argument, questions whether existence as such is a perfection. However, under the criticisms of Gassendi and Kant, this position has been generally abandoned. The second argument is cast in modal terms, arguing that necessity is more appropriate to divine existence than contingency. A God which just happened to be or whose existence was dependent upon external conditions could not be as great as a God conceived to exist unconditionedly and necessarily.

Let us consider Hartshorne's formalization of this second argument in a simplified version:[5]

1. A perfect being could not exist contingently; hence the assertion that it exists could not be contingently but only necessarily true ("Anselm's Principle").
2. Hence, either it is necessarily true that a perfect being exists, or it is impossible.
3. But the existence of a perfect being is not impossible (in-

tuitive postulate, or conclusion from other theistic arguments).

4. Therefore it is necessarily true that a perfect being exists (2, 3, disjunctive syllogism).
5. Whatever is necessarily true is true (modal axiom).
6. Therefore (it is true that) a perfect being exists (4, 5, modus ponens).

In analyzing this argument, John Hick seeks to distinguish between logical and ontological necessity.[6] That which is logically necessary is true analytically, that is, its contradictory is logically impossible. Ontological necessity, on the other hand, refers to ontic independence, the capacity to exist without regard to any conditioning factors. In the *Monologion*[7] Anselm distinguishes between existence from itself *(a se)* and existence from another *(ab alio)* and argues that God could only derive his existence from himself and not from any external cause; the perfection of God entails his "aseity." Duns Scotus also speaks of God as uncausable, since as self-existence, he must be eternal or without temporal limitation. "For if he had begun to exist, or should cease to exist, he must have been caused to exist, or to cease to exist, by some power other than himself; and this would be inconsistent with his aseity."[8]

Hick argues that Anselm understood his argument in terms of ontological necessity, and on these grounds his principle (step 1) is valid, and step 2 follows.

However, from this disjunction, according to which the divine existence is (ontologically) either necessary or impossible, we cannot derive the conclusion that Perfection or God exists. What we can deduce is that if there is a God, he has ontologically necessary (i.e., eternal and self-existence) being. For the coming to exist and the ceasing to exist of an eternal Being are alike percluded; God exists either eternally or not at all. This is the maximum that can validly be derived from the concept of God as existing eternally and *a se*.[9]

To get on with the proof, necessity must be understood in logical terms, as Hartshorne consistently does. In this case, however, everything follows except the initial step, which apparently cannot be established by means of logical necessity.

The argument hinges on the proper interpretation of Hartshorne's formalization, "Nq," where "N" is defined as "it is necessary (logically true) that" and "q" as "(3x)Px" ("There is a perfect being, or perfection exists"). Reading the symbols directly in sequence, we obtain: "it is true by logical necessity that a perfect being exists." This is apparently the way in which Hartshorne intends "Nq" to be read. Then Hartshorne's formalization of step 1, "q strictly implies Nq," must read: "If a perfect being exists, then it is necessarily true that a perfect being exists." As Hick points out, an argument of the form "if p, then it is necessarily true that p" is not universally valid, nor (for the reasons advanced by Gassendi, Kant, and J. N. Findlay) can one treat a purely existential proposition as a logically necessary truth.[10] Note that the statement "a perfect being exists," by itself, is non-modal and therefore susceptible to the objections against Anselm's first argument. What would be required to ward off these objections is the statement "it is necessarily true that a perfect being necessarily exists," but this cannot be simply formulized as "Nq."

In fact, it turns out that there is no direct way in which the distinction between logical and ontological necessity can be formalized. This, in turn, raises the question whether it is proper to demand of formal logic that it make such a distinction. In defending the analyticity of his argument, Hartshore is in effect claiming that "Nq," interpreted as "it is necessary that a perfect being exists," *is* the proper logical rendering of "a perfect being necessarily exists." On Anselmian grounds we can establish the latter as immune to the objection raised against existence as a predicate; can we also effect the needed logical translation?

As I understand him, Hartshorne argues that all necessary statements are analytic, but in opposition to many contemporary thinkers he holds with Leibniz that some analytic statements have metaphysical import.[11] The necessity in question is essentially a systematic necessity, flowing from the intrinsic relationships between the postulates and the theorems. The problem turns on whether there is an appropriate "fit" between such a logical system and the necessary structure of the world. Consider Hartshorne's response to his own posed question:

> Are metaphysical judgments analytic? I reply that, assuming suitable meaning postulates, they can be made that. If it be objected that scientific hypotheses, too, become analytic with suitable meaning postulates, the reply is that only observation prevents science, so taken, from describing an empty universe, whereas it is the task of metaphysics to find meaning postulates which describe the *necessarily non-empty* universe, or the common aspect of all possible states of affairs.[12]

What is common to all possible states of affairs is unconditionedly or ontologically necessary. No possible situation could alter it, nor does its necessity exclude any real possibility. If our metaphysics has been successful in describing what is genuinely common to all situations, then the logical necessity inherent in the systematic relationships of its basic principles does reflect the ontological necessity found in reality. Thus Anselm's principle stated in terms of the unconditioned necessity of metaphysical reality, has its appropriate systematic counterpart, expressible in logical terms.

However, if with Hartshorne, God's existence is purely analytic and nonrestrictive, a bare abstraction compatible with the possible existence of anything whatsoever, then it would seem that we have emptied our affirmation of all significant import. In particular, how can we derive God's concrete actuality from such an empty assertion? Here Hartshorne has recourse to his distinction between what is abstract and necessary in God, as opposed to what is concrete and contingent, a distinction not possible for the classical theism espoused by Anselm. Hartshorne agrees that "the concrete is richer than the abstract, and the more cannot follow by necessity from the less," but denies that this is what the ontological proof intends to do, for it does not address itself to God's concrete actuality.

Let us call the concrete state of a thing its *actuality*. Then my proposition is, actuality is always *more* than bare existence. Existence is that the defined abstract nature is *somehow* concretely actualized; but *how* it is actualized, in what particular state, with what particular *content* not deducible from the abstract definition, constitutes the actuality. Of course, then, it would be contradictory to deduce this content by any proof.[13]

Thus from the ontological argument we cannot deduce God's concrete actuality, but we can infer from the conclusion that the property of divine perfection must somehow necessarily be concretized is some actuality, and that no state of affairs could exist in which this actualization of perfection did not take place.

Thus the unconditionedness of God's existence is a highly abstract property which can be adequately expressed by the logical necessity of our systematic principles. Since Hick's argument depended upon God being ontologically but not logically necessary, that objection fails.

In one of his discussions of the argument, however, Hartshorne remarks: "The proof was not intended to refute every alternative to theism, but only the 'atheistic' alternative, defining atheism as the doctrine that (a) the existence of God is consistently conceivable, but (b) God does not, or for all we know may not, exist in fact."[14] It may be questioned whether any genuine atheist ever held that God was logically possible in the sense that Hartshorne uses the term.

In considering Hartshorne's argument, R. L. Purtill has demonstrated the following general theorem to be valid for any modal system of moderate strength: "If p strictly implies necessary p, then possible p implies p."[15] Anselm's principle is an application of the antecedent clause of this theorem to divine perfection: if God exists, he exists necessarily. All that is needed to demonstrate God's existence is to establish possible divine existence. Here the matter becomes very delicate, for Purtill's theorem is sufficiently general to allow "p" to be interpreted in terms of God's non-existence as well. If God does not exist, by

Anselm's principle his existence would be impossible, since no contingent condition could bring him into being. Then it follows that the possible non-existence of God excludes his existence. In effect, Anselm's principle merely expands what is involved, or raises the ante so to speak, so that the entire issue of God's existence must be resolved on the level of possibility. If God could possibly exist, he must; but if there is the slightest chance that he might not exist, then his existence is utterly impossible. If "atheism" is thereby ruled out, so is the corresponding "theism," defined by the thesis that God does exist, though he might not have. Our "atheist" and "theist" alike had granted the contrary possibility, because these two possibilities are mutually consistent for all ordinary or contingent beings. Even as possibilities, however, the alternatives are exclusive in the case of necessary beings. Confronted by this development, it seems reasonably clear that any genuine atheist would affirm the possibility of God's non-existence rather than the possibility of his existence.

LOGICAL SYSTEMS AND THE ACTUALITY OF GOD

Now it is necessary to be very clear as to what the various modalities of existence can mean in logical terms. A logical system consists in a set of mutually consistent postulates from which various theorems may be deduced. We may speak of entities existing within that logical system in terms of existential propositions, for the modal existential status of an entity is identical with that of its corresponding existential proposition. An entity exists necessarily if its existential proposition is a theorem of the system. An entity possibly exists if its existential proposition is consistent with the postulates; otherwise its existence is impossible. An entity actually exists if its existential proposition is in fact given, whether as a postulate or as an additional proposition consistent with the postulates.

Let us consider only those logical systems which contain Anselm's principle as a theorem or postulate. For these systems, if a perfect entity is possible, it must exist, but if it may possibly not exist, then its existence is impossible. In other words, its existential proposition must either be a theorem of the system or be inconsistent with its original postulates. Consider the logical system defining the domain of cardinal numbers. Here numbers are our entities, and it is possible that there is no perfect number, if we define perfection in Anselm's terms as "that than which nothing greater can be conceived." The rule, "for every n, there is a number n / 1," establishes the possibility that there may be no greatest number. By Anselm's principle it follows that there cannot be any greatest number, for no matter what postulates we add consistent with the original set, we cannot derive its existence.

A metaphysics is a logical system which purports to describe the actual world. By Anselm's principle no metaphysics can assert both the possible existence and the possible non-existence of a perfect being. These two assertions are mutually inconsistent, but it is conceivable with respect to a given metaphysical proposal that either one might be consistent with the existing postulates. In that case we would have to argue that we are dealing with an essentially incomplete metaphysics. To be complete, a metaphysics would have to describe all possible actualities, and in so doing would have to decide whether a perfect actuality was possible. Since, with respect to perfection, possibility entails necessity, we argue that no metaphysics can be complete until it has demonstrated the necessary existence or impossibility of a perfect being. This is not to say, however, that such a perfect being must resemble the Hebraic God; in Plato's thought that perfect being would naturally be the Form of the Good.

The problem with isolated analyses of the ontological argument is that they usually operate within incomplete metaphysical systems in order to give the argument a generality with respect to competing metaphysical alternatives. In the final analysis this will not do, for as long as the affirmation and the denial of God's existence are equally consistent with our metaphysical postulates, we cannot yet determine whether God's existence is possible or impossible. A decision is possible only for those metaphysical alternatives which claim to be complete, surveying all possible actuality. Hence, God's possibility or impossibility must be regarded as a function of a particular complete metaphysical alternative. We cannot argue whether God is logically possible in the abstract; he may be logically possible for one logical system describing a particular metaphysics, but he may be logically impossible for some other alternative.

Hartshorne seems to identify logical possibility with what is true for some possible world. Since metaphysical judgments are analytic, statements about metaphysical possibility are likewise statements about logical possibility, at least in the sense that the logical descriptions of possibility may be correctly used to express metaphysical possibility. In raising the question as to whether God is really possible, Hartshorne must finally be asking whether the statement of possible divine existence is compatible with the postulates of a logically consistent, complete metaphysical system. Then, since it is "the task of metaphysics to find meaning postulates which describe the *necessarily non-empty* universe, or the common aspect of all possible states of affairs,"[16] the only possibility available would have to be those consistent with the necessary structure of actuality. Therefore, for something to be possible it must be capable of existing in some possible world, while metaphysics has the task of describing that which is true of all possible worlds.

A "possible world" for Hartshorne cannot mean a world as consistently described by some alternative metaphysics, for the necessary structure of that world would conflict with the necessary structure of the actual world as described by the true metaphysics. (If there were no conflict, then we would merely be considering two versions of the same metaphysics, not genuine metaphysical alternatives.) In Whitehead's terms, each "possible world" would simply be a possible cosmic epoch, differing from ours in terms of many of its basic conditions but not in terms of its underlying universal categoreal structure. Metaphysical necessity pertains to that which must be true for all possible cosmic epochs. Thus "logical possibility," as it functions in Hartshorne's use of the ontological argument, refers only to that which is possible in terms of that metaphysics which accurately describes reality, excluding that which might be regarded as possible or impossible in terms of some alternative metaphysics. Thus God is not logically possible except in terms of a given metaphysics. For this reason the ontological argument can never stand by itself to demonstrate the existence of a perfect being, apart from demonstrating the appropriateness of that metaphysics by which we affirm the possibility of such divine existence. As Duns Scotus recognized centuries ago, the ontological argument must be supplemented by some sort of cosmological prologue demonstrating that possibility.

We may illustrate our point by way of a geometrical analogy. Suppose the question arises whether triangles are possible the sum of whose interior angles equals more than 180 degrees. Since the interior angles of Euclidean triangles must equal 180 degrees, such triangles are impossible for Euclidean geometry; nevertheless we may discover non-Euclidean geometries where such triangles not only are possible but are the only kinds possible. Possibility is therefore relative to the system adopted.

Does the analogy hold for metaphysics? Hartshorne might wish to argue that metaphysics should more closely resemble the topological domain underlying all the various possible special geometries, while Whitehead would see each consistent metaphysical alternative as analogous to a particular special geometry. The issue finally turns on whether rationalistic criteria can ever be entirely sufficient to describe metaphysical issues. For Hartshorne ultimately there can be only one possible metaphysics, for all others, having in some way gone counter to that which is common to all possible worlds, must be somewhere incoherent or inconsistent. As I read Whitehead, several different metaphysical structures are in principle possible, just as there are several different fully consistent and systematic geometries. We can only determine which geometry actually describes physical space by making very careful measurements, not by challenging the mathematical soundness of the various geometries. Likewise in metaphysics we must appeal to the adequacy and applicability of our proposal to our experience, for reason alone cannot settle the issue.

We have come to the limit of rationality. For there is a categorical limitation which does not spring from any metaphysical reason . . . The general principle of empiricism depends upon the doctrine that there is a principle of concretion
which is not discoverable by abstract reason.[17]

This categorical limitation is cosmic in scope, specifying among
other things "the special logical relation which all events must
conform to."[18] This particularly applies to Whitehead's formal
elements or eternal objects in their internal relatedness to one
another. Here he distinguishes between the eternal object's "individual essence" and its "relational essence." The individual
essence describes its unique quality or particular individuality,
for Whitehead rejects the idealist thesis that properties can be
reduced to a tissue of relations. On the other hand, the relational
essence is necessary because an eternal object "cannot be divorced
from its reference to other eternal objects."[19] The diameter of a
circle cannot be possible apart from its specific internal relationship to the circumference. These internal relations are constitutive of the eternal objects, and as such form a necessary, un-
changeable structure to be exemplified throughout all time, by
all possible actualities. "This relational essence determines how
it is possible for the object to have ingression into actual occasions."[20]

Thus, with respect to their actualization, the eternal objects
must be related to one another in an absolutely universal fashion.
Yet there is no ultimate reason why the way they are internally
related to one another is the only possible way in which they
could have been so related, for each eternal object has an individual essence, and these individual essences, abstractly considered, form a bare multiplicity capable of being structured in
many different ways. Because the demands of actuality require
that one particular pattern of internal-relatedness be chosen,

we must provide a ground for limitation which stands among
the attributes of the substantial activity. This attribute provides the limitation for which no reason can be given: for

all reason flows from it. God is the ultimate limitation, and His existence is the ultimate irrationality. For no reason can be given for just that limitation which it stands in His nature to impose.[21]

The similarities of this argument to Sartre's are striking. Sartre argues that each individual must choose his own "original project" or underlying orientation in terms of which his various, plans and activities acquire value and meaning. Moreover, this choice must be "pre-reflective," for all reflective rationality depends upon some prior basic orientation. Whitehead calls for just such a choice, but on the cosmic scale, and such a decision can only be effected by a cosmic self, God.

As a mathematician and logician, Whitehead could appreciate the tremendous variety and flexibility of different logical systems, each consistent with itself, and some being sufficiently comprehensive to qualify as plausible descriptions of actuality. As the structures of possibility alone could not determine the structure of actuality, some decision had to be made, and this decision required a cosmic decider. This line of reasoning suggests the way in which Whitehead personally was induced to introduce God into his metaphysics, but it does not indicate the full scope of God's role as it emerged in his most philosophical work. As in the case of Hartshorne, our attention will be focused upon the underlying logic of Whitehead's approach as a means of providing us with knowledge about God.

CATEGOREAL ANALYSIS

In *Process and Reality*[22] Whitehead sought to frame a universal categoreal scheme for all actuality. Metaphysics can proceed by exploring the nature and modalities of being, or by examining the generic features appropriate to all beings. Whitehead chose the latter course, adopting the strategy of distinguishing between primary and derivative beings. All beings are entities, but for the sake of coherence or solidarity there is only one class of fully actual entities. All other entities must be referred to this one class for their existence. This strategy is explicitly formalized in terms of the ontological principle, which asserts that "actual entities are the only reasons; so that to search for a reason is to search for one or more actual entities."[23] In the course of describing all the generic features of a typical actual entity, all other derivative entities will be accounted for, and all metaphysical conditions, insofar as they are universal and necessary for all being, will be presented.

Such an approach requires that if God is really actual, he must conform to the general categoreal description applicable to all actuality.

> There is no going behind actual entities to find anything more real. They differ among themselves: God is an actual entity, and so is the most trivial puff of existence in far-off empty space. But, though there are gradations of importance, and diversities of function, yet in the principles which actuality exemplifies all are on the same level. The final facts are, all alike, actual entities.[24]

From the standpoint of *Process and Reality*, God is investigated not as a separate principle, but only insofar as he is a function of the universal categoreal scheme. In reminiscing about Whitehead's teaching at Harvard, William Ernest Hocking reports him saying about his concept of God: "I should never have included it, if it had not been strictly required for descriptive completeness. You must set all your essentials into the foundation. It's no use putting up a set of terms, and then remarking, 'Oh, by the way, I believe there's a God.'"[25]

If from a metaphysical perspective all actualities are alike in that all are equally instantiations of the same generic principles, then we must appeal to empirical evidence in order to show how they differ among themselves. Whitehead makes this appeal with respect to various complex groupings of actual occasions such as protons, atoms, molecules, cells, etc. The sole philosophical task in cosmology is to show how such grouping could be possible in terms of one's generic principles, leaving the issue as to which ones are in fact actualized for empirical investigation. Being wholly contingent, their presence cannot be determined by metaphysical methods, which apply solely to that which is universally and necessarily the case.

Now if all differences between actualities apply only to their contingent aspects, because they are all alike with respect to their necessary aspects, then the difference between God and other actualities could itself refer only to their contingent aspects. But if the difference between God and some finite actuality is merely contingent, then there must be some set of conditions whereby this difference might be overcome. (If there were no such set of conditions, then the difference would have to refer to their necessary aspects.) That means, however, that under certain circumstances God would be indistinguishable from some finite actuality, whose own existence is purely contingent. Thus, if there is no necessary ground for God's distinctiveness, he could exist contingently, and there could be some world in which he might possibly not exist. But as we have seen by Anselm's principle, if God could possibly not exist, then his existence is utterly impossible and must be completely ruled out. Thus a God who only differs in his contingent aspects from other actualities is an impossibility. If God is to be included at all, there must be a systematic, necessary distinction between God and all the actual occasions of the world, and Whitehead appears to make just such a distinction in *Process and Reality*. How can this be squared with the equally insistent categoreal demand requiring the generic similarity of all actualities?

Historically, a good many metaphysical ventures have come to grief over just this point, for it seems extraordinarily difficult to sustain metaphysical regularity with respect to God. If, as I am inclined to feel, Aristotle's characteristic substance is a concrete particular forming a composite of form and matter, then his divine separable substance is clearly an exception. Descartes declared all actuality to be either thinking things *(res cogitans)* or extended things *(res extensa)*—except God. Some theocentric thinkers make a virtue of this divine irregularity. For Thomas

Aquinas, essence and existence, while separate in all other substances, are identified in God. Tillich insists that God as being-
itself is radically different from all other beings in not being a
being. Leibniz was perhaps the most resolute of Whitehead's
predecessors in requiring God to meet the metaphysical demands
imposed upon all actualities. As a simple substance, God must
be one of the monads: the highest monad with absolute clarity
of perception. Since Leibniz denied that any causal interactions
would be possible between infinitesimals, these monads are
windowless, and he must appeal to a pre-established harmony in
order to account for their apparent interaction. Since such absolute coordination among the vast array of substances would be
a feature of all the "better" possible worlds, God, in choosing
the best one, would thereby be actualizing one such pre-established harmony. On what basis does God make his choice? Though
monads presumably act on the basis of their inner principles,
we cannot explain how God's inner principle would correlate with
the particular world chosen, unless there were some higher pre-
established harmony embracing God and his world. If, on the
other hand, God were to be influenced by the nature of the possible worlds he contemplates, in effect he would have windows
toward his creatures. But, as Whitehead protests, "God is not to
be treated as an exception to all metaphysical principles, invoked to save their collapse. He is their chief exemplification."[26]
In the face of historical failure on this point, how can we be
sure that Whitehead himself is not surreptitiously guilty of the
same offense?

GOD AS THE EXEMPLIFICATION OF THE CATEGORIES

In order to show that God is not an exception, we must
demonstrate how he exemplifies all the categories appropriate
to actual entities. We must also show how God is systematically
distinct from the world, i.e. from the totality of all finite actual
occasions. We can be very precise in our terminology here, for
according to Whitehead's usage, God is an actual entity but
not an actual occasion.[27] All actual entities possess both a "mental

pole," a capacity for novelty, and a "physical pole," a receptivity to other actual entities. In actual occasions, the mental pole is dependent upon the physical pole, following "Hume's principle of the derivation of conceptual experience from physical experience."[28] While all actual entities must have both poles, there is no reason of the widest generality why the physical must always precede the mental. Whitehead contends that in the case of God the poles are reversed, with priority being given to the mental pole as the organ of novelty. Thus, there are two classes into which all actual entities can be divided, according to which pole is prior: the divine and the mundane. What obscures this classification from us is the fact that the divine class has only one member while the mundane class consists in an indefinite, perhaps infinite plurality. God and the World are the proper contrasts, the two species of actual entities. The issue becomes distorted if, in our fascination with the multitudinous variety of actual occasions, we see them as constituting the totality of actuality. Then God can appear only as a curious exception.

Our procedure will be to describe those generic features of all actual entities which are applicable to God and to the World. From these we hope to derive their basic contrast. If we can show that all the distinctive differences between God and the World can be systematically derived from this inversion of the two poles, we will have demonstrated that God not only exemplifies the categoreal scheme, but that the systematic distinction between God and all actual occasions is a necessary consequence of that scheme.

In proceeding in this fashion, we do not pretend to be following the way in which Whitehead introduces God in *Process and Reality*. Whitehead is not always fully cognizant of the systematic distinction between God and the World, though he was moving in that direction and can be so systematized. Whitehead started in *Science and the Modern World* with actual occasions and eternal objects derived from the "events" and "objects" of his earlier writing in the philosophy of science. It seems likely that Whitehead framed his categoreal principles with actual occasions primarily in mind, and subsequently applied them to God. We shall consider these principles more explicitly as applying to both God and the World, recognizing that on this level they must remain exceedingly abstract, without any possibility of interpretation by direct reference to experience. It is only after the distinction between the two species, God and World, has been introduced that it becomes possible to test the adequacy and applicability of Whitehead's description to the world we directly confront. If the account of actual occasions does square with our experience, and this account is coherently and systematically correlated with a theory about its logical contrast, God, then we have a firm metaphysical basis for knowing the generic features of God.

Let us consider three basic features pertaining to all actual entities, whether divine or mundane:

1. "The actual entity is the real concrescence of many potentials."[29] The word "concrescence," derived from the Latin verb *concrescere*, "to grow together," is used to designate the process of actualization which is the formation of the concrete. From a Whiteheadean perspective, the 'being' of an actual entity is constituted by its 'becoming.'[30] The completed determinate concrete state of an actuality is only the final phase of this dynamic process. It is properly seen as an aspect of the completed actuality. All entities are therefore "creatures of creativity" in the sense that they are instances of the on-going creative process of unification whereby an initial indeterminate multiplicity becomes a single concrete outcome. They are also creatures in the sense that what they become is a result of this creative process inherent within them. Creativity pertains to what Whitehead describes as 'the category of the Ultimate' because it is "the universal of universals characterizing ultimate matter of fact."[31] All actual entities, in virtue of their actuality (i.e. activity in actualization), exemplify creativity. In turn, creativity exists only as so exemplified and has no separate actuality or existence of its own. Thus, while God can properly be described as a creature of creativity, the creativity in question is his own ac-

tivity of unifying his manifold prehensions into a total experience in the course of his concrescence. While creativity is an ultimate, it is not an independent reality standing over against God.

2. Every actual entity is divisible into prehensions (the 10th category of explanation).[32] "Prehension" is a generalization from apprehension on the model of Leibniz' distinction between 'apperception' and 'perception,' used to indicate the inclusion or grasping of some datum by a subject, whether consciously or unconsciously. The two major species of prehension, physical and conceptual, are distinguishable in terms of their data. What is grasped in a physical prehension is some other actual entity as objectified for that subject. Our direct, sensory awareness of the external world is mediated by such physical prehensions, as are all causal influences. In general, if A causally influences B, then A has become effective in B because B has physically (usually "unconsciously") prehended A. Any experience God might have of the actual world is also in terms of physical prehensions. These physical prehensions constitute the "physical pole" of an actual entity.

Conceptual prehensions (forming its mental pole) have as their data 'pure potentials' or abstract possibilities. They provide the element of novelty, even if it is only the way in which the multiplicity of physical prehensions can be synthesized together into a determinate actuality. Every actual occasion is in a certain sense 'new,' because that occasion, with precisely its determinate relationships to all other actualities, had not previously existed.

Every actual entity requires both physical and conceptual prehensions, and achieves its concrescence by the integration of both. Without conceptual prehensions, there could be no novelty whereby there could be any creative advance to the new. Without physical prehensions, there would be nothing determinate and concrete to synthesize. No amount of concatenation of abstract possibilities by themselves will produce anything concrete; concretion must start by utilizing that which is already concrete.

3. Every actual entity has its own inherent subjectivity. For

"an entity is actual, when it has significance for itself" and "this self-functioning is the real internal constitution of an actual entity."[33]

This "panpsychist" insistence is perhaps the most difficult feature of Whitehead's thought for many to accept, but it is hardly an arbitrary or eccentric thesis. It stems in part from an acceptance of Leibniz' insight that the individual actuality does not have the properties appropriately assignable to aggregates. Since macroscopic objects like books, tables, and typewriters have mass, solidity, hardness, and inertness, it was assumed that their constituent elements must have the same properties. Contemporary physics has destroyed this image for the elementary particles, which are equally conceivable as fields of energy. Aggregates may be lifeless and devoid of any inherent activity without the individual actualities sharing those properties.

In large measure, however, Whitehead's "panpsychism," which is equally a "panphysicalism," stems from his solution to the subject/object split. Subjectivity and objectivity do not designate separate classes of entities, but different aspects of each actual entity seen in terms of temporal modality. Put most succinctly, Whitehead identifies objectivity with pastness and subjectivity with presentness. Every actual entity in process of concrescence enjoys its own subjective immediacy as it unifies its many prehensions into one final satisfaction. Every actual entity becomes past insofar as its actuality is objectified for subsequent actualities. Every subject actualizes itself by prehending other objects, and thereby becomes an object for future subjects.

Each act of self-creation is guided by its "subjective aim," which is its conceptual prehension of the ideal it seeks to actualize. Every concrescence requires a covergence if it is to terminate in a single concrete unity. The subjective aim supplies the direction of that convergence, as the diversity of prehensions are gradually modified by that aim to fuse together into one.

All these factors—concrescence, prehensions (both physical and conceptual), subjectivity, and subjective aim—may be ascribed to God as well as to all other occasions. Whitehead's uncompromising "panpsychist" stance here pays dividends, for it is not necessary to regard divine subjectivity as "wishful anthropomorphizing" or as a "symbolic projection" upon a reality essentially devoid of subjectivity. Divine subjectivity is not in the least exceptionable, but directly follows from the generic description of actuality.

THE CONTRAST BETWEEN GOD AND THE WORLD

All actual entities, including God, have both physical and conceptual prehensions. However, on this level of generality we have refrained from assigning any order among them. This brings us back to our original suggestion, for the totality of physical and conceptual prehensions constitute respectively the physical and mental poles of an actuality. As Whitehead writes, "Any instance of experience is dipolar, whether that instance be God or an actual occasion of the world. The origination of God is from the mental pole, origination of an actual occasion is from the physical pole."[34]

Aristotle, Aquinas, and Hume all argue that there is nothing in the intellect which was not first in the senses. For Hume all ideas are faint copies derived from initial impressions. In the case of actual occasions, Whitehead follows Hume in deriving all conceptual prehensions from an initial multiplicity of physical prehension. Each occasion is finite, dependent upon its causes for its existence. Since the causal relation is simply the obverse of physical prehension, the causes for an occasion's existence can become efficacious only insofar as they are grasped by physical prehension. Without the prehension of past actual occasions there would literally be nothing in the occasion to be rendered concrete, and no concrescence could occur. Since everything in the occasion, including its novel possibilities, must be derived from elsewhere, and physical prehension provides the only means for such derivation, the actual occasion must originate from its physical pole, upon which all is dependent, including the mental pole.

Now we must ask whether it would be possible for all actual entities without exception to originate from their physical poles.

Would the category of the actual occasion be capable of sustaining the entire metaphysical order? Whitehead answers no, in terms of the more sophisticated argument for the principle of concretion developed in *Process and Reality* with reference to subjective aim. The subjective aim provides the incipient subjectivity of the occasion, for it is that by which the occasion decides the character of its concrescence. According to the ontological principle this subjective aim must be derived from somewhere, that is, from some actual entity. It cannot come into being from nowhere, 'out of nothing.' There are only three possibilities: the aim has its origin in (a) the concrescing occasion itself, (b) past actual occasions (contemporary or future occasions could have no influence upon it), or (c) an actual entity which is not an actual occasion. It cannot be derived from the concrescing occasion because it is required at the very outset of that concrescence. There can be no activity of coming together unless some center is aimed at; this aim is not generated by the activity but is presupposed by it as its direction.

Past occasions cannot provide the subjective aim for three reasons. (a) They are simply potentials for inclusion in the concrescence; the way in which they are included does not depend upon them but upon the 'decision' of the concrescing occasion. (b) Each past actuality is simply one among a vast multiplicity of occasions; all together they are *data* for synthesis, but cannot effect the synthesis themselves. (c) Each past actuality is a datum in a vast number of different individual syntheses, and cannot therefore contain any regulative principle for any particular synthesis. Thus, the initial subjective aim, the focus for that particular act of becoming, must be derived from an actuality different in kind from all actual occasions. "In this sense God is the principle of concretion: namely, He is that actual entity from which each temporal concrescence receives that initial aim from which its self-causation starts."[35]

Each actual occasion derives its initial subjective aim, i.e. the possibility of that which it will become, from its physical prehension of God. To provide such aims God must be a reservoir of unrealized possibility, the source of all novelty. This is particularly important for the evolutionary advance, for each new level of complexity must first be introduced as a possibility before it can be actualized. As creator, God's role is to persuade the creature to create itself. God supplies the lures of feeling which urge successive generations of actual occasions toward ever-increasing levels of complexity. If the world were a closed system, there should be a gradual decrease in achieved complexity according to the law of entropy. God's persuasive power in providing novel aims for actualization is precisely that which counterbalances entropy and tips the scales in favor of increased complexity over time.

Thus far we have shown that there must be some source of subjective aims outside the world but we have not yet determined why there should be only one actual entity, God, which originates from its mental pole. By Whitehead's principle "that no two actual entities originate from an identical universe,"[36] there could not be two infinite, all inclusive actualities. Yet, this would not preclude there being several finite actual entities each originating from a different set of possibilities. Here we must have recourse to Whitehead's distinction between the "individual essence" and the "relational essence" of each possibility or eternal object described above.[37] The "individual essence" describes its unique quality or particular individuality: just what it is, whatever that may be. Every possibility, however, is also related to other possibilities in terms of inclusion and subordination, compatibility and incompatibility, similarity and difference. All possible cats must be mammals, all numbers must be odd or even, all triangles must have three sides. These relationships are eternal, fixed for all time, and applicable to all actualities. Yet, there is a certain arbitrariness about them, for it is conceivable that for an entirely different universe they could have been otherwise. These "relational essences" require a reason why they are so and not otherwise; by the ontological principle this reason can only be found in some actual entity. The initial or primordial envisagement of the possibilities provides that reason, thereby determining these essential relationships.

The consistency of the universe depends upon there being

only one universally given pattern of interrelationships among possibilities, for only compatible possibilities can be actualized. Thus, there could only be one primordial envisagement of possibility, and only one actual entity originating from its mental pole. "This ideal realization of potentialities in a primordial actual entity constitutes the metaphysical stability whereby the actual process exemplifies general principles of metaphysics, and attains the ends proper to specific types of emergent order."[38] Two actual entities independently originating from primordial envisagements of possibility could produce compatible possibilities only by an extraordinary, unexplainable coincidence. If there is only one such envisagement, it would be infinite because it could not be limited by any other possibility or actuality. "Unfettered conceptual valuation, 'infinite' in Spinoza's sense of that term, is only possible once in the universe; since that creative act is objectively immortal as an inescapable condition characterizing creative action."[39] By the principle of relativity, that "it belongs to the nature of a 'being' that it is a potential for every 'becoming,' "[40] this primordial envisagement will condition all other actualities.

God differs from actual occasions primarily by being one unique everlasting concrescence while they constitute a great plurality of finite, temporal concrescences. Whitehead and a great many other thinkers hold that there can be no actual infinite—the world at any one stage in its development consists of a finite number of actual entities. Each occasion starts with a finite number of physical prehensions to unify and "the process continues till all prehensions are components in the one determinate integral satisfaction"[41] which terminates that concrescence. Both the rhythmic demands of creativity[42] and the inexhaustibility of God's primordial envisagement insure that this succession of actual occasions will never end. That infinite envisagement provides God with his own subjective aim, the most intense and harmonious realization of all possibility. This insatiable goal requires an everlasting concrescence prehending all actualization for its fulfillment.

In summary, we may say that "God's existence is not generically different from that of other actual entities, except that he is 'primordial.' "[43] This primordial origination from his mental pole accounts for all the metaphysical differences. This reversal of poles also provides a complementarity of roles so well described in "God and the World," the concluding chapter of *Process and Reality*. Process philosophy envisages a dynamic, reciprocal interplay between these two realms, each needing and being fulfilled in the other. The world needs God for the novel possibility which it actualized. God also requires the world for his participation in actuality, for it is only from the world that God can derive the physical prehensions whereby he can sustain his everlasting concrescence.

This dynamic reciprocity of God and the world nicely illustrates the solidarity so characteristic of Whitehead's thought. He demanded of speculative philosophy that its fundamental ideas cohere, that is "presuppose each other so that in isolation they are meaningless."[44] Apart from God, the world as analyzed by the categoreal scheme cannot be rendered fully intelligible. If it could, then we should rightly ask : why need there be God in addition to the world? Why is there not simply the world? The same logic applies equally well to God : either God cannot be rendered intelligible without the world, or no metaphysical reason can be given why there should be any world in addition to God. Insofar as we maintain that God is equally free to create or not create the world, our philosophy is incoherent, for we have introduced an "arbitrary disconnection of first principles."[45] But once we have seen that God needs the world for the enrichment of his being, then we are able to give full affirmation to the secular world. The temporal world provides for a constant, growing enrichment of the eternal simplicity of divine experience. Temporal enrichment and eternal simplicity are not antithetical concepts if eternal simplicity is understood in inclusive and dynamic terms, as we argue Boethius' formula can be.[46]

In this essay we have outlined two procedures whereby process philosophy has sought to know the nature of God : the logic of divine perfection and the method of categoreal analysis. These constitute the major philosophical approaches to God, but one need not stop there. One of the most important findings of Whitehead and Hartshorne is the recognition that God has contingent as well as necessary dimensions. As long as God's dependence upon the world for his experience and knowledge of actuality was not recognized, it was easy to assume that God's nature and activity were wholly necessary. This assumption had several unfortunate consequences.

If God is conceived to have only necessary attributes, it is extraordinarily difficult if not impossible to assign satisfactory complementary roles to reason and revelation. Both describe the same reality, and revelation can play a distinctive and contributive part only by arbitrarily restricting reason in some way. When reason is given full reign, as in Hegel, revelation becomes relegated to a secondary, symbolic presagement of the absolute philosophic truth.

If necessary and therefore independent of contingent historical conditions, God's activity in the world must be conceived in completely universal terms. Thus God must be assumed to act in all places and at all times in precisely the same manner. It then becomes difficult to single out any particular events as peculiarly manifesting divine activity, let alone any decisive action in Christ, except on the basis of purely subjective criteria, such as the witness of those who testify that these events were peculiarly revelatory to them. Particular events can only become symbolic of the divine activity, for God has acted no differently in them than in any other event.

In contrast, if God has contingent aspects as well as necessary ones, the philosophical endeavor to know God is necessarily inadequate, no matter how penetrating our reasoning might be. By its very method philosophy can only determine that which is necessary, which is highly abstract in contrast to the concrete contingency of God. It is as contingently concrete that the God of Abraham, Isaac, and Jacob is more than the God of philosophers. Whiteheadean philosophy can only teach us that God manifests himself to men in the form of initial subjective aims, and not that one of these aims in fact called Abraham forth from Ur of the Chaldeans on the long journey of faith. In all times and places God provides that aim which, if fully actualized by the creature, will provide the greatest richness of achievement. Yet the particular aim provided is dependent upon circumstance, and certain circumstances (notably our responsiveness as creatures) are particularly apt ' for the giving and actualizing of aims peculiarly characteristic of the divine beings.

We should understand 'reason' and 'revelation' in terms of the philosophical investigation of God's universal and necessary activity in all things in contrast to the reception of God's historical, contingent activity as peculiarly manifest in cumulative religious traditions. The Bible does not 'reveal' God's unchanging nature; it rather tells us the story of His particular activity on behalf of one nation. We may discern in that skein of historical circumstance and human response, of deep sensitivity and human outrage, a steady intensification of the divine aim which culminated in the person of Jesus of Nazareth, one who perfectly realized the will of his Father. At the same time we may be confident that God is working in all places providing ideal aims so that other cultures and ways of life are not bereft of their own revelation of God.

1. Frederick Sontag, **Divine Perfection: Possible Ideas of God** (New York: Harper & Brothers, 1962).

2. Aristotle, **Eudemian Ethics** VII, 1244 b - 1245 b, quoted by Arthur O. Lovejoy, **The Great Chain of Being** (Cambridge: Harvard Univ. Press, 1936), p. 43.

3. Aristotle, **Metaphysics XII**, 1074 b 20ff, trans. Richard Hope (New York: Columbia Univ. Press, 1952), p. 266.

4. Anselm, **Proslogion,** trans. Sidney Norton Deane (Chicago: Open Court, 1903).

5. This formalization first appears in Charles Hartshorne, **The Logic of Perfection** (LaSalle, Ill.: Open Court, 1962), p. 51, and is reprinted in **The Many-faced Argument,** eds. John H. Hick and Arthur C. McGill (New York: Macmillan, 1967), pp, 335, 348f. We have adopted the latter version, for here the phrase in step one, "hence the assertion that it exists could not be contingently but only necessarily true," was added

at Hartshorne's request. The above argument is our translation of the following symbolism:

1. $q \to Nq$
6. $Nq \lor N \sim q$
7. $\sim N \sim q$
8. Nq
9. $Nq \to q$
10. q

where "q" stands for "(x)Px" ("There is a perfect being, or perfection exists.") and "N" for "it is necessary (logically true) that." Steps 2-5 have been omitted as quite acceptable, and not here in dispute.

6. "A Critique of the 'Second Argument,' " **The Many-faced Argument**, pp. 341-56.

7. Anselm, **Monologion**, trans. Sidney Norton Deane (Chicago: Open Court, 1903), chap. VI.

8. "A Critique of the 'Second Argument,' " **The Many-faced Argument**, p. 347.

9. **Ibid.**, p. 351.

10. **Ibid.**, pp. 349f.

11. Charles Hartshorne, "Metaphysical Statements as Nonrestrictive and Existential," **The Review of Metaphysics**, XII (1958), 35-47, and "Some Empty Though Important Truths," **The Logic of Perfection** (LaSalle, Ill.: Open Court, 1962), pp. 280-97.

12. Charles Hartshorne, "Present Prospects for Metaphysics," **The Monist**, XLVII (1963), 207f.

13. Charles Hartshorne, "What Did Anselm Discover?" **The Many-faced Argument**, p. 329.

14. Charles Hartshorne, "What the Ontological Proof Does Not Do," **Review of Metaphysics**, XVII (1964), 608.

15. R. L. Purtill, "Hartshorne's Modal Proof," **Journal of Philosophy**, LXIII (1966), 398.

16. See footnote 12.

17. Alfred North Whitehead, **Science and the Modern World** (New York: Macmillan, 1926), p. 257.

18. **Ibid.**, pp. 255f.

19. **Ibid.**, p. 229.

20. **Ibid.**, p. 230.

21. **Ibid.**, pp. 256.

22. Alfred North Whitehead, **Process and Reality** (New York: Macmillan, 1929).

23. **Ibid.**, pp. 36f.

24. **Ibid.**, pp. 27f.

25. "Whitehead as I Knew Him," **Alfred North Whitehead: Essays on His Philosophy**, ed. George L. Kline (Englewood Cliffs, N.J.: Prentice-Hall, 1963), p. 16.

26. Whitehead, **Process and Reality**, p. 521.

27. **Ibid.**, p. 135.

28. **Ibid.**, p. 382.

29. **Ibid.**, p. 33.

30. Ibid., pp. 34f.

31. Ibid., p. 31.

32. Ibid., p. 35.

33. Ibid., p. 38.

34. Ibid., p. 54.

35. Ibid., p. 374. For the argument of this paragraph, see particularly Ivor Leclerc, **Whitehead's Metaphysics, an Introductory Exposition** (London: George Allen & Unwin, 1958), XIV and XVI.

36. Whitehead, **Process and Reality,** pp. 33f.

37. Whitehead, **Science and the Modern World,** pp. 229f. That this distinction is still operative in **Process and Reality,** see Whitehead's letter to Charles Hartshorne on January 2, 1936, reprinted in the Kline anthology, p. 199.

38. Whitehead, **Process and Reality,** p. 64.

39. Ibid., p. 378.

40. Ibid., p. 33.

41. Ibid., p. 39.

42. Here see Donald W. Sherburne's masterful discussion in **A Whiteheadian Aesthetic** (New Haven: Yale Univ. Press, 1961), pp. 9-20.

43. Whitehead, **Process and Reality,** p. 116.

44. Ibid., p. 5.

45. Ibid., p. 9.

46. See "Boethius and Whitehead on Time and Eternity," **International Philosophical Quarterly,** VIII (1968), 38-67.

Process and the Nature of God

◇

by
Charles Hartshorne

TO BEGIN WITH an historical note, the following thinkers have more or less explicitly and consistently believed in a God-in-process or in an in-some-sense-developing deity: Pfleiderer, German Protestant theologian; L'Abbé Bautain, French Roman Catholic; Bergson, at least by implication; Varisco, Italian mathematician and metaphysician; Martin Buber; Karl Barth; James Ward, English psychologist and philosopher; W. R. Matthews, Anglican theologian; A. E. Garvie, English Congregationalist; B. P. Bowne, W. P. Montague, E. S. Brightman, W. E. Hocking, A. N. Whitehead, American or Anglo-American philosophers; John Cobb and Schubert Ogden, American Protestant theologians. In one footnote Heidegger strongly hints at the idea. In the foregoing partial list, to which other names will be added later, I have not included those who, like William James or J. S. Mill, have argued for an indefinitely finite God, who of course would be subject to change. It would seem that even S. Alexander belongs here.

I hold that God, to be worthy of the name, must have an aspect of infinity and immutability. A merely finite and changeable "God" is an idol or fetish. In this essay we are concerned only with the view that God is, in some but not all aspects, open to the acquisition of new qualities. Far from being an extreme view, this is the only way to avoid the two extremes that everything in God or nothing in God is eternally the same.

An apparent justification for the first extreme, that God is unchanging, is the plausible notion that where change is possible decay or degeneration is also. Because, as we ordinarily encounter it, the changeable is corruptible, it would not seem possible for God to change. The argument is weak, since anything as we ordinarily encounter it is inapplicable to deity. Concerning any property, the theistic question always is whether it can have a supremely excellent or "eminent" form unique to God. Divine process can only be eminent process or gain without even the possibility of loss, creation with no possibility of decreation or destruction. In this sense, divine process must be incapable of corruption.

THE AESTHETIC AND CONCRETE DIVINE PROCESS

Can there be such process?

Decay or loss takes two forms: deterioration of character, capacity, or mode of action; and forgetting. The strong become weak, or disintegrate and die; the good become evil. In addition, past joys are largely forgotten, so that it is almost as though they had never been. To form the concept of eminent process, we must deny both the very possibility of deterioration of character and of forgetting. God must always be equally strong and good. He also must forget nothing worth remembering. To the question of whether there is anything not worth remembering, I should answer in the negative. Considering his limited capacity to remember, man must forget many things, and for him some things are not worth remembering. With an unlimited capacity to preserve them, however, all experiences are interesting and worth retaining. Though the ordinary "memory" is mixed with forgetting, whatever God may be, he is not ordinary.

A more plausible objection to the idea of divine process runs that a "perfect" being must be as incapable of gain as of loss, since it must eternally possess whatever is worth possessing. The reasoning is conclusive provided there be no logical objection to the idea of perfection as here interpreted. However, it is not logically possible to possess together everything worth possessing if there are good things which are possible collectively. The classical idea of perfection assumed that though good things as we know them are partly incompossible, for God all values are compossible. But either God can have all possible world-states fully actualized or he cannot; if he cannot, then either world-states give no value to God, or they give less than all possible value. The justification for world-states giving no value to God must be the assumption that he is perfect in the very sense whose possibility is at issue. In addition, this view makes the religious idea of serving God an absurdity.

The contention of process philosophers is that the arguments against divine change in the form of increase of values rest upon arbitrary and, indeed, absurd premises. God can increase in value simply by acquiring new content in the awareness with which he enjoys the new world-states as they come into being. He is not stronger or better or holier, but only richer in experienced content. The gain is aesthetic, not ethical or in power.

When Plato spoke of "absolute beauty," he used the second word in this phrase without analysis or definition. From many attempts at such an analysis, the clearest result has been the phrase "unity in variety" (or variety in unity). Mere unity is not enough. If it were, a musical chord would equal or surpass a symphony, and a single color, the gayest or richest combination of colors. At the other extreme, mere variety is nothing, and could not even be experienced. There must be integrated variety.

An objection sometimes made to the notion of "unity in variety" is that it is possessed by every object and every experience. The answer is twofold. First, as was shown by the above examples, in many experiences there may be too little variety for more than trivial beauty; and second, the real meaning of the phrase is a balance of unity and variety. Where the variety is more striking than the unity, there is an interesting, amusing, tragic, or even ugly object, not a beautiful one; where the unity is more striking than the variety, there is at best a neat object, and at worst a boringly monotonous one. Beauty is the precious mean between mere chaos and mere order. The value of the mean depends upon the level of complexity. A musical chord is as much unified as it is diversified, but the complexity is trivial.

If all this is accepted, then absolute beauty must be absolute variety absolutely unified. Yet, absolute variety has no clear meaning unless it refers to all possible variety. Again we confront incompossible possibilities. I find Whitehead's conclusion from this to be cogent: eminent value in aesthetic terms cannot be an absolute maximum incapable of increase. If the divine experience enjoys any beauty, it is a beauty to which additions are possible.

Yet there is a clear sense in which deity can be eminent aesthetically. Eminence is not the same as absoluteness, or "perfection" in the platonic sense. Eminent means exalted beyond possible rivalry; God must be unsurpassable by any other conceivable reality. Anselm's famous formula almost succeeded in seizing this idea. All that is needed is to take "none greater can be conceived" to mean none greater, other than himself. God must be unsurpassable *by another*. There is no need and no good reason to add, "or even by himself." If God surpasses God, that does nothing to elevate anyone else to his level.

Just how can the beauty of the divine experience be unsurpassable except by itself? Consider the total universe of reality as beautiful. Obviously no one save God, the eminently perceptive being, can distinctly experience this beauty. Any rival to God with its own beauty must be but an item in the total universe. Suppose, too, that the total universe is perpetually increased by new items bringing new contrasts and new harmonies into being. As eminently perceptive of cosmic beauty, God will then acquire new values with each such addition. Thus the perpetual creation of new things other than God has for final purpose the "enrichment of the divine life itself" (Berdyaev). Tillich hints at the same idea: God created universes as steps in the endless process of creating additional values for himself.

If God increases in value, must there not have been a time in the past when God had no aesthetic value at all? If not, the divine past is beginningless, and we confront a form of Kant's paradox of an infinite series which yet ends in the divine present.

Apparently no human theory of ultimates is free from paradox. So far as I can see, process philosophy must take the past as an infinite yet actual sequence. Though logicians and mathematicians disagree as to the tenability of this conception, I am impressed with the objections of the radical finitists but not convinced. As regards the future, I see no difficulty: the future is infinite, but not actual, for the divine increase can reach no final maximum. If anything is absolutely infinite and inexhaustible, possibility must be. Only an actual infinite would be paradoxical.

There is another problem. If God already enjoys the aesthetic richness of an infinite and unforgotten past, how can this infinity be subject to increase? Here there are two answers from which to choose. The first is that numerically there is no increase, but that aesthetic richness is not measured by counting. Add new items to an infinite totality and the mere number of contrasting items is not increased, yet there is qualitative enrichment, for new contrasts are now present. Russell once told me he thought this was tenable. Aesthetically speaking, counting is a secondary function. The second possible answer is that the infinity of the past keeps passing to a higher type, and has always been more than simply infinity. This assumes that the Kantorian hierarchy of infinites can be taken seriously, which is most controversial. Whitehead once suggested this solution to me. I gather, however, that it may not be consistent with another assumption, which I am inclined to agree with, namely, that becoming is "epochal" rather than continuous. Apparently Whitehead does not apply this to divine becoming. As I am not clear with what justification this exception can be made, I incline to the first answer.

If, as I have said, God must not be capable of change in all respects, how shall his immutable aspects be characterized? The concept of eminence provides the answer. God has not become unsurpassable by another, but eternally is so; nor has he become surpassable by himself only in aesthetic enjoyment, for this, too, he eternally is. Though absolute beauty is impossible, absolute immunity to possible rivalry is not impossible.

I have also said that the divine increase is aesthetic not ethical.

Certainly it would be a poor ethical idea of God to consider that he might have been wicked once and only after a struggle became righteous or holy. But absolute goodness is more possible than absolute beauty. The reason for this lies in the logical point that ethical value is abstract, whereas aesthetic value is not. Dealing rightly with others is a merit in measuring which we abstract from many things. We do not ask if the scene the agent contemplated was beautiful, monotonous, chaotic, but only if he did the best in his power to serve the interests at stake. A man can be ethical in an ugly, boring windowless prison cell, but he cannot there enjoy the beauty of a spring landscape with singing birds, fragrant flowers, and happy children playing about him. Aesthetic value is inclusive, and while it depends partly on one's response to others, it depends also on the others.

To suppose that there can be no such distinction for God is to suppose that divine power and freedom annihilate creaturely power and freedom. God does not depend upon what creatures do for his goodness, yet he depends on them for the degree of his aesthetic enjoyment. Goodness is active, but enjoyment of beauty is partly passive. To deny all passivity to God is to cut him off from the aesthetic, and also to make creaturely freedom valueless for him. The objections to this are religious as well as philosophical.

THE ABSTRACT AND THE ETERNAL

Having considered the values of goodness and beauty in eminent form, let us now discuss cognitive value or the value of truth. There is an ambiguity to be avoided here. In one sense cognitive value, like ethical value, is abstract and admits of an absolute maximum. He has absolute knowledge who is free from error and ignorance. It does not matter what sort of universe there is for him to know; if he knows it fully and without error his knowledge is perfect or absolute. There is a further question, however, which concerns the value of this knowledge: is any universe more worth knowing than any other? The abstract perfection of knowledge—its freedom from error and ignorance

—is not its full value. This depends also upon the richness, diversity, and harmony of the reality which is known. It is easy to see that the concrete value of knowledge is a species of aesthetic value. To know the truth is to be in harmony with one's world; but the satisfaction this yields depends partly upon the diversity and harmony of that world itself.

Thus, there are two basic dimensions of eminence: the abstract dimension, admitting of a maximum, absolute, and hence eternally fixed perfection; and a concrete dimension, admitting only of unsurpassability by another with perpetual self-surpassing. The ethical and the abstract-cognitive are really one, as are the aesthetic and concrete cognitive; but the abstract and the concrete are distinct. The traditional doctrine that divine attributes are not really multiple is valid only with this qualification. There is one abstract and one concrete eminence, but the difference between the two is entirely real. As a matter of fact, when our ancestors argued for the real unity of the attributes they did not even consider the concrete dimension of beauty in any clear fashion.

According to the sound Aristotelian and Whiteheadian principle that the abstract is in the concrete, there is but one God, that is, the concrete, self-surpassing, other-surpassing aesthetically eminent God. An abstract aspect of this God is absolutely unsurpassable and immutable. In this view, abstraction is no mere function, but divine as well. God himself distinguishes more clearly than we his abstract from his concrete properties.

Instead of talking about aesthetic value, one could employ a term such as happiness, for which the theological term was usually "bliss." God was supposed to enjoy perfect or absolute bliss. But is it enough for perfect happiness to have no unsatisfied desires or interests. In that case a contented oyster is as close to perfect happiness as we human beings are likely to get. Indeed, a man in deep sleep should be perfectly happy. Another approach to the ideal of happiness is to take the diversity of satisfied desires or interests as a measure of happiness. But then absolute happiness would consist in the full satisfaction of all possible interests. Once more the spector of incompossibility blocks our path. Happiness, like aesthetic enjoyment, with which it coalesces in its eminent form, is too concrete to have a final maximum. The inexhaustible superinfinity of possibility can always be drawn upon. Eminence here can mean only unsurpassability by another, achieved through a mode of self-surpassing which as such is absolutely unsurpassable (because the "as such" introduces abstractness). Fechner brilliantly anticipated this doctrine long ago. God's perfection is in his unique perfectibility. A century passed before anyone else put it so neatly.

It is an old Aristotelian doctrine that what becomes is contingent and what is eternal is necessary. Insofar as God becomes, he is contingent; but insofar as he is eternally the same, he is necessary. Since the unsurpassability of God, including his absolute though abstract ethico-cognitive perfection, is eternal, God exists necessarily. This includes his self-surpassing and otherwise unsurpassable aesthetic capacity as such or in its abstractness. Only the concrete *de facto* aesthetic state is contingent.

To understand necessity it is important to consider the contrasting term contingency with more care than most disputants with Anselm or Descartes, or indeed than these two men themselves, bestowed upon the subject. Contingency, I believe, is the incompossibility (Leibniz) or competition between specific ideas. Red here and now excludes green here and now. My doing this now excludes my doing that now, even though I could have done that instead. Specific ideas compete for existence and something beyond the ideas must cast the decision, but the most general or abstract ideas exclude nothing—except nothing itself. Now, to exclude nothing is not to exclude. The most general ideas are nonexclusive, noncompetitive, and therefore their being exemplified is noncontingent.

This is a definite proposal about contingency. I have yet to see any very good reason for rejecting it, unless it be that the proposal opens the way to an ontological proof. As Donald Williams once said to a student during an oral examination, the fact that a rule makes the ontological proof invalid is not sufficient justification. But the above justification is rather that the rule makes contingency intelligible, and that it enables us to avoid the paradox "there might have been nothing." Among others, Munitz asks what "there" or "have been" would refer to in that case? If nothing, then what is the difference between referring to nothing and not referring? The normal uses of "nothing" are quite different; as Munitz says, they mean "nothing to the given purpose" or under the rubric being considered. "Bare nothing" is used only to bring out a failure of significance.

THE ONTOLOGICAL PROOF FOR GOD

If the most general or abstract ideas cannot lack exemplification, how does this help the ontological proof? The answer is that the definition of God as unsurpassable is as abstract or general as any possible idea. It excludes nothing positive. Take, for instance, unsurpassable cognitive power. It must be able to know any world-state whatever, and would know it were it actualized. It would contradict his unsurpassable cognitive power to suppose a world-state to be possible which would exclude the unsurpassable knower, for the unsurpassable knower could not know such a state. Thus, either the idea of God is absurd, or the idea of his nonexistence is absurd. Taken either way, the issue is *a priori* and rules out all attempts to prove or disprove God empirically. The atheistic argument from the problem of evil, taken as an appeal to observation, cannot possibly be valid. The same holds of any claim to prove God from results of science.

The identifying character of God is completely general or abstract; it is no more exclusive than reality as such or process as such. God is the *individual with strictly universal functions,* unsurpassably relevant, influential, knowing, and hence ubiquitous, coextensive with being, truth, reality, and process. To be is to be for God, to happen is to happen for God. What is and what God knows coincide, what occurs and what God knows as occurrent coincide. The existence of God thus understood could not be exclusive or competitive.

It does not follow that the total concrete reality of God excludes nothing, for that, we have said, is contingent. God decides or acts for this against that freely, and his mere existence does not prejudge the decision. God's action is precisely not his essence and it is here that the tradition erred grievously. His mere existence is, indeed, his essence, but not his concrete actions, decisions, decrees, and responses to the world. By such considerations one can, as I have shown, revise and partly defend the ontological argument. Whitehead entirely failed to note this possibility.

Let us revert to Aristotle's principle that the eternal and the necessary coincide. Johannes Krell, the Socinian theologian, articulated God's eternity in terms, not of immutability, but of necessity: "That is eternal which cannot not exist." If, on the contrary, the external were contingent, how would its eternity be knowable? If its nonexistence is possible, how could one be sure that this possibility never was, and never will be realized? Even God, as eminent process, cannot wait forever to see if he continues to exist. If he knows himself to be eternal, it must be because he sees the impossibility of his not existing. However, it is held that this impossibility may be only conditional: since he does exist and is eminently strong, he can guarantee his everlasting preservation. Let us consider this idea. God always has existed and his death or destruction are impossible; still, it was perfectly possible for him never to have existed. But there does not seem to be a possibility here, since it would have to rest upon no conceivable condition or cause. Had God not existed, nothing would have excluded him from existing; for to suppose this is to conceive him surpassable in power of adaptation to conditions and dependent for his very existence upon another. For the same reason, his actually existing also rests upon no cause or condition, because, being his own principle of existence, there could be no such condition. Thus, to the alternative of God or no God, rational explanation has no application whatever. The immeasurable difference between God and no God is entirely exempted from caused explanation and yet is held to be a contingent matter. I would think that the point of the causal principle is to make the contingent in some measure intelligible. Strict determinism is not needed for this; for no indeterminist supposes that even the freest acts are simple uninfluenced by causal conditions. The explanation for the divine existence is simply that there is no alternative other than a merely verbal one.

The most abstract aspects of reality are eternal. Nothing is more abstract, in the relevant sense, than the unsurpassability of God. For example, God has unsurpassable knowledge, but from this no logic can deduce that he knows Mao. To do that, one must have also as premise that there is the man Mao. Knowledge of particular contingent things does not follow from cognitive unsurpassability, but only from that plus the contingent facts as to what contingent things exist to be known.

God's abstract attributes must be somehow actualized in concrete form, but how and in what form or forms is entirely contingent. God's concrete actuality, such as his actual knowledge of Mao, is not provable but must be experienced. What is provable is that God is somehow concrete and actual; but here the terms "concrete" and "actuality" function as abstractions. The concrete, actual states of divine experience, in an analogical sense, in their particularity utterly escape *a priori* proof, though the bare statement that God exists is innocent of such particularity.

If unsurpassability is abstract enough to entail existence, its correlate, surpassability, is no less abstract. From this I infer both that God exists necessarily, though with contingent concrete states, and that the correlative to God, surpassable being as such, exists necessarily. It forms a class which necessarily has members, though each member is contingent. Thus, calling the eminent process The Creator, and the correlative idea, The Creature, the latter is equally subject to an ontological proof. The vast difference, however, is that "The Creature" names a class, not an individual, even though a class which cannot lack members, while "The Creator" names an individual. In no universe could there be room for a plurality of eminent processes, for no principle of individuation *(principium individuationis)* applies here.

From this it appears that we give up the doctrine that God is free to refrain from creating, free to exist alone *(solus)*. What would be the point of a freedom which is of no value except on condition that it be left eternally unused? Any world is better than none. I suggest that God's freedom is positive. It is a freedom to create this world or that; it is not to create nothing, and so be only potentially a creator. God must create, but he need not create the particular universe which does in fact exist.

The validity of the ontological argument does not mean that it is by itself a sufficient reason for belief. As Leibniz pointed out, any argument from a concept or definition assumes that there is no logical impossibility in the concept. In the case of deity, this is seriously disputed. For more than two thousand years (since Carneades, at least) men have denied that the idea of God can be freed from intrinsic absurdities. The process version of the idea eliminates some traditional antinomies; but one may still wonder if it is free from antinomies of its own. To that extent the ontological proof is not self-sufficient; it depends upon other arguments by which one might combat the Carneadean or positivistic form of atheism. As these other arguments conclude not simply to the possibility but to the reality of God's existence, in a sense we do not need the ontological argument. In this the Thomists have been right, but with the important qualification that Anselm showed how to establish the logical level of the theistic question. Or, he showed us *in what sense* God, if the concept is even logically admissible, exists. For all empirical theistic or atheistic arguments he showed the fallacy by which, if *a posteriori* means empirical, there are no *a posteriori* arguments for or against God's existence, any more than there are for or against "$2+2=4$."

What is peculiar about Anselm's argument is not that it starts with an idea rather than an empirical fact, but that it starts with the very idea of God. There are other ideas, such as contingency, order, value, from which one may argue for the divine existence. However, none of these other arguments needs to use an empirical fact such as the fact that there are changing things. Indeed, is this really an empirical fact if it could not be empirically true that there were not changing things? Experience itself in its very idea implies change. Change is an *a priori* category which could not lack exemplification, any more than could the idea of divine actuality.

Suppose there were no nondivine change or process, what then would there be? Obviously one of the following: nothing at all, divine process alone *(solus)*, or mere immutable being. The first is absurd, the second yields the divine existence, while the third is the paradox of the merely abstract apart from any exemplification—it is the old dubious "platonic" notion of separable forms apart from all particularity or individuality. There is no need for nondivine change or motion as mere fact in theistic argumentation. Similar reasoning holds for the argument from design and also for the moral argument that, in abstraction from God, value judgments are empty gestures in the face of an indifferent cosmos. Plato hints at this argument and Whitehead stresses it. The point is not that in fact there are values, but that there could not not be values, for any interest in truth attributes value to truth and it is vain to speak of a possible truth in which there could be no interest whatever. Plato's concept that the good is superior to being was perhaps a way of stating this. Thinking cannot be less than valuing. Value as such is *a priori*, but it becomes intelligible in theistic terms.

PROCESS IN GOD AND CREATURES

It is time to consider the relations between eminent process and ordinary process. Concrete process, so far as it is knowable, is experiencing. Of processes other than animal, we have only abstract outlines, not concrete intuitions. Thus, in our knowledge an atom appears as a mathematical scheme, a mere outline. To fill in this outline there is no positive alternative to supposing that some exceedingly strange or radically nonhuman forms of experiencing or feeling are taking place in the micro-constituents of matter. This supposition has been made by the great systematizers of process philosophy, not only Whitehead, but also Peirce, Alexander, Bergson, and Varisco. To reject it is merely to say that, beyond the mathematics, we know nothing of real agents in the inanimate world. Russell is clear about this agnostic implication of the rejection of psychicalism. Many others seem not so clear.

Process is experiencing, mostly in nonhuman forms, but including the eminent form. Experiencing always has data or things experienced. In a process view, concrete data can only be other processes, other experiences. Experience is always of experience or "feeling of feeling." I held some such view long before I knew about Whitehead. The data experiences may be either prior experiences of the same enduring individual, or experiences of other individuals. The first is memory, the second, perception. Since in the first moment of an individual life there cannot be memory, perception is the universal form of experiencing, of which memory is a special case.

Perception relates us to the past as much as does memory. Indeed, when we look at the stars we are aware of a past much more remote than any we can remember. There are good logical reasons for denying that, even in bodily sensations, the bodily process given in the experience is literally simultaneous with our experience of it, rather than immediately prior to it. Perception, thus construed, is "impersonal memory," awareness of past process not our own. It may be neutral process, belonging first not to the human, but to the cellular individual, whose feelings are participated in by us. In physical pain we share in sufferings that the cells have just undergone.

The notion of perception as having a temporal and social structure like that of memory in which we sympathize with our past selves is apparently due to Whitehead. I am not sure it was held by anyone earlier. Peirce was unclear on the issue, as I think was Bergson, while Alexander was questionable. This notion of perception as temporal and social effects a wonderful integration of concepts. It eliminates the idea that memory is an oddity because of its pastward reference, or because it relates experience to other experience. All experience has past experience as datum.

How then shall we conceive divine process? It seems that divine process must eminently perceive nondivine experiencing and eminently remember its own prior experiencing. Eminent or unsurpassable perception seems conceivable as complete participation in all experience "as soon as" it has taken place. Thus God has exhaustive impersonal memory of our moments of living, and in this way all process is taken into divine process. Scotus Erigena hinted at something like this; Varisco and Whitehead affirmed it. In this sense eminent process is all-inclusive. It is not any and every process; but in its data it possesses all processes whatever, whether as actual or past. By this route all experience attains immortality, and the apparent nullification of value through death can be dismissed as illusory. Death writes *finis* to the book of life, but it does not destroy the book, or even "cancel half a line."

There is difficulty in relating such a scheme to relativity physics. More than one physicist is considering this question, as are various theologians and philosophers. The matter is still obscure, to me at least. It might appear that there could not be a conflict between theism as *a priori* and physics as an empirical science. It is always hard to be sure just how much of what scientists say is really empirical, and how much of what metaphysicians or theologians say is really required by *a priori* categories.

From a teleological point of view, relativity physics, makes excellent sense, for would it be desirable that signals could "pass" instantaneously to remote parts of the universe, establishing an absolute yet empirical simultaneity? It seems bad enough that we can learn in minutes about events in China or India and have to ask ourselves whether we are our brothers' keepers in that locality also; how much worse if we could learn of catastrophes on another planet. What would "infinite velocity" mean? There are logical as well as empirical problems here. I suspect that any universe would have a relativistic aspect. But I am not able to think clearly about the relations of this aspect to the process view of reality, or any other view for that matter.

It is important to realize that the doctrine of divine change in the form of acquisition was thought of long before Whitehead. It can be and has been reached by many routes other than the one he took. I first reached it, in crude outline, as a kind of fusion or compromise between William James' finitism and Royce's absolutism, with some prodding by my teacher W. E. Hocking, who had himself also reached it, I think, mainly via James and Royce, plus Hegel. Later encouragement came from Bergson, Brightman, and many others, as well as Whitehead. Supporters of the idea are found in Islam and Hinduism, as well as in Judeo-Christian circles.

The most important contribution of Whitehead is perhaps in his theory of perception, ordinary and divine, as means of relating divine to ordinary process. Also helpful is his sharp distinction between the mutable or "consequent" and the immutable or "primordial" aspects of the divine nature, and his clear recognition that although only the former can properly be termed absolute or infinite, the finitude or relativity of the consequent aspect does not imply its inferiority. Quite the contrary, mere infinity or absoluteness is an empty abstraction, "deficient in actuality" or concreteness.

Though his view implies it, Whitehead does not quite say that finitude or relativity has two essentially different forms, an ordinary and an eminent one. Ordinary finitude is better termed "fragmentariness," the status of being only a part of the actual whole of things, or of being localized by having an external environment. We are finite in the radical sense that most finite things are external to us; God as finite is the inclusive finite reality, with no external environment. Ordinary relativity is partial or restricted relativity, the status of being influenced by some other things, not by all. God, as eminently relative, is influenced by all things, just as in his absolute or primordial aspect he is influenced by none. God is the cosmic or universal form of independence and dependence; we are cosmic or universal in neither respect.

A defect of Whitehead's terminology is that the two "natures," primordial and consequent, are ambiguously integrated into the unity of the divine reality. They seem to be two abstractions or essences, both seeking concrete embodiment. The word "nature" suggests this. In a process philosophy no essence or nature is concrete or actual; actuality is in events or states. God as actuality is neither the essence of (unsurpassable) independence nor that of dependence. Primordially God has a consequent aspect, so that dependence is as primordial a property as is independence. God is "not before but with" all creation, which is "a primordial datum for God"; thus always God and the world have been in interaction.

The problem has some analogy with trinitarian questions. I suggest that we distinguish between the abstract natures or principles of divine independence (the Father?) and divine dependence (the Son?) and the de facto state of the actually dependent God (the Spirit?). Concrete actuality as such necessarily means relativity and finitude, though not necessarily fragmentariness or restricted relativity. Concreteness as such is not the same as an actual concrete thing. As Russell very significantly remarked long ago, concreteness is an abstraction. Thus, the general idea of God's being consequent upon and relative to his creatures, who in their way are relative to him, is a mere abstraction, compared to particular states of God relative to particular states of the world. The concrete actuality is our God now, not God in general, who is relative to the world in general. For process thinking the God of Abraham, Isaac, and Jacob is less concrete than our God now, and either one is incomparably more concrete than the mere "consequent nature" of God. God is consequent, no matter what world exists, but he is consequent upon this world only if this world exists. The first is obviously an abstraction, compared to the second.

I have spoken as though there were a plurality of states in the divine process. Whitehead denies that God is a sequential "society" of actualities, and speaks of him as a single actuality. He also says that God "reaches no final completion" and is "always moving on." He further holds that actualities become rather than change, for change is a succession of actualities. I find it impossible to understand how God can be in process without being a society—of course, the eminent society. Here eminence means that memory is complete, without "negative prehensions," and that the perception or impersonal memories are also complete. The alternative is to suppose a succession of "prehensions" in God, not of unitary experiences, but as a single never completed experience which keeps acquiring new data. I do not assimilate this other picture, though it does seem to mitigate the physical relativity difficulty. Lewis Ford defends the single actuality option with ingenuity. Nevertheless, for me God is analogous to a "personally-ordered society," though without negative prehensions.

A great merit of Whitehead, even though Peirce and Bergson anticipated him in this, is to have fully generalized the aspect of freedom or creativity inherent in the idea of God, so that it becomes inseparable from concrete actuality as such. God has divine freedom, man has human freedom, atoms have atomic freedom. Were it the only freedom, eminent freedom would no longer be eminent. Nor can one explain how we could have the concept of freedom or creativity if only God exemplified it in any degree. Moreover, it is purely arbitrary to stop with man and suppose the rest of creation to be simply without freedom. Divine attributes can only be eminent forms of universal or categorical aspects of reality in general. God has eminent power; nothing has simply no power except nothing itself, nonbeing. God has eminent power of decision, of closing otherwise or antecedently open alternatives; nothing has not even the slightest part of this power. If justice is done to the great Leibnizian distinction between active singulars and inactive collectives, we can readily escape having to bother with such things as clouds, rivers, or planets in construing the formula: every single creature is creative, and faces and somehow resolves open alternatives.

Whitehead takes creativity as essentially process, even in God. In my largely pre-Whiteheadian days I wrote a student paper entitled "The Self Its Own Maker." Part of the argument was similar to that which I later found in Whitehead; another part was similar to James' position that to freely make a decision is in some measure literally to make one's own subsequent character. This applies to deity. God freely decides, let there be light. He might have made a different decision, but, once made, the decision is part of God's actuality. To that extent he has made himself what he has not been eternally (which, re-

member means necessarily). Lequier, who, via Renouvier influenced James, reached the same conclusion, though perhaps by
a partly different path. He held that, in creating us, God creates
contingent content for his awareness. He makes himself what he
need not have been, the knower of the creatures we are. Since
we make our own decisions, and thus in some degree make ourselves, we also participate in the divine self-creation; for, as
omniscient, God can know us as freely deciding thus and thus
only if and because we do so decide. We participate in the divine
self-creation. If this is generalized for creator and creature at
large, Lequier's view turns into Whitehead's "creativity" as
"category of the ultimate." Moreover, Lequier said that freedom
in his radical sense should be "the first principle of philosophy."

Whitehead thought that process philosophy requires a rather
extreme platonism, a set of "eternal objects" which God primordially contemplates. I see no necessity for this. There must
be an eternal element, but God's primordial nature, not a set of
entities, is that element. It is a unitary matrix from which all
sorts of multiplicities can emerge in due time. One may think
of it as a continuum, and like many mathematicians, including
Whitehead in his "extensive abstraction," one may view continuity as devoid of ultimate parts. Parts of eternal potentiality are
themselves only potential.

Whitehead says there is an eternal divine ideal for creation,
the ideal of harmony and intensity—let there be beauty and
ever more beauty, beyond any final limit. This ideal is one, un-
generated, and immutable; it is unmoved mover.

Process philosophy has something to offer to those who feel
that mere change, with no eternally fixed standard or motivation,
is an absurdity. A great deal of the negative theology, so nicely
refined by Aquinas, applied truly to the primordial aspect of
God; but the positive content which he sought to give the doctrine by means of analogies belongs to God as consequent, not
to his mere primordial or eternal aspect. With this qualification,
the scholastic natural theology is a valuable heritage. It has defended the possibility of metaphysics against monolithic empiricism and the unsurpassability of God against radical fini-

tisms and relativisms. It has also been partly right in insisting upon the need for other theistic proofs than the ontological, and in defending a realistic epistemology.

DIVINE ATTRIBUTES

What happens to the standard divine attributes in a process philosophy? As the Socinians clearly saw, omniscience can be asserted with the understanding that "knowledge of all things" does not imply knowing all events throughout time as determinate concrete entities. In the process view there is no final totality of definite events, but a new totality each moment. "The universe" has no one fixed reference. The death of a person now living is not an event but a kind of event which is bound to be exemplified somehow, though exactly how is indeterminate. To "know" it as determinate would be error, not knowledge. The degree of determinateness depends upon the degree of determinism true of nature. God alone knows just what the degree is, and until the event itself happens this is all there is to know. The Socinians thus sagaciously reversed the inference from timeless omniscience to the definiteness of the future, and inferred rather the progressiveness of the unsurpassable knowledge from the indefiniteness of the future. As we have seen, there are additional reasons for a process view of divine knowledge.

Omnipotence also admits of a process construction, in terms of unsurpassable power over all. However, not conceivably surpassed power over all is one idea; a sheer monopoly of power or decision-making is quite another. Were the latter genuinely conceivable, it would have to be inferred from the former, but there is good reason to take it as a confused or self-contradictory combination of notions. Thus, unsurpassable power over all things must be the maximal degree or kind of power compatible with a real plurality of powers. God can do for creatures whatever they could not do for themselves or one another, but need to have done somehow.

One application of this is to laws of nature. Only God could set universal limits to multiple creaturely freedom and the conflicts and disorders implicit in multiple freedom. Man more or less orders his human world; he does not and could not establish the basic general order within which alone his decisions could accomplish anything. Moreover, God does not just institute natural laws once for all; he must constantly "persuade" things to obey the laws. This is a continuing action; it is difficult to imagine, but implicit in a reasonable idea of God. As Whitehead and Boutroux have seen, there is no reason to regard natural laws as eternal. Quite the contrary—any definite law is arbitrary, and arbitrary things are not worth eternal maintenance. As with artistic styles, the variations eventually become trivial and a new style is in order, for which reason at due intervals God has to inspire the universe with new modes of behavior.

As Whitehead profoundly argues, God "saves" the universe, both from chaos and from excessive or too prolonged modes of regularity. He inspires things with a tendency toward the golden mean between mere disorder and a too exact regularity or an eventually trivializing persistence in one type of order.

The foregoing may seem to have limited God's control of things to what has traditionally been termed "general providence." Is there no "special providence" having definite individuals or groups in view? This question has two aspects, of which one is commonly forgotten. God's perception is of definite individuals, and his unrestricted memory of his perceptions endows each moment of an individual's life with imperishable value for God. There is nothing abstract or merely general about this. Somehow God must forever find significance in his own life for each individual creaturely experience, once it has occurred. This is a kind of special providence, giving each of our moments of life a unique and everlasting role. The other aspect of special providence would be God's influencing worldly events in some further fashion than that involved in the laws of nature, i.e., influencing them miraculously. Concerning this I have no wisdom, one way or another. I wonder with Hume if we could know such a thing, if it took place. What is more, I am not clear that it would make a better world to have the future depend not only on creaturely freedom, within limits set by natural laws, but also upon divine freedom suspending the laws here and there.

In spite of providence, some conflicts and evils occur; this is inherent in the idea of multiple freedom. No matter how restricted the scope of creaturely decisions, they cannot be made harmless without being made trivial to the same extent. Incompossible goods appeal diversely to diverse creatures; and if two creatures pursue incompatible goals, there is a conflict. The requirement upon cosmic management is not that all risk of conflict and consequent suffering be excluded, for then everything would be excluded. The requirement is rather that the risks be justified by the opportunities for good, for significant harmonies. The laws of nature effect this, we may believe.

What then is the divine goodness or righteousness? To act righteously is to take into account the interests or value possibilities at stake. The Socratic notion that knowledge is already virtue is objectionable only because human knowledge has so many degrees and meanings. The wicked man may "know" what he is doing in a sense, but not in every sense or in the fullest sense. He may be aware of certain value possibilities so long as his own desires do not conflict with their realization and then forget them when conflict arises. Or he may know in a pale abstract way, compared to the concrete vividness with which he envisages some preferred and more or less selfish value. Omniscience eliminates all these possibilities of a gap between knowing and doing. In no degree can unsurpassable knowledge be set aside in decision making; hence divine wisdom and divine goodness are inseparable. Since all achievement is taken into the divine life via complete perception, God could not fail to want creaturely happiness, since he entirely participates in it; he could not want creaturely misery, since he participates in that also. Fechner saw this with brilliant clarity.

An objection that some will certainly make is the following: on the view I have been taking, God's love is really self-interest. Instead, one should say that while we creatures cannot help aiming at our own good, God is superior because he has his good once for all simply in himself. If he aims at our good, that is a sheer gratuitous addition, pure generosity. This, however, is the pseudoconception of perfection that we have rejected. The idea of doing good to others, without hope that this good will necessarily turn out to be in its entirety also one's own, is appropriate only to partly ignorant, mortal, and not unsurpassably loving beings, such as are we. Thus, our children may profit by our efforts for them long after we are dead, or when they are far away, or happy in ways we cannot ourselves fully appreciate. But God does not die and cannot fail to apprehend every achievement in its full concrete value. The issue of selfishness vs. unselfishness is not an issue for God, just because he is God; but it is an issue for us, just because we are not God. God has no nonloving self, we do; he has no ignorant, mortal self, we do. We are but fragments of life and value; God is the inclusive life and value. What could it mean for him to promote a good simply outside his own? Whatever it may be, duty or goodness in that sense is not divine.

A RELIGIOUS WORLD

If the beauty of the world is its value for God, who is the final measure of value, then all things in nature can be looked upon in a religious aspect. This is true, not simply because God is their supreme cause, the supreme creature agent making their existence possible, but because each of them contributes something to the divine self-creation which is the creation. "The creator of all things is also creator of himself," said a pre-Spanish Mexican poet. This ultimate self-creation is achieved through the humbler self-creative activities of the "creatures." Thus, the creator is also supreme creature, and the creatures are also lesser creators. The idea that the sublimest contrast of all could be expressed by the mere assertion and denial of creativity in its active and passive aspects—"uncreated creator," and "uncreative creature"—was an ultrasimple notion. Why should the final secret be as easy as that? Only God is eminently creative of all things, and his existence cannot have been created. So far one may agree with the formula: uncreated creator. But is it any less true that only God can be eminently created, enriched by all things or events; or that the humblest creature is above zero in its capacity of self-determination, individual decision, closing of antecedently open alternatives, and determining of previously indeterminate possibility?

It follows that everything in the world has intrinsic value beyond its utility to man. Regardless of the experiencer's color or racial type, all human experience presents to God a value transcending its evanescent occurrence and human recollection. The legitimate ideals of humanists contain no positive element which a theist must reject. But only the theist can have a rational theory of the importance of human happiness, in view of the mortality of the individual and, for all we can know, of the species. Everyone can feel this importance, but the problem is to think it as well. It seems to me that the nontheist does not go beyond the feeling, or "animal faith." Sartre and Camus admit what theists have long maintained, that human life merely in its own terms is "absurd," meaningless, but an animal cannot feel what this pretends to say. Feeling and impulse continue to affirm importance. I agree with Schweitzer that there is a contradiction of intentions here from which theism is the explicit rational escape. It is the business of philosophy to think what it is impossible not to feel and will.

The foregoing is a theistic argument somewhat analogous to Kant's from the highest good *(summum bonum)*. It avoids postulating human immortality in any sense that is not a mere corollary from the belief in God. It also avoids supposing that there must be rewards and punishments proportional to moral deserts. This notion leads to the sad consequence that, although we are to love others for their own sakes, we must also be justified in doing this by the belief that in the long run we will thereby sacrifice nothing of our own advantage. It cannot be necessary that human disinterestedness should be rewarded, if it really is disinterestedness. Virtue must for itself be the only indispensable reward.

In the eminent case alone is love also self-interest and vice versa. This is because no good which God promotes can remain outside his possession, and because he is the inclusive or all-perceiving reality, not a fragment. Only the fragment must

serve ends beyond its own advantage, and it must do this because it otherwise has no rational end at all, being a fragment in
time as well as in space. The reasonable reward for serving God
is only that no lesser service is reasonable, and there can be no
reason for not being reasonable. In serving himself, God serves
all things, because his participation in all life is unrestricted. From
its corner each creature enjoys glimpses of and contributes to
that beauty which in its integrity is real and permanent only for
God.

Evolutionary Perspectives and the Divine

◊

by
Eulalio Baltazar

ONE OF THE most important philosophico-theological tasks of Christian thought today is to reformulate the notion of God in a manner relevant to modern man. This paper suggests a possible way in which the evolutionary perspective of Teilhard de Chardin can contribute to this formulation. It is less concerned with showing non-Christians the validity of the divine in our evolving world, than with attempting to evolve for Christians a notion of God relevant to an evolving universe. Although this interest is "domestic," it is not without its wider repercussion, for a deeper understanding of the notion of God carries with it its own apologia.

THE PROBLEM: IMMANENCE VS TRANSCENDENCE

The Immanence of God

The one great objection to the formulation of the notion of God in the classical tradition is that a God conceived as eternal, that is as timeless, cannot be really present in time and history. Furthermore, to attain such a God, man would have to abandon the things of earth. As such perceptive thinkers as Nietzsche, Freud, and Marx have shown, this would render man himself inhuman. Ludwig Feuerbach dramatically poses the problem: "the question of the existence or non-existence of God is the question of the non-existence or existence of man."[1]

The aspirations of the modern Christian would seem to be expressed by John A. T. Robinson in *Honest to God* when he suggests that we come to God not by turning away from the world, but by a deeper immersion in it.[2] It appears, however the classical formulation of God in terms of "substance" metaphysics[3] would remove God from the secular. Teilhard de Chardin expressed this tension between the claims of a Platonic expression of Christianity and that of an evolving universe when he asked: "Must one, in order to be united with Christ, keep himself disinterested concerning the progress peculiar to this cosmos?"[4] It was the belief of Teilhard de Chardin that there is a clash between the traditional formulation of a superterrestrial sort of Christianity and modern man's awareness of terrestrial values. He observes: "This is the existential problem in the heart of a Christian where the divine faith which supports all human effort, and the terrestrial passion, which is its sap, inevitably collide."[5] The problem, then, would seem to be that of understanding God's immanence in evolution and in the secular.

Many contemporary thinkers have made important contributions to this common effort. Bonhoeffer speaks of the God of a secular faith, of a "suffering" God,[6] of a God who is radically different from the Absolute God of classical theism. However, this God requires conceptual clarification that Bonhoeffer himself does not furnish. Tillich presents us with a God that tries to go beyond naturalism and supernaturalism.[7] Though "self-transcendent," this God is the ground of being of whatever exists. Yet, Tillich is still bound by such categories of classical metaphysics as that of "being."

While paying tribute to the constructive efforts of Bultmann, Bonhoeffer, and Tillich in their fight against supernaturalism, Schubert Ogden nevertheless notes in them a fundamental weakness. He states that "the conceptuality these theologians employ is insufficiently developed, so that what they mean when they speak of God is left obscure or uncertain or else their conception of God is still determined by the same metaphysical-theological premises by which the supernaturalism they seek to transcend is itself determined."[8] Ogden further observes that this attempt of the death-of-God theologians to base Christian theology on the secularistic premise that God is dead makes an assessment of our cultural situation that is "completely undiscriminating in simply assuming that secularism is an essentially unified and internally consistent outlook."[9] While the attempts of the existential-phenomenological tradition to formulate the notion of God in historical and inter-personal terms has described the immanence of God to a certain extent, they lack the ontological base for any real explanation of God's presence.

Accordingly, it is my belief that there is need for a philosophy of process in which to formulate a notion of God that would make him immanent to a universe in process. This belief is shared by the process philosophers and theologians of the Whiteheadean tradition.[10] However, the inspiration of this paper is drawn from the evolutionary thought of Teilhard de Chardin.

Process and Evolutionary Thought

It would seem that the very nature of Christian revelation as an ongoing process in which "God is still working in the world and revealing himself to men"[11] demands that revelation be cast in the philosophic categories of process. What is more, as theology since Vatican II is seen more in function of culture, it becomes more evident that it is the nature of theology to be adapted to its present culture. Because the thought pattern of modern man is historical and evolutionary a relevant theology today must adopt the evolutionary pattern of thought.

In terms of the cultural situation in America, this would seem to mean process.[12] Consequently, many American Christian thinkers have suggested that their faith be formulated in terms of American philosophy, which has been largely influenced by Darwin, and expressed by Whitehead, Peirce, James, and Dewey.

Protestant process thought in America has largely followed the philosophy of Whitehead. American Catholics who are behind in the development of a process theology, could well adopt

Teilhard's process thought. This is especially true since post-Vatican Counciliar theology, which has become significantly evolutionary in character, has been largely influenced by Teilhard de Chardin.[13] The use of Teilhard's process thought in Catholic theology might also contribute to the dialogue with Marxists,[14] among whom Roger Garaudy believes that the Christian thought exemplified by Teilhard to be quite congenial on many points with Marxist thought.[15]

Teilhard has written neither a treatise on God in the context of evolutionary thought, nor a philosophy of process which explicitly formulates a notion of God. Consequently, the notion of God to be developed here,[16] though taking its inspiration from Teilhard and, I believe, implicit in his writings, may not necessarily be one that Teilhard would accept. This notion of God will be formulated in the context of evolution. It will not be complete, since it is confined to the single problem of the relation between time and eternity in God, or more precisely, to the ontological base for God's presence in a world in process, in short, to the relation between God's immanence and transcendence.

Immanence and Transcendence

It would seem that both of these must be accounted for. It is no solution to deny transcendence in order to emphasize immanence as is done in the myth of the eternal return. The obvious words in Scripture that salvation is beyond this world and that Christ's Kingdom is not of this world cannot be ignored. On the other hand, the Scriptures also say that the Kingdom of God is within you; that God is Emmanuel, i.e., God-with-us. The Incarnation as the presence of God among men is the central fact of the Christian faith. Thus, the New Heaven is also the New Earth. It would be false to this data to uphold immanence at the expense of transcendence.

If in the past the opposite was true, resulting in the dehumanization of man and the devaluation of the things of earth, it is no solution to go to the other extreme of calling for the denial of all religion, and proposing a religionless and completely secular type of Christianity. Merely to distinguish secularity, which makes room for transcendence, from secularism, which does not, leaves unsolved the problem of reconciling transcendence with immanence in the context of secularity. There remains even the same presupposition from which was derived the traditional position it seeks to transcend: the presupposition of a dualism between time and eternity, the phenomenal and the metaphysical, the sacred and the secular. Now, however, what is chosen is the alternate triad of the temporal, the phenomenal, and the secular. Such a solution can only generate a future reaction toward the other extreme, and a dialectic that never finds a resolution.

TIME AND ETERNITY

It would seem that the solution to the problem of the relation between immanence and transcendence is ultimately based on the meaning of time. It was the Greek view of time that established the dichotomy between change and permanence, identifying change with time and permanence with timelessness. This view of time also gave birth to the distinction between the metaphysical or substantial as the region of permanence and the phenomenal or accidental as the region of contingency and change. In order to resolve this dualism, it is necessary to reexamine the traditional notions of time and eternity.

Because of the chasm between God and creation, there would appear to be no essential similarity between time and eternity. As Rudolf Otto observes in his book, *The Idea of the Holy*,[17] God is wholly other. It is paradoxical that there must nonetheless be some similarity between time and eternity, for every agent acts in a way like to himself *(omne agens agit sibi simili)*. If God created time, then time must somehow be in God. The traditional answer is that, like all creature by perfections, time is in God, not univocally as in creatures, but in a more perfect way *(eminenter)*. Precisely what this more perfect way is, is not explained, though it is confidently asserted that a similarity exists between time and eternity by virtue of the analogy of being. But if eternity is viewed as the complete absence of time, instead of a basis for analogy, there would seem to be only total dissimilarity.

It is difficult to see how a timeless God can relate himself to the temporal. How can God be truly immanent in all things that evolve if his eternity situates him outside time? How can he be the Lord of Time if he does not control time from within? How can he be truly compassionate and merciful if he cannot know temporal human existence with all its cares and anxieties.

From the point of view of man whose goal is a participation in God, to be with God would be to participate in his eternity. If eternity is timelessness, this implies a withdrawal from time. Now, because the medieval man regarded time as negative or at least neutral, there was neither theoretical difficulty nor spiritual tension in accepting this dialectic of withdrawal. The modern Christian, however, who sees time as creative, positive and humanizing, finds the dialectic of withdrawal from time quite meaningless. In the traditional view of God's eternity as timelessness, it is impossible to show not only that God is immanent in time and history, but that Christianity truly values the temporal and the secular.

ETERNITY AS FULLNESS OF TIME

As a tentative solution I propose that God's eternity be viewed not as the absence, but as the Fullness of Time. To this there are immediate objections. Is this not tantamount to saying that God is the fullness of contingency and change? Is it not to deny that God is the Immutable, the Unchanging? Is it not the identification of God with Matter, and since matter is the highest form of contingency, transiency, and mutability, would not God then be equated with pure potency? Would not making God temporal like material creation destroy God's transcendence and his Otherness and lead us into pantheism?

These objections show that any valid formulation of God's eternity must safeguard God's Otherness from creatures. To do this, however, it is not necessary that God's eternity be seen as an absence of time. The crux of the issue is whether contingency is of the essence of time, for if contingency were essential, then to say that God is the Fullness of Time is also to say that he is the fullness of contingency.

Even today when evolution is seen as universal, time perhaps unconsciously is excluded from the universal law. But why should not time itself evolve? To consider it to be forever contingent is to look at it statically. Though the oak evolves from an acorn to a non-acorn (full grown oak), the nonliving reality (matter) to the living, the nonsensitive (vegetative) to the sensitive, the sensitive towards the suprasensitive or self-conscious, and so on, we do not recognize that time evolves from contingency to non-contingency or from transiency to immanence.

PHILOSOPHIES AND THEOLOGIES OF TIME

Ancient Philosophies of Time

In order to explore the possibility of the evolution of time, it is necessary to review the evolution in the notion of time itself. In Greek thought, time was seen as negative. It does not evolve or produce new reality. Rather, things are destroyed in time, which is therefore negative. Plato saw time as unreal because it is but a "moving imitation of eternity."[18] Things in time are mere shadows, copies of the eternal ideas which are outside contingency and change. The dialectic of life and knowledge is a departure from this shadowy cave of illusion and change. In the metaphysical system of Plotinus, the sensible world is derived by a fall from the One, and time is but the measure of this degradation.[19] For Aristotle time is closely allied with change of which it is the measure. Aristotle observes that

"it is the nature of *all* change to alter things from their former condition. In time all things come into being and pass away. . . . It is clear then that it must be in itself, as we said before, the condition of destruction rather than of coming into being (for change, in itself, makes things depart from their former condition), and only incidentally of coming into being, and of being."[20] . . ."A thing, then, will be affected by time, just as we are accustomed to say that time wastes things away, and that all things grow old through time, and that there is oblivion owing to the lapse of time, but we do not say the same of getting to know or of becoming young or fair. For time is by its nature the cause rather of decay, since it is the number of change, and change removes what is."[21]

As the Greek view of time was essentially negative and contingent, it would be contrary to the nature of God to have anything to do with it. God's eternity would have to be portrayed as the absence from time. Oscar Cullmann notes that

> For Greek thinking in its Platonic formulation there exists between time and eternity a qualitative difference, which is not completely expressed by speaking of a distinction between limited and unlimited duration of time. For Plato, eternity is not endlessly extended time, but something quite different; it is timelessness. Time in Plato's view is only the *copy* of eternity thus understood.[22]

The result of this Greek view of time for Platonic spirituality is also noted:

> For the Greeks, the idea that redemption is to take place through divine action in the course of events in time is impossible. Redemption in Hellenism can consist only in the fact that we are transferred from existence in this world, an existence bound to the circular course of time, into that Beyond which is removed from time and is already and always available. The Greek conception of blessedness is thus spatial; it is determined by the contrast between this world and the timeless Beyond; it is not a time conception determined by the opposition between Now and Then.[23]

Much of our present-day thinking is rooted in this Hellenism, as is illustrated by the fact that "far and wide the Christian

Church and Christian theology distinguish time and eternity in the Platonic-Greek manner."[24] Cullmann observes that "down through the history of doctrine to the present there can be traced a great misunderstanding, upon the basis of which that is claimed as 'Christian' which in reality is Greek."[25]

As long as the Greek view of time remained unchanged, the logical formulation of God's eternity would be by way of qualitative contrast to time of which it was the complete absence. Though in the Greek pattern of thought, this formulation is valid, it would be a mistake to consider it absolute.

Modern Philosophies of Time

In contrast to the Greek notion of time, the modern notion as positive and evolutionary may furnish the possibility of considering God's eternity as the Fullness of Time. An analysis of this new notion of time will show that time is not essentially contingent or a pure succession. This analysis will draw some confirmation from the Scriptural view of time.

To observe time as evolutionary, it must not be seen as a distinct entity whose essence is pure succession and contingency or as the container of all things that change. As evolutionary, time is not an absolute and homogeneous container of everything; instead it is one with the existence of a thing as process. To observe time, then, one must observe the evolutionary process itself.

In the process of evolution, time has not remained essentially contingent, but has evolved from contingency to noncontingency or from transiency to immanence. By immanence we mean that the movement does not flow out of the thing but has its term within the thing itself; the movement is perfective of the thing, and time is the measure of stability and noncontingency.

At the lowest level of the evolutionary process, although time is quite transient inasmuch as the movement of sub-atomic particles is quite random and chaotic, time already has some degree of immanence. The phenomena of radioactivity and polymerization, the fundamental process of cellularization, and such activities as nutrition, growth, reproduction, and irritability are obvious examples of immanent movement. As we ascend towards animal life, in sense cognition and sense appetite the faculties which originate the operation are themselves perfected and manifest a higher form of immanence. More important, cognition and appetite in animals make possible for the first time a conscious gathering of time. By its memory the animal is able to gather the past and make it coexist with the present so that time does not completely flow away as in the infrasensitive level and contingency in part is overcome. Compared to the randomness of sub-atomic particles, the temporality of animal life is oriented; to a degree it terminates in a maturation of time. However, the animal does not fully control its time. Although it is able to determine the forms of its activity, the animal, ruled purely by instinct, cannot consciously control and direct these forms toward a goal.

Man is able to gather together the past and the present and somehow grasp the future. Of all the animals, only man can foresee; only he can propose a goal and direct his actions towards that goal. Compared to the infrahuman forms, in man there is a measure of the fullness of time. The lower forms lead to man precisely inasmuch as they are able to participate in his time dimension, which for the lower forms is their "eternity."

Theology and Time

Even the immanence in man still contains contingency, and if man were the end of the whole evolutionary process time would still be contingent. However, at the conscious level or, to use Teilhard's term, at the level of noogenesis man is still evolving and open to the future. According to Teilhard, whose thought follows St. Paul's, in man time is evolving toward Christian time. The meaning and essence of time is to be found in Christ, who, as the Scriptures say, is the Fullness of Time. In Christ, time is no longer contingent, no longer passing, negative, and destructive; it is positive, creative, and salvific. In him time has evolved into its fullness—the eternal.

Those in the graced state of union with Christ by that very fact possess a measure of eternity, because grace is a participation in Christian time. But the Church is still in pilgrimage and growing toward the fullness of Christian time (the *pleroma Christi*). She could not grow if she were not in time, nor could she attain more of eternity if eternity were the absence of time. The liturgy, with its seasons and cycles celebrating the process of birth, death, and resurrection of Christ, is this participation and attainment of the fullness of Christian time. The New Testament position that the liturgy will go on in heaven would seem to rule out eternity being the absence of time.

The Biblical notion of eternity, as Cullmann noted above, is not timelessness but endless time.

Primitive Christianity knows nothing of a timeless God. The "eternal" God is he who was in the beginning, is now, and will be in all the future, "who is, who was, and who will be" (Rev. 1:4). Accordingly, his eternity can and must be expressed in this "naive" way, in terms of endless time.[26]

EVOLUTION AND GOD AS THE FULLNESS OF TIME

The attempt to show God's eternity in terms of temporality is not new. The process philosophers and theologians of the Whiteheadean tradition,[27] for example, speak of the temporality of God, as does Heidegger. To speak thus is closer to the view of the Scriptures than is the hellenic view of God's atemporality.

Unfortunately, these thinkers equate temporality with finitude, growth, and contingency, so that God is said to grow. This would seem to harbor the same defect which Schubert Ogden noted in Bonhoeffer, Bultmann, Tillich, and the death-of-God theologians, namely, that of being bound by the hellenic categories. Thus, they accepted without question the common sense view that time is by nature contingent and finite. Consequently, in predicating temporality of God, they are forced to hold that God grows and is contingent and finite in his being and knowledge, while at the same time holding his ontological priority as the infinite and the absolute.[28]

It it not clear to me how this identity or coincidence of opposites is possible. Instead it would seem more true to see God's temporality in the light of an evolutionary view of time in which time evolves from contingency to noncontingency, from the lack of time to the fullness of time. With an evolutionary view of time, such as that of Teilhard, it is possible to predicate temporality of God without necessarily admitting that he grows. We note from observation that at the full term of a process which is also the fullness of time, as in the full term of pregnancy which the Scriptures speak of as the fullness of time, (as when the fullness of time came for Mary, she gave forth her first born son), there is no longer growth—the basis of contingency. The fullness of time of a process coincides with the fullness of growth and hence with its cessation. This is also the fullness of being, and when one has the fullness of being, obviously, there is no becoming.

This does not mean, however, an absence of time, for becoming or contingency is not the essence of time. Rather, fullness of being is one with the essence of time. This can be seen if it is remembered that in the context of process the meaning of a thing is not in the first but in the full stage, for it is there that a thing is fully differentiated, fully evolved, and fully revealed for what it is. Thus, for example, the seed is revealed in the fruit, and we call the seed by the fruit, as an apple seed. So, too, time as evolutionary is revealed in its omega or term. As we have seen, time evolves toward noncontingency or immanence; hence, paradoxically, the true meaning of time is noncontingency or the fullness of growth and being. It is therefore possible to predicate temporality of God without necessarily implying that God grows and is finite.

Probing more deeply into presupposition of the traditional view of time, including the views of Hartshorne and Ogden, one finds that time is taken to be already time; time, as we have it here and now, is considered as the fullness of time. Consequently, the march of time toward the future is either toward the absence of time as in the classical or hellenic, or toward unending time or growth as for Hartshorne and Ogden. Both of these views presuppose a static time that does not evolve. Why, however should not time itself evolve? Time itself is, so to speak, in time. If it too must evolve, then one would expect to find time at its initial stage in the undeveloped state of timelessness or lack of time; and at its fully developed state one would expect the fullness of time, for evolution is from the lesser to the greater state of being.

In contrast to the traditional view that starts with the fullness of time and ends with eternity as timelessness, this position reverses the dialectic. It starts with timelessness and ends in eternity as the fullness of time. The consequence of this revolution in outlook is that our present time is really a state of timelessness, which is to say that it is also the period for the acquisition of time.

There seems to be no adequate basis for holding that our time is the fullness of time. In fact, it could not be such, since it still lacks the future. If all things in time are process, then they also lack time since they still lack the future. Furthermore, the evolution of time itself is a movement from timelessness to the fullness of time. Thus, in matter and in vegetative life, there is a lack of time in the sense that time flows out; there is no gathering of past, present, and future as in man who can unify them by his consciousness.

There would also seem to be no adequate basis for the position that the essence of time is change or growth. This view is based on the belief that time is timeless in its very essence as change; everything changes except change itself. This, however, would seem to be a static view of time. The essence of time is not change or growth, but the fullness of growth, and hence the cessation of change. This does not mean that time ceases to be, but that time ceases to change or develop when it has attained its fullness. What follows is not a cessation of activity, but a fullness of activity consequent on fullness of growth and being.

A more basic objection to the view of some process thinkers that God grows is their equation of evolution with interminable becoming which never ends in the emergence or maturation of being. This view of process is not only unintelligible if in process it is the end that is the principle of intelligibility, it is also without empirical foundation. In all known cases there is always a term or stage of maturation in process or development; for example, the fruit as the term of the seed, rebirth in the case of the fetus, or the adult for the child. Besides being unintelligible, a view of reality in which becoming is not qualitatively transformed into being is also nonevolutionary and, hence, static. In evolution, there is qualitative transformation and not merely quantitative increase. Thus, the acorn is qualitatively transformed into an oak, the nonliving into the living, the nonsensitive into the sensitive, the sensitive into the rational. A view of process as interminable becoming would have the acorn remaining interminably an acorn, albeit, a super-acorn. Such a growth is not evolutionary, since there is no qualitative transformation of becoming into being. This contention falls into the same static view that philosophers of being have been accused of, namely, freezing being in all stages of its change so that there is no becoming. In this case, however, it is becoming that is frozen so that it does not evolve into being.

One may object that it is precisely by remaining with becoming that we maintain a dynamic view of reality, and that if becoming were to terminate in being the result would be a static view. In this objecton there would seem to be a hidden fallacy. It is presupposed that in order to contrast philosophically the dynamic outlook of our age with the static pre-evolutionary view it is necessary to show reality as perpetually becoming, rather than as perpetually being as in the static view. However, the real difference between a non-evolutionary or static and the evolutionary or dynamic view is that in the latter view beings come into existence by birth. They have a history and becoming is necessary for the emergence of being. In the former view, beings come into existence ready-made, finished, and hence, already being; there is no becoming in time. Theologically, the static view holds for an instantaneous creation of reality; the dynamic view holds for a temporal one such that evolution itself is God's creative action expressed in time.

What should be distinguished therefore is not being, on the one hand, and becoming, on the other, but two different notions of being. In the evolutionary view, "being" is synonymous with maturity or the fullness of growth; thus, it implies a previous becoming which the notion of "being" in the static view does not. In the latter view, becoming, maturation, and history are not essential to the constitution and meaning of being.

The failure to distinguish between the two notions of being is what necessarily commits some process thinkers to opting for a perpetual becoming. They regard this as the only way of distinguishing a dynamic from a static view based on being. Having committed themselves to "becoming" as of greater ontological and cultural value than "being," they would logically attribute this higher value to God. Within their context one cannot say that becoming terminates in being without also saying that the static is of greater value than the dynamic, and the immutable greater than the mutable.

The process philosophers and theologians of the Whitedeadian tradition would seem to be correct in holding that in a culture where the dynamic is of a higher value than the static, the notion of God must be formulated in the dynamic context. However, this does not necessarily commit one to speaking of God as a perpetual Becoming and as a Changing Reality. Within the evolutionary context familiar to modern man, the maturation of growth is of greater value than perpetual growth. For example, the adult is of a higher order and value than the child; the newborn than the unborn, the fruit than the seed, the fully developed than the undeveloped, the mature than the immature. It is not perpetual becoming that is of greater value, but rather the maturation of becoming. In accordance with the hierarchy of values in an evolutionary context, we must logically attribute to God the state of the fullness of growth, rather than the stage of becoming. In the very context of the evolutionary process the stage of becoming implies the possibility of failure, immaturity, and, hence, imperfection.

THINKING AND SPEAKING OF GOD

Semantically, since we must speak of our temporal existence as a stage of becoming, we must speak of God's existence in relation to ours as the goal of our becoming or as the source of our fullness and maturity. It would be improper to speak of God as being also in the process of growth, for this would destroy God's otherness and his transcendence in relation to us.

God as Ground

In selecting a model with which to think of God in relation to us, we might choose that of the ground and of ourselves as seeds. It is the seed that grows, that becomes; the ground is the source of growth, of maturation, of the fullness of time of the seed. Since the ground is not a super-seed in relation to an ordinary seed it itself does not grow.

Though our starting point in thinking about God is our own subjectivity and the social character of personality, the relation of God to man is not that between persons in society where both grow. In that case, God's transcendence and universality would be preserved by saying that he is a super-person who would be first in his capacity to grow and supreme in his relativity.[29] Just as the otherness of the ground from the seed is not otherness of one seed from another, so the otherness of God from the human person is not that of a super-person from an ordinary one. God is beyond person; the Ground of personality; he is as different as is the ground from the seed.

To properly think of God, we have to think dialectically and employ what the early Christian thinkers call negative thinking. The failure to appreciate this technique leads some process thinkers to conclude that, because the human person grows, God also must grow and become.

This is not to imply that God is not affected by human actions, that he is totally aloof and unconcerned, or that he is not some-how saddened and even diminished by human failings or en-riched and fulfilled by his encounter with good men. On this point the process thinkers of the Whiteheadian tradition rightly criticize the classic notion of an aloof and totally unconcerned God.

On the other hand, this does not mean that God grows or becomes. Once again the dialectic between the ground and the seed can help us see how God is affected by his encounter with men. Earlier it was noted that it is the seed and not the ground that grows. There is, however, a sense in which it can be said that the ground becomes more or less productive when there are more or less fruit-bearing trees growing on it, for the ground is a co-cause of the fruition of the trees. Just as the ground can be said to be more or less productive, God who is the Ground of our beings, can be said to be affected by our human acts in such a way that he is somehow enriched or diminished by them. Nevertheless, just as we do not speak of the ground as growing or increasing in size, so we cannot speak of God as growing, as if he becomes more godly. As the ground is the perpetual source of productivity and fullness of time for things that grow, so God is an eternity of creativity and is the Fullness of Time for all becoming.

The Unlimited Line

The traditional view as expressed by Boethius is that eternity is best represented by a point, since it is the simultaneous posses-sion of an unending life.[30] This position starts from what appears to us to be the false premise that time is succession and eternity the absence of succession and, consequently, the absence of time. In the traditional view the point represents the absence of time, not its fullness.

In his book, *Christ and Time* Cullman proposes that the con-trast between time and eternity for the Hebrew view is best represented as the difference between a limited line and an un-limited one. The advantage of Cullman's imagery of eternity as a limitless line is its suggestion, in contrast to the classic view, that eternity is not the absence of time, but infinite time. However, there are defects in the imagery of eternity as a limitless line. First of all, Cullmann denies the qualitative difference between time and eternity, since for him a qualitative difference means the absence of one in the other. In so doing, he fails to show the chasm that exists between God's existence and creaturely existence. This brings him to the other extreme of seemingly identifying the two, and incurring the danger of pantheism.

Another objection to the imagery of a limitless line is that such a line has no goal and consequently is unknowable and meaningless. Furthermore, a line that is unending is unfinished and, therefore, contingent. Thus, an unending line would seem to be a defective image for representing God's eternity.

The Omega Point

In the context of process, the difference between time and eternity is the difference between the line and the Omega point.[31] This imagery is able to show the qualitative difference between time and eternity while at the same time showing their continuity. The Omega point, as the fullness and crowning point of the linear process, is continuous with that process; but being the end point it is outside the line and hence transcendent.

Is not the Omega point merely another name for the classic notion of point as representing eternity? To answer this question, let us analyze the nature of the Omega point. Its first characteristic is that it is noncontingent. Since it is the term of the process and the Absolute Future it ceases to move forward and there is no beyond. Thus both the Omega point and the classic notion of point agree on the characteristic of eternity as noncontingent. It might be objected that representing eternity as the Omega point implies immobility and that this would hardly represent the true God, who is most fully mobile and active, and is represented as an eternal procession by Christian thought. True, in the context of transient motion or pure succession, the end point represents immobility, for it does not contain what came before. But in the context of process or evolution the past is carried on into the present and the present into the future, so that the absolute future as a point is the region of the fullest time. Thus, while the classic point represents the absence of time, the Omega point implies fullness of time. The basis for this difference is the differing view of time. The classic view sees time only as pure succession or change, while this view sees it as evolutionary, that is, tending towards the fullness of time.

Because the Omega point is the region of the fullness of time, it is also the region of the fullness of being, and hence of activity and mobility rather than of inactivity and passivity. Because the fullness of one's activity is gauged by the degree to which the self is given in the activity, the fullness of activity is attained when the self is totally given in the act. This is done only when the self is made totally present by being totally grasped. For this, however, one must attain all of one's past, present and future, that is one must have the fullness of time. Thus to have the fullness of time is to have the fullness of activity. At the Omega point, activity and being are identical since the total self is present completely and fully in its activity.

The total grasp of oneself implies total knowledge and the full revelation of oneself with the consequence that complete freedom and fullness of love are possible. As Omega point, God is the fullness of activity where act and being are identical; he is the fullness of freedom and the fullness of love as St. John tells us.

In contrast to the Omega point, the previous stages of evolution, the fullness of being, are the region of night and day, of light and shadow, and, therefore, of doubt, error, and contingency. At the Omega point, there is only light—no shadows. Christ as Omega is truly represented in the Scriptures as the Light come to enlighten our darkness; He is the Truth and the Life.

Thus far the transcendent character of the Omega point in relation to the previous stages has been emphasized. The absolute immanence of the Omega point should not be forgotten. Since the Omega point is the fullness of time, it is present to all of time. The previous stages of evolution were absent to themselves because they were absent to their future in which the fullness of being was to be attained. The Omega point is not only fully present to itself, but, because it is Absolute Future, it is also fully present to the other stages. In fact, it is more immanent to these stages than the stages are to themselves, for the meaning of the previous stages are precisely in the Omega. The Omega is the logical principle of immanence insofar as it is the principle of intelligibility, but it is also the ontological principle, since the absence of the Omega means the cessation in being of the past and the present. The Omega is, therefore, both center and depth of being. Because the Omega possesses all time, it is the Presence and the Lord of all time. Christ is rightly seen by the Scriptures as the Presence and the Lord of History. As Omega point, he is the principle of providence, salvation and redemption, because the Omega is present to all the stages and is able to direct and accompany the stages in their journey to the Absolute Future. Hence, Christ, in addition to being the Truth and the Life, is appropriately called the Way.

THE SECULAR AND THE SACRED

A practical application of the newly formulated notion of God as the Fullness of Time concerns the relation between the Scriptural statement that Christ's Kingdom and our salvation are beyond this world, on the one hand, and secularity and the values of this world, on the other. If one starts with this world as being in a state of timelessness and is serious about evolution and development, it makes sense to go beyond the world, for the world is not fully itself. It must abandon itself in order to attain itself, just as the seed must abandon its undeveloped and "timeless" state in order to attain its fuller and more authentic being in the plant.[32] To go beyond the world is not to withdraw from time, for this point of departure was not the world as already having the fullness of time.

The traditional view which starts with the world as already fully itself is quite logical in the conclusion that to abandon the world is to abandon time, and that to go beyond the world is to attain timelessness, since it starts with time as already in its full-ness. In such cases the process of divinization and redemption would be one of dehumanization—an abandonment of the human, the timely, the secular. The resolution of this impass is not to deny transcendence and hold that the world has no beyond. This would save man from the dehumanization consequent upon the traditional view only by developing another form of dehumani-zation which would deny transcendence to man and his world and absolutize this world after the manner of the proponents of secularity who absolutize this world as already secular.

Instead, it should be noted that if the world is not yet fully itself, then it is not fully secular. To go beyond this world is really to become more immanent to the world, since the beyond is the fullness of being of the world. This is possible because the world is not yet its real and full self. What the proponents of secularity have not appreciated is the implications of evolution for their theologizing and philosophizing.

Once we accept the evolutionary pattern of thought, it is not hard to see that to be transcendent is to be immanent, and to be immanent is to be transcendent. To go beyond the world and oneself is to be truly "worldly" and human; to go beyond the present time is really to attain the Fullness of Time. The New Heaven is truly the New Earth, as the New Testament concludes.

◊

1. Quoted from Henri de Lubac, **The Drama of Atheist Humanism,** trans. E. M. Riley (New York: Sheed & Ward, 1951), p. 27.

2. John A. T. Robinson, **Honest to God** (Philadelphia: Westminster Press, 1963), p. 47.

3. David B. Burrell, "God: Language and Transcendence," **Common-weal,** LXXXV (1967), 514.

4. See **La vie cosmique,** 1916. Quoted from C. Tresmontant, **Pierre Teilhard de Chardin** (Baltimore: Helicon Press, 1959), p. 59.

5. **Ibid.**

6. Dietrich Bonhoeffer, **Letters and Papers From Prison,** ed. Eberhard Bethge, trans. R. H. Fuller (London: SCM Press, 1953), p. 164.

7. Paul Tillich, **Systematic Theology** (Chicago: Univ. of Chicago Press, 1957), II, pp. 5-10.

8. Schubert Ogden, **The Reality of God** (New York: Harper & Row, 1963), p. 53.

9. **Ibid.**, p. 15.

10. Leslie Dewart, **The Future of Belief** (New York: Herder & Herder, 1966).

11. Gabriel Moran, "The God of Revelation," **Commonweal**, LXXXV (1967), 501.

12. John A. Kouwenhoven, "What's American about America?" in **Essay**, ed. Jans P. Buth (Belmont, Calif.: Wadsworth Pub. Co., 1962), pp. 36-51. Kouwenhoven observes that skyscrapers, the gridiron town plan, the assembly-line production, the comic strips, jazz, etc., are closely related to one another—they are composed of simple and infinitely repeatable units; they are open-ended. He concludes: "America is process. And in so far as people have been 'American'—as distinguished from being (as most of us, in at least some of our activities, have been) mere carriers of transplanted cultural traditions—the concern with process has been reflected in the work of their heads and hearts and hands." (p. 50)

13. See the article of Gerard Vanderhaar, "The Status of Scholastic Theology Today," **Proceedings of the Catholic Theological Society of America**, XXI (1966), 71-93, and Robert T. Francoeur, "Pierre Teilhard de Chardin," **U.S. Catholic**, XXXII (1966), 31-36. There is no reason why Catholic theology in America cannot employ Whiteheadean categories for its reformulation, though Teilhard's thought would seem more adequate. Being processive, it would also seem to be sufficiently relevant to American culture.

14. Norman Pittenger, "A Contemporary Trend in North American Theology: Process-Thought and Christian Faith," **Religion in Life**, XXXIV (1965), 500-510. Pittenger observes a resemblance of American process-thought with its attention to the evolutionary perspective, on the one hand, and that of Teilhard, on the other.

15. Roger Garaudy, **From Anathema to Dialogue**, trans. Luke O'Neill (New York: Herder & Herder, 1966).

16. Cfr. E. Baltazar, **Teilhard and the Supernatural** (Baltimore: Helicon, 1966), Part II.

17. Rudolf Otto, **The Idea of the Holy** (New York: Oxford Univ. Press, 1958).

18. **Timaeus**, 37 d. **The Dialogues of Plato**, trans. B. Jowett (New York: Random House, 1937).

19. **Plotinus: The Enneads**, trans. Stephen MacKenna (New York: Pantheon, 1930), 3: 7, 7.

20. **Physics**, IV, 222 b, **The Basic Works of Aristotle**, trans. Richard McKeon (New York: Random House, 1941).

21. **Ibid.**, 221 a.

22. Oscar Cullmann, **Christ and Time**, trans. F. V. Filson (Philadelphia: Westminster, 1950), p. 61.

23. **Ibid.**, p. 52.

24. **Ibid.**, p. 61.

25. **Ibid.**, p. 54.

26. **Ibid.**, p. 63.

27. For example, Charles Hartshorne, Schubert Ogden, Bernard Meland, Daniel Day Williams, Bernard M. Loomer, and John Cobb, Jr.

28. Ogden, **The Reality of God**, pp. 60, 65.

29. Charles Hartshorne, **Reality as Social Process** (Boston: Beacon, 1953).

30. Cf. Boethius, **De Consolatione Philosophiae, V** (Cambridge, Mass.: Harvard Univ. Press, 1962): "nunc stans," "interminabilis vitae tota simul et perfecta possessio."

31. This is a Teilhardian term which represents the final focal point of convergence of the evolutionary process. It coincides with the Incarnate Christ in whom all will find their meaning, existence and fullness of activity.

32. The analogy of the seed dying in order to attain the new life in the plant is, incidentally, the example St. Paul uses to bring home to us the mechanics of the redemptive process (I Cor. 15:35-50) applicable not only to man but to the world which, according to Paul, is also groaning to be redeemed.

Part II

Person

Heidegger and the Possibility of Authentic Christianity

◇

by

Thomas Langan

THOUGH CHRISTIANITY has long since ceased to be the central effective force giving its character to our time, there continues to be professed Christians. Are they merely hanging on to what is over and done with?

As a believing Christian myself, I hold that Christian faith is somehow still an authentic[1] possibility, even in this epoch which Heidegger describes as that nihilistic night of "the planetary domination of technique."[2] If one were to accept Heidegger's analysis of our time as the epoch in which God has withdrawn, how could one still pretend to be a Christian, a member of a community of love manifesting the presence of Christ?

With help especially from several key texts and a reading of *Being and Time* which puts resoluteness, properness and improperness in perspective, I believe Heidegger can be interpreted in a way which, while faithful to his deepest inspiration, allows the possibility of authentic Christian existence today.

THE HISTORICITY OF THE OPENING WITHIN WHICH GODS AND MEN RELATE

As the human existence *(Dasein)* comes to some self-awareness, it discovers itself as already having interpreted the world and itself through having assumed tasks which the world held

[169]

up to it as possibilities.³ By taking the interpretative horizons of the given everyday world for granted, we deploy these commonly interpreted possibilities thoughtlessly.

In our own time, however, the granting of those horizons has at last been brought into question. The historicity of the epochal opening of an essential time-space has been grasped; it has been understood that the individual agent is not master of his world but rather depends on its gifts for his very possibilities. It is these which he carries forward in "ek-sisting": quite literally the future itself *(Zukunft)* announces itself to the Dasein *(sich kunftet zu uns)*⁴—comes toward us out of what has already been.⁵

At the foundation of the entire suite of handed-down and still stored up possibilities⁶ stands the Source *(die Quelle)*,⁷ from which the tradition acquires its unity. Since the beginning of the tradition, Western man has moved within the temporally unfolding horizons of that Opening which was first vouchsafed us 2500 years ago. To this, as essential time-space we are beholden for what we are and for the ways the gods and God have been able to appear to us. This is so even though the Opening itself has until now been ignored because nature, man and the gods, which were illumined within it, drew all attention to themselves and away from the illumining. The night of forgetfulness of this founding Opening grew dark as the ground of all sense came to be sought first in some super thing beyond the things of our experience and finally in the subjective will willing itself. The times turned patently nihilistic and generated an extreme denial of any being-be-holden. Suddenly *(Jezt aber tagt's!)*⁸ this very absence of the Opening is so palpable that we are called to remember it and the Source to which the tradition owes its existence. Remembering, the Poet is called to name the Source of the Opening: Holderlin sings of it as *das Heilige*.⁹

CONTEMPORARY NIHILISM AND THE WITHDRAWAL OF GOD

When one affirms the historicity of the interpretation horizons, within which nature, man and the gods can appear to us, two opposed extremes must be avoided as misunderstandings.

On the one hand, it is not intended to suggest that the gods or the God in their historical manifestations and withdrawals are dependent on man, as projections of his fancy or whatever. On the contrary, man is not even dependent on himself for his own fundamental possibilities of interpretating the gods and the possibilities of interpreting man. These are given to us individual existents with the interpretative horizons of the historical time-space in which we discover ourselves as always already having been "thrown."

It is not by human decision that a new epoch is inaugurated; no one and no group of existents has *caused* the modern era of technological-bureaucratic organization in which nature itself is looked upon as a storehouse of energy. Rather, this era has emerged from the tradition; it is always already there surrounding us, eliciting our vision and action along its pathways.

Is this to suggest that a Hegelian necessity reigns throughout the development of historical horizons within which alone the gods and man himself can appear? That is the opposite extreme interpretation to be avoided. The necessity *(Not-wendigkeit)* manifest in the movement *(Be-wegung)* of history is not that of the Hegelian *Aufhebung*. The past is not brought forward into the more recent stages by subsumption and preservation in a synthesis which is more true, in the sense of more self-conscious, than what has gone before.[10] It is present not as a memory *(Erinnerung)* to be retained, but as a possibility challenging the existence to make it his own *(sich aneignen)*. As the ground of these possibilities is itself always obscured by the very things it illumines, history does not develop from the Source in the direction of a necessarily greater awareness of itself. On the contrary, its own obscuring of itself has favoured contemporary voluntarism, by leading mankind to interpret itself as will for will's sake, for whom God is dead.

Thus, the necessity *(Not-wendigkeit)* Heidegger discovers as unifying history does not found a closed system, for it does not exclude further possibility—creating determinations from taking place within the fundamental Opening of the tradition-founding *Geschick*—the destiny that is sent from the beginning. Nevertheless, all such further determinations necessarily are in some way developments of the founding possibility or the original Need *(die ursprüngliche Not)*. The creative acts of Dasein are grounded in the possibility which comes to him from the interpretative horizons of the epoch essential-space *(Wesensraum)* into which he is thrown. This does not mean that the way he takes up these possibilities and extends them into the future is indifferent. On the contrary, the way the later fundamental possibilities of the tradition come to future Dasein depends on whether present Dasein responds to the call of the deepest possibilities for him to make them his own. If he does not, they remain improperly covered over *(bedeckt)*, the dissimulation of Being deepens, and mankind becomes ever more lost to itself and the gods more remote.

Is this to suggest then that the withdrawal of God which dominates our time is somehow for the tradition both an essential possibility, in the proper sense a necessity, and also something for which we are in someway responsible?

The withdrawal of the God is a basic aspect of the nihilism accompanying the fulfillment of the metaphysical tradition. In the beginning Being illumined things in a way which made a metaphysical interpretation of the totality of things possible. The improper appropriation of the possibility held open by Being took the form of a search for a ground of all the things of our experience *(ta phusika)* in a most existing entity *(das Seienste des Seienden)* which, as cause of all other things, had somehow to be beyond *(Meta)* them in a supersensible world. When Christendom *(das Christentum)* sought to appropriate the faith through thinking, it did so mostly by improperly thinking the faith metaphysically: for theology, God became *ens realissimum* and First Cause. The modern subjectivist turn followed. But its possibility was there from the beginning in the metaphysically conceived distinction between ground and grounded and in the ambiguity of the relation of being and thinking. With the rejection of an increasingly unbelievable supersensible ground, the subject was interpreted as the ultimate source of value. The necessary outcome was the withdrawal of God, for whom there was literally no more place in the world.

This is the sort of world into which we have been thrown, but it is a world which comes to us as possibility. We can respond to it either improperly, by giving in to the superficial interpretations lying ready at hand, or properly, seeking the most proper *(eigenste)* possibility, which can only be taken up through confronting the total sense of the entire field of possibility. Only thinking back *(der Schritt zurück)* through the tradition to its origin in search of the essence of the metaphysical movement can bring us near the fundamental or the more proper possibility.

These then are the two faces of contemporary nihilism with its necessary corollary, the withdrawal of God. At first, it seems to invite us to atheism and subjectivist value-creation; but the very blackness of the night in which we find ourselves is an epochal call of Being: the possibility of asking how this could happen. How could it be that the gods and the God, once so present and effective in forming the essence of whole epochs, now find no place in the scheme of things?

If to thoughtful Dasein the epoch begins to appear, at least on its bureaucratic-technologic-atheistic-dehumanizing surface, as a menace to survival of virtually everything Western man has traditionally cherished, where is he to turn for salvation? Clearly, he cannot follow the crowd along what appears a sure and spectacular road to destruction. Does hope lie somehow in the exceptional? That thought does not trouble the man of Christian faith, for Christians have always felt called to the exceptional; since Christ's answer to Pilate, "My kingdom is not of this world," Christians have always felt strangers in every epoch and every milieu. Hegel accuses the Roman Christians of stoicist escapism, and a Heideggerian could answer that Christians are simple meta-physicians par excellence, placing their hope in a supersensible entity that is indeed "not of this world." But that is not the most thoughtful answer the Heideggerian reflection has

to offer. I would like to show this now, by raising the question:
Can Christian faith itself be appropriated as essential possibility
in the present epoch?

IS CHRISTIAN FAITH AN ANACHRONISM IN THE PRESENT EPOCH?

It is true that Christianity is no longer the central effective
force giving its characteristic stamp to the epoch,[11] but it should
be asked whether authentic faith has ever been an essential part
of the essential space *(Wesensraum)* of any epoch? Heidegger can
sound at times like Harnack. I propose first to present his rather
Protestant anti-institutional position without comment; later in
the paper I shall show matters to be more complicated and less
stilted, as we think through the distinction between authentic
faith and worldly churchdom, between authentic institution as
family of loving Christians and the worldly power of the Church.
In the Middle Ages, writes Heidegger, the effective force which
organized society as state and Church was not "the Christly"
(das Christliche) but rather "Christendom" *(das Christentum),*
the hierarchical, feudal and ecclesiastical establishment whose
theology was metaphysical. As early as the missionary activity
of Paul and the writing of the Gospels, the Christly life *(das
christliche Leben)* was being transformed into the worldly
establishment, "the historical, worldly-political appearance of
the Church and its claim to power *(Machtanspruch)* within the
formation of occidental mankind and its modern culture."[12]

How seriously are we to take the hint offered here that the
Christly life is no more to be confused with the epochal power
(Macht) than theology is with faith?[13] The text from the essay,
"Nietzsche's Pronouncement, 'God is dead,' " continues:

Christendom in this sense (i.e. as a tentative of worldly
power) and Christliness *(Christlichkeit)* of New Testament
faith are not the same. Even a non-Christly life can affirm
Christendom and use it as an instrument of power, just as,
conversely, a Christly life does not necessarily have need of

Christendom. Therefore a controversy with Christendom is in no way a fight with the Christly, just as little as a critique of theology is per force a critique of belief, of which theology can be an explication *(Auslegung)*. One moves in the depths of fights between Weltanschauungen so long as this essential distinction is ignored.[14]

A subsequent text from the same essay explains "the metaphysical sense of Nietzsche's pronouncement, God is dead," in these terms: "the supersensible world of ends and measures does not quicken or bear life any more. That world itself has become lifeless: dead." Then Heidegger adds this crucial consideration: "Christly belief will be here and there. But the love which rules in such a world is not the effectively real *(wirken-wirksame)* principle of what is now happening."[15]

One could, of course, discount these texts as sops to the sensibilities of religious contemporaries. On the other hand, one could take them as reminders that human existence is not simply reducible to the major improper epochal possibilities most obviously characteristic of the era into which one is thrown. Such an interpretation accords with the deep sense of Heidegger's *Denken*. If we accept such an interpretation, then I believe we should also take very seriously this rare mention of love, here said to be ruling the Christly world.

In the existential analytic of the Dasein presented in *Being and Time*, which element of the analysis lays the foundation for the phenomenon here called "Christian love"? We find it in the description of the being together of authentic Dasein. This relation is termed "proper solicitude" *(eigentliche Füsorge)*; it is described as one Dasein "leaping out ahead" of another's concrete possibilities in order, by freeing the other for his possibilities, to enable him to become properly himself.[16] In a later passage, it is explained that resolute proper Dasein is not isolated from the world (a basic point overlooked by some inadequate Heidegger interpretations) but is rather first through resoluteness brought into its own proper being-in-the-world. Here Heidegger adds,

Through this self-elected possibility of being, the Dasein frees itself for its world. Resoluteness itself allows Dasein to permit the co-existing other 'to be', to live his own most proper possibility and to co-operate with him in unlocking this possibility of being through freeing solicitude which leaps out ahead.[17]

The ground of the possibility of proper concern for the other is, then, a certain self-concern, the resolute taking oneself in hand which requires that one's most proper possibilities be allowed to stand out against the background of the whole field of one's possibilities. As those possibilities are so many calls to being-in-the-world, they include necessarily the possibility of being with the others. That is to say, part of the very possibility of my own existence as being-in-the-world is the other's being different, as well as my being different from him within the common horizons of a partly shared destiny. We have here not only the ontological foundation of what the Christian calls "love" but also the ground of a doctrine of authentic institution, as we shall presently develop it.

The central importance here of concrete possibility must not be overlooked. The other, with whom we are to co-exist through resolutely allowing him to be himself while we affirm our own uniqueness, is neither *Dasein* in general nor a class or a generation, but another individual in his "irreplaceable, ineluctable uniqueness." To be sure, we share common epochal, generational, national horizons with him;[18] we are thrown together into the same state of affairs *(Lage)* as co-citizens of the world of technology; more particularly, we may be thrown into complementary roles in the same institution. But it is not in virtue of such commonality of institutions, establishments, groups and societies by which I relate to the other *eigentlich* that I free him for his *eigenste Seinkönnen*,—his most proper possibility of being. Most basically, I do so through concrete encounter with him in his uniqueness.

In a slightly different context where Heidegger is describing resolute Dasein as calling up his essential possibilities from the past (*Wiederholung,* repetition), to explain just what is recalled he adds, parenthetically, "That the Dasein elects his heroes."[19]

One cannot pursue the question we have asked uniquely on the ontological level, occupied by *Being and Time,* for it is an ontic question concerned with the properness of our own faith in this actual epoch. At issue is concrete Being-possibility (*Seinkönnen*)—as it always is when one descends to the level of actual existence where particular choices have to be made. Because, since *Being and Time* Heidegger's concerns have been all with the remembering and rethinking of the sense of Being's revelation-dissimulation of itself in the metaphysical tradition, the resulting ontological analyses can be of only limited help in answering an ontic question. I say of limited help, rather than no help at all, because, as we shall see in a moment, every ontic question requires a proper ontological situating.

How are we to interpret the remark about the need for the resolute Dasein to choose his heroes? We have just seen that however widespread the epochal, the traditional, the societal possibilities, all come together only in the individual's unique interpreting-eksisting: there alone can they take up an actual ontic existence. Now possibility is repeatable only concretely: a particular Dasein projects a possibility in his dealing with the world (*handeln*)[20] which earlier Dasein have opened up through their existential acts. "Heroes" manifest concrete proper past possibility[21]; the "election" (*Wahl*) of a hero is the appropriation and reconcretisation of that possibility through taking it up as one's own pro-ject (*An-eignen as entwerfen*).

In Dasein's task of appropriating the possibilities held out to him by the world, two levels of *Nachdenken*—of rememberingly thinking back—are to be co-ordained. On the one hand, our situation is epochal, and to understand this epochal situation reflection on the sense of the entire tradition is necessary. Today, a Christian cannot ignore technology, nihilism, and the absence of God from many lives as the effective force of the epoch; he must discern what is possible epochally. On the other hand, our situation is individual; whatever the epochal possibilities, we can take them up only personally. Hence, the overriding importance of encounter with concrete Dasein, from whom we learn what are the actually livable forms of the possible. In sollicitude *(Fürsorge)* we relate properly to concrete Dasein, not only to those with whom we are thrown in a common world now, but to Dasein that has already been in its past proper possibility *(dagewesenem Dasein in seiner gewesenen eigentlichen Möglich keit)*.[22] As all knowable possibilities, even what appear the most eye-catching and up-to-date possibilities, are founded in what has already been, we should not be surprised if we discover that the deeper possibilities open to us are embodied concretely by Dasein who may have existed long ago.

Does it make sense to speak of having sollicitude for past Dasein? As all possibility handed over to us already is the way it is and therefore is in a certain sense past, I can say that the friend with whom I was just speaking is (i.e., always has been) in such-and-such a way. There are also Dasein who are "over and done with," and for whom there is no question of my "leaping out ahead" to free them to be themselves in the sense of my being for them a solicitous call of conscience. But in *Wiederholung,* in taking up again as my own the possibility of Dasein that has already been, the need of allowing the other to be other even in this case remains crucial. The other's acts must be incorporated into my own existence without the other's ceasing to be affirmed in his difference. Whether past or still living, the other must not be a tool to what are essentially my own voluntaristically fabricated ends. Receptivity implies the respect of listening to the other precisely in what may be most foreign about it and yet astonishingly may prove germain. The deepest sense of the word *fürsorge* is clearly fulfilled by such respectful emulating.

What then distinguishes the proper hero from the improper form of possibility held up to us by the inauthentic "them"? We have just suggested that heroes could be chosen from far back in the tradition, but whom should we choose for our heroes?

In the past of every proper Dasein there is something we can emulate. But surely there is more to the choice of heroes than a call to emulate all in human existence that has been noble and still remains repeatable.

In the choice of heroes, I can see three factors. First, in our encounters, there is a certain "Throwness," that is, we can elect only those we happen to know. (For Christians the importance of evangelisation stems from this basic principle.) Secondly, a proper hero is not to be fabricated out of fragments of lives and isolated heroic acts composed by us into a *collage*. Rather it is the integrity of a resolute Dasein in its unity which alone reveals the truth of proper possibility. The hallmark of such existence is integrity in the sense of resolute Dasein which, having taken his existence in hand in the light of the possibility which is most essentially his own, projects only that which consistently helps to develop that most essential possibility. But as all possibility comes to him as possibility in the world, he is genuinely receptive to what it has to offer and lovingly open to all whom he encounters; his concern reaches out to embrace the vast sweep of existence, past and to come. Hence the third consideration: in choosing a hero we should look for the existent who, because of the reach of his concern, is genuinely a man for all times. He must hold up to our emulation what we most need to learn: openness to Being through respect for all it illumines.

It may seem that we have wandered far from our initial theme: the Holy as Source beyond both gods and men. On the contrary, I would like to show now that, by his very mode of existence, the truly adequate hero brings us face to face with the question of the mystery of the Opening within which alone encounter with the God and authentic self-interpretation become possible. The hero cannot be fully what we have described without approaching the mystery of the Opening, for the hero's authentic resoluteness is an encounter with the Holy. Resoluteness is a pro-jection into the not-yet *(das Dagewesene)* in the light of one's most proper *(eigenste)* possibility. What this dry formula actually calls for is astonishing, absolute and, in its full and pure achievement, rare. The kind of openness to the full range of received possibility for which it calls requires embracing the full sphere of what potentially lies open.

This will to embrace the totality of the field of possibility brings the hero to an encounter with the limits of the horizons of the Opening. As there is no going beyond these dimensions, this rare and *ängstlich* experience is an encounter with the Absolute, for confrontation with the entire field of one's possibilities, from the throwness of birth to that "possibility of impossibility" which is death, is recognition of dependence on the gift of Being for all that we are. Against that background the resolute Dasein seeks out its most proper *(eigenste)* possibility, that is, the uniqueness of its own position in the world. Such a coming face-to-face with oneself is a new event or founding; it carries forward the totality into the not yet which is essential and in its manifestations eminently worth preserving by later Dasein. In this sense it can be said that resolute Dasein's encounter with the ultimate dimensions founds that which remains. Hölderlin ends his great poem, *"Andenken,"* with the line: *"Was bleibet aber stiften die Dichter,"* "but what remains the poets found." For late Hölderlin the poet is always hero-poet whose going-to-the-limits is the ultimate resolute act which, as act, necessarily expresses itself.

Because of the radical newness which characterizes every absolute encounter, the traditional means of expression must be de-centered and recentered to achieve the new expression to which they contribute their accumulated sense and through which they receive a new life. Although later Heidegger expresses his vision in terms of thinking *(Denken)* and saying *(Sagen)*, the dealing *(Handeln)* and existing *(Existieren)* of *Being and Time* remain presupposed as the act of the Hero which the poet's word expresses. In the present essay I would bring out the sollicitudes *(Fürsorgen)* which binds resolute Dasein to one another.[23]

From this it should be clear that authentic heroes never

become anachronisms: what they found remains, for that is what is worth repeating. However, insofar as epochal horizons are improper *(ineigentlich)*, preserved in the mode of *das Man,* can Heroes ever be at one in their visions with any epoch? As the epochal forms are hidden, fallen manifestations of the Hero's resolute encounters with the "not yet," his existence is to us a call to render properly our own what at first had been only in the mode of "their" everyday improper solicitations.

These few reflections make it possible to establish that Jesus as the Hero of Christian faith is not an anachronism. For the Christian, however, that is not enough, for to faith Jesus is not just *a* hero, He is the Christ. This is an ontic claim for his unique status as Hero of all heroes, as a manifestation of the Divinity against which time cannot prevail. Is such a claim ontologically acceptable? It would seem to demand that we see in Christ a kind of central, unsurpassable moment in history. At first glance, this might appear irreconcilable with the historicity of Being, but not if the matter is thought through. One aspect of this claim need cause no difficulty for the Heideggerian *Denken:* That a moment of history should be a unique event to which all subsequent Dasein are called to return in recalling thought *(Nachdenken)* and that love is the very essence of the Heideggerian *E-vent (Ereignis)* and the very measure of its essentiality. Every crucial, epochal E-vent is such a unique point of reference. What is different and disturbing about the Christian claim is that the Christ be God dwelling among men, that He be both God and man. The scandal of the Christian claim, then, is not that Christ is unique and that we are to emulate him, but that He is uniquely unique, i.e. absolute. The absoluteness here claimed is something more than that encounter with the ultimate horizontal dimensions of existence we have seen characterizing every hero. In the Christ is manifested something about the Source itself of those historical horizons, within which the divine can be encountered and man can interpret himself and be in a world of nature and instruments. Can Heidegger's thought, despite the undoubted fact that the thinker himself has never taken a step along such a path, be interpreted in a way that allows a place for this eneluctable element of Christian faith?

THE CHRIST AND THE HOLY

The founding revelation of Being which opens the entire Western tradition is a gift, *ein Geschick,* as Heidegger says. The word is admirable, for it recalls both the fact that this initial opening of a horizon of inquiry was sent *(schicken, geschickt)* to us from the Source, and the fact that, as the tradition-founding moment, it determines the Destiny *(das Geschick)* of the West. The beginning of our history *(Geschichte)* is itself an E-vent, a happening *(ein Geschehnis)* at a moment in time.

All subsequent moments in the tradition follow necessarily from the founding moment. We have taken pains to show that the necessity assuring the unity of the tradition is neither closed nor mechanical. Indeed, each great epoch-founding E-vent within the tradition requires a further *Geschick* for, as an act of projection into the "not yet," resolute Dasein's encounter with the horizontal limits always owes thanks to a gift of the Source. This is not to suggest that just anything can overtake us at any moment. The creative aspect of the encounter, at the world-limits, with one's destiny is always understandable after the event as having been prepared by a long past, and as having been present at the moment of accomplishment precisely as possibility. Nevertheless, the new E-vent remains a gift insofar as it is an accomplishment, an ex-tension, the opening of new possibility.

For such an ontology there is no *a priori* reason to object to Christian belief when it holds that at a certain time and place within the tradition, in an essential place *(Ort)*, there occurred the *Geschick* of a *Da-sein*, a self-interpreting existent, just as historical in His concreteness as any other, to whom it was given to radiate through word and deed the Godhead dwelling in him. (I would add that the history preserved in the books of the Old Testament could be interpreted as part of the preparation of the space for the Advent of that E-vent.)

The problem would seem to be rather on the side of the Christian. How can he accept the notion that the Holy transcends every manifestation of God and every interpretation man makes of himself?[24]

To be sure, any *metaphysical* interpretation of such a contention would at once render it totally unacceptable to Christian faith. To think of the Christian God in some way causally dependent on a superentity, the Holy, would amount to nothing more than a denial of the absoluteness of God. But any metaphysical interpretation would be equally fatal to Heidegger's intention.

The question is this: Can Heidegger's non-metaphysical thought be interpreted in a way which would let the Christ be one with God and let God be absolute?

The Holy is transcendent Source of the interpretative horizons of the tradition—the *Ort* within which the gods and the God can appear and withdraw and within which man can interpret himself and his relations to nature and instruments. For Christian faith the founding moment of the *Geschick* sent by the Holy is not unique, but twofold. Besides the opening of a space of inquiry manifesting itself in the early Greek thought of Being as Presence of that which is present and of the totality of things as *phusis* or *cosmos,* there is the other founding moment, remembered and handed down *(tradere)* in the Pentateuch, of the encounter on Sinai. The subsequent moments of encounter with the Absolute are *Geschicke* within that one traditional time-space founded in the people of Israel. The most astonishing of these is Jesus' revelation, through word and act, that He is one with the Father and the Spirit, that He proceeds from the Father and that from the Father and Him proceeds the Spirit. Only within the epochal time-space of the living tradition of Israel can such a revelation *be.* Though the fruit of long preparation, like every epochal *Geschick* it goes beyond what had been, for it was ultimately given to Jesus, as to no other, to transcend the limits through anguished *(ängstlich-Gesthemane)* confrontation. The Resurrection is Christ's going beyond Dasein's ultimate limit, death. His conquering that limit reveals to all who believe that the historical dimensions of their existence, while indeed their beginning, do not enclose their most proper *(eigenste)* possibility.

What, in Heideggerian terms, is the essence of the claim that Jesus is the Christ and that the Christ is God? This revelation is granted as a gift of God at a moment in time, within the epochal *Ort* of the tradition. The Fatherhead of God means that the Source, which is at work through the horizon-opening gifts of history, cares for us individual existents who can only happen within those horizons and are, indeed, its children. Caring is then no longer limited to *Dasein*. Without compromising the transcendence of the Source, of which we continue to have no intuition, we are privileged to know that, however it may be, it cares. This means that the possibilities opened by heroic Dasein, above all those of Jesus, Hero of heroes, have a sense, which is that of our salvation. The *Seinsgeschicke* are not indifferent to our welfare but intended for our fullest human development. Through Jesus, Providence brings about the institution of the Church within which all men are called to a life of love. What is held out to us is the vision of the possibility of an authentic institution in which each would call forth in the other his most proper possibilities. Such would be the reign of the Spirit.

How does the tradition founded in the revelation of Being through the early Greek thinkers merge with the tradition of belief, descendent from the founding encounter at Sinai and from Jesus' revelation? Properly, *(eigentlich)*, in the thought of those believers who, rememberingly-repeating the concrete possibilities opened by Jesus, interpret them in terms of the thought of Being; improperly *(ineigentlich)*, when aspects of the possibility opened by Jesus are thought metaphysically, which allows it to fall into the mode of the thingly *(Vorhandenes)*. When Paul or John, faithful to the most proper possibility of their existence, express their experience in Greek terms, the authenticity of their encounter with the Source requires that they de-center and re-center the Greek categories so that what they say is not limited merely to metaphysics' forgetting of

Being. In contrast, at times theologians can use things Christian as part of a religious and philosophical problem-solving exercise. Such inauthenticity would be like the ecclesiastical schemer's use of the faithful to achieve worldly political aims. The great fathers and doctors are more than metaphysicians when their thought is animated by their heroic, i.e. saintly, encounter with the Holy along the way of Jesus. Loving Christians relate to each other within the authentic institution in a way which sees their respective roles aiding, not hindering, their full human development.

Christian faith thus obliges us to travel far on paths strange to Heidegger. That he might find unacceptable all that follows here from the ontic claim of Christian faith is no reason for judging it ontologically incompatible with the Heideggerian *Denken*. If I am correct, a Christian thought, both re-calling the most proper possibilities of Heidegger's vision and faithful to what it has been given us to remember of the Christ, may prove authentic, as some have thought but which I once doubted.

◊

1. **Ineigentlich** is usually translated in this paper as "improper" and **eigentlich** as "proper," rather than as "inauthentic" and "authentic," to underscore the notion that what was in **eigentlich** has become mine. **Being and Time**, trans. J. Macquarrie and E. Robinson (New York: Harper, 1962: hereafter s2), speaks of the process of appropriative (**aneignen)** possibility.

2. Especially important for this undertaking is the essay "Nietzsches wort, 'Gott ist tod!' " in Holzwege, 2nd. ed. (Frankfurt am main: Vittorio Klostermann, 1950), pp. 193-247. Hereafter, **HW**.

3. **Sein und zeit**, 7th. ed. (Tubingen: Max Niemeyer, 1953), p. 307-308.

4. SZ, p. 322.

5. "Andenken," in **Erläuterungen zu Hölderlins Dichtung**, 4th ed. (Frankfurt am main: V. Klostermann, 1971), pp. 100 and 113 (in 1st. ed., pp. 95 and 107). Hereafter EHD.

6. "Das noch aufgesparte gewesene," see "Die onto-theologische Verfassung der Metaphysik," in **Identität und Differenz** (Pfüllingen: G. Neske, 1957), p. 44.

7. Holderlin in **"Andenken"** names it "die Quelle": "Mancher trägt scheue, an die quelle zu ghen." Heidegger's commentary is in EHD, pp. 129-133.

8. The line is from Hölderlin's "Andenken": "But now it dawns."

9. In "Wie wenn am Feiertage . . ." we read: Jezt aber tagts! Ich harrt und sah es kommen, und was ich sah, das Heilige sei mein Wort. For Heidegger's commentary on this important ruin, see EHD, pp. 49-77. For "das Heilige," see EHD, pp. 59, 63, 104-106.

10. This is discussed more fully in my article, "Heidegger beyond Hegel," in the International edition of **Filosofia**, XIX (1968), 737ff.

11. "Nicht das wirkend-wirksame Prinzip dessen, was jetzt geschieht." HW, p. 234.

12. HW, pp. 202-203.

13. HW, p. 203.

14. **Loc. cit.**

15. HW, p. 234.

16. SZ, p. 122.

17. SZ, p. 298.

18. SZ, p. 384-385.

19. SZ, p. 385.

20. SZ, p. 300.

21. SZ, p. 394.

22. SZ, **loc. cit.**

23. There is a danger of over-intellectualisation in making language "Being's house." An institution as **Sittlichkeit,** as a set of habits, is incoropated in more than its express statutes.

24. EHD, p. 108.

Person and/or World As the Source of Religious Insight

by
Maurice Nédoncelle

FROM SENSE PERCEPTION TO BEING AND TO THE DIVINE

Sense Perception and One's Body

SENSE PERCEPTION, it would seem, should be spoken of only in the plural, for by it at any one moment my attention is diffused among many percepts. By them I grasp a number of pieces or partial factors, whether visible or tangible, audible or of smell, or of taste—and of muscular or visceral kind. Furthermore, even if in the process of receiving them, I seize and organize them, they remain a given that existed before I did. Hence, my information remains always posterior to their reality, and I can never dominate their multiplicity.

Nevertheless, as can be seen by the very fact that they manifest themselves to me in this manner, they constitute a world which differs from me much as would a spectacle that unfolds before me or a visual or non-visual drama of which I become a witness and even, in a sense, an accomplice. This world possesses a number of special characteristics.

1. The first is that the pieces or fragments perceived are only parts and do not of themselves suffice to constitute a whole or a world. In each perception there arises the conviction that what

has been perceived is only a part of a whole which has not yet
been perceived. The notion of extended reality as that which has
"parts outside of parts" is verified not only within the boundaries
of what has been perceived but extends beyond that series of
given factors to a potentially unlimited field of things that are
yet to be perceived. Consequently, the diversity of the sensible
world is unified in space and time only imperfectly and in diverse
manners. Reality thus presents not only a clear and defined image,
but has an obscure and undefined side corresponding to my ignorance and to the limitations of my efforts.

2. The second characteristic of the sensible world is that it
intrudes upon me to make me a part of it. The sign of this in-
trusion is my body, because this is an object of sense perception.[1]
My body appears to me in a paradox that is constitutive of perception, being simultaneously the instrument and part of the
object of perception. Because my body is a part of that object,
and hence of the spectacle and the reality of the everyday world,
I am a part of that world. Thus, to the degree that I am able to
perceive, I am a part of the world because the common characteristic of objects is to be one part outside of another and related to
a whole. And if I am a part of a whole, I am contained by that
whole but am not that whole itself.

3. However, the parts are not simply juxtaposed; the very
opposition by which they attain their individuality shows that
they interact causally. Considering only the relations of absence
or presence between two objects, A and B, four combinations
are possible: A-B, not A-B, A-not B, and not A-not B. On the
basis of the most simple forms of causal relations between these
two elements, the causal relations can be defined as the fact that
the presence or absence of one is the source of presence or absence
for that or for the other term. This allows for sixteen possibilities
(from A comes A or not A, or B or not B, etc. . .). The pattern
becomes more complex if the possibility of a dual causality is introduced (from A proceeds AB or not AB, etc. . .), or to a still
greater degree if one inverses the order of the couples (from A
proceeds BA or not BA, etc. . .). It is unnecessary here to develop
this pattern of causality which already manifests a progressive

complexity even when only two terms are used. However, it is already apparent that this pattern becomes a formalism by which one can conceive the individual and collective development of elements perceived. What should be noted here is that the world of perception is one of causally organized parts, and that as regards my bodily nature, I am a constituent part of that world.

4. In what sense am I part of this world and how am I to understand it? The immediate impression given by perception is that my body is a central and privileged part of the world in relation to which all the rest is organized or at least perceivable and comprehensible. As Pradines notes, the "senses of participation" (such as coenesthesia) suggest this more on an affective basis, while the "sense of distance" (such as sight) suggest it more on a cognitive basis. Vision especially, with its variation in the size of images depends upon their distance, shows the almost magic variability of the elements in the panorama related to one's body. More exactly, because we are able to extend or retract our limbs, this variability is related to a point from which we start and which continually falls back as we wish to seize it completely, since the eye does not see itself.

However, the understanding of the perceptive pattern can be reversed so that my body loses its central importance and is engulfed by the world. In fact, the basis for this inversion was laid in the previous perceptive centering upon the body. That perspective could never be absolute. On the contrary, its relativity was manifest both by the continual motion of the parts of the non-corporeal world and by the continual recession of my body considered as the center when I wished to consider that center itself and place it entirely within the perceptive network. However, if the inversion of the body-centered view is indicated within that perceptive itself, it is realized there neither in sensation nor in imagination, that is, in neither the clear nor the obscure aspects of extended reality. Rather, it is realized in intellection by which we remove ourselves from constituting the center and interrelate the various elements so that they form the objective world as an ordered relationship between things.

Nevertheless, the world which is seen as engulfing me as just one point among many never completely succeeds in so doing, and this for two reasons. First of all because the world remains incomplete and enigmatic; it remains incapable of being formulated in laws which exhaustively express its cosmic elements. The cosmos remains open; it escapes the limitations of the objective factors discovered concerning it. Second, the paradox mentioned above is never able to be eliminated. My body which is a part of the perceived or perceivable pattern remains an instrument of the act by which I perceive. What is more, it takes refuge in my subjectivity at the moment at which it would be about to evaporate into objectivity.

The above vacillation between the two interpretations of the network of perception is a strange one. Having begun in search of a circle with a center, I found an ellipse with two entrances. I can direct my attention by preference to one, but cannot make the other disappear. What makes this duality very special is that if I choose to relate everything to my body, I remain on the level of sense perception, whereas if I choose to relate all to an autonomous world of reciprocally related objects, I move to the intelligible level where the real becomes the result of a system of theoretical requirements. What is most disconcerting about this duality is that, though the two entrances of the ellipse are on different levels, they depend upon each other: sense perception contains the seeds of intelligence, and the intelligible world cannot indefinitely remain a pattern of theoretical exigencies. From time to time and indirectly it must be experimentally verified.

The Being of the World and the Divine

Certainly by beginning from sense perception, the world I discover can be affirmed to be real. Nevertheless, I cannot claim that it is complete in the strong sense of the term, though at first sight I would have spoken of it in this manner. There seems to be a radical insufficiency to the world in view of which it is not feasible to choose the world as a base on which to build immediately a proof for the existence of God. The indetermination of the world is too ambiguous to provide a sure foundation for the work of theology. At least as a mediating link, there is need for the idea of being. Though the world is not a whole, it is a reality. Even though I do not know whether it is substance or accident, contingent or necessary, and though I am not able to follow the path of being in itself to its end, the world follows this path far enough to enable me to say it exists. What is more, its form of being is sufficiently determined to enable me to ask if it implies a God.

This investigation of being in the world or of the world in being requires a prior elucidation of the nature of being. If being were the existent or existents of the world, it is possible that these pieces would not be self-sufficient, but it would not be evident that this insufficiency required a God. However, being is not an existent or group of existents; rather it is the first and last relation of each existent with itself and with other existents. This relation is not arbitrarily applied from without; it is indispensable to every existent in order that the existent's distinctive reality be defined and be able to situate itself in the world. This relation is dynamic and constitutive, but because it transposes the existent or existents into itself, it remains anonymous and is constituted by this very act. Being, which traces out the world in all its senses and at all its levels, manifests itself in the beings of the world without their knowing it, like a language which does not come from its words but which conditions all their relations. By this very fact it is uniquely present at the root of all.

Can this Porphyrian being and universal mediator, without which existents—however dense they might be—would fall into nothing, be called God? If we abstracted from person as much as possible, as we have until now, it is not possible to say that the being on which the world rests is that act of the Being par excellence which is God. However, we can discern in this being a prefiguring of God, that it: a divine. It is necessary to justify this assertion.

1. One cannot say that being in the world, which to us appears as the being of the world, is the act of God. The reason for this is that we have no means of deciding directly whether

or not the insufficiency of things which exist in the world requires a transcendent cause. Nor is it possible to say whether the idea of cause, such as was defined above, limits itself to meaning that one being is the determining condition for the presence or absence of another being. In brief, we cannot say whether causality extends above, within, or between beings. Beginning from things that exist in the world, one can only pose this question.

2. Nevertheless, we can perceive in things existing in the world a divine or a prefiguring of God because being, of whatever sort, immediately reveals an intelligible order. The world has a fundamental harmony accompanied by power and wisdom, as is manifested in its presence to every existent, in its unlimited power of relating things, and in the very fact that, while penetrating all existents, it is able to express, transpose, and unite them, without appearing as anything separate or in its own right. Being insensible to evil, which neither touches the divine nor is touched by Him, the divine plans and orders all things; it is always pure in that which is impure, the permanent beauty of the cosmos, and the way which opens new ways and rewards those who follow them. The divine is nature both as giving birth to what is new and is itself unfolding, not by creation but in an endlessly reversible cycle.

True, some call this principle of harmony God; it is the divine of which philosophers speak. Others, however, refer to it as divine and still consider themselves atheists because they consider God to be more than the divine of which philosophers speak. I shall call it the precursor or prefigurement of God, for it is the most that one can achieve when he begins from sense perception with the ontological reflection based upon it. Using the ordinary meaning of second causes, one cannot consider the precursor to be the absolute source or goal of things that exist. That notion does not even arise out of the insufficiency of being, but is found within them at their very foundation. Whatever they may be, by the very fact that they are, the source is present as their breath, their very atmosphere. Neither made like an inanimate thing or engendered as are living things, the divine is co-extensive with everything that is and with every living thing that is born. Although it can be called one, it is at the root of all multiplicity as the unspoken face in all faces, itself remaining unchanged throughout all the changes it makes possible. If one says that it is here, it can equally well be said to be there and to be betwen here and there; and if it is immutable in its nature, it is infinitely mobile in its presence. Thus, while retaining its own identity, the divine is the source of the identity of all others. These, however, do not become the divine, which is rather their basic identity with themselves and their relations with other beings. It is the Reason *(Logos)* of Nature, the supple mediator of the world, the first approximation of God, and the God before person.

FROM PERSON TO GOD

Once I realize that I am not a part of the world of sense perception everything changes. From the fact that not all was reducible to the objectivising process which constituted the consciousness of my body within the pattern of this world, it was already clear that the world could not be a universe in the proper sense of that term. That universe lacked the subject which perceives it but which it itself cannot include.[2]

The feeling of existing in the world also is immediately transformed. Though this existence is still manifested by awareness of the body, there is no longer that strangeness by which one speaks of the body in the third person and which allows us to share images with the world. The new relation is manifested by that intimateness by which my body is me and I am that body. Nevertheless, this type of integration of the body with subjectivity is not the whole of subjectivity but only one particular act or mode. Subjectivity is not fully achieved unless it is personal, and it becomes fully personal only by going beyond the corporeal feeling it includes and beyond the world of perception by which it is represented.

Here the thought process *(cogito)* is not limited to the mathematical model, but is a unique reality implying a vocation, a structure, and a history.[3]

I do not maintain that the proof of the existence of God becomes evident from the moment one recognizes this uniqueness of persons. However, I certainly would say that the proof which I am going to present would not make any sense without a prior recognition of this principle. I would even add that I would not consider valid any proof that is separated from this principle.

Person and Nature[4]

The first stage of the reflection which leads toward a philosophical belief in God is constituted by an awareness that my reality and yours, as untouched, unique, and unlimited openings upon being, are out of any proportion to the resources of nature. By definition, a personal center escapes the limitations, the similarities, and the contrasts which accompany beings on the levels of biology or animal psychology. The person judges the world and is capable of indefinite growth in his own identity. Even in hating himself, he cannot renounce himself. This alliance of a unique destiny and an unlimited openness is, without doubt, only a wish in us, but the orientation toward this goal rules out from the beginning any absolute break between appearance and reality in me. In this sense, from the beginning we are what we are to become, and this by an act which radically surpasses anything in the sensible world. Certainly we live in this world and make it exist in our bodily and psychic functions, but the principle which specifies these is not limited to them; it is that unique reality that we are by the very fact that we have being. For us sensible factors can only be aids or obstacles, not causes or goals.

A similar line of reasoning can be established concerning interpersonal relations. Even if men are destined to a total intercommunication, they do not create it, but receive it as a promise or as a task. The immense influence that men exert one upon the other can be real only if they have already been given their respective beings. Evidently, it is not procreation which explains this being, for that is only its context and occasion. That is why at times we can depersonalize ourselves so well when with others and come closer to ourselves in solitude. The very idea of inter-personal relations is not ours; we receive and utilize it, whether for good or evil. The degree of our presence to others depends on us, but the presence itself is a gift which surpasses us and which, thus, always retains something undefinable that cannot be con-verted into concepts or analyzed into its particular characteristics.

Person and god

The second stage of the reflection that leads to God consists in recognizing that we do not understand and explain ourselves if there is no god who is closer to us than we are to ourselves. For the moment, I will use but a small 'g' or, if you wish, the term *'daimon.'*

1. There is a strong temptation to protest that this is only a type of project image or auxiliary construct, rather than a being which makes me be for and by myself. But a projected image does not precede the being of a thing, whereas our appreciation of ourselves implies a source that is not simply derived as a shadow. We are aware of being immediately and perpetually dominated by the norm which imposes our phenomenal character and which we ratify by the very fact of affirming ourselves in the first act of our existence. In the same manner, an auxiliary construct made by us would only furnish a support, whereas the god of personal awareness is not a support produced by us, even when we ratify him. Our 'god' is antecedent to us. He surpasses us independently of ourselves and even when we violently opposed him, without ever ceasing either to affirm him or to be affirmed by him. The theme (the divine) is given; our existence is only a series of variations or responses unequal to themselves and amongst themselves. Whether faithful or not, even in the protests or the negligences of infidelity, they will be incapable of negating the theme since, in a word, they are slaves to their very identity.

Finally, neither a projected image nor an auxiliary structure can be a cause, whereas it is precisely a reality in the order of cause that experience manifests. I know that I am wanted, and I know this not in the repressive manner of a false belief resulting from a pathological projection, but in a sense that is both more radical and inevitable and more discreet and rational. Reflection certifies the initial experience which obliged me to recognize in myself someone other than myself, and it is only in this interior realization that I grasp the causality in its entirety. Elsewhere, I perceive causality only in its superficial forms of interpersonal action or of natural phenomena. It is only in my being that I learn what it is to be totally produced, to be the living *exitus* of an infallible grace which wishes me to be free and on which even my revolt depends. Undeniably, my *daimon* places me in existence at each moment, but it situates me in a position that is open to both defeat and to progress. It divides me between an ideal and a factual self, and strangely interlaces the functions of the two. I perceive that I am the cause of my actions and of their adequacy or deficiency in relation to me; but this is not the most profound revelation of causality that I possess. The most profound revelation I have of causality is that of being a unique effect and of being dominated by a cause which absolutely envelops and specifies me.

The experience of the causality which I exercise is not the same as that of causality which makes me capable of exercising it. The latter is accessible to me only by looking, as it were, behind and above, since I cannot cause in the same way as the cause of my being, that is, by creating a thing in its totality. No doubt the being that is engendered is not by that very fact inferior to the one who engenders it, for there can be as much dignity in receiving as in giving. Thus, it is therefore not because I am wanted that I am inferior to the cause of my being, but because I cannot respond equally or be the total source of any being.

2. Must one say that this cause or *daimon* is personal? I cannot reduce it to myself, even though I am rooted in it and identify myself with its creative will. Nevertheless, I must refer to it as a thou, though in a sense which surpasses all worldly analogy, for it is the only thou which constantly understands me and is continuous with all my acts and states. It would be contradictory to assimilate it to an impersonal principle since it is

eminently what I am. In fact, it would be more probable to fear that in realizing myself completely I might dissolve my person into his, except that this new fear is overcome by the fact that his action is to make me to be. Furthermore, the elementary and worldly forms of causality already manifest a curve through the realm of the living and their levels of psyches towards a manner of influencing whereby the cause is conscious of itself and of the other. In human relations, personal consciousness is in no way definitively diminished by the fecundity of its operations, but is even increased by the slightest influence it exercises upon other consciousnesses. It would be strange for the convergence of act and of person suddenly to disappear at the summit after having been progressively affirmed at each degree leading up to it, for this would be to collapse abruptly at the very origin of human beings within whom person is realized most distinctly and without assignable limits.

God and god

The third stage of our road toward God consists in asking ourselves if the *daimon* is different for each consciousness or if it is the same for all: is my god (with a small 'g') God (with a capital 'G')? I shall refrain from ridiculing polytheism which, at the level at which we place ourselves, is a profound and elegant hypothesis and accounts so well for the plurality of nature and of humanity. However, it does so too easily and disregards at least two things. On the one hand, in all of our encounters there is an abrupt presence of God as an undivided unity appearing in the midst of our meetings while remaining perceptible in those states in which union is lacking. In short, the respective gods of each of our persons are the faces of the same God and we cannot hypostatize each of its reflections in our mirrors. On the other hand, to safeguard each aspect of the divine in its uniqueness, polytheism bypasses the problem of the (uncreated) uniqueness of all uniquenesses (personal identities) and is condemned to substituting for it either a general idea or a world soul. Thus we are led back to that earlier notion of a divine which is manifestly inadequate to the legitimate and inevitable requirements for God which have become manifest at this point in our itinerary.

God is not only personal because he creates our persons; he is so by the intimate nature of his divinity and in a unique manner, without adding himself as an additional or even first link to the series of persons we form among men. He is supra-personal, not infra-personal. His perfect immanence and our obvious weakness make the relationship we have with him unequal. Nevertheless, there is always a reciprocal relation between Him and us. The life of spirit, when it develops itself, shows that that relationship never tends to lessen. Thus, on that point, philosophical reflection confirms the testimony of religious invocation.

Is it possible to go further and to forsee something of the intimate life of God? Certainly, for God cannot give being to a person without in a certain manner giving himself as well. We have considered Him as the uncreated uniqueness of created uniqueness, but nothing excludes the possibility of a plurality of supra-personal centers in God.

Contrary to a frequently held thesis in the history of philosophy, we have been led to conclude that the person is not personal because he has limits, but that he is personal because he is an end or goal in himself. Thus the 'other' is for this person not a limit, but a source of this very finality (or goal orientation). If it is true that the not-I is not necessary to the I to which it is associated in our experience, it is nevertheless impossible to identify and conceive the I without a thou. If God is supra-personal, how could there be a kind of 'I' eternally alone? In that case He could be saved from this solitude only by our creation and there would thus be two gods: the one impersonal, before creation, and, as it were, during creation; the personal, after creation, and dependent upon it. Even if the created persons were eternal, they would not make God as source personal.

In fact, our reflection has led us in an altogether different direction. We have established neither that there could be a change in God's nature, nor that divinity has only a surface personality. Duality enters not through God, but through ourselves. From God comes unity, and it is he who rescues us from being simply discontinuous phenomena. It does not seem possible to admit that we are co-eternal and necessary to God in a way which suffices to give him a thou equal to his own divine eminence. Thus, we can recognize him to be fully personal, as our reflection demands, only if he is multipersonal by an intimate disposition of his being. Only this hypothesis, before which philosophy falls silent, corresponds to the analyses and the thrust of philosophy.

INTUITION OF THE GIVER

Reflection overcomes poor relations and re-establishes contact between their elements; it proceeds from an intuition which it purifies and by which, once purified, it is replaced. In a similar way, the philosophical road to God ends with a religious experience, just as it usually starts out with one. As we are neither in the darkness, nor in the noonday sun, the ascetic and aesthetic must alternate on all levels of our existence. What is universally valid in a proof of God does not come from the generality possessed by species and genera, but from the fact that God is in each of us by the presence in each personal consciousness of a unique and supreme Being that reason seeks to verify and express. This presence, which at first is obscure to reflection, progressively disengages itself by means of a sacred contemplation when we consent to take off our shoes, as it were, in order to enter the sanctuary of our soul.

Personal Past

Many men are certain of the existence of God for motives related to their own intimate life. They believe in divine Providence because they see its operation in their life and perceive it at some turning point in their past that is known to them alone. Such a claim would be debatable if it were based on simple and profane advantages. However, it becomes much more respectable and even peremptory when the person who is testifying is capable of the kind of spiritual verification which results, not from frightened egoism, but from the desire to conform to an interior objectivity. I believe in God not because my neighbor was killed in an accident while I was spared: this raw fact can prove nothing but the absurdity of events. I believe in God because I see a will in the course of events, because I know that at certain moments I was gently but firmly led by Him where I did not want to go. There is no automatic union of God with the happiness or with the tragedy of this world; but there is a way in which God breaks in upon us and transforms events by the meaning with which he suffuses them. He acts sometimes as the conqueror who imposes himself upon our restive will and sometimes as a friend who summons forth our highest responses. When I look back over my past years, this is how I meet God. It is easy to dispute the value of such a conviction, and an individual alone with his love is always disarmed. Nonetheless, this conviction can be justified by replacing the immediate impression in its context and submitting it to a criticism which, though of a strictly private order, is nonetheless valid. One might not violate an axiom of logic by denying that such encounters possess the value evidence of the action of God, but in so doing one is aware of a lack of sensitivity. To go to God one must reason, but he must also reach out for all indications.

God as Present

It is not only reflection upon one's own past which makes one aware of the presence of God's action. This awareness can also arise from the intimations of the present and from the way in which they point toward the future. For man God is a guide; he is the Being which is eternally before (and leading) the world.

He is the supreme final cause (or goal) and no doubt he is most commonly recognized as the sole adequate goal of a personal and even a cosmic order. Only he can sustain the spirit and enthusiasm he inspires, for only he can give us the strength and the means to go all the way to him, without falling back into ourselves or even lower than ourselves.

Such a God speaks to us by offering himself while we search for him and try to decipher his message in all that happens. Nevertheless, he remains at a distance and we grope for him, being more sensitive to his radiance than to himself. On one hand, the order of our relations with Him is free, as are those of a grown-up child with his Father. But, on the other hand, this noble religion is weak in its foundation, for it implies a kind of exile. The grown-up child addresses himself to a Father who is distant and this remoteness is due not only to the limitations of sensibility, which I understand here not as gross physical emotion but in its most refined significance beyond prosaic pleasures and sorrows. The distance from God is due also to the limitations of thought, which must always be transcending darkness, hesitating between two possibilities, and confronting the ambivalence of its condition and the equivocation of its reflection.

Mystical Presence

Could there be a still more sublime intuition of God, a mystical relation to Him, or an appreciation not only of his gifts but of the presence of God himself?

At first the one who comes from God is not aware of his source but of himself; he is absorbed in what he senses and in his own action and forgets the person (the Thou) which is his cause. Though this pattern of ingratitude is formed constantly throughout our career as human beings, there remains a marginal consciousness of being caused, which constitutes an invitation to metaphysical analysis and a certain perception of Being. However, this mystical illumination does not depend upon a long and technical metaphysical analysis. If one accepts grace, that is, if one responds to divine initiative, the reflexive method of the metaphysician normally should continue into a mystical illumination and arrive at the final phase of the human-divine relationship.

This final phase is still unclear It would seem that the more penetrating the effect of the divine, the more likely one is to forget its source. But this is true only in the first phase of the activity of an awakening personal consciousness. The supernatural presence of God is revealed with the greatest immediacy especially in the intuition of what theologians call actual grace, that is, in the initial indications of God's friendship and its transformation of our nature, as well as in the very fruitful contacts with God through the theological virtues and the gifts of the Holy Spirit. Thus, in many ways the whole of man is most intimately united with the divine being. Here, the gift is the very self of the Giver, who, in turn, is the fulness of love itself. In this way the interpersonal relation overcomes ungrateful nature, for there is no longer a separation between the gift and He who gives it.

To approach God mystically, one must not depend upon one's own works, the *ego poietikon,* but on God who is their source. For the mystic, the negation of self consists in his overcoming the usual natural ingratitude and relating himself personally to his source. In so doing his actions are purified, the essence of his soul is divinised, and in his essential being rather than merely in his peripheral powers his deviations and deficiencies are corrected. The ego is simultaneously affirmed in its own right and seen in relation to God so that, not God exists because I conceive him *(cogito ergo Deus est),* but I conceive of God conceiving of me *(cogito Deum me cogitantem).* In this way my existence is seen in a clearer light so that, without ceasing to be itself, it does cease being ungrateful to its source. At this point for the mystic the end becomes the beginning, he no longer searches for the support of his being, and, though mediation remains, distance disappears. His basic consciousness is open to the presence of God. If he could maintain himself in this heavenly state, he would come to appreciate everything and everyone, for his essence would adhere to that of God, and the whole limited pattern of his knowledge as well as of his operations would be transformed; his phychic trend would be reversed, that is, no more falling away upon its separate self but ever moving godwards.

In order to retain this intuition in its entirety while on earth, one must not attempt its total expression: what is essential is never said. To this idea, which in certain respects summarizes Plotinus' notion of hierarchical emanation, one might add another that is not accepted by Plontinus, but which is the law of the Cross and related to the Incarnation: by accepting in love its condition, the inferior order which comes from and expresses God paradoxically becomes capable of infinity and, so to speak, becomes God.

In this way there also takes place that interpersonal communion of created persons desired by God. Everything happens as if God had wanted to hide himself as much as possible so that we could love him freely, he hides our strongest bond to him so that we can discover it; he even proposes to us the being which he imposes upon us so that we can impose the being that he proposes. He might even invite mankind, which has risen to the idea of God in its philosophy, to give birth to God himself in its history.

THE RECOVERY OF THE DIVINE IN GOD

Returning now to our point of departure, it was noted there that the divine to which man has access through the sensible world manifested itself in terms of beings as the source of their harmony. Though on the basis of the traditional equivalence between being and transcendental values, being was synonymous to the true, the good, and the beautiful, none of these notions on that level led to a personal God. This does not imply that God cannot be spoken of in terms of those values, but to do so demands that they be approached in a new manner.

Values in a Non-personal and a Personal Context

First of all and hypothetically, these transcendentals would have to be considered on a metaphysical and a personal level. They would no longer be characteristics of nature alone but of personal subjects as such, that is, of existents who do not belong merely to the sensible world. The transcendentals did not prevent the beings in that world from fighting, tearing each other apart, decomposing, or dying. In that realm indifference regarding what happened to beings was the rule, tempered by a merely mathematical harmony which allowed for the most tragic developments and exchanges. The tragedy did not blemish this harmony because it did not contradict it.

However, values which directly concern persons acquire new content and status. They both determine and are determined, and this is done both in and by a consciousness. Their dynamism does not consist simply in being interiorly or exteriorly transmitted, but in giving rise to ideas within a free person who must respond either by ratifying or by rejecting them. In effect, it is characteristic of a person to have personally to appropriate the being he receives.[5] The extension and the intensity of these values increase as they begin to suffuse the relations of persons with themselves and with others, for persons are centered which no longer open only to things outside themselves as do things that are mere parts of a larger whole. Each one virtually includes all else and escapes reduction to the status of a mere part in at least one essential point. In each, the coincidence of knowledge and reality in the one primitive act makes them responsible for their being, so that they create anew the relations into which they enter and thus become their values.[6]

Personal Values and the Manifestation of God

In the transcendental system as developed in terms of the

personal, the primacy of the existent with regard to being is clearer than it was in the development in terms of the sensible world. Values now become the trustees of a message which emanates from the supreme existent, that is, from God. Through all the axiological stages which reflect the actions of human beings, through even the negations of value which hinder this act even while related to it, there remains invincibly manifest the relation of God to his creatures, that is, the being of God and the cortege of transcendental values, which is the hidden presence of the supreme Existent. In this sense, value is the anonymous communicability of God, identical to Him inasmuch as it originated with Him, but different from Him insofar as it is the mediating act of his presence to things other than himself.

As attributes of the divine, value is communicated to others according to their capacity to receive it. As the capacity of the sensible world for God was poor, the reflection of God in the divine, present in this world, could only be poor. However, the divine capacity of human persons for God is quite different being both boundless in its past realization and infinite in its promise for the future. Value fills the gap between the thinking thought and the thought thought, between the willing will and the willed will, just as it steeps persons in their vocation to perfect interrelationship. The divine attributes which we perceive in the anonymous multitude of values can also seek to return in their entirety to God himself who draws every being and the whole being back unto Himself, for the face of God, as the fulfillment of hope, is to be revealed to all existents.[7]

Atheism and Personal Values

In the present state in which the person is incarnate, Power and Glory, Truth and Justice, and all the other ultimate values remain providentially ambiguous. If they are sincere, atheists always set one ultimate value as absolute or unconditioned, be it only Truth. But they cannot reduce the values to being mere determinations of natural being without denying their absolute character and, in so doing, contradicting their own position, for to consider a value as absolute is to recognize that it mysteriously goes beyond its explicit determination. To subordinate oneself unconditionally to a value, to be ready, for example, to sacrifice everything rather than betray truth or justice, is to restore to that value the character of being a divine attribute. More than that, it is affirmation of faith in a living synthesis of the attributes, the substitution of the idol by a glimpse of God, a passage from the divine to God.

This transition is especially remarkable when the value under consideration is interpersonal love, because this love unites Being and the existent in a privileged manner. Charity is the most synthetic in the series of values. It not only dominates and dialectically unifies the entire kingdom of anonymous values, it bridges the gap between the anonymous and the personal orders. It bridges even that between the forms of impersonal (which must not be confused with the anonymous) and personal realities (whose anonymity is either an expressive form or a mundane phase). Love opens a passage between ideas and things, on the one hand, and all consciousness on the other. However, disheartening might have been the original experience of evil, love is the only hope of recovery. As love, God is that point at which the existent opens fully onto being in the personal act par excellence which is eternally simple and can adopt us for eternity.

If value is the veil of the divine attribute and if the passage from the attribute to God is possible, atheism has a positive content inasmuch as it adopts, without knowing it, a theistic perspective. It does this, first, by conforming itself to the unavoidable condition which obliges the believer to see God in the prism of the various attributes. By stressing one of these attributes (which might be at times neglected by the believer), atheists draw one's attention in such a direction that one is preserved from narrow-mindedness or habit. Thus there is a distinctive advantage to—not a confused theology of "the death of God"—but the traditional theology of the "hidden God." What is more, this verifies the thesis of many from St. Anselm to Maurice Blondel that to think is to think God and, consequently, that there are no real atheists, but only idolaters. So concludes the philosophical analysis when it is carried to the very completion of its term.

The unbeliever will perhaps be unhappy to be given this gift by the believer and will ask to be left alone. But the believer could well answer by pointing out that even in its name a-theist expresses a reference to God, and that the affirmation of God is thus prior to its negation. In reality, neither adversary can leave the other alone, for, whether they like it or not, they are indispensable to each other. Destined to meet in human society, they are found together in the heart and mind of each man.

FINAL REMARKS ON THE ARGUMENT OF CAUSALITY

The road to God which we have followed was that of the final cause (or goal). There are possible misinterpretations on the subject.

1. We have not used the notion of cause as it is used ordinarily in the natural sciences, that is, as one phenomenon which is a condition determining another phenomenon (as in the following example: given the position and the speed of a body in motion at moment T-O, what will be that position and that speed at moment T-1?). This much is clear.

2. Nor have we used a principle of causality which we would have first had to describe and justify with its sometimes massive presuppositions and corollaries (as, for example, the affirmation that the effect cannot be superior or equal to its cause, which is only an axiom and of merely limited scope). Our reading of the metaphysical facts shows that the sensible world does not account for the first appearance or the continuation in existence of the person; the interaction of interhuman powers indicates an analogous helplessness; and finally human egos are seen to depend not upon a purely formal and transcendental Ego, but from a divine Thou which gives them their reality and obliges them to affirm it themselves. In this entire progression, we have done nothing more than reflexively analyze experience, locate the different ontic strata, and determine their nature.

3. In the personal order causality explains the origin of

consciousnesses, of which a partial source is found in interpersonal communication and whose total source is found in divine creation. The cause—efficient and final together—does not abandon the effect, nor can the effect be completely cut off from this cause. Rather than the effects being able to be detached from the cause, they are like rays continuous with the cause. The breaks in this continuity are only apparent and its obliteration is only superficial. What is more, the rays are coextensive with the persons they unite and whose images they retain as they manifest them either directly or indirectly. Whether the consciousness begins in a sequence in which one contributes to another, or whether it is found in the creation of a person by God, the consciousnesses tend to become synchronized so that their reciprocal action is rendered immortal. In this sense, to recognize God is to allow oneself to be immortalized by Him and to desire that, if He consents, the response of the creature might even give birth to Him.

1. This approach to the problem of one's body is by way of perception, but it is related to an operational approach. For a less schematic study of this, see the stimulating reflections by A. M. Tymieniecka, "Den Wendepunkt der Phönomenologie entgenen," **Philosophische Rundschau,** XIV (1967), 182-208.

2. One might object that I grasp myself and other persons as persons only by means of the vehicle of sense perception. Though this might be disputed, I will not do so here. I admit without hesitation that, because the human person is incarnate, in order to grasp him one must proceed by way of something non-personal in the sensible order. Nevertheless, I maintain that this detour does not substantially modify the uniqueness of the person and of his intuition. For example, even if the thought **(cogito)** arises from sense knowledge, it immediately discards the alienation which characterizes sensible reality. The physical nature in which we are immerged threatens us with explusion at every instant and affords only the precarious shelter of a mortal life. In descending towards death, however, we think and will in a light which is entirely different from nature. By imposing upon us a new type of reflection, based upon my openness to myself and upon the consequences which flow from this, the very axis of the world is reversed.

3. All of life and of philosophy depends on this uniqueness which we must personally discover and which requires that we treat ourselves as the very object of our thought processes. We are quite conscious of this. When, for example, we love in another his very self rather than simply certain of the particular characteristics he possesses, everything suddenly becomes very serious. Both the other person and we ourselves immediately know this, though we may refuse to admit the consequences which would take us much further than we think.

4. The following pages, 00-00 are drawn from my **Conscience et Logos** (Paris: Editions de l'Epi, 1961), pp. 128-38, by permission of the publisher.

5. To express this new order of things, it would be advisable to use a different vocabulary depending on whether it is a question of worldly being or of personal being: the first is a connection received in the existent or the existents that it concerns, the second is a **relation** that is both received and basically willed by the person or persons.

6. Being personal and interpersonal, they can no longer remain in the world of sense images without shattering it because of its violent contrast with their own exigencies. It is not that persons cannot work in terms of the sensible world even if they feel out of their element there, or that they cannot concentrate on the realm of nature, since the radical univocity of being allows them to enter everything. But the comparison of persons to nature manifests their difference from nature and the comparative poverty, in ontological terms, of the latter. The perpetual threat of bodily death manifests rather than compromising the originality of the person, for it shows that consciousness has no adequate rest home in a world that is for it neither sufficiently broad nor permanent.

7. From the ontological point of view, it would be necessary to expatiate on the following items: 1) The nature of the primordial connection or relation of each existent with itself and with the other existents. 2) The metaphysical status of being with regard to the uncreated Existent and the created existents. 3) The metaphysical status of being with regard to the surrounding ultimate values. 4) The bond of being with the Logos as mediator. 5) The way which being can be conceived as an aspect of the "we." This aspect begins in the reflection upon sensible data since this reflection cannot be severed from the personal order in which it must be explicitly acknowledged to lie, achieving itself in God. 6) Lastly, condition of existents.

Ontology of Mystery and Ontology of Covenant: Phenomenology As Directing the Mind to A Divine

◇

by
Moshe Schwarcz

IN THE VAST contemporary literature on existential philosophies, very few allusions have been made to two great literary and philosophical phenomena of our time: the first is the thought of Gabriel Marcel, the Christian, and the second is that of Martin Buber, the Jewish Existentialist. There are striking similarities between them not only in the inner structure and texture of their thought and their literary temper, but also in the way they react to the historical events of our age. Both represent a certain type of philosophy of faith as a response to the disastrous outcomes of the scientific-systematic oriented western culture.

In their philosophical endeavor, both Marcel and Buber pave the way toward a dimension that might be conceived only in its dynamic, as transcending the static and abstract realm of objects. The source of this dynamic is the Absolute Being or a Divine, designated as the Eternal Thou, who moves and motivates the abundant and inexhaustible concreteness of being.

Both agree that the way of knowledge that leads us to the ultimate source of being is not a kind of "theory of knowledge," since the mind cannot objectively define the structure of reality (Marcel). The way to the source of being lies rather in a certain intuitively experienced and creatively performed "participation"

[211]

or co-presence, which realizes its concrete determination in such anthropological "existentiale" as love, hope, and fidelity.

Nevertheless, these basic structural similarities should not prevent us from detecting some principal differences in their pattern of thought. These result partly from their specific philosophical heritage and problem-situation and partly from their respectively permeating spiritual-religious environment.[1]

With regard to the former aspect, the pheonomenological procedure and thomistic-scholasticism were two decisive factors in Marcel's thought. Buber, on the other hand, presents a dialogical philosophy which follows the thought-patterns of the Bible, Jewish mysticism, and Chasidism. Thus, the outcry for concreteness and for really lived experiences, so strongly heard in these two thinkers, has found its metaphysical echoes in Marcel's "Ontology of Mystery." Here the mysterious source of being appears to be an encompassing pneumatic power or *ens realissimum,* though not in the scholastic sense. The same echoes are found in Buber's "Ontology of Meeting," or personalistic encounter, wherein the testimony of the *covenant* between God and Man functions as the sign of a "nominalistic" or dialogical ontology. In short, whereas, despite his sharp critique of the western philosophical tradition, Marcel still stands in the mainstream of the metaphysical contemplation of *being qua being,* Buber prefers to go along the "narrow ridge" of the undisclosed certainty of meeting, that is not expressible in any metaphysical terms. That this difference is a crucial point in the philosophies of Marcel and Buber will be exemplified by the problematics of philosophy and religion in this paper.

MARTIN BUBER: A PHILOSOPHY OF CO-VENANT

Faith and Philosophy

One point, which is basic in Buber's philosophy of religion and expressed emphatically in his lecture on religion and philosophy,[2] is that the elucidation of the relationship between religion and philosophy is not attainable by mutual delimitation.

In that approach religion would find meaning when philosophy has already accomplished its work, or vice verse. However, it is unacceptable to base a philosophy of religion on the assumption of an intrinsic or essential kinship of this type between religion and philosophy, as did Hegel, for initially it denies any approach whereby the intelligible aspect of faith is stressed. What is required from a philosopher is not *delimitation,* conditioned by the affirmation that religion and philosophy are two bordering aspects of one and the same surface, but *determination* on the basis of their unique characteristics.

This methodological remark, made by Buber in a lecture which forms the early version of "Eclipse of God," opens the way to a scrutiny of the relationship between Buber and Marcel. Being "theistic" existentialists, both wish to determine, on the basis of really lived and concrete experiences, the very nature of religious belief. They endow belief with the intrinsic power of the revival of the genuine spiritual sources of mankind and bring back "religiousness" from petrified and external manifestations to the actual and concrete experiences, which underlie any religious manifestations. However, the ways in which Buber and Marcel do this differ in their reflective or meditative concomitants.

In the "Conclusion" of his most systematized book, *Mystery of Being,* Marcel writes:

> We must emphasize the *intelligible aspect of faith;* and in doing so, we shall be obliged to diverge very considerably from the views both of the Danish philosopher and even perhaps of the writer in whom we may well be inclined to see his precursor—I mean Pascal; for there is a connection which binds together faith and the spirit of truth.[3]

This binding connection between faith and (philosophical) truth is assumed by Marcel to be in strictest opposition to Kierkegaard and his theology of the paradox. In addition, it is in rather sharp contrast to the scholastic interpretation of this linkage.

Buber, on the other hand, though opposing Kierkegaard on

many points such as the suspension of the ethical, remains close to him in his suspension of the "onto-logical" as a way of thinking or an aim of understanding. Buber goes beyond Kierkegaard by eliminating the sharply pointed reminder of the "meditative" content, which is implicitly expressed in Kierkegaard's paradox. Faith, according to Buber, is not being against reason but beyond reason; it is a completely new and independent determination, which cannot be conceived even by means of some meta-ontological concepts.

Instead of the ontological approach to Being, which centers upon the "meditative movement" of reflexion, called by Marcel "second reflexion," Buber emphasizes the "evocative movement" based on the primacy of the practical.[4] In this shift from the meditative to the evocative, Buber follows the footsteps of many modern Jewish philosophers who emphatically deny the "concordance between metaphysics and religion," and stress the primacy of the ethical in religion. Such philosophers would include L. Steinheim in the 19th century and H. Cohen in the 20th century. They were guided, as was Buber, by the idea of monotheism, which becomes most problematic in the light of the ontological tradition of western philosophy.

Nominalism and a Concrete Philosophy of God

Buber's critical approach to the western philosophical heritage has been brought to the surface most clearly by his reference to the medieval scholastic dispute regarding the so-called *Universals*. Buber looked upon this struggle not merely as one of the central events of the "Christian philosophy," but also as the expression of the essence of philosophy and of the struggle between religion and philosophy. "The central event of Christian philosophy, the scholastic dispute over the reality or unreality of universals, was in essence a philosophical struggle between religion and philosophy and that is its lasting significance."[5]

The nominalistic standpoint, which ascribes reality only to the concrete particulars and not to the universals, is basically identical to the religious viewpoint. The realist standpoint, which ascribes reality only to the universals or essences, conveys the genuine philosophical outlook upon reality. Buber's point is that western philosophy, from its very beginning in Greece until its most recent representatives in modern thinking, is distinguished by one basic characteristic defined as the universal-eidetic insight into the realm of things.

This philosophical attitude is a perennial attempt to evade the "pre-philosophical" situation in which the mind was habituated to concrete human situations. The very nature of reasoning, in the form conveyed by the Greeks, is seen in the objectification or "opticizing" of reality, whereby the human mind relates to being in much the same purely neutral way it relates to scenery. Thus in its historical significance, the way of knowledge points to an ontological structure that cannot be primordial. Therein we detect and follow the effort of the human mind to conceive the world as an object *(Gegenstand)* and to isolate the mind as a conceiving subject from the world. This is exemplified in the history of western philosophy which traces the development from a strictly objective way of perceiving the realm of things (in Greece), through the subjective validation of the realm of objects (Descartes-Kant), to the total denial of any "absolutum" (Nietzsche, Sartre). In so doing this history manifests itself as a direct offspring of the realistic approach of the western philosophy.[6]

Buber sees in the philosophic "realism" the clue for the misunderstanding of the genuine religious experiences and, primarily, of God's Being or Nature. Within the realm of so-called philosophical ontology God must be conceived in abstract and universal terms. "Philosophy is grounded on the presupposition that one sees the absolute in universals."[7] For Buber, this means the voluntary expulsion of man from the original "grasping of God." Thus, he relates this tragic phenomenon of the "Eclipse of God" in the modern mind to the platonic-eidetic approach which has dominated the western philosophical mind since its dawn in Greek philosophy.

For this reason, the critique of nominalism against realism in medieval philosophy is highly appreciated by Buber because it gave expression to a philosophical protest against the dominion of the traditional ontological approach. He saw it as a necessary step toward overcoming the intellectual obstacle which barred the way to a genuine understanding and determination of religion. Buber went one step further by saying that, in opposition to philosophy, when religion "has to define itself philosophically" it can do so as "the covenant of the absolute with the particular, with the concrete."[8]

The importance of the above-noted "philosophical" definition of religion is in the equation of the biblical notion of the covenant with a "concrete philosophy," identified by Buber with the "covenant of the absolute with the particular." As F. Kaufmann put it correctly, the specific function of the "covenant" is that of "a bond that unites, not a bond that fetters its members in the syndesmos of being; neither absolute dependence of man nor a limitation of the sovereignty of God."[9] Thus the notion of the covenant suggests the idea that religion in its purest manifestation might give support only to such an ontological position, through which the absolute and the concrete respectively maintain their real uniqueness.

According to Buber, the very essence of the Jewish monotheistic-religion is conveyed by the unconditional realization of an encounter between God and Man as "two actual beings." According to his characterization of the genuine meaning of the biblical faith, Buber sees in the "God of Israel" an ontologically unqualifiable Being.

> What is meant by religion is not the massive fullness of statements, concepts and activities that one customarily describes by this name . . . Religion is essentially the *act of holding fast to God*. And that does not mean holding fast to an image that one has made of God, nor even holding fast to the faith in God that one has conceived. It *means holding fast to the existing God*.[10]

This passage emphasizes with utmost clarity the Buberian idea of religiousness: since God as an existant Being is pure actuality or unrestricted presence, religion means the "act of holding tast to God," that is to say, a meeting with God not as a specific "content," but as a "Presence as power."[11]

The Specific "Content" of God's Revelation to Man

The elimination of the meditative factor as a primary aspect of revelation raises the question of the medium of the human being in which Buber's nominalistic ontology might be anchored. A basic and characteristic feature of Buber's "religious nominalism" is his treatment of the *transition* from the reflective—meditative inquiry in ontology to the dialogical one. He is one of the eminent leaders of dialogical philosophy or, as Rosenzweig called it, *Sprachdenken*. The basic contention of this current in modern thought is that speech is an inter-mediary reality, a realm of "*Zwischen*" or relations. As Buber put it in his short essay "The Word that is Spoken," the very nature of speech is its capacity of addressing man and of grasping him to make him a partner. "Language never existed before address: it could become monologue only after dialogue broke off or broke down."[12]

One should distinguish between language as the objectified layers of genuine speech and language as the spoken word, which does not dilute the actuality of speech calling to and being called by a fellow-man. Only the latter can be stated as the primary word I-Thou; the former is the form of I-It and the language of "thinghood" rather than of real relationship.[13]

Nevertheless, Buber accepts speech as the true signum of reality not because of its representational nature, but for its evocative power as the purest, though not the only, means of stating and testifying the relational characteristics of Being. It is the acme of a universal and all inclusive relationship which is the only principle of reality. Speech is therefore the most successful "metaphor" that might be found in order to realize the evocative quality of reality.

Yet, reality cannot be completely "represented" in language. The world of relations pervades three distinct spheres: our life with nature; our life with men; and our life with spiritual beings.[14] A relationship can be considered explicit in language only in our life with human beings, though mutual relatedness still is present in our life with nature at a lower level, and with spiritual beings in art and religion at a higher level. Nevertheless, mutuality does not occur at the level of meditative-reflective thinking.

The crucial difference between Marcel and Buber at this point is revealing. According to Marcel there exists a dialogical situation in the intellectual activity of the soul, meaning the recollections of the unlimited scope of Being by the "vitalized" form of reflexion or the *pensee pensante*.[15] Buber, on the contrary, emphasizes the phenomenon of encounter as inclusive in regard to all aspects of life, except the meditative-reflective.

As we shall see later, Marcel argues that Buber "denaturizes" speech by making it the "ideogram" of reality, because the very essence of language is to effect the transformation of Thou to thinghood.[16] This claim that Buber "denaturizes" Being by the means of language would be justified only if he had designated Being in positive ontological terms. But, as has been pointed out above, Buber's intention was to neglect the ontological approach even within the Marcellian frame of reference of an ontology of mystery. The claim that Buber "denaturizes" speech is no more correct than the opposite argument which criticizes Buber for making language merely a medium, a means of real encounter, a sign which even in its purest realization points to a genuine *"Be-gegnung"* or, to speak theologically, to the Eternal-unfathomable-Thou.[17] This contention that he makes language only a symbol *(Zeichen)* and not an authentic body of religious knowledge would be valid only if Buber had accepted the idea that meaning is inherent in the meditative or cognitive aspect of Being. In fact, this was denied explicitly by Buber:

> The religious *essence* in every religion can be found in its highest *certainty*. That is the certainty that the meaning of existence is open and accessible in the actual lived concrete, not above the struggle with reality but in it. . . . *Meaning* is to be experienced in living *action* and suffering itself, in the unreduced immediacy of the moment. Of course, he who aims

at the experiencing of experience will necessarily miss the meaning, for he destroys the spontaneity of the mystery.[18]

Together with the rationalistic inquiry into the nature of being, Buber denies any theory of meaning which identifies the meaning of religion with the realm of essences. Revelation, or reality qua co-venance, requires a new approach to meaning, whereby adequacy is no longer understood as *adequatio rei et intellectus,* but as certainty or authenticity of the "living action."

Language as "spoken word" or as a "primary-act" *(Ur-akt),* through which "revelation" or the "pure form of meeting" gains any reliable standing, is the steadfast approval of the "religious essence." The meaning of the genuine religious experience is expressed with unsurpassable clarity in the reply of the people of Israel on Sinai: "We will do it, we will hear it."[19] Buber explains this biblical verse, which stands at the very core of the covenant, as the replacement of the descriptive religious utterance by the evocative attitude of real engagement. "The meaning is found through the engagement of one's own person; it only reveals itself as one takes part in its revelation."[20]

We may conclude then that in his "Ontology of Co-venant" Buber looks upon the human Being as directed to a Divine by giving decisive importance to the directing act as the only constitutive factor of meaning and value. Ultimately, every genuine relationship within the realm of human existence is a concrete and unique testimony for the convenant that exists between the absolute and the particular, between God and Man. One cannot grasp anything beyond the immediate experience of the act of meeting, unless he falls back to a reflecting attitude, which might only be the afterthought (absence) of the presence. With regard to this dilemma Marcel's "Ontology of Mystery" represents a unique, though different philosophical standpoint.

GABRIEL MARCEL AND THE PRESENCE OF GOD

Presence vs Dialogic

Marcel's attitude toward Buber's dialogical philosophy is clearly and explicitly stated in his essay on Buber, "I and Thou."[21] In reading the controversy between Marcel and Buber, one might easily be convinced that both have left behind what makes their philosophies basically distinct in order to stress some similarities and dissimilarities within the limits of their common approach to philosophy. Marcel touches on certain weak points in Buber's teaching in a way that reflects his own philosophical point of view, his Ontology of Mystery, which is doubtfully applicable to Buber's Ontology of Covenant. In his reply to Marcel, Buber does not detect clearly enough the hidden assumptions of his critical remarks. My purpose here is to point out, rather roughly the underlying assumptions of these important polemics.

Marcel claims:

> To be sure, the fundamental intuition of Buber remains to my mind absolutely correct. But the whole question is to know how it *can be translated into discourse without being denatured*. It is this transposition which raises the most serious difficulties and therein probably lies the fundamental reason why the discovery of Feuerbach recalled by Buber remained so long without fruit.[22]

The fundamental intuition, which seems both to Marcel and to Buber to be absolutely correct is the consideration of the Thou as the ultimate principle of Being. This is the source of their common pursuit of rescue from "either the impasse of an individualism which considers man solely in reference to himself or the other impasse of a collectivism which has eyes only for society."[23]

Like Buber, Marcel has seen the realm of Thou as a unique dimension of Being, by which it is realized as "presence." Both have emphasized that the starting point of any spiritual approach to being should be the acknowledgment of a certain fullness of life that

> "can in no circumstances be that of my own personal experience considered in an exclusively private aspect, considered

inasmuch as it is *just mine;* rather must it be that of a whole which is implied by the relation to the *with,* by the togetherness."[24]

Marcel and Buber equally share the conviction of a "primitive assurance" or certainty of the presence of being that might be revealed in its purity only in every lived experience here and now. This immediate realization of presence infinitely transcends all possible verification "because it exists in an immediacy beyond all conceivable mediation."[25]

The question has been raised by Marcel, however, as to whether the transposition of this genuine intuition into discourse or dialogical terms does not affect the "denaturizing" of Being. On this very basic point Marcel considers himself as not following Buber.

It is necessary to keep in mind that Marcel, by speaking of "denaturizing," indicates the detachment from reality as such by means of a quasi "simulacrum," that is, a picture which represents an already fixed object in concepts or brings about the very fixation of reality, as we find in any discourse. In order to qualify this primary relationship in the realm of being, Marcel uses the notion of "appresentation" coined by Heidegger. "It is a necessary condition of all appresentation that the appresenting being should be placed in the middle of a light that will allow something to appear to that being to be made manifest to it."[26] This focal point, which throws light upon being, is not "the word that is spoken" but the "spirit of truth" or the all-inclusive pneumatic nature which underlies every possible relationship.

At this point we must clarify the meaning of the "spirit of truth" in Marcel's philosophy. It cannot be identified with any objectifiable truth, since therein being is converted into object and the immediate relation to being is lost. For the same reason it cannot be identical with language, as happened to be the case in such dialogical philosophies as those of F. Rosenzweig, F. Ebner, and M. Buber. "Human speech, as Bergson perceived with his usual depth of vision, is naturally adapted to the statement of spatial relationships, which are relationships, fundamentally, of mere juxtaposition. And that very sentence, indeed, illustrates this inadequacy of language to the truths of the inner life."[27] Thus Marcel stands far from the current of dialogical philosophy.

The spirit of truth is revealed only by means of the immediate presentation of "the inner life," which "can be reinstated only when the speech impulse has been driven, or drawn, downwards[28] In a more positive manner, Marcel phrases his intention by saying "I address the second person when what I address can respond to me in some way—*and that response cannot be translated into words.* The purest form of invocation— prayer— embodied imperfectly in the uttered word, is a certain kind of inner transfiguration, a mystery influx, an ineffable peace."[29]

Hence the spirit of truth, by transcending dialogics, reveals the realm of intersubjectivity through which real encounter is possible. "To encounter someone is not merely to cross his path but to be, for the moment at least, *near* to or with him."[30]

Incarnation

In order to understand what this "nearness" really means for Marcel it is important to turn to a uniquely Marcellian category of Ontology, the notion of "incarnation". Though this category is not necessarily bound up with the Christian dogma of "re-incarnation," there is no category that might point out more clearly than this the basic difference between Buber and Marcel, in spite of their common insight or intuition into the co-presence or co-esse. This central notion, which appeared in Marcel's philosophy in various connotations, bears as its broadest meaning the idea that "A blindfold knowledge of Being in general is implied in all particular knowledge."[31] One cannot relate in a meaningful way to any particular being without being conditioned by being itself. "Incarnation—the central 'given' of metaphysics: Incarnation is the situation of a being who appears to himself, as it were, *bound* to a body. This 'given' is opaque to itself: opposition to the *cogito*."[32]

The notion of "ex-sistence" already and expressly includes the "centrifugal" tendency of the human being. "I exist, I certainly mean something more than this; I vaguely imply that I am not only for myself but I manifest myself, or rather am manifested. . . . I exist: that means I have something by which I can be known or identified."[33]

The immediate manifestation of my existence is my unique co-essence with my body. Between my body and Me there is neither separation, nor fusion, nor relation, but an unobjectifiable participation. At this stage the idea of incarnation is the experience of Spirit as being in an undissoluble way connected with body. Descartes' supposed distinction between body and mind destroys the vitality of the mind and its power to know reality. However, the broader sense of being qua incarnation points beyond to my "present existence" as an "existential orbit" or a "magnetic field" to which an "infinite variety of anything I can think of as existing" is related.[34]

Therefore, the more I am aware of my presence the more I am an existing being. There is a strict reciprocity between the two. By the existent, as by "my body," I mean that a long chain of spatial, temporal, and spatio-temporal relations are compressed by imagination to the point where they become co-present with me.[35]

Co-presence understood as "incarnate being" in the above-mentioned meaning is no longer a strictly relational term. Its very meaning is participation, understood as the immanent ontic cause for every possible relationship. Accordingly, "to communicate" could not mean primarily to hold dialogue or to converse, for participation "means that the other person ceases to be for me someone with whom I converse, he ceases to intervene between me and myself; this self with whom I had coalesced in order to observe and judge him, while yet remaining separate, has fused into the living unity he now forms with me."[36]

This clarifies the first critical point made by Marcel against Buber in the earlier passage: the intuition of the presence cannot be translated into discourse without being "denatured." Even in its dialogical patterns, language is to some extent an alienating factor, a means of separating me from myself and from my fellow men, who belong to my "existential orbit" not less than myself. If nature is conceived in Marcel's philosophy as "as world in which everything is in communication, in which everything is bound together"[37] in a living unity, language must objectify this unity in a specific form. To put it in another way: if Marcel's starting point is "a certain fullness of life,"[38] then language itself must be understood as transforming the Thou into an It. Buber's answer to Marcel, that "if I really say 'Thou', then I as little mean by it a thing as when I say 'I' to myself,"[39] is not at all relevant to the polemics. Since the basic question is whether, by addressing the "Thou" or by being addressed by him, I am engaged primarily in an intersubjective nexus rooted in an intelligible milieu, or am ontologically in an absolute and un-motivated position. At this point there seems to be an uncompromisable difference between Ontology of Co-venant and Ontology of Mystery. Whereas in the Ontology of Co-venant, "human life and humanity come into being in genuine meetings,"[40] in the Ontology of Mystery the genuine meeting is the outward realization of Being.

Marcel makes their different approaches more clear in his next criticism of Buber's philosophy of relation.

Man's Relation to God

Marcel's next contention against Buber is that *"Beziehung"* or encounter between one subject and another must be conditioned by a primordial ontic unity which makes possible any inter-relationship of different terms. "In the beginning is a certain felt unity which becomes progressively articulated so as to make room for an ensemble involving interrelated terms."[41] Marcel denies Buber's principle that "In the beginning was the relation." This can also be put in another way: Although phenomenologically Marcel emphasizes encounter or meeting in a seemingly Buberian sense, ontologically Marcel strives to reach the inner kernel that makes any committed behavior meaningful. The phenomenological procedure in Marcel's philosophy is not only bound to the on-tological goal of realizing the mysterious source of being, but is also "regulated" by that mysterious reality. ". . . the more we are able *to know* the individual being, the more we shall be oriented, and as it were directed towards a grasp of being as such."[42]

In this Marcellian insight into the problem of being can be found the explanation of the so-called "ontological exigence" or "need for Transcendence." The term is totally unfit for the context of Buber's philosophy. In his "Autobiography" Marcel describes the specific character of his ontological approach by saying: "My effort can be best described as an attempt to establish a concept which precludes all equation of *being* with *Ding* (thing) while *upholding the ontological* without going back to the category of substance, which I regarded with profound mistrust."[43]

Marcel is not less critical of any ontology of *"Ding"* than Buber, for according to Marcel a *Ding* is a petrified form of a vivid experience, a short-cut of a lived reality. We are accustomed to think of experience as "a sort of given, more or less shapeless substance,"[44] but genuine human experience is not an "object" *(Gegen-stand)* or an obstacle which is placed before me, facing me and blocking my way, in such a way that I can in a pure mental act of understanding overcome or solve it. Only if I limit the whole realm of experience to the narrow and ever fixed plan of the "problematic" might being be identified with thinghood.

Marcel does not uphold the ontological position in behalf of traditional ontology. His intention is to reform metaphysics by considering Being "as the principle of inexhaustibility,"[45] that is, he intends "to restore its ontological weight to human experience."[46]

Being is no longer conceived as a closed system, but as self-transcending experience, that is to say, a concrete experience which brings man to "the heart" of his existence.

The heart of my existence is what is at the center of what we might also call my vital interests; it is that by which I live, and which, moreover, is usually not an object of clear awareness of me. The community between *Thou* and *Me,* or the co-belonging, is the more real, the more essential, *the closer it is to this heart.*"[47]

In opposition to Buber, the community between I and Thou is not an exclusive creation of the "meeting" or a strictly unconditional encounter between two partners. It is an instantaneously revealed "co-belonging to the same history,"[48] or the bearing of the same destiny of *"homo viator"*—the wayfarer.

Marcel gives the following concrete example. The stranger seated beside me in the train or in the restaurant to whom I say nothing does not belong to my history. The fact that we eat the same food is not enough to create a community among us. But an unexpected stop of the train which threatens to have existential consequences for both of us might be enough to give birth to this community.[49]

This example proves that "community" is conditioned by our engagement "in a certain adventure," though in order to experience it we have to free ourselves from our "egocentric topography" and from our "habitual perspectives."[50]

Thus the "need for Transcendence" reflects "our condition in this world" to "remain a wanderer, an itinerant being, who cannot come to absolute rest except by a fiction."[51] Science and the whole ontological and theological tradition based on the static and objectified category of substance helped us to create the fiction of "thinghood," and thus to reject the supernatural power. Therein historical man *(homo historicus)* became natural man *(homo naturalis).*[52]

The duty of philosophic reflection is to oppose with all its strength the fiction of taking experience for granted and to devote itself "to the production of currents whereby life can be reborn in regions of mind which have yielded to apathy and are exposed to decomposition."[53]

Transcendence vs Immanence

In Marcel's essay on Buber there is a brief statement of the advance gained by the progressive articulation of "felt unity" into "interrelated terms." "This transformation, indeed, will not take place without incurring an impoverishment or kind of drying up of the realm of experience. But that is only the inevitable price of a major advance. That advance makes of the realm of experience a place in which verification becomes possible and in which the very word "truth" acquires a meaning, whereas at the level of felt unity it had none."[54]

The quoted passage stresses once more, in a very condensed form, a basic difference between Marcel and Buber which has multiple implications in their respective philosophies. At this point the distinction of "first reflection" and "second reflection," also called by Marcel *pensee pensante* and *pensee pensee*, is most relevant. The distinction clearly manifests how remote Marcel is from Buber's view of ontological meaning and verification.

In Marcel's philosophy the above destruction fills up the dimension of the meta-problematic, that is, the intermediary layer between the objective problematic or the realm of Having and the metaphysical problematic or the realm of Being. Buber thinks in dichotomic terms: I-Thou and I-It are two "primary words" which are not inter-connected. Marcel's thought is triadic: between the realm of It (Having) and the realm of Thou (Being) there is a third realm of concrete-metaphysical experience, which first makes possible the "ascension" from "pure having" to "real being." The whole scope of this ascending dialectic is rooted in the idea of "ontological mystery." To Marcel this means that ultimately only "the Mysterious and the Ontological are identical,"[55] and that assumed identity affects the ascending dynamic of existence. The Mysterious does not deprive the Ontological of its intelligibility, but it does make "knowledge" to be "environed by being."[56]

In the Ontology of Mystery the primacy of being over knowledge is postulated not by removing knowledge from itself, but by making knowledge to be "involved" in Being. Therefore, says Marcel, "A mystery . . . is something in which I find myself caught up," having as "its essential part that it should be acknowledged."[57]

Thus Being, the ultimate source of experience and "concreteness," becomes per se the primary ground *(Ur-Grund)* of knowledge. "A mystery is a problem which encroaches upon its own data, invading them, as it were, and thereby transcending itself as a simple problem."[58] "Knowledge is contingent on a participation in being."[59] The realm of knowledge and the realm of Being are not so disparate that transition from the former to the latter is impossible. In this context, Marcel's positive approach to the "intelligible aspect of faith," mentioned at the beginning of our discussion, becomes meaningful.

Obviously, knowledge cannot be identified with any absolutized knowledge or rational philosophy which might be objectively verifiable. The realm of experience, wherein verification becomes possible by means of "definition" or "objective determination," merely brings about a disintegration of reality and, thus, affects only despair and misery. "First reflection" illegitimately transcends reality through breaking its spontaneous and creatively integrating unity into distinct and intentionally interconnected terms (subject-object). The objectively performed way of thinking by the means of concept and conscious formations cannot realize the primary unity that exists between life and thought, creativity and clarity, spontaneity and reflection.

In this light there appears the importance of "second reflection." Faith is guided by the "blindfold" faculty of the original intuition *(intuitus originarius)*. This notion is from Kant's *Critique of Judgment*, but the immediate influence upon Marcel seemingly is that of Schelling's "intellectual intuition" *(Intellectuelle Anschaung)*. Faith enables us to materialize the immanent unity of Being. Second reflection relates to the first by eliminating the various antinomies that are put before us in the very procedure of objectified thinking. In the *Journal Metaphysique* Marcel spoke of faith as an act through which the "spirit fills up the gap between the knowing and the empirical Me *(moi)* by affirming their transcendent conection."[60]

Spirit is not identical with reflection or with any thinking faculty, but is its inner ground. Both the first and second procedure of reflection are kept together in an ascending dialectic by the all-embracing spirit. That pneumatic inclusiveness provides that "every reflection (at least potentially) is a reflection upon it; that reflection is at the same time any particular moment together with the power of transcending that moment whatsoever."[61]

The transcending power of the second reflection makes the very procedure of knowledge a mirror of the inexhaustible reality. In reference to the objective knowledge of first reflection it might be said that by the means of reflection reflection is "suspended," or rather "sub-jected." "Such a reflection of the second degree or power, whose object is another original reflection, is to my mind synonymous with philosophy itself viewed as an effort to restore the concrete beyond the disconnected and discontinuous determinations of abstract thought."[62] "Metaphysical thought (is) reflection trained on mystery."[63]

This expresses the inner connection between metaphysics and faith. Faith is not an intelligible, that is, unreflective act, but the utmost realization or actualization of intelligibility. Obviously one cannot conceive it as fidelity to some objectified doctrines of any traditional religion. It must be identified with a "living" and "dedoctrinizing" factor, "creative fidelity" which provides to "interrelated terms" the extent of flexibility that is required by the genuine "ontological order."

The whole scope of knowledge has to be conceived as awareness of the self-transcending articulation of Being. Phenomenologically this is the reflective procedure of verification, while ontologically it is the "self-judgment" of Being and the attestation of Spirit.

The highest value of the metaphysical knowledge is concretized at its best in the human existentiale of fidelity which was interpreted by Marcel as "the faithful following, through darkness of a light by which we have been guided and which is no longer visible to us directly."[64]

Thus we may conclude that the Mind, being directed to a Divine, is the self-realization *(Ens manifestum Sui)* of the Divine. This final remark points to what would seem to be the greatest difference between Marcel and Buber. To Marcel the genuine relationship or Encounter between human beings which is expressed in love and, at a higher level, in fidelity is sustained by the all-inclusive Immanence of the Divine. The definition of God by Marcel and by Buber as "the Absolute Thou who never can become It"[65] is not intended to stress the transcendence of God as the "wholly other." Rather it qualifies Being, as such, as the intrinsic power which makes the realm of experience transcend itself in a procedure of recollecting the lost actuality and creativity of Being within the objectified world.

The "inter-subjective nexus" realizes the procedure of re-union, and thus suspends itself through resolving into the realm of genuine Being. In other words, the realm of Thou or of relatedness is the means for experiencing the realness of Being. No other way exists to reveal the plentitude of concrete life apart from the I-Thou nexus, since in opposition to abstract-logical thinking there is in the inter-subjective nexus an immediate participation in the concrete, personal reality. If for Buber language replaced reflection, or "theoria" through its evocative capacity, for Marcel there is a double theoretical function in each genuine "dialogical" attitude. On the one hand, in regard to the logical form of thinking, it becomes meta-problematic. In objective intentionality transcendence was structural and logical. Here in meta-problematical relatedness it becomes evident that the true meaning of the self-transcendence in thinking is striving toward otherness. On the other hand, "theoria" on the highest level is attained through the metaphysical insight that the "metaproblematic is the mysterious" and ultimately transcendent source of both thinking and being.

Buber wishes explicitly to eliminate the cognitive-theoretical element from the realm of Encounter. In the act of meeting the personalistic real uniqueness of the "interrelated terms" is not resolved either in the *"Ur-grund"* of Being or in the *"Ur-grund"* of Thought. Both Thought and Being are transcended in the uncontingent act of meeting in true revelation.

The religious ideal of covenant *(B'rith)* implies according to Buber, the radical denial of any type of mystical unity *(Unio Mystica)*, by replacing "theoria" or the dimension of Thought by the ethical and practical realization of Being.

Faith is an attitude toward and a struggle for the truth, that is, the correlate of an authentically lived life. I commit myself to the Thou not because of the "nearness" or "substantial" together-ness of ourselves but for being the absolute other. In short, in Buber the ontological realm is identical with the I-Thou relation and not vice versa as in Marcel. With Schelling we could phrase that difference as follows: while for Buber the eminent ontological order is the all-inclusive transcendence, for Marcel it is "tran-scendence transformed into the immanent" *(das immanent gemachte Transcendente)*.[66]

Paradox vs Equilibrium

In the final passage in his Essay, "I and Thou," Marcel pays tribute to Buber in the name of a "living equilibrium" that exists between "reason" and "revelation," not only in his own, but also in Buber's thought. Obviously Marcel has interpreted Buber's philosophy in the spirit of his own teaching. At least, with regard to the principal question of the relationship be-tween philosophy and religion, Marcel assumes that Buber in-clines to favor a "living equilibrium" by which "man is nourished at eternal sources."[67]

We have emphasized our serious hesitation concerning any attempt to assign to Buber a method of correlation or councili-ation between philosophy and religion, even if philosophy is conceived not in its narrow scholastic meaning of objectified thinking, but in the genuine Marcellian meaning of "reflection trained on Mystery." In his own frame of reference, by assuming determination instead of delimitation as the only legitimate method of religious knowledge, Buber has underlined a position that is paradoxical, instead of being the quasi "living equilibrium" of religion and reason. Therefore, faith cannot be characterized to any extent as "second reflection."

In setting up his nominalistic ontology and the ontology of

covenant, Buber removes the philosophical dimension of "Ground of Being" or "Being as such" understood as the pure actuality of concrete existence. At this point he stays far away from Marcel's Ontology of Mystery, P. Tillich's Ontology of *New Being*[68] and F. Rosenzweig's Dialogical Ontology.

In this context, we wish to make an incidental historical philosophical remark. It is a striking fact that Marcel, Tillich, and the Jewish philosopher, F. Rosenzweig, all of whom were under the direct influence of Schelling, are outstanding representatives of a kind of "Positive-Philosophie" whereby new methods of reflection were thought of in behalf of the mutual validation of philosophy and religion. These thinkers identified this reflective method with faith or "religious knowledge" since all of them accepted in principle the intelligibility of faith.

Among these three philosophers only Rosenzweig has related faith to language, assuming the uniqueness of language in bringing about the new orientation which is founded by revelation. By reliance upon language as the very core of religious knowledge Rosenzweig has confirmed the binding connection between faith, as revealed also in the Judaic-Christian concept of the Covenant, and philosophy. He is distinguished among the new followers of Schelling by remaining free from the assumption of an all-inclusive pneumatic unision as the inner ground of the possibility of correlation. God-Man-World are three unique "elements" of Being which became "united" in "correlated terms."

The relationship between Marcel and traditional Christianity became subject to divergent opinions just as Buber became a controversial figure among Jews. Marcel has admitted that he could not have formulated his theoretical categories apart from Christian influence, contending that "We cannot reason . . . as though there were not behind us centuries of Christianity."[69] The same can be said of Buber; he might not have to reason as though there were not behind him long generations of Judaic tradition.

Being a *homo historicus,* and thus being attracted by their respectively unique "existential orbit," both have reacted upon the intellectual and moralistic deficiency of their time by a revival of an ontological attitude inspired by their "intelligible milieu." The Ontology of Mystery of Marcel, which according to his own statement was shaped within "para-Christian zones,"[70] proves that it has been affected also by the unconscious radiation of Christian revelation. Therefore, Marcel's Ontology was intended to point out that, although revelation is not conceivable unless it is addressed to a being who is involved or committed, the very possibility of this commitment is based on the idea that "Supernatural life must . . . find a hold *in* the natural."

Buber's Ontology of Covenant, though formed systematically in "para-Judaic zones," attests to its immanent connection with Judaism by assuming the possibility of involvement on the basis that the supernatural must find a hold not *in* but *with* the natural.

◇

1. Marcel denounced "religious Esperantism," saying that "the subject of faith cannot be treated as a modality of thought in general." See G. Marcel, **The Philosophy of Existentialism** (New York: Citadel Press, 1961), p. 120.

2. Delivered at the Annual Meeting of the Schopenhauer Association. See **Jahrbuch der Schopenhauer Gesellschaft für das Jahr 1929**, p. 220.

3. G. Marcel, **The Mystery of Being** (London: Harvil Press, 1951), II, pp. 198-99.

4. See F. Kaufmann, "Buber's Philosophy of Religion," in **The Philosophy of Martin Buber**, ed. Paul A. Schilpp (Library of Living Philosophers; LaSalle, Ill.: Open Court, 1967), p. 214.

5. M. Buber **Eclipse of God,** (New York: Harper, 1962), p. 41.

6. **Ibid.**

7. **Ibid.**

8. **Ibid.**

9. **The Philosophy of Martin Buber,** ed. Schilpp, p. 229.

10. Buber, **Eclipse of God,** p. 123.

11. M. Buber, **I and Thou** (New York: Scribner, 1958), p. 110.

12. M. Buber, **The Way of Response,** ed. N. N. Glatzer (New York: Schocken, 1966), p. 103.

13. Buber, **I and Thou,** p. 6.

14. **Ibid.**

15. "Encounters can also occur on the level of thought." See G. Marcel, **Creative Fidelity** (New York: Farrar, Straus, 1964), pp. 12-13.

16. G. Marcel, "I and Thou," in **The Philosophy of Martin Buber**, p. 44.

17. See Casper Bernhard, **Das dialogische Denken** (Freiburg: Herder, 1967), p. 301.

18. Buber, **Eclipse of God**, p. 35. The italics in the quoted passage are mine.

19. Deut 5:24.

20. Buber, **Eclipse of God**, p. 36.

21. G. Marcel, "I and Thou," in **The Philosophy of Martin Buber**, pp. 41-48. See also Buber's reply in the same volume, pp. 689-744.

22. **Ibid.**, p. 45.

23. **Ibid.**, p. 42.

24. Marcel, **The Mystery of Being**, II, p. 9.

25. Marcel, **The Philosophy of Existentialism**, p. 15.

26. Marcel, **The Mystery of Being**, I, p. 87.

27. **Ibid.**, I, p. 158.

28. **Ibid.**

29. Marcel, **Creative Fidelity**, p. 32.

30. **Ibid.**, p. 12.

31. G. Marcel, **Being and Having** (New York: Harper & Row, 1965), p. 28.

32. **Ibid.**, p. 12.

33. Marcel, **Creative Fidelity**, p. 17.

34. **Ibid.**, p. 18.

35. **Ibid.**

36. **Ibid.**, p. 33.

37. Marcel, **The Mystery of Being**, II, p. 17. In this metaphysical insight Marcel comes very near to Leibniz's "sympnoia panta," although it serves by Leibniz as a rational co-relational term.

38. **Ibid.**, p. 9.

39. **The Philosophy of Martin Buber**, ed. Schilpp, p. 706.

40. M. Buber, **The Knowledge of Man** (New York: Harper & Row, 1965), p. 69.

41. **The Philosophy of Martin Buber**, ed. Schilpp, p. 45.

42. Marcel, **Creative Fidelity**, p. 48.

43. G. Marcel, **Philosophy of Existence** (New York: Philosophical Library, 1949), p. 127.

44. Marcel, **The Mystery of Being**, I, p. 57.

45. Marcel, **Being and Having** (New York: Harper & Row, 1965), p. 102.

46. **Ibid.**, p. 103.

47. **The Philosophy of Martin Buber**, ed. Schilpp, p. 46.

48. **Ibid.**

49. **Ibid.**

50. Marcel, **The Philosophy of Existentialism**, p. 41.

51. Marcel, **The Mystery of Being**, I, p. 104.

52. Marcel, **Creative Fidelity**, p. 180.

53. **Ibid.**, p. 12.

54. **The Philosophy of Martin Buber**, ed. Schilpp, p. 45.

55. Marcel, **Being and Having**, p. 101.

56. Marcel, **The Philosophy of Existentialism**, p. 18.

57. Marcel, **Being and Having**, p. 100.
58. Marcel, **The Philosophy of Existentialism**, p. 19.
59. **Ibid.**, p. 18.
60. "L'esprit comble le vide entre le moi pensant et le moi empirique en affirmant leur liaison transcendante." **Journal Metaphysique** (Paris: Gallimard, 1927), p. 45.
61. **Ibid.**, p. 43.
62. Marcel, **Creative Fidelity**, p. 22.
63. Marcel, **Being and Having**, p. 100.
64. Marcel, **The Philosophy of Existentialism**, p. 98.
65. Marcel, **Journal Metaphysique**, p. 136: "Dieu est is toi absolu qui ne peut jamais devenir un lui." Martin Buber, **I and Thou**, p. 112: "The Eternal Thou can by its nature not become It."
66. F. W. J. Schelling, **Werke**, (München: Ch. Bede und R. Oldenbourg, 1927), II. 3, 170.
67. **Ibid.**, p. 48.
68. Paul Tillich, **New Being** (New York: Scribner, 1955).
69. Marcel, **The Philosophy of Existentialism**, p. 45.
70. **Ibid.**

Classical Philosophy and
The Meaning of God

◊

by
Augustin P. Leonard, O.P.

INVALID CRITICISMS OF CLASSICAL THEISM

NOTHING IS SO common today as is the *a priori* and dogmatic rejection of the "proofs" of the existence of God. In his
day St. Anselm of Canterbury had tried to convince by a single
and irrefutable argument the "fool" who says in his heart "there
is no God." This fool has since grown a very large and ecumenical
family including atheists, Jews, Catholics and Protestants. Rarely, however, have the members of this family taken the same
trouble as the monk, Gaunilo, who wrote a criticism of St. Anselm:
In Behalf of the Fool,[1] which then forced the Saint to write a reply.
Instead they often assume, but in no way demonstrate, an impossibility for the human reason to discover the existence of
God, though "to stop thinking of elephants is not the same as
thinking that there are none."[2] Enthralled by "relevance" and
"meaningfulness," many in the fool's family seem to fall headlong
into that paralogism. One sometimes wonders if they even read
the texts.

On Missing the Encounter with Classical Theism

What Charles Hartshorne writes on St. Anselm could be said
of many classical writers who proposed arguments for the
existence of God. Their critics "present their wretched little

[237]

caricatures as serious accounts of the subject. . . . If Anselm is to be refuted, it should be for what he said, taken in something like the context which he provided, and not for something someone else said he said, or a fragment of what he said, torn wholly out of context."[3]

Even if, impressed by St. Thomas' criticism that the transition from essence to existence in the so-called ontological argument is illegitimate, one disagrees with St. Anselm and Charles Hartshorne, it is still a delight to see somebody dealing accurately with the argument. Furthermore, if Thomas Aquinas knew of Anselm only the strings of quotations which were so frequent in the Middle Ages, one might be obliged to doubt that Thomas Aquinas did in fact understand Anselm and to reconsider the whole problem. If the same must be said of Immanuel Kant, who also ignored the *Proslogion,* the problem might not be as simple as it appears to the fool's family.[4]

The real weakness of the fool's family lies in the assumption that David Hume and Immanuel Kant have done the job for them, once and for all. They sleep peacefully wrapped in the doubts of their ancestors and could hardly be said to be trying to find out by themselves. Though one would hope that this is exaggerated one finds Ronald Hepburn writing: "If we are convinced that Hume and Kant and their successors have once and for all refuted the arguments of rational apologetics, we are faced with a choice between agnosticism (or atheism) and the discovery of an alternative method of justifying belief."[5] Here, two redeeming features save human intelligence from total incapacity and reduction to the world of things, objects and tools. The first is the recognition of the need for some justification for belief, and the second is the attempt to do this in a new way.

Some minds still rebel against the superficial empiricism of Hume and the formalistic moralism of Kant. Nevertheless, there is something strange in the devotion of modern minds—in the terms of C. J. Jung it may be a temporary and necessary psychopathological imbalance—to the founding fathers of empiricism and moralism,[6] and to "a Supreme Being to give effect to practical laws."[7] This suggests the most appalling conception of God.

Often it has been noted that Hume and Kant were working in the framework of the Newtonian physics. The causality with which they are concerned is the mechanistic and observable causality between cause and effect in the empirical world. That this cannot be predicated of God is quite understandable. The causality of Aristotle and Thomas Aquinas is of a different type. In the case of Aristotle it is organic; and in the case of Thomas Aquinas it is ontological and existential.[8] To be the cause of the heating of the water is quite different from being the cause of the totality of being and existence. The word "cause" is obviously analogical; it in each case denotes a totally different effect and a totally different type of causality. Gabriel Marcel points out that the term "cause" is a bad word to use analogically for in the modern mind it is freighted with mechanistic undertones. As a consequence, it may be better to substitute for causality the terms "communication" or "generosity."[9]

Yet many more important factors than causality are involved. The very approach is often unphilosophical in its use of Hume and Kant as "authorities" or "Fathers" of the philosophical sect. This is similar to the use of Aristotle in the Middle Ages or to the infrequent mood of Jacques Martain when, in *Le Paysan de la Garonne,* he bravely claims that "Skepticism, Nominalism, Empiricism, Kantianism, Idealism, Pragmatism, Positivism, Dialectical Materialism or Existentialism . . . (do not cross) . . . the threshold at which philosophic knowledge starts. . . . They speak much and they say a lot of remarkable things, but they are still in a prenatal state."[10] There is no difference between this position and the modern dogmatism which believes that Hume and Kant have disposed of the philosophical problem of the existence of God.[11]

Charles Hartshorne would agree with Jacques Maritain that Hume and Kant have not necessarily said the last word on theism and metaphysics. Though "Kant's own queer and truncated sort of metaphysics" may be decisive against the classical metaphysics of being and substance, Hartshorne would not consider it decisive against Neoclassical metaphysics or the theism of Peirce, Bergson, and Whitehead which takes as the primary categories of thought (without necessarily excluding the "secondary abstractions"?) : "creative becoming, event, relativity, and possibility."[12] In this view the Greeks and the scholastics who followed are responsible for a conception of God as the Unmoved Mover *(Movens Immobile)*, Subsistent Being Itself *(Ipsum Esse per se subsistens)*,[13] and the immutable and perfect actuality of Existence, which does not allow for change, relativity or possibility *in God*. Though it is often said that such a notion of God does not allow for these properties in participated beings, obviously, if God is the perfect Actuality of Existence, everything else is mutable, relative, contingent.

Classical Theism and the Meaning of God for the World.

The truly serious problem that lies at the base of the difference between classical and neoclassical metaphysics concerns, not the categories of being and becoming, but the meaning of God for the world and human existence. How can God be concerned about the world and love men without changing in order to "respond to them differentially?"[14] In order to preserve the transcendence of God, Thomas Aquinas held that the relationship between God and his creatures is not real in God, but only in creatures; in God it is only a "relation of reason," *(secundum rationem tantum.)*[15] This may mean only that God is not dependent on the creatures and cannot be determined by them. The fullness of goodness can only communicate his own goodness; from the point of view of the creator, the relationship between creator and creatures is one of sheer generosity. Nevertheless, it may be doubted that the best way to express this generosity is by calling the relationship one of reason only *(secundum rationem tantum)*.

No doubt other weaknesses can be found in the traditional proofs of the existence of God. These weaknesses are obvious in Plato and Aristotle who inspired the arguments for the existence of God. There are in Plato different levels of divine existence and it is very diffcult to determine their order and the relationships. Is the supreme goodness, beyond the Ideas[16] and essences, really personal? One recent commentator has concluded that "Platonism does not really reach God."[17] The participation between the Ideas and the sensible world is formal and not a true causality; the Platonic God is not really personal; and his relationship with the inferior *Demiourgos* of the *Timaeus*, who fashions the world according to the model of the Ideas, is mysterious. Nevertheless, Robin thinks that it is possible that Plato has attributed to the supreme goodness the highest personality.[18]

Aristotle begins his consideration of God by first discovering something which moves, without being moved, being eternal, substance, and actuality. But "life also belongs to God; for the actuality of thought is life, and God is that actuality; and God's self-dependent actuality is life most good and eternal. We say therefore that God is a living being, eternal, most good, so that life and duration continuous and eternal belong to God; for this is God" *(touto gar o theos)*.[19] In the dry Aristotle, there is a sense of wonder before this great discovery. "If, then, God is always in that good state in which we sometimes are, this compels our wonder; and if in a better this compels it yet more. And God *is* in a better state."[20] Finally God must be given the noblest activity, thinking, and the only fitting object of that activity, himself. "Therefore it must be of itself that the divine thought thinks (since it is the most excellent of things) and its thinking is a thinking on thinking *(kai estin he noesis noeseos noesis)*.[21]

There is ambiguity here, for the relationship between this most excellent and thinking being with the fifty-five or forty-seven celestial and eternal bodies subtracts something of the unicity and personality of the Prime Mover. Moreover, as is well known, the Aristotelian God does not create the world because it is eternal, nor does he provide for it or even know it. The final cause "produces motion as being loved" *(kinei de os eromenon)*.[22] Nevertheless, when one reads his ancient texts anew with some historical sense and an awareness of human creativity, one cannot help being full of wonder, as was Aristotle before his own ingenuity and the object of his discovery. Nor can one help admiring, as Bernard Lonergan puts it: "the Greek miracle that effected the triumph of *logos* over *mythos*."[23]

Two reasons might be singled out for the importance of the

Greek discovery. The first is the initiation by the Greeks of metaphysical thinking, the question of being and becoming, of unity and multiplicity, and many others, without which it would seem very difficult even to ask the question that eventually leads to the existence of God. This is the central problem, for the powerful influence of empiricism upon those who accept it makes this question meaningless. In the Copleston-Russell debate, Russell makes his point as follows: "I should say that the universe is just there, and that's all."[24] Against somebody who does not see the question, no argument is possible; one can only describe the experience wherein the question arises: why is there being? Many scientists have no idea of such a question. They repeat confidently that the universe is self-sufficient, infinite in space and time, and does not require anything other than the particular explanations given in science.[25]

A number of factors militate against this position. First, it is rather odd to limit *a priori* the questioning desire of the human intellect, especially when it is so obvious in the Greek inventors of philosophy. Second, such a scientist position supposes an explicit or implicit metaphysical materialism, in which matter itself is given such attributes of the divinity as self-sufficiency, eternity, infinity, and creativity, if not intelligence. The same may be said of History or Evolution, which sometimes appear as immanent divinities, independent of men's decisions and responsibilities, having a life of their own, and like the Hegelian "cunning of Reason," pursuing their own goals. Third, these presuppositions are often assumed to be self-evident without any justification, especially a scientific demonstration. Fourth, an eternal and infinite series of finite effects, supposing that the idea of an eternal and infinite series of real, concrete, and finite things is not self-contradictory,[26] still does not solve the problem of the existence of such effects. The question of creation is independent from the question of the duration of its effects.

Finally, though science from its point of view and relying on its particular methodology may consider the universe as a self-sufficient entity, ontological enquiry is not built on the "gaps" of the scientific explanation; it asks another question. This question is well expressed by M. Merleau-Ponty in his posthumous book: "there is being, there is world, there is *something;* in the strong sense in which the Greek language speaks of Tὸ λέδειν, there is cohesion, there is meaning."[27] "The *truth* of science, far from making philosophy useless, is only founded and guaranteed by a relation of transcendence to Being, a belonging of the subject and the object of science to a pre-objective Being."[28] While the ontological question does not presume the theistic or atheistic answer, it at least makes the dialogue between them possible. It is this ontological question that is the first and permanent lesson inherited from the Greeks.

A second reason for the importance of the Greek discovery becomes manifest when it is observed that the discovery of a Supreme Goodness or a living thought by the Pagan philosophers can hardly be ascribed to the influence of the Jewish-Christian revelation. This seems to testify to a possibility written in the very essence of man and, with the brutality of a fact, dismisses some arguments proposed against the possibility of a philosophical theism. For example, the main argument of John Hick in the *Existence of God* is that the *a posteriori* theistic proofs "necessarily beg the question, in that a person who accepts their premises already acknowledges the reality of God."[29] Why must the consideration that there *is* something beg the question or rest "upon a fundamental act of faith, faith in the ultimate 'rationality' of existence."[30] The position that it does so is basically the very common fideistic attitude that the atheistic or theistic answer to the question of existence is a matter of faith. In such a case, both choices would be basically irrational, although both ancient and modern philosophers don't stop giving reasons for a seemingly impossible enterprise.

THE LIMITATIONS OF CLASSICAL THEISM

The main objection against theism is not simply a fideistic attitude, but a criticism of the Classical tradition as a whole. Having stressed the relevance of this tradition, its critique must now be studied in order to emphasize the limitations of classical theism. Paradoxically the objections are developed according to two contradictory lines. One has its roots in respect for the transcendence of God, while the other insists upon the immanence of God. In both lines the meaning of God for human experience is not isolated from the merely technical aspect of the validity of the theistic arguments.

Classical Thought and Transcendence.

In the first line Martin Heidegger is a commanding figure. According to Heidegger, the whole history of Western metaphysics since Plato is a history of the "forgetfulness of Being." There is, therefore, an abyss between metaphysics and the fundamental or founding ontology to which Heidegger wishes to return. Metaphysical systems had always been concerned about an aspect of being or about the rational categories of being, but they had not dealt with Being itself. Thus the idea was substituted for being, and *ousia* was interpreted as a substance,[31] rather than as presence. A rationalization of the perception of being has been substituted for the basic thought, which should be an openness to being.

Moreover Western metaphysics has always been involved in the subject-object polarity. If Being is treated simply as an object of reason, it is necessarily reduced to what may be known and metaphysical truth becomes the correspondence between the human concept and reality *(adaequatio rei et intellectus)*. Finally reality is limited to what man can grasp in a rationalistic and conceptual thinking.

Another aspect of "the task of destroying the history of ontology" lies in the relationship between Being and time. "Time must be brought to light—and genuinely conceived—as the horizon for all understanding of Being and for any way of interpreting it."[32] Man and his understanding of Being is essentially temporal and historical, and hence is much more in the manner of St. Augustine than in the fashion of the Greeks and the Scholastics.

That metaphysics is abstract, categorical, and rationalistic, that it "objectifies" reality, and that it does not take into account the historicity of man and his thought—these three ideas have been applied by Heidegger and many of his disciples to the problem of God.[33] For Heidegger the traditional notion of the First Cause is linked to the condemned metaphysics, which is concerned with the being of a particular entity, but not with the truth of Being. "The Transcendent is supra-sensible entity. This entity is conceived as the supreme entity, in the sense of the first cause of all entity. One thinks of God as this first cause."[34]

It is precisely the death of such entities and values, which are concepts bound to the *physis,* that was announced by Nietzsche. It is metaphysics, not fundamental ontology, which is by its nature "onto-theo-logical" and introduces into philosophy God as self-explanatory *(causa sui).*[35]

> This is the fitting name for the God in philosophy. To this God man can neither pray nor sacrifice. Before the *causa sui* man can neither fall to his knees in awe nor sing and dance. Accordingly, godless thinking that must give up the god of philosophy, god as *causa sui,* is perhaps nearer to the divine God. This means only that such thinking is freer for him than onto-theo-logics would like to admit. This comment may let some small light fall on the path toward which a thinking that carries through the step backwards, back out of metaphysics into the essence of metaphysics, is moving.[36]

Heidegger's thought is neither atheistic nor theistic; it waits in suspense. It is clear that his Being is not God, since for the earlier Heidegger, Being was finite, while for the later Heidegger it remains indeterminate. Being is anterior to God or the gods. "But Being—what is Being? Being is what it itself is *(Es ist Es selbst).* This is what the thought of the future must learn to experience and to express. Being is not God or a world's ground *(Weltgrund).* Being is farther removed than all entity and nevertheless nearer to man than any entity, be it a rock, an animal, a work of art, a machine, be it an angel or God."[37] In this passage, where God is *a* being alongside an animal or an angel, Heidegger may be speaking of the God who in Western metaphysics is known as a foundation or part of the world of being. His own thought may be that the true essence of the divinity is not yet discovered. "It is only starting from the truth of Being that the essence of the Sacred may be thought. It is only from the essence of the Sacred that one must think the essence of the Divinity. It is only in the light of the essence of the Divinity that one may think and express what the word 'God' can name."[38]

Christians who use the vocabulary of Heidegger in order to escape the criticism bearing on the classical tradition certainly distort the original and largely incomprehensible meaning of Being. The Heideggerian Being is neither the God of creation who alone makes a created and real participation in being understandable, or the transcendental concept of being in general. John Macquarrie states that because Heidegger's Being tends to replace God and his attributes, he is actually making the inverse move to the claim that God should replace Being.[39] Maintaining the value of philosophical theology, he elegantly substitutes an existential-ontological theism to a "traditional (or metaphysical) theism," in which God is not *a* being but Being itself. In a different manner Heinrich Ott substitutes the Barthian God of creation to the Heideggerian Being.[40] What needs clarification in these attempts is the meaning of Being. It seems to me to be largely a matter of semantics when one discusses Being versus *a* Being, or the "is-ness" of God versus his "existence."

What is obvious is that the Classical tradition in its Greek part has broken down in modern philosophy. Is this also true of the Medieval part of that tradition; is this merely an hellenization of Christianity?

What is the true value of the conclusions of the five ways of St. Thomas according to which God is the Prime Mover, the First Efficient Cause, the Being necessary *per se,* the cause of being, goodness and all perfections, and the Intelligence which ordains every being to its end?[41] Following Heidegger, who certainly involves the Schoolmen in his critique of the Classical tradition, John Macquarrie thinks that the theistic arguments fail in going from particular beings to another exalted, particular being which is God.[42] In the case of St. Thomas this is obviously a misreading. God is not the first number in the series of beings; he is outside of and transcends the series of beings. St. Thomas writes; "The name 'who is' does not determine any modality of being, but it relates in an indeterminate fashion to all modalities of being and consequently it designates the infinite ocean of substance."[43] It is very difficult to put "the infinite ocean of being," Being Itself *(Ipsum Esse)*, in any ladder or scale.

For St. Thomas the knowledge of God, even in faith, and *a fortiori* through reason, is by way of causality *(via causalitatis)*, negation *(negationis)*, remotion *(remotionis)* and eminence *(eminentiae)*. This means that there is no human concept or idea which can give an adequate representation of what God is. To quote: "the divine substance exceeds immensely all the forms that our intelligence can reach. Thus we cannot perceive that substance in knowing what it is. We have nevertheless a certain knowledge of it, in knowing what it is not."[44] St. Thomas keeps a very sophisticated and, hence, misunderstood balance between a thorough agnosticism which denies that the human mind is created to know even very imperfectly in this life, and an anthropomorphism which indulges in fancy imaginations about God. I fail to see how one can confuse the Subsistent Being Itself *(Ipsum Esse subsistens)* and the Actuality of Being, with a stop-gap God or one who is "out there." Of course, it is first necessary to understand the fundamental question of existence and being, which, again, is the whole problem.

Another common objection to the traditional ways of finding God is that St. Thomas makes a great illogical leap between the Necessary Being and what we know in the Judeo-Christian tradition as God when he concludes: "and that we call God," or "and that everybody calls God." These critics do not seem to be aware that for St. Thomas the word or the name "God" has absolutely nothing sacred in it. It is not a proper, but a common and analogical name which can be applied by the Pagans to a tree, an animal or themselves.[45] The real question therefore is not a matter of semantics; it is the question of what one puts under the name "God." There is therefore no illogical leap between the

Necessary Being and God, because the name "God" is completely irrelevant. There is no proper name for God, because we do not know what he is.

In this the Schoolmen were taking a clue from the book of Exodus: "Then Moses said to God, 'I am to go, then, to the sons of Israel and say to them, "The God of your fathers has sent me to you. But if they ask me what his name is, what am I to tell them?" And God said to Moses, "I Am who I Am."[46] The different translations of this famous verse do not make any difference, because the proper name of "God" is unknown. Being itself *(Ipsum Esse)* does not seem to be a bad name, because it includes Action itself, Truth itself, and any other perfections we can think of. In order to act and to be truthful, one has to be.

Classical Thought and Immanence.

In the matter of the traditional arguments for the existence of God, Gabriel Marcel is the rare philosopher in the modern times who has had a balanced view. "In the final analysis, it is because the unity of man has been shattered, because his world is broken—that we confront this scandal of proofs which are logically irrefutable but which in fact exhibit a lack of any persuasive power."[47] This is a very accurate description of the present situation: the arguments are irrefutable, but they are not convincing. "Thus we confront the paradox that generally proof is efficacious only when we can if necessary do without it; while on the other hand, it will always seem circular to the person to whom it is directed and who must be persuaded."[48] Such momentous decisions as the acknowledgement of the existence of God are not based entirely on a rational demonstration, even if that demonstration cannot be proved inaccurate, inconsequential, or invalid. The absolute value given to man in contempoary atheism is not a consequence of ontology; rather, atheistic ontology is a consequence of the absolute value given to man.[49] In this historical situation, it is the burden of a theistic philosophy to present its case in such a manner, that it will bring sense, meaning, and value to contemporary man. In this light a few observations can be presented. No Christian is obliged to engage in a philosophical investigation of the existence of God. Even the First Vatican Council statement that it is possible for the human reason to find God does not mean that everyone may feel inclined to check that possibility. If one does philosophize concerning God, ways other than those of classical thought are open, as is testified by Maurice Blondel, Lavelle, Le Senne, Whitehead and many others.

The classical theistic arguments themselves are not "proofs" in the modern sense. "Demonstrations" in an Aristotelian sense, in which the logical necessity between propositions makes "science," do exist, but it is doubtful that on the ontological level there are any "proofs." The theistic arguments are "ways" in which man must engage himself not only with his reason, but with his desire. Plato guessed it in his dialectic of love; even Aristotle had a sense of "wonder"; and the Moslems, Jews and Christians were driven by a passion which St. Thomas admirably explained as the desire of God. Man has a natural aptitude to know and to love God, and this aptitude is in the very nature of the human mind *(mens)*. The quest of God will never be ended, because man is essentially openness to the Transcendent. Without that possibility written in the very structure of man, even a revelation from God would not be understood.

If the quest for God is the product of a passionate intelligence, the theistic arguments should show this. They should start with one of the phenomenological analyses of human existence of which there are admirable examples in Heidegger, Gabriel Marcel, Sartre, or Camus. Whereas many traditional works take for granted the question of existence or being, it is only slow and patient analysis of a human situation which shows finally and ultimately the horizon of being.

Today the question is far from being obvious. People must be led by a description of the tragedy and the triumph of their life to the decisive question, without which the answer does not make sense. Whereas placing the starting point in natural phenomena like motion or causality would drive the mind to a Prime Mover or a First Efficient Cause, placing in it human existence would lead the mind to a loving "Thou" or a generous freedom which is creative, provident, and naturally inclined to reveal itself.

It might also be said that traditional theism is too much concerned about what God is in himself or his ontological attributes, and not enough about the moral attributes or what God is for us. The "in-itself" in traditional theism has always been much more emphasized than the "for us." This is the basic problem raised by the Neoclassical Metaphysics and other tendencies stressing the immanence of God. To see in an ontological way the "in-itself" of God and the "for us" is still an unsolved problem. To strike out simply the eternity and the immutability of God, or the ominipotence and omniscience is not philosophical. The real problem is to reconcile in God himself eternity and history, self-sufficiency and generosity. In this very difficult problem, philosophy will have to let itself be enlightened by the mystery of the Incarnation. Kierkegaard had a profound intuition when he said that the news of the day are the swaddling clothes of eternity. To get rid of eternity, as is so common today, is no solution, for the "now" of today has no reality if it is not the presence of Eternity in time.

◊

1. Anselm, **Proslogium, Monologium; An Appendix In Behalf of the Fool by Gaunilon; and Cur Deus Homo,** trans. S. N. Deane (Chicago: Open Court, 1903).

2. Charles Hartshorne, "Introduction to Saint Anselm," **Basic Writings** (2nd ed.; La Salle, Illinois: Open Court, 1962), p. 11.

3. **Ibid.,** p. 2.

4. Arthur C. McGill, "Recent Discussions of Anselm's Argument," in **The Many Faced Argument,** eds. John Hick and Arthur C. McGill (New York: Macmillan, 1967), p. 38, nn. 17-18.

5. **Metaphysical Beliefs,** ed. A. MacIntyre (London: SCM Press, 1957), p. 89, quoted in John Macquarrie, **God-Talk, An Examination of the Language and Logic of Theology** (New York: Harper & Row, 1967), p. 109.

6. The necessary link between empiricism and moralism (in its worst aspects) would be worth investigating. It is the highest ontological vision

which gives man his dignity and its inner freedom. If man is condemned to an exclusive empirical knowledge, he is also condemned to "moral duties." This might explain many features of American life and its international politics.

7. Immanuel Kant, **Critique of Pure Reason,** trans. F. Max Müller (New York: Doubleday, 1966), p. 396. There is, of course, a moral argument for the existence of God. Kant saw very well the importance of practical reason in problems of values, and the absoluteness of the human person leading to the foundation of an absolute moral value. See John-Henry Walgrave, **La preuve de l'existence de Dieu par la conscience morale et l'expérience des valeurs,** in L'existence de Dieu (Paris: Casterman, 1961).

8. See for instance J. M. LeBlond, **L'usage theologique de la notion de causalité,** in **De la connaissance de Dieu, Recherches de philosophie** (Paris: Desclée De Brouwer, 1958), III-IV, 15-26.

9. Gabriel Marcel, **Ibid.,** p. 27.

10. Jacques Maritain, **Peasant of the Garonne** (New York: Holt, 1968), pp. 29-30.

11. It should be noted that after explaining the five ways of Thomas Aquinas, Maritain proceeds to give a sixth way to the existence of God. This way is based on the Augustinian paradox that in a contingent being the activity of thinking as spiritual and intemporal implies, in a transcendent and pre-existent way, "being, thought and personality." This is akin, as Maritain remarks, to the Hindu metaphysical and mystical relationship Atman-Brahman. Maritain also acknowledges that the ways of "the practical intellect," which are not demonstrative but belonging "to an existential and prephilosophic order," discover God as Beauty and Goodness. This recognition of the ways of the practical intellect, which have never been fully accepted and developed in Catholic philosophy, manifests a Maritain who is less dogmatic than his introductory statements imply.

12. Charles Hartshorne, **The Logic of Perfection and Other Essays in Neoclassical Metaphysics** (LaSalle, Illinois: Open Court, 1962), p. xiii.

13. Thomas Aquinas, **Summa Theologica** (New York: Benziger Brothers, 1947), I, q. 4, a. 2, ad 2.

14. Hartshorne, **The Logic of Perfection and Other Essays in Neoclassical Metaphysics,** p. 36.

15. Thomas Aquinas, **Summa Theologica,** I, q. 13, a. 7, c.

16. **Republic,** VI, 509 b; cfr. Leon Robin, **Platon** (Paris: Alcan, 1935), p. 249.

17. Maurice Cordvez, "Le Dieu de Platon," **Revue Philosophique de Louvain,** LXV (1967), 5-35.

18. Robin, **Platon,** p. 251.

19. **Metaphysics,** 1079 b 26-30, trans. W. D. Ross, **Aristotle's Metaphysics** in **The Works of Aristotle** (2nd ed.; Oxford: Clarendon Press, 1928), VIII.

20. **Metaphysics,** 1072 b 23-25.

21. **Metaphysics,** 1074 b 30.

22. **Metaphysics,** 1082 b 3.

23. Bernard J. F. Lonergan, "The Dehellenization of Dogma," in **The Future of Belief Debate**, ed. Gregory Baum (New York: Herder & Herder, 1967), p. 78.

24. **The Existence of God**, ed. John Hick (New York: Macmillan, 1964), p. 175.

25. Raymond J. Nogar, **The Land of the Absurd** (New York: Herder & Herder, 1966), p. 73.

26. See the discussion of this point in F. Van Steenberghen, **Le Dieu Caché** (Louvain: Nauwelaerts, 1961), pp. 201-10.

27. M. Merleau-Ponty, **Le visible et l'invisible** (Paris: Gallimard, 1964), p. 121.

28. **Ibid.**, p. 279.

29. John Hick, **The Existence of God**, p. 5.

30. **Ibid.**, p. 6.

31. Martin Heidegger, **An Introduction to Metaphysics**, trans. Ralph Manheim (New York: Doubleday, 1961), pp. 151 ff.

32. Martin Heidegger, **Being and Time**, trans. John Macquarrie and E. Robinson (New York: Harper & Brothers, 1962), p. 39.

33. Paul Tillich, **Systematic Theology** (London: Nisbet, 1953), I, 227 ff.

34. Martin Heidegger, **Lettre sur l'humanisme**, trad. Roger Munier (Paris: Aubier, 1964), p. 127.

35. An expression endlessly repeated and never used, as far as I know, by St. Thomas because it is contradictory to be the cause of one-self.

36. Martin Heidegger, **Essays in Metaphysics** (New York: Philosophical Library, 1960), p. 65. I am using the better translations of James M. Robinson, **The Later Heidegger and Theology** (New York: Harper & Row, 1963), p. 37.

37. Heidegger, **Lettre sur l'humanisme**, p. 72.

38. Heidegger, **Essays in Metaphysics**, p. 130.

39. John Macquarrie, **Principles of Christian Theology** (New York: Charles Scribner's Sons, 1966), pp. 105 ff.

40. Robinson, **The Later Heidegger and Theology**, passim.

41. Thomas Aquinas, **Summa Theologica**, I, q. 2, a. 3.

42. Macquarrie, **Principles of Christian Theology**, p. 107.

43. Thomas Aquinas, **Summa Theologica**, I, q. 13, a. 11.

44. Thomas Aquinas, **Summa Contra Gentiles** (London: Burns, Oates & Washbourne, 1923), I, 14.

45. Thomas Aquinas, **Summa Theologica**, I, q. 13, a. 11.

46. Ex. 3:14.

47. Gabriel Marcel, **Creative Fidelity**, trans. Robert Rosthal (New York: Farrar, Straus and Co., 1964), p. 180.

48. **Ibid.**, p. 179.

49. Jules Girardi, "Atheisme et theisme face au probleme de la valeur absolue de l'homme," **Revue Philosophique de Louvain**, LXV (1967), 211.

Freedom and Christian Philosophy

◊

by
L.-B. Geiger, O.P.

NOTIONS OF FREEDOM

THE THEME OF the relationship between man and God concerned man's mind long before it achieved a state of reflection sufficient to formulate this relationship clearly and express it intelligibly. Though this theme first appeared in mythology, its forms of expression were ignored for a long time by philosophers precisely because philosophy had been born in Greece with the intention of rising above the level of mythology. Nevertheless there was the myth of Prometheus, the jealousy of the gods, and the justice of fate which forces anyone back into the common lot who seeks to elevate himself above this level. Finally there was the theme of *hybris* which constitutes a powerful temptation as fatal as a poison causing the loss of reason, and plunging the imbiber blindly into enterprises in which he will be destroyed as certainly as the son of Atreus, plagued by his cruel but relentless fate.

This is not the place to consider in detail either the content or the significance of these myths or others which have flowed from them. But in them one sees clearly that:

(1) the rational creature is conscious of the existence of limits within which he feels himself enclosed or ensnared;

(2) by the very same token he is also conscious of the presence

within himself of a certain force which is restrained by these limits and at the same time extends itself to break forth beyond them, as if there exists a natural conflict between the development for which the human being feels himself destined and the condition of the universe in which he finds himself placed; and

(3) in these myths and in much later periods this conflict, instead of being experienced, understood, and formulated in technical terms, was understood as man's encounter with the gods, or more generally, with the world of the divine.

The progress of man thus appeared in its ensemble as an undertaking which is at once both necessary and fatal. It is necessary since it is based upon an interior force which constitutes a sort of irresistible temptation. It is fatal because based upon a dangerous, even sacrilegious, undertaking which leads man to struggle with powerful forces whose resources he neither understands nor comprehends, forces whose jealousy and spirit of vengeance he thinks he knows.

Such a situation is understandable on the supposition that the human being finds himself in the presence of a world of gods upon whom he does not depend in his very being. This would be a world of divinities identical to those of all peoples who know nothing of creation properly so called. In this supposition the world of the gods would be perhaps a more perfect and happier one, but it could only be juxtaposed to the universe of men. One could easily understand that these gods, if they were not already the product of human anger, would desire to preserve the realm and the prerogatives which distinguish them from men, that is, to prevent any presumptuous undertaking which would wrest their exclusive enjoyment from them. Accordingly these gods would have to be moved in a completely natural manner, as would any social class which seeks to distinguish itself from inferior classes by a desire to possess exclusively the powers and the knowledge which give them their specific character.

As long as man accepts such a view of things, he would consider himself to be in the tragic position of being necessarily driven to scale Olympus. A relentless force would counsel him to break forth from the situation which is his, to free himself from the limits which encompass his knowledge and from the shackles which prevent him from enjoying the good of life to the degree that he desires. He would be torn between, on the one hand, the thirst which is part of his very being and, on the other hand, the limitations against which he struggles. Success in pushing back such limits would give him the impression of having reached out far beyond his measure, and leave him with the feeling of having undertaken a more or less sacrilegious venture.

One of the central affirmations of the Christian faith, inherited from the Old Testament, is that the true God created heaven and earth and all that they contain with such good pleasure that he looked upon each of his works as good, even as very good. Man, for his part, was not haphazardly formed, but made by God himself to his image and likeness. He was entrusted to rule the entire universe and commanded to go forth, to multiply, and to inhabit the earth.

When the apostles went forth to preach the good news to the pagan world, they took care to stress the degree to which the doctrine which they announced in the name of Jesus Christ marked men's liberation from all the powers, elements, and fate which weighed so heavily upon the conscience of the hellenistic world. "You are citizens of the city of the saints, you are of the house of God," sons of God and coheirs with Christ. The new doctrine was received with joy. In fact, it gave the first Christians the consciousness of being at last free of all the forms of slavery in which, not only the worship of the gods, but the doctrine of the philosophers had held them.

Within the last century one of the most constant reproaches voiced against religion in general and Christian thought in particular is precisely that it is an enemy of man's true freedom. For this reason, atheism itself no longer takes exception to this or that point in the proofs of the existence of God. Instead, it bases itself upon the simple evidence of men's freedom in order to draw from it the conclusion that one must choose either man and his freedom, or God. If God exists, man cannot be free. But man is free; and from all the evidence concerning the constituents of his most authentic being, he must be free and wishes to be so. Thus God does not and cannot exist.

In fact, even the idea of God must be suppressed to render possible authentic human existence. Mechanistic determinism thought itself able to found the negation of God upon the demonstration of the incompatibility of, on the one hand, divine action and human liberty to interrupt or simply to modify the rigorous interlocking of causes and effects and, on the other hand, those laws which govern their succession. In opposition to this position, a large part of modern and contemporary philosophy has considered it necessary to deny the existence and the possibility of God in order to remain faithful to the most evident reality: human freedom. Hence, today man finds himself once again in the presence of an antinomy between men's liberation and religion. It is as if the very word religion could be taken only according to one of its etymological meanings to signify bond with all that the word could suggest of restraint or rein, and consequently of a principle antagonistic to the zeal for freedom.

It is not the purpose of this paper to treat in its entirety or in its various aspects the problem of the relationship between religion and the irresistible desire of humanity to contribute to the process of evolution by efforts aimed at conquering or avoiding limitations. For the mass of humanity space exploration is a most expressive symbol of this. Tentative analogies can be found in all the domains of human activities, technical and artistic, and in scientific as well as psychological or anthropological theories.

This paper limits itself to the more precise and certainly more difficult problems of human freedom properly so called. Without a doubt, the process of liberation must lead to greater liberty. But one can conceive the possibility, even the necessity, of a sustained effort for liberation which is not founded on a formal claim for interior liberty, and especially for liberty as conceived by a large part of philosophy. Moreover certain advocates of liberation have refused the privilege of true liberty or freedom to

the individual, seeing in it a vestige of bourgeois and individual-
istic philosophy which, guided by a sense of history, they feel
must give way to truly anonymous and superhuman force.

Within the general problem of the liberation of man, that of
freedom constitutes a particular question with its own proper
characteristics. To the general notion of opposition to limits or
to exterior constraint, it adds the idea of a profound liberation of
man from all which could influence him in any way whatsoever.
Indeed, this freedom must be considered not as a force launched
against the universe which impedes it, but rather as a force
whose source is capable of giving meaning to its activity and to
the effects which it produces.

The precise problem of freedom as it actually presents itself
to Christian philosophy will be the object of the following reflections. They will show:

(1) how and why a certain interpretation and claim for freedom leads a part of contemporary thought to atheism;

(2) how, on the contrary, reflection on this same freedom,
and its importance for a sane understanding of man,
leads other contemporary thinkers to discover there the
need for a religious attitude, without which freedom would
cease to be what it truly is; and

(3) how to draw out from this twofold exposition the conclusions which follow for a Christian philosophy of freedom
and its relationship with God.

FREEDOM: A FOUNDATION FOR ATHEISM

The establishing of freedom as a base of atheism is part of a
movement which dates from the past and of which Feuerbach is
increasingly given the honor of being the initiator. Recent works
such as those of Arvon caution against oversimplifying the thought
of this philosopher. However, he clearly held that a human being
cannot find himself fully unless he leaves behind him the alienation in which he abdicated his best qualities to a God of his own

making. Man gave up the personal pursuit of an ideal of humanity, and did this for a being existing only in his imagination. It is important, therefore, to denounce the alienation, even to annul it, and then to liquidate this God who exists only in one's ignorance.

This theory of alienation was used in the general Marxist social doctrines of class struggle and of the development of humanity. This would be fully reconciled with itself once all causes of the distinction and opposition of human beings had been eliminated by the communist society. Spread abroad amongst the most diverse levels of society, this theory has taken hold among all peoples and continents where Marxist influence has managed to infiltrate. By it, the idea of an ineluctable conflict between the desire to progress and the true freedom of man, on the one hand, and religion, on the other hand, has come to be accepted as evidence by a growing segment of humanity, educated or not.

The theme of alienation, at least in Marxism, remains necessarily related to an understanding of history as unable to be influenced by any individual. In Marxism, it is not formally men's liberty which is at issue and which opposes him to God, but men's liberation precisely with reference to God and all that his faith in God implies. Marxism looks at the evolution of humanity and the realization of its true end, rather than at the conditions of true liberty.

Sartre's position is quite different. He places himself primarily on the side of the individual and emphasizes liberty before any other aspect of the real. According to him, a philosophy such as that of Heidegger, which does not take this as its point of departure, must condemn itself never to find it. Whatever their differences may be, the philosophies of existence along with the phenomenologists and against Cartesians and rationalists have insisted that it is the opening to the world which is first given and from which one must start, if he does not wish to be weighed down by mere abstractions. Men are not, first of all, isolated substances which must search to open themselves to the world. Initially and by reason of the intentional structure of conscience they are present, or even more exactly, presence to the world.

For Sartre such a point of departure is pregnant with danger.

Is one not falling back into philosophies of being, indeed into the realism and all its consequences over which contemporary thought has triumphed? The point of departure of the philosophies of existence appears to be beyond doubt. If one adopts this and does not wish to abandon the evident liberty of conscience which is the typical mode of being of conscience, one is bound to conclude that conscience does not rise up before a given world with its diverse given meanings which can be read as one reads a book. For Sartre, consciousness is born like a disease of decompression of being. It is a pure initiative filled with meaning by itself and therefore only for itself. On the basis of this first step, the world itself emerges into existence with meaning which it has only by me and for me.

It is not necessary to insist on the extreme consequences with which Sartre has been obliged to invest his principles, namely:

(1) that consciousness should not have any other title than nothing ("néant") in order to avoid everything which might contaminate the pure development of liberty as he conceives it;

(2) that every objective value has to be rejected, on the pretext that such objective values would dominate my decision from without; and

(3) that God must be rejected because the idea of creation, applied to liberty, is contradictory: a free being, by definition, being in opposition to its creator from the very moment in which he is free and poses an act of liberty.

The important facts to be emphasized here are two. First, in the philosophy of Sartre neither liberty nor liberation are simply an operation or activity brought about by a human being, who for his part is a being determined by his nature. A being which is able to pose a single free act must be fully free in its very being. He has, therefore, neither nature nor being, but only nothing. In this lies the novelty of his thought, in opposition to the atheism or anti-theism of the Greeks and moderns.

Secondly, only by reason of his interpretation of liberty does the being of man logically involve the absolute rejection of all objective values and dependence on God. Sartre can be shown to stand in a long tradition which, under the guise of the liberty of the human conscience, thinks almost exclusively in physical images and terms. Liberty is described as an energy or a power to launch something, including to launch the meaning of launching itself. Liberty, then, is simply the point of origin, and this origin must necessarily be a pure one. If it is not pure, it simply is not, for all that is not pure origin in itself is negation of this purity, and, therefore, of liberty. Since values impose a certain pressure, they would negate liberty. Similarly, if the action of God causes liberty to exist, it must make liberty be a being by another, which is the very negation of liberty.[1]

CONTEMPORARY RELIGIOUS PHILOSOPHY OF LIBERTY

One can show very simply that a particularly simple interpretation is at the base of Sartre's negation by calling upon other philosophies of existence, such as those of Gabriel Marcel or Louis Lavelle, and their interpretations of the same given, that is, human liberty.

First of all, instead of the simplified image of Sartre, they understand freedom in its authentic context of spiritual reality. Certainly freedom implies a certain independence or separation. However, freedom as it really exists appears primarily to be related to an encounter with value properly speaking, that is, with absolute value or good in itself. Value does not impose itself. It invites and calls one to accept and agree; but it leaves one perfectly free to consider this agreement or to refuse it. At the same time, value offers for one's consideration a choice as to how one should be himself. This should be precisely by responding to value, rather than to some vulgar desire of satisfaction or possession, whether of power or pleasure.

This is a first liberation. However, it is completed only at the instant when one decides freely to make of himself, both by and for himself, an act of love and realization of the world of value, taken in its varying an hierarchical order. More fundamentally than a breaching or independence, understood in a purely negative sense, liberty of freedom presents itself to one's mind as a link, a response, and an assent. This is made to the value as value on the one hand, and, on the other, to that possibility within oneself by which he is able to respond to that value. It is as if one's innermost self made one recognize a dormant facility to materialize or to actuate that value in making it one's own by the free decision to henceforward will the good according to the truth.

At the same time, far from refusing any link whatsoever with any source which gives it being, freedom shows itself to be present in one by some Liberty or Act. While remaining distinct because Absolute, instead of remaining alien like some distinct cause, this freedom presents itself as that in which one continually participates to be and to be free.

Rather then efficient cause, the contemporary philosophers mentioned prefer to take recourse in the Platonic term: participation. However, they do not use it in the order between the objects of knowledge, that is, in an intelligible universe to be contemplated. Instead, they place it in the spiritual experience of one's activity, that is, on the side of the subject and not on that of the object. Thus, it expresses that experience, whose evidence was already expressed by the *Memoria* of St. Augustine and the latter's theme of *"Deus intimior me meipso."* This experience consists in an activity which is most authentically one's own, free, and thus, in a sense, most independent. At the same time it allows one to see most clearly that he is not its first source, but that it subsists in him from a source in which he lives, moves, and exists. This source is seen as conferring on one precisely that freedom which consists in a free response to the truth of the good as intuitively confronted, and as cleansed from the obscurities of instinct and its longing. Lavelle and Marcel do not hesitate to name this source God.

It remains necessary to discuss the difficult problem of values, specifically the question of their mode of being. If they are treated as the equivalent of things or even of Platonic Ideas, as if they were a gallery of pictures in a museum, then once again liberty runs the risk of falling back into a purely natural level of things.

It should be noted, however, that nobody, not even Sartre himself, has succeeded in realizing by the individual consciousness itself the total creation of his first step or leap and of his values. The "pour-soi," the consciousness or "néant" (nothing) rises up necessarily as a kind of obsession of the "en-soi" and leap ("projet") which is at the same time both free as the "pour-soi" and solid as the "en-soi." It is not a leap that one might choose or even invent. It is rather the absurd leap of nobody. It is the result of the absurd accident which is the birth of the "pour-soi." In order to avoid creation Sartre takes refuge in a kind of mythology.

Traditional philosophy is less extravagant in words, but more in agreement with reality, in defining liberty from the beginning as this mysterious agreement of oneself with a possibility which seems to come from within. This invites one to identify himself by choice with a possibility of oneself which does not itself depend for its being on one's choice.

A CHRISTIAN PHILOSOPHY OF FREEDOM

It is time now to draw some conclusions from these general ideas. It should be remembered, first of all, that one of the most difficult points in the religious conception of liberty is that same truth of creation which has appeared to converts from paganism to the Christian faith as the very sign of their liberation. On the contrary, to existential atheism as in general for a great number of philosophers, this truth appears as the very negation of liberty itself. This is so because it implies the dependence of creation on a cause, and hence on a being quite other than the creatures it causes to move and have their being. It seems to make one no more free than a remotely controlled machine. This then implies that the theme of liberty runs the risk of shutting off access to the sphere of religion for two distinct, but closely related reasons:

(1) the conception of liberty itself;
(2) the idea of our liberty being dependent upon the creative actions of God.

Let us briefly examine these points.

Concerning liberty itself, what is essential has already been stated. It is very important to present liberty under its true colors and to avoid simplifications. These may be useful for the imagination; but for many they impede rather than open the way to true liberty, since they imply a conception of liberty on a physical, rather than on a true spiritual basis. Such a message, far from constituting an invitation to growth and development in spiritual stature and to a certain and uninterrupted creation, appears as a promise of security bought at the price of higher aspirations.

However, the conception of liberty is not the only difficulty which confronts many contemporaries in reconciling their faith in liberty with the idea of God. It is indeed their idea of God and creative action that is equally involved. Here one touches upon the agonizing problems which all theologians know only too well, namely, the relationship of grace and liberty, physical promotion, divine concurrence, predestination, and human responsibility.

The intention here is not to take up again, even briefly, an exposé of theological themes involved, but simply to make the following observation. Supposing one conceived for himself as exact a conception of one's true liberty as possible. One would confront almost insurmountable difficulties if he proceeded to place, either in front or outside of this liberty, a God who is its cause. Such a God would cause as the sun causes the warming of the atmosphere, or even as a living being of this universe begets another living being from which it is completely distinct and independent. Either one does not speak of God in relation to one's liberty and satisfies oneself by a phenomenological presentation of given human experience, or one speaks of God. In the latter case, one must try, at least, to avoid those most egregious errors which, from their very nature, inevitably and irrevocably obscure the very data of the problem.

In this regard, one should call to mind the essential role that St. Thomas assigns to negative theology within the whole of theology. The words that open the treatise on the essence or the nature of God in the *Summa Theologica* itself should be taken quite seriously: "After having shown the existence of God, let us study the essence of God, that is to say, that which God is or rather that which he is not."[2] In the *Summa contra Gentiles*,[3] he observes that, in contrast to the knowledge of finite beings at which one arrives by the addition of positive differences, it is rather by a group of negations, made progressively more precise, that one attempts to discern the mystery of God. This is done without ever being able to obtain a positive grasp which, if had of the absolutely simple being, would necessarily be a direct vision of God himself.

If the affirmations of St. Thomas and of all the great theologians have any meaning, they say at least this: the word God designates a being whose fullness of being and perfection necessarily escapes the grasp of any created intellect. He is always incomprehensible, even for an intellect admitted by grace to the vision of God. Far from discouraging the spirit who loves God, this evidence of God's transcendence increases one's reverence and adoration, and the authenticity of one's love. Such is the condition of man's intelligence confronted with the word God; and he must never forget it. It must always be taken into account whenever one deals with a problem of anthropology or of ethics, and especially when one deals with the problem of freedom. This means that one must not work on the relation of freedom and of God without having realized the unique position that the word God occupies in the universe of one's mind.

Therefore, one cannot allow himself or his listeners to think that the freedom of man and God occupy in one sentence the same position as any subject or predicate. If God is the transcendent Being, the plenitude and source of all good and being, he cannot be exterior to anything in the univocal sense of spatial exteriority. He cannot be alien to anything or juxtaposed to anything, for he has no position. He is, on the contrary, interior to everything. More precisely, he is intimately present to everything that is, continually giving it true being. This is the presence that the theologians have taken so much trouble to specify. The very transcendence of God by which he is completely different from all that is finite implies his immanence, rather than opposing itself to it. The transcendence is not an infinite estrangement, which would terminate by coinciding with total absence and nothingness. It is rather the positive plenitude which necessarily comprises all perfection. By that very fact, it distinguishes itself from all finite being while at the same time being its permanent and superabundant source.

God cannot, therefore, be simply represented as something opposed to one's freedom, for this would imply an image which would lead to false perspectives. He is necessarily present as the very principle of one's freedom, not in order to limit or falsify it by his influence, but precisely to make it be: to give that authentic freedom of which one is aware. Certainly, it is impossible for one to think of his freedom and of God at the same time without danger of error. To deny it or to be astonished at it would be once again to forget that God transcends one's knowledge. Any philosopher or theologian, who would esteem himself capable of embracing God and his creatures in one perfect glance, would implicitly affirm that he is more than God. He would be the true super-God, judging and contemplating in one instant both God of whom he speaks and his works.

The first movement of freedom, then, will not be to revolt against God. Rather it will be to give thanks both that this gift is and that one finally knows that it is. The only way to be able to appreciate one's liberty, both as one's own and as rooted in an inexhaustible source, is precisely to understand that freedom as a free gift of oneself is a grace continually conferred on us by a source which is Gift by essence. A freedom which wishes only to be efficacy or will to power will seek above all to assert itself in opposing itself to anything. A liberty which understands itself as a free gift cannot but understand itself as participation in the Gift by essence. from which it is distinct, without being separated.

This less simplified conception of the relationship between one's freedom and its divine source permits one to avoid a great number of false problems relative to dependence upon the creative action of God. Certainly the mystery must remain if it is true that it could be clarified only if one clearly understood God and his relation to his work. But one can and must clearly say at least the following.

Freedom and Dependence

The notion of creation transcends efficient causality and places one once more in the field of analogy. To create is to make to be purely and simply, not to transform any preexistent material. A mechanic can construct a car which functions according to established laws and without his intervention to turn the pistons and wheels at each moment. Likewise, if an act is truly creative, it will posit true beings absolutely in the act of being and each will have the properties and nature demanded by its degree of being. Therefore, if God makes a freedom to be, the least one can say is that it is an authentic freedom which functions truly as freedom.

The continuous act, by which God gives freedom its being, will neither destroy it nor prevent it from being what it is and from functioning according to what it is, because it is precisely by that continuous gift that one's freedom is freedom. Such a dependence on its source results precisely in man's freedom being freedom: free in its being as well as in its act.

It remains true that the expression "efficient cause" or "creative cause" is suspect to many philosophers, Christian or not, because of the mechanical images that it inevitably suggests. Therefore, some have preferred to have recourse to other comparisons such as the relation which unites a work of art, a poem, or a piece of music to its author. Surely, the work depends on its author as an expression and a gift but not in a mechanical way. If in a certain sense the work is independent of the author and may continue to exist once the author has disappeared, it remains nevertheless the expression of his love of beauty which brought this work into being.

Other authors, such as Lavelle and Marcel, prefer the idea of participation. Be that as it may, the important point is not to believe that physical images are essential for the presentation of the notion of creation or the idea of the dependence of the creature upon God. This would make it more difficult, if not quite impossible, to reach Christian thought for minds sensible above all to the eminent dignity of our liberty and to the spiritual reality which it implies as its permanent principle. One should say the same for the notions of nature and substance. They may also imply images, which is correct and necessary. Nevertheless, these images make them liable to error in translating the realities of the spiritual order or of metaphysics.

Freedom and Law

There is an obstacle which one often creates for oneself without wishing it. This takes place when one is faced with the spiritual understanding of freedom, no longer under the aspect of dependence, but under that of the laws and norms. In doing this, one runs the risk of proposing God as a limit or an impediment against which one's freedom must inevitably stumble, and in which one's freedom finds an exterior limit which it can never surpass. This also is an image, and it is one which presents God first of all as in some way exterior to one's freedom. This image also presupposes that one's freedom should be without any other content than a gratuitous gesture: that it should be without law, without deliberation, without any other purpose than to show the will; that it should be no more than the absolute incoordination of gratuitous caprice.

However, far from being true freedom, this lack of coordination would be simply the physical or physiological decompression of energy, necessitated by its own pressure. This would remain in the domain of spontaneity, and in no way express that of freedom. True liberty appeals to and forms its own law. This is so in the same way in which a true scientist, in opposition to a dreamer, includes in the love of truth flowing from his spiritual spontaneity a rigorously demanding fidelity both to the object, which he tries to see correctly formed in his mind, and to the methods, which have proved their efficacy. To be truly free is not to be opposed to laws or values, but only to those laws and values forced upon one from outside and which one must fulfill out of fear of punishment or hope of gratification. This could never be the case where true freedom is faced with good or with laws understood in their true essence.

For St. Thomas, however, all true law is finally founded on the natural law. This in turn is essentially nothing other than the tending towards good and end which was marked by God himself on every creature as the true expression of its nature. Freedom has no other law than to be free. But if it be a matter of the mind, and in no way of a fluctuating energy, then freedom implies in that wish to be free which is its law the wish to know the truth of the good toward which the whole action takes place.

In this light, the law of God does not appear as a barrier against which one necessarily sees the aspiration of his liberty destroyed. There is no extrinsic frontier to one's liberty and he can desire everything, the good and the evil. But good cannot do otherwise than to appear as that which ought to be, and evil as that which ought not to be. If one considers that as a barrier then it must be recognized that freedom indeed has its limits. Not to recognize these limits, or to be unable or unwilling to take account of them, is to be unable to act freely in the full sense of that word. It would be the same as making some blind gesture or one of whose worth one has no idea, and then resigning oneself bravely to the consequences. Under the pretext of a more pure freedom, the consequences would be produced without having dared to look the situation in the face.

It is true that, at the same time, one both does and does not propose one's own law for oneself. As St. Augustine exclaims: who belongs more truly to oneself than oneself, and who is less one's own than oneself if one is what one is by another! Therefore, one must avoid relating freedom to law as a vital movement to a limit which operates from outside, or as a moving object which collides with an obstacle. Trees also are bound by certain limits, but it is in no way necessary to frame them with metal frames or to point out to them how large they must be or what shape they must assume, as one would do with blocks of cement. It is their own vital spontaneity which keeps them within their proper limits.

Finally, one must in no way conceive God as exercising external surveillance over one's actions in the same way in which parents either recompense or punish their children by watching whether or not they behave according to the rules set down. A God who would be obliged to spy on man in such a way, in order to assure the proper distribution of his sanctions according to man's good or evil behavior or according to the account man renders of himself, would be anything except God. It is well known how damaging to the mind of those who have realized the eminent dignity of the God-given free act is the presentation of a God-directed moral as a sanction, repentance, reparation, or merit added, so to speak, from outside to the proper value of the moral act.

CONCLUSION

To sum up, it can be said that the theme of human freedom meets religion in two perspectives: first, in its origin where it meets God as Creator, and, secondly, where freedom stands before God as lawgiver and judge. Freedom depends upon God for its very being; it must recognize him as its author and as the author of moral law.

On these two aspects, contemporary thought poses somewhat new problems which Christian philosophy must recognize. Most assuredly, the truth given to men by God must not be modified to the passing whim. On the other hand, one should be ready to recognize that there are some legitimate demands being made to give high value to the truth in the very manner in which one presents that truth. One must not confuse the truth with the more or less adequate expressions given to it, for by doing so one

10

would risk confusing those expressions with truth itself and, consequently, falsifying the picture. One would then be like the pharisees who, by their blind fidelity to the letter, imposed heavy burdens on men's shoulders. Jesus himself declared it impossible to bear such burdens and wished in his love to remove them in order to liberate the human race.

In the same way, one must always be assiduous in freeing the true spirit of Christian philosophy from inadequate expression and formulae. This is neither a desire to hide the truth nor a servile fear of wounding men's susceptibilities. Quite the contrary; it must be done in order to permit all facets of philosophy to be presented to one's contemporaries in a true and authentic form.

◇

1. See L. B. Geiger. "Philosophie realiste et liberté," in **Philosophie et spiritualité** (Paris: Desclée, 1963), II, 35-59.

2. Thomas Aquinas, **Summa Theologica** (New York: Benziger, 1947), I, q. 3, prol.

3. Thomas Aquinas, **Summa Contra Gentiles** (London: Burns, Oats & Washbourne, 1923), I, c. 14.

Part III

Language

God, Necessity and Falsifiability

◊

by
Kai Nielsen

IT IS DIFFICULT to know where to start in talking about
religion. People are puzzled about it and taken up with it in
very different ways, but many philosophers' deepest perplexities
turn on whether they can make any tolerable sense out of key
religious concepts. Where they want to believe, this sometimes
leads even to a profound emotional harassment, for in certain
moods at any rate the most fundamental concepts of their religion seem quite meaningless to them.

In its own right, this reaction is philosophically puzzling,
since for the most part both believers and non-believers, as participants in the same culture with the same forms of life, know
how to use religious discourse. In our culture, they both have a
participant's grasp of God-talk. At this level there is no significant lack of understanding; they both know how to operate with
religious discourse. But knowing how to use this self-involving
form of discourse does not imply that there is no bewilderment
about its use. Both believers and non-believers alike are baffled
by what it is all about.

It is no longer news that a very pervasive kind of disbelief
consists in the conviction that key segments of God-talk are not
stammering efforts to talk about an ultimate mystery, but meaningless or incoherent stretches of discourse. God-talk, it is held,

does not succeed in fulfilling the putative cosmological claims which believers confusedly think they are making when they use such language. Non-Neanderthal believers, on the other hand, though deeply perplexed by the language will continue to claim on pain of ceasing to be believers that, though such talk is perplexing, it is not utterly meaningless or incoherent. In reality such utterances do have a kind of substantive content which enables their users to make intelligible, affirmative, cosmological assertions concerning a mysterious ultimate reality. Though they are mystifying utterances, they manage to present themselves as factual claims, that is as true or false utterances about what there is. The believer must take his stand here, but this is precisely where many a religious sceptic is sceptical.[1]

There is a natural response and defensive stratagem on the part of the religious believer that cannot be allowed. I have in mind the kind of fideism which would claim that though the believer's utterances are meaningless, he can believe them anyway. This is nonsense if anything is,[2] for unless we know at least in some minimal sense what it is we are to believe, it is logically impossible for us to either believe or disbelieve. I cannot believe or fail to believe in some putative proposition unless I understand to at least some extent the meaning of p. Whether we like it or not, we are faced with the very central and fundamental question of whether God-talk does have sufficient intelligibility to give it enough coherence to make faith justifiable. Can we show that God-talk has the kind of intelligibility which would make reasonable, philosophically informed, and perceptive human beings become or remain Jews, Christians, or Moslems?

While religious sceptics do not think that religious discourse has this kind of intelligibility, believers obviously think that it does. How could we rationally decide whether God-talk has sufficient intelligibility to make Christian, Jewish, or Islamic belief acceptable options among the conflicting ways of life?

THEOLOGY OF FALSIFICATION: A. FLEW

Part of the issue here emerges from the much discussed "theology and falsification" issue and from what has been dubbed Flew's challenge.[3] Suppose two fast friends, a believer and a sceptic, are standing together aboard ship on a starry night. The believer remarks to his friend, "How can you really deny that God made all this?" The sceptic replies that awe-inspiring and vast as all this is, he cannot see the hand of God in it. "From a human point of view," the sceptic continues, "there are perfections as well as imperfections and order as well as disorder in nature, but there is no reason to say God created or ordained it all." Whatever the believer points to as evidence for God's creative activity, the sceptic interprets naturalistically. On close observation they seem to be using different terminology to describe the same phenomena. Finally, an observer of this discussion begins to wonder if there is anything more than a purely verbal and attitudinal difference between the believer and his sceptical friend. When the believer asserts "God made all this" or "God loves his children," what is he asserting that is different from the assertions of the sceptic with his thoroughly naturalistic orientation?

Surely, if he is doing anything more than talking about natural phenomena in a high-toned manner, he must show the difference between asserting and denying such putative statements as God created the heavens and the earth and God loves his children. If this cannot be done—if it is not possible to show at least what conceivable experiences count for and against the claim that God created the heavens and the earth and that God loves his children—then these putative statements are devoid of factual and cosmological significance. They purport to make factual statements and are actually used by believers with that intent. Nevertheless, they are devoid of factual content if no experiential statements, not even statements recording what it is logically possible to experience, count for or against their truth.

However, as Flew points out, this at least seems to be just the situation we are in vis-à-vis religion. Sophisticated believers so use such key bits of God-talk that nothing counts or even is allowed to count against their truth. If even in principle nothing can count against their truth then neither can anything count for their truth. Thus, in reality such theistic claims are devoid of factual or cosmological significance. Flew's challenge comes to this: the theist seems to use such key theistic utterances as "God created the heavens and the earth" or even "There is a God" in such a way that they are compatible with anything that could conceivably transpire. If this is so, then they are devoid of factual significance. To show that they do have the kind of factual significance and intelligibility the believer requires, the believer must show what conceivable turn of events would count against his putative assertions. He must describe a conceivable turn of events which, if it were to transpire, would be sufficient to warrant the claim that it is not the case that God created the heavens and the earth and it is not the case that God loves mankind.

Of course, as a believer he does not believe that such states will occur. However, if his God-talk is to have factual content, he must not rule out the logical possibility that one could specify an empirically identifiable state of affairs, which, were it to transpire, would warrant the assertion "There is no God." "God does not love his children" or "God did not create the heavens and the earth."

Much modern scepticism and religious perplexity revolves upon the conviction that theists cannot adequately meet this challenge. Non-anthropomorphites cannot state in straightforward empirical terms under what conceivable conditions they would give up making such key theistic claims. Thus they seem not to be making any real claims at all.

Many have assumed that such a challenge is not really serious because in a somewhat hidden form it presupposes the correctness of the new thoroughly discredited logical empiricist claim that an utterance is at least cognitively meaningless unless it is verifiable (confirmable or infirmable) in principle. But no such general criterion of meaning is presupposed or even involved in Flew's challenge or in my argument. What is involved is the following: an utterance is devoid of *factual* content—and thus can make no factual assertion—if it is not directly or indirectly confirmable or infirmable in principle. This essay will examine the reasonableness of this assumption.

Many would categorically deny that this is a proper assumption when the subject of our discourse is God. God has the kind of existence, if He exists at all, that makes it impossible to characterize the logic of God-talk in such a manner. God is a necessary being; His non-existence is inconceivable. If He exists, He exists necessarily. Thus, His existence is either logically necessary or impossible. Because there can be no question of an experimental or empirical identification of God, Flew's challenge is not to the point. The only possible identification of God would be a purely conceptual one. If this can be done at all, it will be accomplished through a conceptual analysis which will establish that "There is a God" is *logically* necessary and "There is no God" is a contradiction.

Such a claim leads us to the topic of necessary existence. To evade Flew's challenge, one must establish that the concept of necessary existence or necessary being is a coherent one, that God has necessary existence, and that a purely conceptual identification of God is possible. This will answer the most pressing questions about the intelligibility and coherence of God-talk.

GOD AS A LOGICALLY NECESSARY BEING: C. HARTSHORNE

I agree that if God exists His existence is necessary. More to the present point, I also agree that if the word "God," as it has come to function in the Jewish-Christian-Islamic tradition, is expressive of a coherent concept, it must be possible to make sense of the notion of necessary existence. But the crucial question remains: can one make sense of necessary existence.

On a certain understanding of Anselm, Malcolm and Hartshorne have tried to explicate and defend a concept of necessary existence. It commits them to regarding God as a logically necessary being and to treating "There is a God" and "God exists" as analytic statements, that is, as statements expressing logical necessities.[4] Though some of the arguments are subtle, because I have discussed the issue at length elsewhere and Malcolm and Hartshorne have been devastatingly criticized by others, I shall be moving here too brusquely and dismissively really to get to the bottom of that issue.[5] Nevertheless, before progressing to my major topic, I wish to indicate the lay of the land and provide some grounds for believing that another conception of necessary existence needs to be appealed to, if this appeal is to serve as an adequate model for explicating the concept of God.

In brief, it is propositions or statements, not beings, that are logically necessary, because it is to propositions or statements rather than to beings or forces that such predicates are applicable. It makes no more sense to speak of a being which is logically necessary than it does to speak of a stone being alienated. Furthermore, there are no existential statements that are logically necessary. J. N. Findlay is perfectly right: if God is treated as a logically necessary being—as having logically necessary existence —then the concept of God, like the concept of a round square, becomes self-contradictory. We would thus know for certain that God's existence is impossible, for the very concept of a logically necessary being is self-contradictory.[6]

Wherever "x" denotes a being or Being, it is never self-contradictory to deny that there is an x. The negation of an existential statement is never a self-contradiction. It is indeed true that "God is eternal" is analytic; it is also analytic to say that God could not cease to exist or come to exist. Thus, "God died" or "God ceased to exist," when taken literally, is a contradiction in terms.[7] By definition God is eternal, and it does not make sense to assert that an eternal being ceased to exist. Nevertheless, it is perfectly intelligible and consistent to assert that there are no eternal beings, and from conceptual analysis alone, it would follow that if there are no eternal beings now, there never was and never will be. This does not establish the truth of the existential statement "There is an eternal being" or the falsity of "There are no eternal beings." Assuming the intelligibility of the phrase "eternal being," conceptual analysis alone cannot establish the existence or non-existence of such beings. Thus, it cannot establish the existence of God.

Though Malcolm has claimed that the denial of *a priori* existential statements is only a dogma, no convincing example of an *a priori* existential statement has ever been given. Hume's famous remarks in this regard in his *Dialogues Concerning Natural Religion*[8] would seem to be a truism, namely, that whatever can consistently be said to exist can consistently be said not to exist. When I assert that x exists, I can also consistently deny that statement. As Findlay shows, this is independent of whether there are synthetic *a priori* statements for in contrast to existential statements those which are said to be synthetic *a priori* do not categorically assert the existence of anything.[9] The synthetic *a priori* statements "Nothing can be red and green all over" and "Every event has a cause," do not make the categorical assertion that anything exists. Knowing the truth of the second assertion does not tell us if there are any events. We know only that if there are any events, they have causes. No existential statement can be logically necessary. The very concept of "a logically necessary being" is self-contradictory.

METAPHYSICAL STATEMENTS: M. CHARLESWORTH

Many would meet Flew's challenge by simply denying that, in order to be factual, an assertion must be verifiable or falsifiable in principle or, as I prefer to put it, confirmable or infirmable in principle. They concede that empirical propositions must be in principle confirmable or infirmable, but add as a counterbalancing factor that one must not assume gratuitously that only empirical propositions have factual or descriptive meaning.[10] Why can there not be unverifiable statements of fact; why can there not be metaphysical factual statements that are neither confirmable nor infirmable in principle; does not the word "empirical" qualify facts? It will be argued that I, Flew, and a host of others are still caught up in a dogmatic and unjustified positivistic spirit. There are certain factual statements, which many have called "metaphysical statements," that are in perfectly good logical order but are not even in principle confirmable or infirmable.

It is surely incumbent upon me to examine some arguments for that claim. One is made by M. J. Charlesworth in his "Linguistic Analysis and Language About God."[11] Charlesworth points out that it is one thing to say that an assertion is a meaningful statement of fact only if we know what would count against its truths; it is "quite another thing altogether to say that an assertion is meaningful only if we know what would count against its truth in the way in which we know what would count against the truth of an empirical assertion."[12] Believers who are at all orthodox take "God will protect me and judge me" to be a factual statement. It is indeed true, Charlesworth agrees, that to be a genuine factual statement (to make a meaningful factual assertion) something must count against its being true. It is also true that to understand such utterances we must know what would count against their being true.[13]

So far there is agreement between Charlesworth, Flew and myself. But, Charlesworth adds, not all "counting against their truth" need be linked to empirical verification. In the case of metaphysical statements, including key theistic assertions, we know what would count against their being true in the sense that "their validity is shown by showing the self-contradictoriness of their contradictories."[14] If, for example, we can show that the assertion "Everything happens by pure chance" is absurd, then "the metaphysical statement that the world exhibits 'order' or 'design' is meaningful."[15] Metaphysical statements do have meaningful opposites; they do make a non-vacuous contrast: "What is denied by metaphysical statements is some kind of absurdity or self-contradictory 'state of affairs' and this, so to speak, is not nothing."[16]

This argument has several flaws. To show that "stones are females" is absurd, does not show that "stones are males" or "stones are not females" is meaningful. "It is false that procrastination drinks melancholy" or "It is not the case that colorless green ideas divorce" are no more meaningful than "Procrastination drinks melancholy" or "Colorless green ideas divorce." All we have done is to put the negative sign, which itself is quite intelligible, before a meaningless collocation of words. Where what we are denying is a contradiction, we should remark that a contradiction cannot be in every sense meaningless. We must understand at least that, given the meanings of the individual words in question, we cannot string words together in this way and assert anything. But being meaningful in this way cannot carry the implication of being assertive. If a given utterance contains a genuine self-contradiction, it cannot be used for stating anything that can be true or false. To try to do so would be to attempt the impossible, namely, to assert at one and the same time and in the same respect the truth of mutually incompatible propositional elements. In effect, a self-contradictory utterance functions to negate itself and thus it cannot assert; it is self-cancelling and ends by affirming nothing at all. Such a sentence unsays what it says and so ends by failing to assert anything. A self-contradictory utterance does not discuss or classify anything; thus it could not possibly assert anything.

When Charlesworth says that the denial of a metaphysical statement asserts a "self-contradictory 'state of affairs,'" he puts "state of affairs" in quotation marks. He does this because he must realize, however dimly, that a state of affairs, a fact, can no more be contradictory than a colorless idea can be green. A self-contradictory statement in principle lacks the power to refer; that is, it is senseless to speak of its referent. Thus its denial cannot refer either, because it does not actually deny that a certain state of affairs obtains. Contradiction and self-contradiction are features of languages, not of facts.

In this connection, a defense of Charlesworth might assert that "if necessarily false statements assert what can in principle never be the case, the denial of such a statement must assert what in principle must always be the case."[17] In reality, however, Charlesworth cannot be defended in that way, because "can in principle never be the case" means "logically impossible to be the case." In turn, this implies "it makes no sense to speak of something being the case here." When I deny the statement, I do not assert that another state of affairs must be the case. I simply give one to understand that words cannot intelligibly be so used.

At the very most, it might be claimed that I disguisedly asserted something about the meanings of words. If I deny that there are any married bachelors or colorless green ideas, I am proclaiming that it is senseless to speak of married bachelors or colorless green ideas. I am not asserting that there must be bachelors or green things, and since "unmarried bachelors" and "colored greens" are pleonastic, I am not asserting that there must be married bachelors or colored greens either. "Unmarried" and "colored" do not really qualify their noun here; they are, in such a linguistic environment, *Ersatz* adjectives which do no linguistic or conceptual work.

If Charlesworth drops the part about "self-contradictory 'state of affairs'" and restricts his claim to "metaphysical statements deny some kind of absurdity," he has said something too vague to be of any philosophical value. If I deny that the moon is made of green cheese or that Nelson Rockerfeller could swim across the Atlantic, I deny an absurdity, but it certainly does not follow that I have made a metaphysical statement. I have instead simply uttered an empirical truism. What special kind of absurdities do metaphysical statements deny? From Charlesworth's example, it would seem that they deny statements whose meaning is, to put it mildly, very unclear. An example is his "Everything in the world happens by pure chance." Assuming that "Everything happens by pure chance" is not self-contradictory or empirically false, what kind of absurdity does it have? It has the kind of absurdity as does "Procrastination drinks melancholy," namely, that while it seems to assert—it has a declarative form—we do not have a use for it anymore than we have a use for "Procrastination drinks."

My above remarks need the following qualification. The two phrases differ in that in certain quite non-metaphysical contexts there is a humdrum use for "pure chance" which Nagel has shown to be perfectly compatible with determinism. It is the use of chance in a sentence like "It was by pure chance that we met at the Klausen pass."[18] If we construe "Everything happens by pure chance" in that way, it indeed becomes a genuine statement; but it also becomes an absurdly false empirical statement. Thus, its denial is not a metaphysical statement either. There is no other use for "pure chance," or at least no other use has been given. Where it is not an empirical absurdity or a contradictory notion, it has no determinate meaning. Like "Procrastination drinks melancholy" or "Disenchanted stone couples suffer alienation," it is without a determinate meaning or use in any *Sprachspiel;* and hence its denial is also without such a use. Since this is so, it cannot be used to assert what is the case or what must be the case.

At one point Charlesworth says that we show the truth of metaphysical statements "by showing the self-contradictoriness of their contradictories." In this case we have, in addition to the above difficulties, others as well. We have shown metaphysical statements to be analytic and, by definition, analytic statements are devoid of factual or substantive content.[19] Charlesworth is correct in pointing out that not all analytic statements are tautologies. However, he is mistaken in thinking that only tautologies, e.g., "A is A," assert nothing at all or are not assertions. Tautologies "do not deny anything, either a possible state of affairs or an impossible 'state of affairs,'" but "Bachelors are unmarried" does not, as I have shown, deny anything either. "A logically impossible state of affairs," like "a round square," is a senseless collocation of words.[20] Anyone who understands the meanings of the constituent terms understands that nothing could answer to that putative description. (It, of course, should not be confused with more mundane uses of language which are perfectly in order, e.g., "The situation in Vietnam is an impossible state of affairs.") "Bachelors are unmarried" signals (indirectly indicates) that certain linguistic conventions are being observed and that for any words with equivalent uses in the same or a different language, it would not make sense to deny such a statement.

Charlesworth maintains that accounts like mine are accounts in which "an arbitrary metaphysical assumption" has been unwittingly or surreptitiously introduced. In view of my above argument, Charlesworth surely needs to give us in precise detail exactly what metaphysical assumption or assumptions have been made.[21] I do not see that I have done anything of the sort here. It seems to me that in arguing against Charlesworth, I have only appealed to the logic or style of functioning of the English language. I would not want to say that my arguments are in any way simply relative to the English language, for certainly what I have said here could be translated into German or French without loss of cognitive content. In fine, I did not make metaphysical assumptions in anything I have said here; I simply appealed to the uses of language.

T. CORBISHLEY VS NOWELL-SMITH ON EMPIRICAL LIMITATIONS

In the original university discussion of Flew's challenge, Thomas Corbishley tried to meet the challenge directly by showing that there are factual statements which are neither confirmable nor infirmable even in principle. I feel that Nowell-Smith's reply to Corbishley utterly devastated his central contentions. However, since others disagree and the issue is a fundamental one, I shall briefly review the arguments.

Corbishley argues that Flew's "notion of what constitutes a fact is in need of enlargement," and that Flew is right in claiming that God is not observable.[22] "There is a God" is not equivalent to or entailed by any statements concerning observable phenomena. Corbishley remarks that he would "gladly concede to Mr. Flew that when I assert that God is a fact, I do not mean by that statement that God is observable in the sense in which gardeners are observable."[23] Even in principle God is not directly observable. Corbishley should have added that since He is not in principle directly observable, He cannot be indirectly observable either. But Corbishley maintains that God is a fact in a "deeper sense" than any contingent thing is a fact. He believes that it is a fact, and practically speaking an undubitable fact, that God exists, because if God were not, "nothing would ever happen at all."[24]

Since this is so, Corbishley meets Flew's challenge in the following way: ". . . in reply to the question 'What would have to occur or to have occurred to constitute for you a disproof of the love of, or of the existence of, God' the only thing to be said is, quite literally, 'Nothing.' "[25] Corbishley takes the question of God's existence to be the key metaphysical question: he maintains that only "the non-existence of anything at all would constitute for me a disproof of the existence of God."[26] Given the fact that "that condition is just not possible," is it not evident that "There is a God" has factual intelligibility and is manifestly true? Flew's very way of posing the question begs the whole issue. There can be no situations which are incompatible with God's existence, for if there are any situations at all (and there are), then God exists. Given the range of application of the word "God," we cannot apply the principle of non-vacuous contrast, which is applicable to ordinary descriptive statements. Given what God is, it is logically impossible that there could be a state of affairs incompatible with His existence. "God exists" and "I exist" are not the sort of assertions for which it is "possible to find out anything that could be regarded as 'counting against' or being incompatible with their truth."[27]

Corbishley contends that Flew makes this challenge only as he does because he uncritically presupposes the common empirical dogma that "unless facts are visible, audible, tangible or somehow observable by sense-experimentation, they are not only ungettable: they just are not facts."[28] Indeed, if x is properly called "a gardener" or "a policeman," then x must surely be something that can be seen. But, Corbishley asks, what is the justification for claiming "that all facts must be of the same class as gardeners or policemen?" To reply "that only the empirically observable is of value for philosophizing" is to make another dogmatic metaphysical statement that, like "I exist" or "There is a God," is not open to falsification. We must firmly recognize that there are many factual statements not open to empirical confirmation or disconfirmation. Corbishley maintains that there are plain factual statements which are compatible with any and every conceivable empirical state of affairs. "God exists" or "There is a God" are such statements. Thus Flew's challenge is simply irrelevant to them.

There are a host of difficulties in Corbishley's attempt to meet Flew's challenge. P. H. Nowell-Smith only points out a few; but, as Nowell-Smith avers, there are many more. Those which come out in attempts to meet Nowell-Smith's reply and arguments of that type will be examined in the next section. In the remainder of this section I shall reproduce the crucial (and to my mind quite adequate) substance of Nowell-Smith's rejoinder, leaving further and more complicated points to the subsequent discussion.

Nowell-Smith remarks that "Corbishley does not answer Flew's main contentions; he evades them and he feels justified in so doing because he attributes to Flew a crude sensationalism which he thinks is self-refuting."[29] As we have seen, Corbishley thinks that Flew holds that "an unobservable fact is not a fact."[30] This would make it impossible for Flew to believe that there are magnetic fields; but Flew, like anyone else in the modern world who has his wits about him, believes that there are such realities. Moreover, it would be absurd for him not to believe in their reality, and for this reason we are strongly inclined to agree with Corbishley that there must be something wrong with Flew's empiricist philosophical principles.

However, Nowell-Smith counters that such a criticism is wide of the mark, for Flew need not say that things like magnetic fields, opinions or other minds must be observable in order to be facts. "All he requires is that it should be possible to produce evidence for or against their existence; and this can easily be done. A pattern of iron filings is evidence for a magnetic field and Flew's paper is evidence for the existence . . . of his opinions."[31] Although some empiricists have tried, we cannot identify the meaning of abstract entities, e.g., Flew's opinions, magnetic fields, orthodoxy or the British Constitution "with their actual and hypothetical manifestations." Nowell-Smith points out that Flew does not commit this error. "He makes no attempt to develop a theory on this point."[32] He only argues, and rightly so, that if such statements as "a magnetic field can be set up by induction" or "the British Constitution is unsatisfactory" make sense, we must "be able to say, at least roughly, what would count as evidence for or against them."[33] Contrary to Corbishley, this does not commit one to the claim that only what can be observed can exist.

It is Corbishley's preoccupation with this issue that blinds him to the point of Flew's parable. The point of the parable is just this:

> God is invoked as an explanation. But if an explanation, of whatever sort, be it empirical or metaphysical, is to explain it must explain why things are like this *and not like that*. Newton's laws explain the movement of the earth; they would not be an explanation if they were true no matter how the earth moved. . . . And for the same reason, the hypothesis that God exists can only explain what happens on earth provided that it explains why this happens and not that.[34]

Indeed tautologies and other analytic statements and propositions that become true by being uttered, e.g., "I am now speaking," are not falsifiable in principle. Here Flew's challenge is irrelevant. But "There is a God" is not analytic and "surely Corbishley does not want to maintain that 'There is a God' is necessarily true because it becomes true by being uttered."[35]

Nowell-Smith makes a further important point about "There is a God" that is very frequently overlooked. Contrary to what Corbishley maintains, "the proposition that God exists must follow and not precede propositions about what God is and does."[36] Before we can sensibly ask whether God exists, we must have some idea of "what it is that is said to exist."[37] Because an existential statement asserts "that there is (or is not) a subject of a certain kind," we must know or at least have some idea of what kind. If our God-talk is to be intelligible, we must give or it must be possible to give the criteria that governs the use of "God." How are we to do that? What are we talking about when we use the word "God"?

Corbishley does not treat "God" as something that can be taught by ostension, for he does not want to say that God can be directly apprehended. In some sense we are to infer the existence of God from experience. We say God must exist because of Y, and Y could not exist without God's existing. (It is like "There are people on the island because there are footprints there, and there could be no footprints if there were no people.") But we have to know what it is we are to infer in order to be able to assert that there is a God. For such an inference to be possible, there must be an intelligible set of conditions associated with "God," and it is here that we face classic difficulties.

One condition that is associated with "God" is "love." God is said to love all mankind. We then discover that "God loves all mankind" is taken by the faithful, or at least by the theologically sophisticated faithful, to be compatible with any and every empirically specifiable state of affairs. No matter what happens, no matter how horrible the situation we envision, it is still held to be compatible with "God loves all mankind." At this juncture, Nowell-Smith asks, what does the word "love" mean in "God loves all mankind" if "God is said to love no matter what happens."[38] The point that Corbishley misses is this: since we cannot ostensively teach "God" in order to be able to assert intelligibly that there is a God, we must come to know what "God" means through descriptions. We must teach and learn the meaning of "God" intralinguistically. Perhaps "God" is but an umbrella term for certain definite descriptions, but at any rate we learn the meaning of "God" intralinguistically by ascertaining that certain conditions are associated with "God." "Love" is one of them. To be able to understand the Jewish-Christian use of "God" we must be able to understand what it means to say "God loves his children." But in order to understand such a statement, we must understand what counts for and against its truth. As Nowell-Smith well says:

We do *not* ask that God's love should be identical with human love; but to be called "love" at all, it must be distinguishable from hate. Even if we believe that God never does, has or will hate his children we must know what sort of situation would lead us to say that he does, even though this situation never arises. Unless "God loves" is contrasted with something it is meaningless.[39]

Behind this claim of Nowell-Smith is a general conceptual

point about descriptive discourse. If a word in a sentence is descriptive (functions descriptively), it "not only means what it does but also excludes what it does not mean."[40] In making factual statements we must utilize what Nowell-Smith calls descriptive sentences; but a descriptive sentence is quite comparable to a descriptive word. To be intelligible, they both must exclude something and have a positive meaning. In fact, this inclusion and exclusion are two sides of the same coin. "A descriptive sentence not only describes a state of affairs but excludes contradictory states of affairs."[41] When it is said that a factual statement must be falsifiable in principle, we are given to understand that it is a statement made by the employment of such a sentence, *viz.* "a descriptive sentence." Only such sentences could be used to make falsifiable statements. To understand "God" we must be able to understand sentences like "God loves his children," "God is angry with men for their sins," "God is merciful to those who are truly penitent," "God is a jealous God," and the like. If "God" is used in an intelligible manner, these sentences must be descriptive sentences. Since this is so, we must be able to meet Flew's challenge and say what would have to occur to constitute evidence against the love of God. Corbishley has not shown how the believer can either meet or justifiably evade Flew's challenge. He has not shown how we can prove that our crucial God-talk has a proper sense if one cannot meet this challenge.

C. DALY, W. NORRIS CLARKE, AND ARGUMENTS OF UNIVERSAL INTELLIGIBILITY

C. B. Daly finds Nowell-Smith's arguments unconvincing and responds in a way that is reasonably typical of a number of metaphysicians.[42] Nowell-Smith argued that for something to be a genuine explanation of any sort "it must explain why things are like this and not like that." To this Daly replies:

But if the theist's reason for asserting the existence of God is the finitude of contingency of any and all finite being, then quite obviously the assertion is not open to empirical verification or falsification in the sense intended and the proposed tests display an enormous *ignoratio elenchi.* Flew's falsificatory occurrences occur in an already existing world whose *existence* is taken for granted; the theist invokes God as the *Cause of the existence of the world.* Nowell-Smith supposes that the "God-hypothesis" will imply one kind of world: the "no-God-hypothesis" a different kind of world. But the theist's proposition is that on the "no-God-hypothesis" there is no kind of a world. Father Corbishley, S. J., was perfectly right in retorting to Flew: "In reply to the question 'What would have to occur or to have occurred to constitute for you a disproof of the love of, and of the existence of God?' the only thing to be said is, quite literally, 'Nothing.' The Theist declares, if there is any kind of world, God exists. His alternative is, either God or nothing. He invokes God, not to explain why the world is 'like this, and not like that,' but to explain how there can be a world at all."[43]

In a similar vein W. Norris Clarke has argued that the principle embedded in Flew's challenge is not "applicable to arguments of universal intelligible exigency."[44] If we look at the actual logic of God-talk, he claims, we will see why. When believers reason about their belief, as when they try to establish the existence of God, it is quite natural for them to reason as follows: "All finite beings demand an infinite of self-sufficient being as their necessary ground of intelligibility. Given finite beings, it necessarily follows that there is an infinite being." If they do reason this way—and many religious people do—the very logic of their argument requires that they assert that every finite or contingent being requires an infinite ultimate cause or ground. Since this is so, it is hardly appropriate to ask the believer who has made that argument to name a finite state of affairs which would count against this claim.

The finite state of affairs would have to be intelligible to be so specified, and it is the believer's precise point here that no finite state of affairs is intelligible without the infinite as its ground. The argument proceeds from this general character of finitude or contingency; hence no particular grouping of finite or contingent beings affects the issue so long as they are still finite. Thus, Daly and Clarke both conclude that the only way to falsify the argument is by attacking the validity of the argument. This can be done only by showing that there is nothing intrinsic to finitude such that finite beings, to be understood at all adequately, must be understood as requiring the infinite as their sufficient reason. God is thus asserted as the necessary conclusion of an argument, not as a contingent fact of experience.

There are a myriad of difficulties and perplexities about these claims. First a general point: both Fathers Daly and Clarke seem to be pulling themselves up by their own bootstraps. In speaking of arguments, demonstrations, proofs and the like, they are assuming the intelligibility of the premises and conclusion while it is just this which is at issue. What is the meaning of Father Clarke's first premise, *viz* "All finite beings demand an infinite or self sufficient being as their necessary ground of intelligibility"? It is precisely such utterances that raise a problem about the intelligibility of God-talk. People are puzzled about the phrase "infinite or self-sufficient being." They are finite beings; they know what it is to demand a raise, or a divorce, or an end to hostilities in Vietnam; they even know vaguely what it is to demand the moon. But what, if anything, does it mean to demand an infinite or self-sufficient being?

What are people talking about when they talk about "an infinite being" or "a self-sufficient being"? Fred says "There is a glacier on Neptune," Maria denies that there are any glaciers there. We understand their utterances; we know what is at issue; and we know what would decide the issue, although at present we may not know how to decide that issue. But if Father Clarke says "There really is an infinite being" and Corliss Lamont says "No, there isn't," the problem of what really is at issue between them arises. What is Father Clarke affirming and Lamont denying?

What, if anything, does "infinite being" refer to? "Infinite being" ostensibly refers, but what it supposedly refers to cannot be observed even in principle. Perhaps it no more succeeds in referring than do "round-square" or "contradictory state of affairs" or "roglid"? How could it actually refer, if even in principle we cannot distinguish observing, encountering, and apprehending such a being from failing to observe, ecounter, or apprehend such a being? Both Clarke and Lamont recognize that there are finite beings, though Lamont may not like talking about them in this way. They might even both agree that these finite beings demand an infinite being as their necessary ground of intelligibility, though Lamont could say that nevertheless there is no such infinite being. "Men and other finite beings exist and they seek a necessary ground of intelligibility, but there is no necessary ground of intelligibility and there is no infinite being." He might add "Even if there were a necessary ground of intelligibility, men need not seek it in an infinite being." These last two utterances do not seem to be incoherent or unintelligible; they most certainly do not appear to be contradictory. If they are contradictory, their denials would be analytic and surely Clarke would not want that.

Would Father Clarke seriously try to maintain that either (1) "If there are finite beings then there is an infinite being" or (2) "If there are finite beings and if there is a necessary ground of intelligibility, then there is an infinite being" has the same tight logical force as "If there are red pencils then there are colored pencils" or "If there are valleys then there is some ground above the valley"? If he does, he is maintaining that they are analytic, and is therefore faced with the fact that his crucial premises are actually truths of language. From truths of language, no truths of non-linguistic fact can follow.

If, like Father Copleston, he denies that they have that tight logical force then, given that we logically cannot observe an infinite being and that no empirically identifiable state of affairs will indirectly verify it, how can Clarke claim that he has ground for asserting that his premise is true and Lamont's false? If their truth conditions are the same, how can he even distinguish them? That they are verbally different no one denies, but so too are "Marie sweats" and "Marie glows." Isn't the only difference between what Clarke and Lamont say is that Father Clarke likes to use "infinite being" with all its emotive overtones, while Lamont does not? If the above argument is right, can there be any more difference between them on substantive grounds than between Hans and Erik when Hans asserts 'He took the elevator' and Erik asserts "He took the lift?"

The believer, of course, wants to claim that he is asserting something more than the non-believer, but if the above is correct, he is unable to say or explain what more he is asserting. His key phrase certainly at least appears to be devoid of cognitive meaning. It purports to refer to something that is not naturalistically specifiable, but it fails to indicate what it would be like for either a believer or an non-believer to know or to have reason to believe that such a reference has been successfully made.

In order to initiate his theistic argument so that we can inspect its validity, its premises must be intelligible in the requisite sense. This is precisely the logically prior question that Clarke tries to bypass. However, as my above argument shows, it cannot be so readily bypassed or in fact bypassed at all, for there are very serious questions concerning the intelligibility of his premises.

INTELLIGIBILITY AND THEISTIC REASONING

This point is of sufficient importance to approach it from a different direction. Corbishley, Daly and Clarke argue that since every finite being and presumably every conceivable finite being as well requires an infinite and ultimate cause or ground, then no disconfirming or falsifying evidence could occur for the statement "There is an infinite ground of all finite things." Any mentionable piece of evidence would refer to a finite being and every finite being, if it is to be intelligible and thus recognizable, requires an infinite cause or ground. The existence of anything at all counts as evidence and, presumably, conclusive evidence for the existence of God (an infinite and self-sufficient being). The existence of nothing at all or the non-existence of the world would establish the falsity of "There is a God." Thus, given the scope of "There is a God" or "There is an infinite being," it is concluded that Flew's test is not a fair one.

For the sake of continuing the discussion, I will put aside my earlier arguments which do indeed have force here. It still can be pointed out that it is precisely the factual intelligibility of utterances with such an unrestricted generality that Flew's and Nowell-Smith's arguments challenge. "There is a God" or "There is an infinite ground of the world" are said to connote (a) "Every and any finite being requires an infinite and ultimate ground." But (a) could not be a factual assertion or statement, for it does not assert that things are like this and not like that. It does not characterize or assert a distinctive state of affairs at all. As Flew and Nowell-Smith show, these features are exactly the hallmark (defining characteristics) of factual statements. Yet (a) and "There is a God" and "God acts in the world" are presumably all factual statements, that is, they are thought by believers to be factual statements. Since they do not have the logic of factual statements, they cannot actually be factual statements. The believer's beliefs about the logical status of his religious utterances are mistaken.

It will not suffice for Clarke or Daly to reply that (a) and "There is a God" are both very unusual factual statements, i.e., statements of supernatural, transempirical, or transcendent fact, for the very intelligibility of these phrases is one of the crucial points in question. Simply to assume their intelligibility would be another instance of lifting oneself up by one's own bootstraps. We understand something of the logical behavior of factual statements; these theistic statements are not used in that manner. To be told they are special "metaphysical," "non-spatiotemporal," "supernatural" factual statements does not help us, for if we are vague about the meaning of "God" we will be equally puzzled by the meaning of these phrases.[45]

Daly cannot adequately defend such philosophical theology by claiming that the theist "invokes God, not to explain why the world is 'like this and not like that' but to explain how there can *be* a world at all," for theists claim that, mysterious as it is, it is a fact that God exists. Presumably this is used to explain another fact, namely that the world exists or that there is a world.[46] As we have seen, "There is a God" is not a factual statement. If this is so, neither is "There is a world" a factual statement; it does not characterize or assert the existence of a state of affairs. Its denial, "There is nothing" or "It is not the case that the world exists" fails to describe even a conceivable state of affairs. Thus, "There is a world" cannot be a factual statement. As we have seen, a factual statement must have an intelligible opposite which also asserts a state of affairs. "There is a world" does not have such an intelligible opposite, i.e., its denial is not a descriptive statement. Appearances to the contrary, neither "There is a God" nor "There is a world," are actually used to make factual statements.[47]

Even if all my previous arguments are rejected as inadequate, there are still grave defects in Clarke's and Daly's contentions. Apart from the difficulty of speaking intelligibly of an "infinite being" or a "totally self-sufficient being," it appears to be quite possible that finite beings could demand or require "an infinite or self-sufficient being as their necessary ground of intelligibility" without their demands or requirements being met. A man might demand loyalty from his employees as a necessary ground for his peace of mind; if he was at peace with himself, we could conclude that it is likely that employees are loyal. Similarly, if "finite beings" is intelligible and an infinite being is a necessary ground for its intelligibility, then we can conclude that an infinite being exists. But why say that an infinite being is a necessary ground for the intelligibility of finite beings? My watch is a finite being and I am a finite being. That I have a watch and that there are such artifacts is made perfectly intelligible in terms of human purposes (why people have such artifacts), the activities of watchmakers, the behavior of springs and wheels, etc. My existence is made perfectly intelligible in terms of the activities of my parents, environment, biological and psychological capacities, and the like. Similar things hold for other finite beings:

everyday observation, and understanding of the different aims of people, and an understanding of scientific explanations make their existence perfectly intelligible. Surely many ordinary sense, finite beings and finite states of affairs can be and are made intelligible without any recourse to God or theology at all.

At this point Daly's argument becomes pertinent. He contends that it is not what or how finite beings or states of affairs are, but that they are which requires a self-sufficient, infinite being. We need an explanation of why there are contingent or finite realities at all. According to Daly, we must invoke God to explain why there is a world at all. In that sense only God can make finite, contingent existence intelligible.

By now the verbal legerdemain in such a contention has also been exposed. We know there are finite beings. We also know that they are intelligible, that is to say, we know that there is no conceptual ban on understanding why any of them are the way they are and behave the way they do. In fact, our knowledge of them is considerable. But if finite beings demand or require an infinite being for their very intelligibility, then we seem forced to admit that there is an infinite self-sufficient being. However, reflection on the actual ways in which we understand finite beings, individual things and processes, and the corpus of our scientific laws and generalizations makes it evident that we do not require an infinite being to make sense out of them or to make them intelligible.

It is said that we do not go deeply enough in this quest, but simply explain one fact by another. We invoke laws, together with statements of initial conditions, to explain particular occurrences. We explain some laws in terms of other laws, but finally our laws are not backed by further laws. Their support ultimately rests on descriptions of the way things are. Those who use existentialist terms could speak here of "brute facticity." Similarly and typically, we explain human actions by exhibiting their rationale.[48] But finally, in search of ever deeper explanations, we would simply have to appeal to descriptions of the norms of human behavior, how they arose, and the human wants to which they minister. Again we are reduced to "brute facticity," to a description of the way things are.

Such explanations, no matter how good, will not satisfy Daly or Clarke, for to terminate the request for explanations in this way does not, they believe, press deeply enough. It does not, they maintain, make finite beings really intelligible, since we are finally left with the brute fact that there are finite beings. As Daly puts it, we have not explained ". . . the most radical and fundamental fact about any fact, the fact that it is."[49] Accepting this remark at face value is to let language play a trick on us. Even if we do not and cannot explain finite beings in this so-called "deeper sense," it does not follow that we have not made them intelligible in any of the standard senses of "explain."

It is an evident fact of experience that in these senses they are intelligible, but it is not at all evident that finite beings are intelligible in that further metaphysical sense. That there is anything at all might be just the very "mystery of existence" which will never be explained.[50] It may perhaps be true that *if* it is to have an explanation, it must be explained in terms of an infinite and self-sufficient being. But why assume that there is such an explanation or that reality is intelligible in that way? To say that there must be a reason for everything is to invoke a principle that, to say the least, is not self-evident and may not hold in all domains.[51] It is reasonable to expect that any individual occurrence has a cause or that all human actions have some sort of rationale or at least some motivating conditions. That is, we explain how, what, and why things are by means of other things of a perfectly contingent sort.[52] But why extend the principle of reason to a radically new and thoroughly mysterious context, that is, to explain that there is anything at all? Why assume, as do so many theists, that there must be a reason, ground, or cause for the fact that there is anything at all? Why even assume that there actually are such *ultimate* explanations? Perhaps an appeal to God, "the Cause of the existence of the world," is simply an appeal to an empty formula that appears to explain without really doing so. This possibility has not been ruled out or rendered at all implausible by Corbishley, Clarke or Daly.

LANGUAGE AND THEISTIC REASONING

That this last possibility may be an actuality is reinforced by the fact that Corbishley, Clarke, and Daly have difficulty in getting their argument stated in an intelligible fashion. Daly speaks of "God as the Cause of the existence of the world."[53] Here "cause" is used in an idiosyncratic and perhaps even in an unintelligible way. To say that "The sun caused the snow to melt," "Overwork caused his collapse," or "Economic instability helped cause the rise of Hitler" is to assert that a relationship holds between two independently identifiable states of affairs. As they rightly insist, God is not independently identifiable and the world is not a state of affairs, for "the world" is an umbrella term for all the finite things that there are. Thus necessary conditions for an intelligible employment of "cause" are absent in the phrase "the Cause of the world." Yet they take this phrase as essential in elucidating "God." Even if the world were "a kind of thing" that could be identified, what causes the world still cannot be independently identified.

Language has gone on a holiday in an even more obvious manner in a further remark of Daly's. He begins in a controversial but tolerably straightforward way by remarking that when the believer asserts there is a God and the atheist denies it, they are not simply differing in their picture preferences or in attitude. "The difference is, in the fullest sense, one as to what is so, and therefore as to the facts."[54] However, in the next remark he slides into nonsense disguised in the same way as the nonsense of "This sentence is false." The offending sentence is this: "The difference is as to what precisely is the most radical and fundamental fact about any fact, the fact that it is."[55] In other words, Daly is trying to say "It is a fact that facts are." But isn't that fact, if it is a fact, simply a further fact, i.e., one of the facts in the class of facts? If so, then that facts are is not a further fact about facts. If, on the one hand, it is simply a fact that facts are, then it is a member of the class of facts and as such it is denoted by "facts are." If so, then how can it be a further fact about the whole class of facts that facts are? If, on the other hand, it is not a fact that facts are, then the statement "It is a fact that there are facts" is false. Moreover, if it logically cannot be a fact that facts are, then "The fact that any fact is" or "A fact that facts are" is not only an odd bit of English, but a collocation of words without an intelligible use.

This can be seen in still another way. Compare

(1) There are facts.
          and
(2) There are no facts.

Assuming that (1) can be asserted or denied, to assert (2) (if (2) can be asserted at all) is to deny (1). But (1) for Daly is supposedly a metaphysical statement of fact. Thus, (2), as a proper denial of it, must be on the same logical level and thus must be a "metaphysical statement of fact." This cannot be, for (2) is nonsense. Suppose we say "There are no facts" is true, i.e., it asserts a fact. Then it is false, for there is a fact. Suppose we try to assert instead that "There are no facts" is false; then again there are facts. We unsay what we say, for we tried to assert that there are no facts. But "true" and "false" are complementary terms. It makes sense to say that a factual statement is false only if it also makes sense to say that it is true. As we have seen, it makes no sense to assert that (2) is true; thus it cannot make sense to assert that (2) is false. Far from being, as Daly must believe, an obviously false factual statement, (2), like "This sentence is false," is a bit of disguised nonsense. In this case, (2) is also non-sense, for (1) is the denial of (2) and hence is on the same logical level. Or, if it is felt that somehow it is too strong to claim that (1) is nonsense, it is at least plain that (1) cannot be a factual statement, metaphysical or otherwise, for it must be on the same level as (2), which has been shown not to be a factual assertion of any kind.

It does not help Daly if (2) is said to be nonsense by way of being self-contradictory or to be meaningful in the way self-contradictions are. In such an assertion, appearances to the contrary, (1) must be analytic, as the denial of a self-contradiction. In that case (1) is indeed meaningful, not as a substantive statement of fact, metaphysical or otherwise, but as a truth of language or as a conceptual remark depending for its rapport on linguistic conventions.

The above arguments are designed to show that certain key putative statements made by Daly cannot even be meaningful substantive assertions; thus he cannot really have a case. If for some reason my arguments here are mistaken, it has been shown that, even if Daly's statements are somehow meaningful after all, we still have no good reason for believing that finite beings can only be explained by reference to an infinite, self-sufficient cause or ground of all finite existence or that there is or even can be any explanation of why there is anything at all.

RELEVANCE OF FALSIFIABILITY THEORY TO THEISTIC ISSUES

We should also note some further defects in Clarke's argument. Clarke speaks of falsifying an argument, but an argument cannot be true or false. It can be valid or invalid, sound or unsound, conclusive or inconclusive. This is the manner used for logical appraisal of arguments. By contrast, statements can be falsified or verified, though they cannot be valid or invalid. To attack or defend the validity of the argument is to beg what exactly is in question, namely that there is an argument, i.e., a formal ordering of meaningful statements, that can be either valid or invalid. Flew and I have questioned whether in such talk there are cognitively meaningful or, as the believer intends, factually significant statements which could serve as premises in an argument. Clarke's very setting up of his claim begs the question; it assumes that he does have an argument which is either valid or invalid, and thus must have meaningful statements as premises. This last difficulty may simply be a slip on Clarke's part that could be avoided by a more careful statement of his case. Nevertheless, this needs to be done.

Finally, let me return for one last time to Daly. Daly remarks:

> The Flew and Nowell-Smith tests belong to science, not to metaphysics. They leave the metaphysical question unasked, and they therefore beg all the questions. For in asking "Why is the world like this, when it might have been like that?" they refuse to see that that question could not arise unless we first had answered the question, "Why is there anything at all, when there might have been nothing?"[56]

This is wrong on two quite obvious counts. When my wife asserts "We have no coffee" she is not making a scientific statement. Yet "the Flew and Nowell-Smith tests" are applicable to her remark: we can say what it would be like for it to be false and it asserts "that things stand thus and thus and not otherwise." More importantly, it is plainly not the case that we must have answered the question, "Why is there anything at all when there might have been nothing?" before we can answer the question "Why is the world like this when it might have been like that?" I haven't the faintest idea concerning the answer to the question: "Why is there anything at all? I am not even certain that it is an intelligible question. It can indeed be emotionally significant, but that is another matter. But it may not be a literal question; in fact, I am inclined to agree with Tillich that it is not a literal or genuine question at all.[57] I can and do raise certain questions concerning why the world is one way rather than another. Sometimes I even answer them, e.g., "Why is there no coffee in the pantry?" "Because I forgot to bring some home from the store yesterday"; or "Why do you constantly break your lead when you write?" "Because you bear down so hard." These are trivial, but they are questions of the requisite type nonetheless. More general questions about why the world is like it is, e.g., "Why do frustrated people respond with aggression?" and "Why is there no lasting peace in the Near East?" can be asked and sometimes answered by people who have no understanding at all of Daly's metaphysical question.

11

There is no reason for saying, as Daly does, that Flew's challenge displays an "enormous *ignoratio elenchi.*"[58] It is not only that "There is a transcendent cause of the world" is not open in a straightforward sense to empirical verification and confirmation; Daly has not been able to show what it would be like for it to have any kind of test at all. He claims that while "the theist's language is adequate to the facts of experience, the atheist's is not." But he has not been able to show how or even that this is so; he does not illustrate how it fits consistently with his further claim that it is a mistake to assume that "the God-hypothesis" will imply one kind of world and "non-God-hypothesis" another.[59] If they both imply the same kind of world, what does it mean to say that one is more "adequate to the facts of experience" than the other? If they both imply the same kind of world, neither need ignore any of the facts of experience or select arbitrarily from the facts of experience.

More basically, Daly claims, as do Corbishley and Clarke, that (1) 'On the "no-God-hypothesis" there is no kind of world' and (2) "If there is any kind of world God exists" are both fundamental truths. But they have not shown that it is self-contradictory or nonsensical to assert (3) "We live in a Godless world" or (4) "Though there is no God, we do live in a world with reflective but often cruel human beings." If they cannot do this, and ruling out empirical verification as they do, how can they know or have any grounds for believing that (1) and (2) are true or even have any truth-values? Moreover, if they did establish that (3) or (4) are self-contradictory then (1) and (2) would be analytic. In that case, (1) and (2) would be devoid of the factual/metaphysical significance so essential for their case.

My examinations of this issue, so central to any account of God-talk and the quest for God, may have seemed wearisome. As Charlesworth, Corbishley, Daly, and Clarke are trying to do what is plainly impossible anyway, why waste time with the details of their views. My answer is threefold: they, and many others, clearly do not think they are trying to do what is impossible. As representatives of an ancient, socially effective institution, their arguments against a claim to end all such metaphysical arguments need to be given careful consideration. If what I said here has not advanced philosophy, it should have advanced understanding between philosophers. Secondly, some of their responses to the "Theology and Falsification issue" are indeed natural and influential responses that deserve an effective reply.[60] Whether I have succeeded in doing that here, the reader must decide for himself.

Thirdly, it is felt in certain circles that a view like mine is still a partial holdover from a largely discredited positivism. Some feel that attention to a more metaphysically oriented approach would show the superficiality of my view. In discussion, Professor John Macquarrie has even remarked that my view is "old fashioned." Fashions change and I am little concerned with whether it is or is not "old fashioned." I am concerned with whether what I say is so and with whether it is indeed superficial. I have tried to show here that it is not superficial and that the criticism directed against such an analytic approach by the Catholic philosophers I have discussed will not withstand critical scrutiny. Perhaps there are better criticisms directed against this approach by philosophers working from a Catholic background, but they remain unknown to me. I issue here an open invitation to improve on these arguments and meet this analytic challenge. If my arguments have been near their mark, the verification/falsification argument remains an unmet challenge to theists. For theistic religion to meet the expectations of their adherents, "There is a cause of the universe" and "There is an unfathomable Divine Love which governs the order of history" must be shown to have a factual status. But theistic utterances of this sort are devoid of factual significance.

1. Some of the key considerations here have been brought out by Paul Edwards and Ronald Hepburn. See Edwards' article "Atheism," pp. 174-89. and Hepburn's "Agnosticism." pp. 56-59, in **The Encyclopedia of Philosophy,** ed. Paul Edwards (New York: Macmillan, 1966), Vol. 1.

2. See my "Wittgensteinian Fideism," **Philosophy,** XLII (1967), 191-210.

3. I have characterized Flew's challenge rather fully in my "On Fixing the Reference Range of 'God,' " **Religious Studies,** II (1966), 13-30. For

the original statement of it see Antony Flew, "Theology and Falsification," in **New Essays in Philosophical Theology**, eds. A. Flew and A. MacIntyre (London: SCM Press, 1955), pp. 96-99.

4. Norman Malcolm, "Anselm's Ontological Arguments," Philosophical **Review**, LXIX (1960), 41-62; and Charles Hartshorne, **The Logic of Perfection** (LaSalle, Ill.: Open Court, 1963).

5. In Chapter 8 of my **The Quest for God**, forthcoming. See also here the criticisms of Malcolm's position in the **Philosophical Review**, LXX (1961), 56-109; Robert Coburn in "Professor Malcolm on God," **Australasian Journal of Philosophy**, XLI (1963), and John O. Nelsen. "Modal Logic and the Ontological Proof for God's Existence," **The Review of Metaphysics**, XVII (1963), 235-42.

6. J. N. Findlay, "Can God's Existence Be Disproved?", in **New Essays in Philosophical Theology**, eds. A. Flew and A. MacIntyre (New York: Macmillan, 1964), pp. 47-56.

7. Nietzsche, of course, never intended it literally. In his **The Joyful Wisdom** (New York: Ungar, 1960), he remarks that to say "God is dead" is to say "that the belief in the Christian God has become unworthy of belief."

8. David Hume, **Dialogues Concerning Natural Religion** (New York: Hafner, 1948).

9. J. N. Findlay, "Can God's Existence Be Disproved?", pp. 71-75.

10. See F. C. Copleston's remarks on this in his debate with A. J. Ayer. A. J. Ayer and F. C. Copleston, "Logical Postivism—A Debate," in **A Modern Introduction to Philosophy**, eds. Paul Edwards and Arthur Pap (New York: Free Press, 1965), pp. 726-50.

11. M. J. Charlesworth, "Linguistic Analysis and Language About God," **International Philosophical Quarterly**, I (1961), 139-67.

12. Ibid., p. 165.

13. Ibid., p. 140.

14. Ibid., p. 165.

15. Ibid.

16. Ibid., p. 163.

17. F. R. Harrison, "Mr. Geach's Interpretation of the 'Five Ways,' " **Sophia**, III (1964), 35.

18. Earnest Nagel, "Determinism in History," **Philosophy and Phenomenological Research**, XX (1959-1960), 291-317.

19. M. J. Charlesworth, "Linguistic Analysis and Language About God," p. 165.

20. Ibid.

21. Ibid., p. 140.

22. Thomas Corbishley, S.J., "Theology and Falsification," **The University**, no. 1 (1950-1951), 9.

23. Ibid.

24. Ibid., p. 10.

25. Ibid.

26. Ibid.

27. Ibid.

28. Ibid., p. 11.

29. P.H. Nowell-Smith, "Theology and Falsification," **The University,** no. 1 (1950-1951), p. 12.

30. **Ibid.**

31. **Ibid.,** p. 13.

32. **Ibid.**

33. **Ibid.**

34. **Ibid.,** pp. 13-14.

35. **Ibid.,** p. 14.

36. **Ibid.**

37. **Ibid.,** p. 15.

38. **Ibid.**

39. **Ibid.,** p. 16.

40. **Ibid.**

41. **Ibid.**

42. C. B. Daly, "The Knowableness of God," **Philosophical Studies,** IX (1959), 90-137.

43. **Ibid.,** pp. 103-104.

44. In a private communication to me. But see also W. Norris Clarke, "Analytic Philosophy and Language About God," in this volume.

45. The best that could be done here is to appeal to what is sometimes called the **sui generis** character of the language or what is less piously called the idiosyncracy platitude, viz., that "every mode of discourse has its own logic." Making such an assumption, one might argue that the sense of "fact" and "factual statement" in God-talk is different than in other areas. One is either aware of what these facts are or one is not. Ultimately one can only understand them in their own terms. I have tried to give grounds for rejecting such a view in my "Wittgensteinian Fideism."

46. C. B. Daly, "The Knowableness of God," p. 104.

47. I am, of course, speaking of non-anthropomorphic concepts of God. Where God, like Zeus, is conceived anthropomorphically, it is simply false that there is such a God.

48. See here William Dray, **Laws and Explanation in History** (London: Oxford Univ. Press, 1957), Chaps. III and V; and William Dray, "The Historical Explanation of Actions Reconsidered," pp. 105-35, and Kai Nielsen, "Rational Explanations in History," pp. 296-324, in **Philosophy and History,** ed. Sidney Hook (New York: New York Univ. Press, 1963).

49. C. B. Daly, "The Knowableness of God," p. 105.

50. See here Milton K. Munitz, **The Mystery of Existence** (New York: Meredith, 1965).

51. See Arthur Danto, "Faith, Language, and Religious Experience: A Dialogue," in **Religious Experience and Truth,** ed. Sidney Hook (New York: New York Univ. Press, 1961), pp. 137-49.

52. Kurt Baier, **The Meaning of Life** (Canberra: University College, 1957).

53. C. B. Daly, "The Knowableness of God," p. 103.

54. Ibid., p. 105.

55. **Ibid.**

56. **Ibid.**

57. In **Philosophical Interrogations** I asked Tillich if this "question" could conceivably be answered and whether, if it were logically impossible to answer it, it could literally be a question. Tillich replied, "There is no doubt that the question, 'Why is there something, why not nothing?', is not a question in the proper logical sense of the word. There is no answer to it, as I myself have concluded by referring to Kant's mythical God who asks this question with respect to himself and cannot answer it." Paul Tillich, "Interrogations," in **Philosophical Interrogations**, eds. Sydney and Beatrice Rome (New York: Holt, Rinehart & Winston, 1964), p. 403.

58. C. B. Daly, "The Knowableness of God," p. 103.

59. **Ibid.**, p. 105.

60. I have tried to come to grips with more direct efforts to answer Flew's challenge rather than to challenge its presuppositions in my "Religion and Commitment," in **Problems of Religious Knowledge and Language**, eds. W. T. Blackstone and R. H. Ayers, forthcoming; Kai Nielsen, "Eschatological Verification," **Canadian Journal of Theology**, IX (1963), 271-81; "God and Verification Again," **Canadian Journal of Theology**, XI (1965) 135-42; and "On Fixing the Reference Range of 'God,' " **Religious Studies**, II (1966), 13-36. I am indebted to Kenneth Stern and John Miller for their helpful comments on an earlier version of this essay.

Analytic Philosophy and Language About God

◇

by
W. Norris Clarke, S.J.

IN STUDYING THE relation of contemporary philosophical movements to religious renewal, in the spirit of *aggiornamento* of Popes John and Paul and the Second Vatican Council, it seems a little strange to reflect upon analytic philosophy. Surely there could hardly be two more opposite poles than the coolly detached, impersonal attitude of contemporary analytic philosophy and the warmly personal, committed attitude of religion. Yet it has always been the case that every significant movement in philosophy has influenced Christian thought and through it Christian religious attitudes. In the present case it can be genuinely fruitful both for Christian philosophy and religious renewal to meet the challenge of this particular contemporary philosophical movement.

The reason is this. Man's knowledge of God is always a delicate, even a precarious balance; it is an inner tension between knowing and unknowing, between the positive and the negative. The best that even positive knowledge can do is to point toward a God hidden in mystery, without ever grasping or understanding Him clearly in finite concepts. As St. Thomas keeps insisting, in phrases that never cease partially to scandalize some: "The essence of God, what God is, is totally unknown to us."[1] But whenever man has moved forward, through the efforts of some great thinker like St. Thomas, to a new level of precision in the positive knowledge of God, as time goes on he tends to settle down comfortably.

He begins to lose the awareness of the precariousness and tension within his finite knowledge of the Infinite; in a word, he begins to think that he knows more about God than he actually does. This seems inevitable as the hard-won achievement of one thinker turns into the traditional doctrine of a school which, after a while, requires more effort to question than to accept.

It is here that one can note the beneficial role of challenge from the outside. If it is met squarely, it often shakes up too easily held certitudes and makes one rethink freshly and creatively the whole problem. This very effort plunges one back into that austere but fruitful semi-darkness in which it becomes necessary to reach out again anxiously with one's mind in order to reconquer or rediscover that in which one's human knowledge of God, with its vital tension between knowing and unknowing, darkness and light, really consists. It is in just such an existential atmosphere of personal intellectual and volitional reaching out towards the hidden God that the religious attitude of faith can experience a fresh and vital renewal.

Something like this can happen from the confrontation between, on the one hand, the traditionally accepted philosophical and religious knowledge of God and, on the other, what at first sight appears to be a dangerously threatening challenge to the meaningfulness of this knowledge from contemporary logical and linguistic analysis. The following will sketch in broad lines both that in which this challenge consists and the way in which it can contribute to a renewal of Christian philosophy. The breadth of the strokes required to give a composite picture will imply some lack of nuance and inevitable oversimplification of issues.

ANALYTIC PHILOSOPHY: A GENERAL DESCRIPTION

The particular concern in this paper is with the school of "ordinary language" or "linguistic analysis" philosophy, which forms part of the general current of analytic philosophy that has developed within the last twenty-five years. The aim which generally characterizes this movement is, not to construct philosophical explanation or systems of its own, but rather to analyze precisely the meaning and logical propriety of already existing language: whether this be the language of science, or of philosophy, or of theology, or simply the philosophically relevant categories of ordinary everyday language. We might for convenience divide the movement into three main streams, though each overlaps the other at not a few points.

Logical Empiricism. The first branch of the movement is logical positivism, often known as logical empiricism since it adds modern logical techniques to the old empiricism. It stems from the Vienna Circle group founded just before World War II by Schlick, Carnap, and others. This school, for all its logical and empirical claims, turned out to be in fact a doctrinaire or a priori anti-metaphysical position, based on the famous verification principle of meaning. According to this theory, a concept or proposition had meaning only if it could be verified or reduced in some way to publicly verifiable sense experience. This, of course, dispensed in principle with any discussion of non-observable entities like God, the soul, the intellect, or any metaphysical principles which by their nature are inaccessible to sense experience.

The extremism of this particular school quickly came under fire for arbitrariness from all sides, so that it has been forced into a steady retreat from its original claims. Historians objected that the past was robbed of all proper meaning, since it was reduced to mean nothing other than the present evidence for propositions containing verbs in the past tense. Scientists objected that highly theoretical conceptual constructs and hypotheses indispensable to contemporary science but not directly verifiable in experiments were rendered meaningless. Philosophers objected that the very verification principle of meaning itself, being a universal negative, could never be verified in any experience or set of experiences: hence, the highly embarrassing consequence that the verification principle was itself meaningless. As a result, logical positivists had to withdraw their assertion of the verification principle of meaning as a truth. It was reduced to the status of a rule, which is neither true nor false, but a freely adopted way of achieving an end. Hence, it cannot be imposed on someone unless he wants to achieve this given end and no other means is possible—questions, obviously, which cannot be settled by invoking the rule itself.

The doctrine in its characteristic original form has now been abandoned by all save a few. One finds scarcely any philosopher on the American or British scene who is now willing to call himself a logical positivist. Its quasi-official laying to rest was presided over recently by one of the best known spokesmen for the movement, Herbert Feigl of the University of Minnesota, in his highly significant—and charmingly frank—Presidential Address for the Western Division of the American Philosophical Association for 1962-63, in which he reviewed his whole career as a philosopher and recounted the steps of his gradual withdrawal from logical positivism.[3] Nevertheless, it is important to recognize that its spirit is still very much alive in various more subtle forms and, as will be noted below, indirectly influences not a few thinkers.

Symbolic Logic and Semantics. The second main branch of the movement is composed of the various branches of technical analytic philosophy, strongest in this country, but existing also in the Scandinavian countries, Switzerland, Holland, Italy, and elsewhere. This comprises the schools of symbolic logic and semantics, principally those interested in constructing precise artificial languages for more rigorous logical and conceptual analysis of the language of science and allied fields. This group will not be of direct concern here either, since it has not to any notable extent applied its techniques to the analysis of philosophical or religious language about God.

Linguistic Analysis. The group which is here of direct concern is the third, often called the "ordinary language" school or "linguistic analysis" philosophy.[4] It objects to being considered as one single school, committed to a fixed body of identical doctrines. Originating in England with G. E. Moore and still the dominant philosophy there, this general stream of orientation is not interested in constructing new artificial languages. Rather, it analyzes the precise meaning of the basic categories of ordinary language and applies them to other areas of discourse or "language games," such as philosophy, theology, law, and to a certain extent even science. It considers the ordinary or everyday language of a people to be the fundamental matrix from which all other more specialized and artificially constructed modes of language take birth and to which recourse must be had to explain their meanings and rules. In particular, ordinary language is also the ultimate, at least negative, regulative norm or court of appeal for checking the meaningfulness and relevance of all philosophical language.

The central operative insight which gave birth to this movement and still sustains its development was the discovery that at least some traditional philosophical problems or hotly controverted positions are not the result of any problems forced upon one by reality itself. Instead they arise from language confusion or muddles, stemming from "category mistakes" or the misuse of terms distorted from their natural context in ordinary language. In these cases some term has been taken out of the ordinary language context in which it is "at home" and applied in some new context. In the process the term has been twisted into at least a partially new meaning, yet holding on to enough of the old meaning to give the impression that it is still the same term or concept that is being discussed. The result is that the new use of the old term conceals within it several disparate or incompatible meanings, often jumbling several different categories into one. This produces a language muddle or category mistake, which can breed endless false and insoluble problems.

The worst of it is that the philosopher in question either does not realize what he has done most of the time and hence cannot get out of his difficulty by himself (like a fly in a bottle, says Wittgenstein) or, if he does realize it, keeps playing on the double meaning of his term in order to keep his problem or novel position going. Because philosophers in the past have not been aware of what they are doing linguistically, they have raised pseudo-problems of all sorts. These remain insoluble because the very language in which they were formulated contains hidden category confusions or even nonsense propositions, as though one were to ask, "How fast can numbers run?" or "What color are sentences?" Obviously no answer is possible to such questions because they are meaningless from the start.

Because the language muddles of philosophers are more subtle and hard to detect than the above examples they need special "therapy." Thus to ask, "Is perhaps my whole life just a dream or illusion?" involves a linguistic muddle, even though it sounds like a deep and difficult problem. The ordinary language use of the term 'dreaming' is to describe certain particular types of experience which are distinguished from the others called 'waking.' It is by nature a contrast word, deriving its meaning from contrast with a meaningful opposite. Therefore, to ask whether the totality of my experiences might consist in dreaming would be to destroy the contrasting correlative of 'dreaming' and thus rob 'dreaming' itself of any specifiable meaning. If the suggested hypothesis were true, the term 'dreaming' would never have existed in its present meaning at all or would at once lose its standard meaning.

Similarly, to ask "What is time?" is to make a category mistake. In ordinary language 'time' is used in sentences like: "What time is it?" or "How much time does this take?" But one does not say, "What is time?" One asks "What is a cabbage?" or "What is a gnu?" because these are things or substance words. But 'time' does not function like a thing word at all. For the philosopher to try and make it function as such, as he does when he asks "What is time?", is to confuse two different linguistic and conceptual categories. It produces a muddled question to which no clear answer can be given. Similar analyses could be made of questions like: "Is space or time real?" or "Can time be speeded up or does it flow at a steady pace?"

When confronted with the contention of certain idealists that "Time is unreal," one of G. E. Moore's favorite refutations was to ask, "Oh, you mean that I didn't eat my lunch after my breakfast, that I ate my lunch at the same time that I ate my breakfast?" If the philosopher protested this was not what he meant, Moore would answer that if he did not mean this then he had changed the ordinary meaning of 'time' without indicating what the new meaning was.

The initial insight was quite sound in observing that some philosophical problems either conceal or have arisen as a result of language muddles by using a term native to one context or category in another and incompatible one without warning of a change of meaning. From this original modest position of G. E. Moore himself, linguistic analysts drifted rapidly toward the position that most, if not all, philosophical problems result from language muddles. Hence, they can be "solved," or rather dissolved by the careful analysis of the meaning of the term used which would restore them to the original living "language game" or native habitat from which they had been lifted.

This general linguistic analysis school can be divided roughly into two main branches, one *negative* and the other *positive*. The first works on the premise that *all* philosophical problems are cases of linguistic muddles or pseudo-problems. The work of the linguistic analysis "philosopher" is therefore one of linguistic "therapy": to dissolve these muddles as they arise, and then to stop. He would have nothing positive to say on his own. Thus when, if ever, he has completed this task, he will have eliminated philosophy itself. This current stems from Wittgenstein in the second phase of his *Philosophical Investigations,* after the repudiation of the *Tractatus.* It was for a while, perhaps, the dominant trend in this extreme negative form, but has slowly become more moderate and tends now to blend a good deal with the more positive current.

The positive branch, which is now more widespread, has a primary positive aim in addition to the above indispensable role of negative therapy. Its intent is to map out by positive analysis the authentic meaning of the main categories of ordinary language, so that whatever real problems remain in philosophy can be worked on without confusion and with a better chance of attaining whatever solutions are possible. At least it will be possible to understand clearly what is meant by the great basic categories or types of terms used in ordinary language. The same techniques can in principle be applied to any living language game, such as the law, science, and according to some even religious language. This program of negative therapy plus positive elucidation of living language is today certainly the dominant trend in linguistic analysis both in England and elsewhere.

By way of personal evaluation, it might be added that as long as one does not reduce philosophy exclusively to linguistic analysis, there are very valuable contributions which can be made both by the negative and positive techniques of this approach. Much purification and clarification of philosophical thought and language can result if philosophers constantly check up on themselves by asking: What do I really mean when I make this statement or assert this position? Am I merely changing the language or making a proposal for language revision when I put forward this position; or am I really expressing a new truth? Does my position render meaningless or inconsistent any basic category or ordinary language such as statements of motion, space or time, consciousness, or personal responsibility?

It has now become clear that Aristotle and St. Thomas both made far more extensive and effective use of such techniques than has till recently been suspected. Thus Aristotle refutes the Megaric position that nothing is possible save what is actual by showing that this would render meaningless the basic language categories of habit, skill, and capacity, in such a way that when a musician is not actually playing one would have to say not "He can play the harp," but rather "He cannot do so." St. Thomas puts forward as one of his main arguments against plurality of substantial forms in man that it would render invalid the essential predication "Man is an animal." Since one does in fact speak this way quite meaningfully, any theory which destroys the meaning of such a predication must quite rightly be considered ipso facto false for him without any further argument needed.[5]

The negative techniques are also peculiarly effective in dissolving by purely internal analysis any all-out reductionist theory of reality, such as, "Everything is material," "Everything is living," or "All my experience is a dream." If such terms as 'material' and 'living' which were made up as restrictive contrast words to distinguish one kind of being from another now include all possible types of being, either it becomes impossible to say just what they do mean or they become doctrines expressing a mere hope for the future. Thus if 'material' does not mean physico-chemical as we now know it but also includes human consciousness, which we cannot yet reduce to physico-chemical laws, then 'material' means simply 'whatever is,' or 'one hopes some day to reduce it all to physico-chemical laws like those now known.' Even then it is not clear what meaning the last phrase can have. The more sophisticated position, however, that everything is inseparable from physico-chemical operations is not susceptible to the same easy dissolution.

Application to Language about God

Both of these linguistic analysis groups have turned their attention in recent years with special intensity to what is certainly the most challenging, puzzling, and problem-laden area of human language: language about God, both religious and philosophical. One of the reasons why they found this field peculiarly apt for their type of analysis is the fact that almost all the terms used to speak of God, such as cause, personal, knowing, good, and provident, are drawn from ordinary language. Yet it is precisely here that the resources of human language are strained to the utmost in the attempt to express through these words a domain beyond human experience.

The results of this application of linguistic analysis to language about God have been partly negative and partly positive. The negative ones have been, if not the majority, at least the best known and the most discussed. They are also the most challenging, and therefore the most stimulating to the renewal of our philosophical, theological, and religious thinking about God. Hence, what follows will concentrate principally upon them.[6]

Impossibility of Proving the Existence of God. The first challenge of linguistic analysis to traditional thinking about.

God has to do with the possibility of proving the existence of God philosophically. On this point ordinary language analysis joins with practically all the schools of analytic philosophy and with most schools of contemporary philosophy in agreeing that it is impossible to give anything like a formal proof of the existence of God. In particular, it declares all the traditional proofs either positively invalid or simply not rigorous proofs in any acceptable modern sense of the term.[7]

This widespread agreement among contemporary philosophical schools seems worthy of reflection. It is true that many of the particular objections against the traditional metaphysical proofs are themselves commanded by explicit or implicit metaphysical attitudes drawn from classical modern philosophers like Hume and Kant, or from the more or less hidden postulates of logical positivism. These can be ignored here, since they are hardy perennials already well known. More significant is the general reason behind all these denials, namely, that the notion of proof is understood in a much more rigorous and formal way today than in the past. This is the result of the intense cultivation of logic and semantics in our day, with its development of keener logical tools and a greater sensitivity to the hidden postulates which lie behind various types of arguments.

Thus the argument from effect to cause and especially to a transcendent cause of a higher order is the heart of practically all traditional proofs for the existence of God from Aristotle on. Nevertheless, it would not be considered by most modern philosphers, even theists, as a proof capable of formulation in rigorous formal logical terms and reducible to the basic logical principles of contradiction and excluded middle. The reason for this is that it presupposes the distinct postulate, irreducible to contradiction, of the principle of sufficient reason or the intelligibility of being. This, in turn, must be given the status, not of a logically analytic proposition, but of a primitive postulate or synthetic a priori which is impervious to any further logical reduction. It posits the ultimate a priori of a primordial harmony and correlation of mind with reality, of the intellectual order and its exigencies with the ontological order.

This implies the assertion, which includes in one vast exceptionless sweep the whole of being, that nothing whatsoever that would be positively and radically unintelligible—such as, for example, a being coming into existence without any cause—can possibly exist in the real order. The immediate corollary of this principle is that if one finds any being or aspect of a being which by itself alone would clearly show itself to be unintelligible, then somewhere else in being there is a sufficient reason for this being in need. This latter is what is called a cause, and every being lacking the sufficient reason for its own existence must have another real being as cause.

Now it is quite true that as soon as one begins to exercise his intellect in order to understand and explain reality and to solve real problems, he is in fact, at least implicitly, using or living this principle. It would be impossible to carry on the life of the intelligence without accepting it in practice. Furthermore, every successful use of it in a particular case goes to build up an endlessly growing partial confirmation.

What the contemporary analysis of proof has made it possible to realize more clearly is that the assertion of the principle of sufficient reason or intelligibility in all its unqualified universality is not as transparently self-evident a truth as the principle of contradiction, which finite created minds can grasp in such a way as to be able to dominate it fully and see clearly here and now why it is and must be the case. To attain this clarity concerning the principle of intelligibility one would have to be the primordial identity of both being and intelligence and the ultimate source and correlator of all beings and intellects, that is, God himself. It is not possible to prove this principle by appeal to any other truth, since all explanation and all proof that is not purely formal and reducible to the principle of contradiction presupposes it.

This evidently rejects as a *petitio principi* all attempts by modern scholastics (the ancients had the sense never to attempt such a thing) to reduce the principle of sufficient reason or causality to that of contradiction. It is indeed unintelligible to assert that something can come into existence completely out of nothing with no cause at all. Still this is in no way a logical contradiction or reducible to one, since it never asserts that being is nothing or that nothing is being. The principle of contradiction is static, like all logic; the principle of sufficient reason and its immediate corollary of causality are dynamic, like all existential explanation.

The finite intelligence of man is here brought up against the experience, which is highly fruitful both philosophically and religiously, of being plunged into the awe-inspiring mystery of its own finitude. It is the inescapable exigency that man must somehow humbly accept his nature and in particular the nature of his intellect as a given, a gift, somehow efficaciously pre-oriented and adapted to a conscious luminous possession of an order of being that, correlatively, is also simultaneously pre-adapted to intellectual possession by human consciousness. Thus, at the roots of man's entire intellectual life there is uncovered a radical act of what might be called natural faith, in the sense of commitment to what cannot fully be seen and justified without residue by one's own powers, in response to a mysterious summons or invitation issuing from the depths of the innate natural dynamism of one's created intelligence.

Only in terms of this radical act of natural faith in one's own human nature as a gift to be accepted can one, through reason and philosophy, make the leap of intelligence to God, or in fact the explanatory leap from any existential effect to its unperceived cause. All proofs of God are ultimately reducible to this: "If being is intelligible, then God is. But being is intelligible. Therefore God is." The minor is inseparable from the basic existential option, commitment, and risk outlined above. This option is an eminently reasonable one—in fact the only reasonable one—to make. But because it is not a purely formal logical necessity and not yet a total vision, it still involves an element of commitment beyond vision, and hence of risk.

The ancients for the most part, and especially the medievals, made this commitment spontaneously and naturally, being content to leave it implicit or take it for granted as outside of philosophical discussion. Perhaps the latter were not fully aware of how far their existentially prior commitment to Christian revelation predisposed them powerfully towards this logically prior act of natural faith in their own intelligences. Modern man, pitilessly self-conscious and living in a pluralistic world of belief and unbelief, can no longer take this underlying act of faith for granted. He must bring it out into the open and make his commitment or rejection of it fully explicit and self-conscious. He must be fully aware of the existential risk involved in living the life of intelligence at all and in freely accepting the responsibility for its assumption.

Thus, by a strangely ironical paradox, contemporary analytic philosophy, with its coolly impersonal methods of logical analysis, joins hands with its apparent opposites, continental existentialism and personalism. Both challenge the pretensions of nineteenth-century rationalism, including its manifestations within Catholic philosophy itself. This contemporary assessment of the limited role and efficacy of strict rational proof in the life of the mind is one of the most potent and pervasive influences of contemporary philosophy on current religious attitudes, among Catholics as well as others. The end of the age of rationalism in Catholic philosophy and theology has been widely heralded.

This sheds a new light on the old problem of the relations between faith and reason. It points to the fact that, without some pre-philosophical commitment of faith to an ultimate Source and Correlator of both finite being and human intelligence, it may be too difficult for self-doubting modern man to make the humble natural act of faith in his own finite intelligence as a given to be accepted. Without this he cannot help but fall into scepticism, even with regard to this-worldly achievements of his own mind. May it indeed be necessary, as Anselm insisted, that I must believe in order that I may understand?

Meaninglessness of Language about God. It is time now to proceed to some of the more particular challenges of the linguistic analysts to the validity of language about God. In general these challenges stem from the claim that language about God is by the nature of the case either incorrigibly confused or else positively meaningless. It may indeed express sincere emotional attitudes and perhaps specifically unique religious feelings, but it cannot suffice to express meaningless objective assertions about something or someone in the real order.

The fundamental reason is always the same. Religious or philosophical language about God is built up by borrowing terms from some other field or established human discourse, principally that of ordinary human experience. These are then transposed with a new twist in meaning to express something totally beyond and different from the area of experience which the terms were originally made up to express, and in which any understanding of their meaning must always remain imbedded. The old meaning no longer strictly applies, and there is no way of specifying the new meaning in terms of any common experience, since the new entity is by definition beyond all human experience. To attempt to construct new meaning in this way with no new experience in which to ground them or by which to test them is to attempt to fly without wings or to think in a vacuum; it can lead only to confusion, vacuousness, or downright nonsense. It should be carefully noted that in this approach it is not a question of proving propositions about God to be false, but simply of dismissing them as semantic nonsense or doubletalk.

Is 'God' a Name or a Description? Let us take a brief look first at one technical objection of this sort. It maintains that the term 'God' as used in religious and much philosophical language is an inextricable confusion of two quite distinct and irreducible linguistic and conceptual categories: proper names and descriptions. A proper name, like 'John,' designates a singular individual but does not describe him; it has reference but no meaning. On the other hand, a description or descriptive term, like 'man,' 'the Creator of the universe,' or 'an infinite being' signifies a meaning, but does not itself designate any referent or bearer of the description. In fact, it is quite possible that none exists. Thus one can ask, "Is there an infinite being, or a dinosaur?" and answer quite meaningfully—whether truly or falsely is another question—"No, there is not." A name points out some actual bearer, but does not describe it. A description expresses a meaning, but neither points out any actual bearer nor even asserts

that there is one. The two kinds of terms function quite differently; they have a different logical grammar.

Turning to language about God, especially religious language,
one discovers that the term 'God' functions simultaneously or in
quick alternation as both name and description. Thus 'God' is
used just like 'John' to designate and actually address in invocation that concrete being whom one believes to be the Creator
of the universe. The proof is that it is used without any article:
one does not say 'a God' or 'the God,' like 'a man,' or 'the Creator
of the universe' and one addresses Him in prayer, "O God, help
me," exactly as "O Mary, help us." Yet in other uses, sometimes within the same sentence, 'God' also functions as a
description. Thus, especially in philosophical language, but also
in catechism explanations or theology, one says "By 'God' I
mean the infinite Creator of all things," or "I will prove that
God exists." The latter proposition means, of course, "I will prove
that something exists which verifies the meaning or the description understood by the term 'God.' "

The analysts argue that religious people and theistic philosophers cannot have it both ways. They must use 'God' either as a
name or as a description, but not as both. Since, in fact, they do
use both they never know exactly what they are doing, especially
since they give no warning that they are shifting from one use
to another or any hint that they are aware of so doing. Hence,
they do not realize that they are talking nonsense as long as
they continue to talk only about God. This does not appear until
one introduces examples from ordinary language into the forms
of language applied to God, at which point the nonsense suddenly
emerges into the open. Thus it would be clearly absurd to say
in ordinary language, "John means a rational animal," or "I
will prove that John exists."[8]

This objection does not seem to be a very difficult one to
handle, though many analysts make a great deal of it and one
who is not used to their kind of thinking can easily be confused
when first encountering this type of objection. It is quite possible
to use a term correctly and meaningfully in practice and yet
not be able to give the correct explicit analysis of what one is

actually doing. The present instance is a perfect case in point. In several different groups to whom I have spoken on this subject I have asked the audience without warning to choose which function, name, or description they thought corresponded best to their own actual usage. In every case roughly one-half voted for name, the other for description, and each was surprised at the other.

Analysts themselves are divided on the issue. Many, including most of those who deny the meaningfulness of language about God, insist that it really functions as a name. My own view and that of I. M. Bochenski, O.P.,[9] the universally esteemed logician, is that if one accepts this position he places himself in a most uncomfortable corner in which he will have considerable difficulty in clearing himself of the charge of linguistic and conceptual confusion.

It would seem that the term 'God' functions rather as a description than as a name. The decisive evidence is that one can always ask, "What does 'God' mean?" and give an answer in terms of a description. This would be impossible if the term were really being used as a proper name. True, it is a description of a rather special sort, yet not without some parallels in ordinary language. Because its meaning allows it to be verified by only a single referent, one can gradually come to drop the article, which originally accompanied the term 'god' like any other description. Thus one begins to use it as a convenient substitute for a name in direct address: "O God. . . ." The same occasionally is done with other descriptive terms that have only one referent. Thus one can say in religious or even poetic discourse, "O Sun, warm us with thy rays this day," or "O moon. . . ."

One reason for this double usage is that strictly speaking— at least in the West since the Judaeo-Christian monotheistic tradition, we have had no proper name for God. Nor do we wish to give him one, since he cannot be pointed out or defined and does not need to be distinguished from other presumably real gods, as in polytheistic paganism.

But whatever solution one adopts, one lesson should emerge from this first brief encounter with linguistic analysis: that of the rich complexity and uniqueness of language—and therefore of thought—about God. This manifests the care with which one must explain what he is actually doing when speaking about him and how easy it is to get mixed up in such attempts at explanation.

God as 'Necessary Being.' A second and more difficult challenge is that which maintains that the traditional description of God as 'necessary Being' is meaningless: a flagrant example of a "category mistake" or linguistic muddle. The term 'necessary' in modern logic and semantics has been clearly identified as a model term referring to propositions, not directly to things. It is used properly when one says, for example, "It is necessary that X is Y," or " 'X is Y' is a necessary proposition," or " 'X is Y' cannot not be true," and possibly even " 'God exists' is a necessary proposition." But it is nonsense to say "God is a necessary Being," just as it would be to say, "God is a declarative being, an analytic being, or a proposition."[10]

There are several ways of trying to answer this. One is to admit that 'God is a necessary Being' is really only a shorthand expression for " 'God exists' is a necessary proposition." However, this leads one into serious trouble, for strictly speaking a 'necessary proposition' means an analytic proposition whose truth is self-evident from the mere analysis of the terms. Surely one could not hold that in this case, unless he held either the ontological argument or some immediate intuition of the divine essence here below.

Others have held that 'God exists' is a necessary proposition in the sense of being necessarily true as a conclusion from the fact that creatures exist. But this terminology is not successful, for all it means is that the proposition 'God exists' follows necessarily from the proposition 'creatures exist.' However, just because one proposition follows necessarily from another does not make the former a necessary proposition in the strict and proper sense of the term. The analysts are correct in affirming that no existential proposition can be a necessary or analytic proposition for man, except perhaps and for very special reasons the proposition 'I exist.'

Others have followed what seems a wiser course. They maintain that just because modern logicians have agreed on the meaning of 'necessary' as a term referring to propositions only does not imply that this is the only possible meaning of the term throughout the history of philosophy. The traditional meaning of 'necessary being' has been this: a being which cannot not exist. There is no intrinsic reason why such a meaning, if consistently adhered to and clearly specified, is not a legitimate one. It would have as much claim to acceptance as the modern logical one, though the latter may be more convenient at present for a variety of other reasons, partly due to changing conventions.

One must be careful, however, in interpreting the above definition. 'Cannot not exist' can never be taken in an absolute and unconditioned sense, as though self-contained and independent of all other propositions or truths. For man in this life it can only mean: God cannot not exist, granted that one knows that creatures exist and imply God as their necessary condition of possibility. Remove one's knowledge of creatures as the point of departure or of reference, and one's knowledge of God's existence, except for special direct mystical knowledge, also disappears. Hence the necessity of God's existence as known by us is never known as a necessary proposition by itself, but only as a necessary conclusion of another contingent proposition, "Creatures, or finite things, exist." If creatures, then God; but creatures; therefore God.

Such necessity is a necessity of fact only, not of essence or *de jure,* because we can never know as an unconditionally necessary proposition that something must exist.[11] We must discover first the fact of some existence and then draw out its necessary implications. This factual necessity, or necessity implied in a non-necessary fact, is quite different from the modern and more strict understanding of 'necessary.' Hence it is not clear that much is gained any longer in using this terminology of 'necessary being' as applied to God.

It is noteworthy that St. Thomas himself never uses it as an attribute proper to God.[12] This came in only through the Augustinian tradition stemming from Anselm. It became fixed as a primary attribute of God only in modern scholasticism through which it spread to other modern philosophers in the rationalist tradition which tended to deduce or at least explain the existence of God as somehow flowing from his essence. Duns Scotus is a prime example of this procedure, even though he stays clear of the ontological argument in its pure form. St. Thomas in no way deduces the existence of God from his essence, but rather defines his essence completely in terms of his existence: God is *ipsum Esse Subsistens,* pure subsistent Act of Existence. In a sense he has no essence at all because he has no limiting principle.[13]

It might be argued against the above that once one knows that creatures exist and that therefore God must exist in fact, one can argue that he could never have begun and can never cease to exist. Hence, one knows that by his nature God must always exist and cannot not exist. This is quite true in a sense. But what it really affirms is not that there must absolutely be a God in view of what his own nature is, but rather that granted God must exist, his nature must be such that he cannot at any time come into or lose the existence it is already known to have. In a word, granted that he exists, his existence is of the self-sufficient type, independent of any other and hence eternal. 'Self-sufficient' and 'eternal' express this more accurately and with less chance of ambiguity for modern philosophers than 'necessary being.' Nevertheless, if the term is carefully limited to necessity of fact as explained above, it is still quite legitimate in itself and maintains a link with a tradition of modern philosophy and scholasticism, though not with St. Thomas.

One might insist, however, that once one knows that God's essence is to exist, it can be said that his existence is necessary because of his nature. To my mind, this is not at all true. To say "God's essence is to exist, or is his existence" is in no way for human minds the same as, or reducible to, the affirmation "God exists." The first does not mean "God's essence is such that he must exist," for this is something which a man cannot know absolutely in itself. At least for a Thomist it means rather: "Granted that God's essence exists, or supposing that it did, it would have to be pure subsistent act of existing." It is impossible for man's mind to fuse into a single proposition both the existence of an essence and what kind of essence it is. The "logical grammar" of attributive and existential propositions is irreducibly different. Whether or not in the case of God one can fuse the two in a single act of purely intellectual insight is another and very difficult question. Certainly one cannot express this in any human concepts or propositions, let alone in one and the same proposition. To attempt to do so is to lay oneself open to well-nigh unanswerable charges by the analysts of linguistic muddles or category confusions.

In conclusion, it would seem more satisfactory and safe to describe God as 'self-sufficient and eternal' than as 'necessary being.' This is due to the many nasty logical traps that can lurk inside the latter. It is also due to the extreme difficulty in getting modern philosophers to understand the traditional meaning of the term or to abandon their own now strongly rooted usage of 'necessary' as applying to propositions only and not to things.

Falsification Theory of Meaning. The next challenge is based on the so-called "falsification theory of meaning" now very much in vogue among analysts.[14] This is a considerably more subtle and sophisticated successor to the now largely discredited verification theory of meaning proposed by the logical positivists, as noted earlier. The latter was a crudely empiricist criterion. Whether or not the former is only an undercover variation of the latter in more refined and moderate terms, as some maintain, is still very much a subject of dispute.

According to the falsification principle of meaning, a term or proposition has no meaning unless it is possible to specify what its opposite would be, in the case of a term or concept, or what would falsify it, in the case of a proposition. In a word, to be meaningful necessarily implies excluding some other meaning or possible state of affairs. For example, suppose one were to say, "X is a loving husband," and then someone objected that X beats his wife regularly, humiliates her in public, does not provide for her, and has affairs with other women. Now, if no matter what facts about the behavior of X were brought up, one kept answering, "Oh, that is compatible with what I mean by a good husband," the original statement would have been without meaning. In other words, if one refuses to accept any state of affairs at all as falsifying or counting against the truth of an assertion, then the statement becomes meaningless or vacuous. If it excludes no possible state of affairs, then it adds no distinguishable intelligible content and becomes indistinguishable from asserting "X is a husband," or even "X is a bad husband."

There is clearly something to this principle, as the example shows. It is particularly useful for judging the fruitfulness of scientific theories and concepts. An hypothesis or theory which no possible experiment could falsify would be completely useless to a scientist, since there would be no way to test it. No definite predictions could be made from it, since all possible outcomes would be equally compatible with it. It is also clear that it applies quite generally to all particular or restrictive concepts which distinguish one thing from another. The crucial question is whether it applies absolutely and necessarily to all concepts and propositions, no matter how universal and ultimate, such as being or God.

This principle might be applied to propositions about God. One says that God is an all-loving, all-provident Father. In the case of a human father one can test an assertion like this by specifying certain falsifying conditions which, if verified, would lead one to judge that the statement was false. For example, he might allow his children to be tortured, starved, or injured in accidents when he could prevent these misfortunes. However, when one applies this test to God and asks the believer to specify what he would consider as decisive evidence counting against his belief in God's love or providence towards himself or other men, he discovers that the believer suddenly refuses to play the game or keeps changing the rules. He is quite willing to point to various events in his life, such as escaping death by an improbable chance, as marks of God's providence. But when asked, "Well, suppose you, or your children, had not been so spared; suppose this or this or this distaster had happened to them or you, would this have meant that God did not love or watch over you?," the truly committed believer always answers, "Oh no, that too would come under God's providence, only in a more hidden way."

If one keeps on this way, it turns out that no matter how one heaps up disasters of the most catastrophic and heart-rending nature the believer on principle will not accept any possible specifiable state of this universe as telling decisively against his belief that God is provident and loving. In that case, the analysts conclude, his propositions have become meaningless, because vacuous. Their terms no longer bear any recognizable resemblance to the original meaning they had in the ordinary language situations which gave them birth. In fact, they have no specifiable meaning at all. To say, "The universe is governed by divine providence or love" now becomes indistinguishable from saying, "The universe is the way it is," or "Things happen the way they happen." 'Providence' now means nothing more than whatever way things actually happen. So it is with other divine attributes. Their attribution to God becomes, not false, but simply empty of all meaning.

This presents a most salutary challenge to the depth and accuracy of one's understanding of just what he does or should mean when he makes such statements about God. Two main avenues of response lie open and have been followed up by theistic philosophers. One is to accept the falsification theory of meaning, and then locate the falsifying (or verifying) conditions in the next life. When confronted with this type of response, many analysts suddenly bring into the open the hidden empiricist bias or presuppositions underlying their thought by insisting that the falsifying evidence must lie in some empirically describable state of affairs in this life. Their reasons are that one can know nothing about conditions in another life, if there is one, nor can one even speak meaningfully at all about personal survival in a mode of life unimaginably different from this which one's whole language has been built to express.

But even when this hidden empiricist limitation on what will be accepted as evidence is not insisted upon, it is no easy job to specify now just what the absolutely decisive falsifying (or verifying) conditions in another life would be for divine providence or love. An other-worldly empirical test for the divine attributes is no easy thing to lay down. Somehow one's religious and psychological instincts indicate that it would be possible to know that it is not all a hoax. But there are peculiar logical and conceptual difficulties in formulating this clearly. Analysts would seem to have had somewhat the better of it in their arguments with theists who have attempted this path.[15]

The other and preferable way of responding to the objection is to refuse absolutely to accept any empirical test for or against the attributes of God, above all in this life. The truly religious believer must first make a total loving commitment of himself to God as the kind of being or person one can and should completely trust. Then one believes firmly that God will be infinitely loving and provident over him in all things simply because he believes that God is this kind of being. One has made a total commitment to Him, giving Him a complete blank check, so to speak, as to just *how* He chooses to execute in detail this providence. In other words, one trusts ahead of time that everything will be under God's providence for one's good, without laying down any humanly conceived empirical conditions or tests by which His love will be judged.

Of course some adequate humanly reasonable evidence, either through argument, personal religious experience, or the evaluation of the trustworthiness of some revealing messenger (Christ), is needed in order to hold that God exists as God, that He is of such a nature as to deserve one's total commitment. But once this is believed any such cautious empirical calculations based on our finite human reason would be quite out of place within the authentic religious attitude. They would, in fact, be equivalent to a kind of practical atheism or unbelief.

Similarily the theistic philosopher will refuse on principle to lay down any empirical falsifying or verifying conditions for the divine attributes. He will assert them simply because they follow by a priori metaphysical necessity once the existence of an infinitely perfect Creator of all things has been established. If there is a God at all, then one can and should assert that He must be infinitely loving and providential. To do otherwise would be to contradict His nature. One does not and cannot know from human reason alone just what these attributes mean in any concretely specifiable empirical detail. This would require a knowl-edge of the infinite wisdom and power of God equal to His own knowledge of Himself, and on the face of it this would be a contradiction. Hence, if one understands properly the nature of man's knowledge of God, he should not attempt to inject any determinate empirical content at all into his concepts about God or His attributes. There is only an indeterminate analogical point-ing to an unspecifiable infinitely "Better" than all one knows in experience.

The great fruitfulness of coming to grips with an objection like this is that it exposes any hidden empiricism in one's phil-osophical thinking or religious attitudes with respect to God. When put to such a test, many apparently quite religious people find that their belief in God's providence or love has actually been based or conditioned more than they realized on a con-cealed empirical test such as: when they prayed a certain piece of good fortune befell them or a certain disaster was averted from themselves or their dear ones. When it turns out that one of their implicitly accepted falsifying conditions does actually become verified, they then revolt against God or even reject His existence, saying "This I will not accept, this is the limit of my endurance," or "I cannot believe that God would allow this to happen to me; hence He cannot exist."

This attribute resembles much more the Roman legal-contrac-tual type of religion, *"Do ut des"* (I offer you this sacrifice in order that you give me this favor in return), than authentic Christianity or genuine personal religion of any kind. This searching challenge of the analysts in the name of the falsification principle of meaning can force one to clarify both the quality of his religious belief and his understanding of just what he does mean when he speaks of the various attributes of God.

How Give Meaning to Predicates about God? The next and last main challenge is a very general and fundamental one. It undoubtedly gives the most trouble to contemporary analytic-minded philosophers, including theists, when they try to make sense, or, as they say, "do the analysis," of language about God. It is the difficulty of showing how any definite specifiable meaning can be given to language about God, including not only attributes like 'personal,' and 'loving,' but also the basic proposition itself, "God exists."

The objection arises from a consideration of the general way in which meaning is given to terms. For purely formal logical and mathematical terms, meaning is stipulated by construction and not intended to describe any real entities. But all terms describing real entities must be derived from some mode of human experience in dealing with the world and ourselves, in which is included scientific experimentation. Their meaning depends on their usage in some one of the established "language games" or ways in which men express their various modes of contact with reality.

The trouble with metaphysical language in general and language about God in particular is that it takes terms endowed with meanings derived from one language game, predominantly ordinary experience, and shifts them to express something notably different, in fact infinitely beyond, their original referents. In so doing it necessarily modifies their original meaning. The difficulty which arises is how one might give meaningful content to the new aspect or dimension of the old meaning. The source cannot be the same as that of the old meaning, one's own experience, because that is just what one is transcending in this new application and the very reason why the meaning is being partly changed. It cannot be the new dimension of reality, because it is by definition beyond one's experience. It cannot be constructed, since all construction is based on materials derived originally from experience, and everything in God is by definition infinitely beyond and other than one's experience. Neither can it be experimentally tested in any way. Hence the new meaning given to terms in order to apply them to something beyond one's experience, like God, turns out to be irremediably vacuous.

The device of analogy cannot be of any real help in this case. An analogous term is one that, according to the standard definition, is applied to several subjects according to a meaning partly the same and partly different in each case. This is all very well when one can know directly in themselves all of the subjects to which one applies the term. By direct comparison of the referents among themselves one can control the partial changes in meaning in the different cases. But in the case of God one cannot at all know him directly or properly as he is in himself. Hence one cannot compare him with the other analogates in order to determine just how the meaning of the analogous term differs when applied to Him.

The famous Thomistic analogy of proper proportionality is of no assistance whatsoever here. All it tells one is that God's existence, knowledge, or love is proportioned to His essence, just as anyone's characteristics are proportioned to his essence. This is true but trivial since it delivers only a purely formal relation, empty of any specifiable content, and with no rule for determining what the terms used could possibly mean as realized in God. The conclusion of all this is, the analysts claim, that neither theistic philosophers nor religious people know what they really mean when they talk about God. Some analysts conclude from this that language about God is simply meaningless. Others note that it must have some meaning because religious, though not philosophical, language has for a long time been a lived language game.

This positive meaning is then variously interpreted. The most common interpretation is that religious language, though ostensibly about God as some entity other than the worshipper, is really only in indirect description of the worshipper's own feelings and attitudes, or characteristic external expressions of these inner dispositions. Thus when the worshipper says, "God is the Supreme Being, my loving Father, and good," what his language really means, whether he understands it or not, is "I have feelings, and perform corresponding ritual actions, of adoration, submission, trust, and prayer," or, in general, "I behave thus, and do these actions with these inner feelings."[16]

This fundamental difficulty is further compounded by the demand made by most analysts as a general principle of meaning analysis. They demand that the meaning of such terms as 'God,' 'exists,' 'infinite' and 'infinitely good' as applied to God be clearly analyzed and defined before any process of proving that

God exists or possesses such and such attributes is undertaken. First tell me, says the analyst, just what 'God' means and how this content carries genuine meaning, before starting to prove that such a being exists. Otherwise one never knows just what he is trying to prove or whether one has succeeded.

THE MEANING OF RELIGIOUS KNOWLEDGE

This is the general and rather formidable indictment. In sketching out the possibilities of answering it, it will be well to proceed from the easier to the more difficult items.

The Subject. The attempt to analyze the meaning of religious language as being really about the worshipper, not about the worshipped or God himself, is clearly unsuccessful. Many analysts themselves have seen this and many other philosophers, particularly phenomenologists, have underlined it. The reason is simple and decisive. The meaning of religious language in this theory simply is not that intended by the people who actually use the language. Whether mistakenly or not, the religious believer who speaks about God and addresses Him in prayer is firmly convinced that he is speaking about and to a real entity quite independent of and superior to himself. This is what he intends to do by his language; it is the meaning given to it by the user. It would be a model of defective philosophical analysis of language, which is intended to bring out the meaning of the language as lived, if it were to go explicitly counter to the meaning intended by the user in favor of one held only by interpreters who are themselves not participants in the language game. One simple test is the fact that no religious person who accepted this analysis as correct could any longer with psychological integrity and sincerity go on using the language as he did before.

The Terms. The demand by analysts that the meanings of the term 'God' and of the various attributes as applied to Him must be defined clearly first, before proceeding to prove His existence or His possession of these attributes, must be rejected on principle by theistic philosophers. This procedure of precise definition of terms is quite appropriate to logic, mathematics, most areas of science, and many other domains of human thought and discourse, including not a few areas of philosophy.

It is an a priori and totalitarian type of analysis to insist that all proofs in whatever field must always proceed rigidly by this same identical method. This does not do justice to the special, open, heuristic type of concepts that must be, and habitually are used in pushing the frontiers of experience into new and hitherto unexplored areas or in probing hypothetically into areas of causes hidden beyond one's experience. The exploration beyond our present frontiers is essential to the continued expansion of human horizons characteristic of man throughout his history, and especially of modern man. This cannot be done without the systematic use of intentionally open, partly indeterminate, heuristic concepts, or, as it has been put, without "the systematic use of vague language."

In the case of God, the precise meaning of the term appears only at the end of the proof and in function of it. This meaning is elaborated through the very working out of the proof and the term 'God' is really only a concise summary of the conclusion of the proof itself. The proper philosophical approach to discovering or proving the existence of God is not to ask, "Can I prove the existence of God?" This would be to come by the word of another upon an already existing dispute, rather than to come to grips directly with the problem as it presents itself in authentic philosophical fashion.

The proper mode of procedure is to start with the world of one's experience and ask concerning the necessary conditions of possibility for explaining its existence and nature. The first step is to show that this whole finite world cannot contain within itself the sufficient reason for its own existence. As outlined in a previous section above, the principle of sufficient reason or intelligibility is the dynamo of one's whole intellectual life and to it one should have made a fundamental commitment. If one is not to jettison this he must make the basic inference that there must be some adequate explanatory cause somewhere in reality "above" and distinct from (that is, transcending) this world-to-be-explained.

One now proceeds by heuristic concepts, somewhat as is done

in mathematics when undertaking to solve a problem. "Let X be the real entity which is needed to solve this problem, possessing whatever properties or attributes are required to fulfill this function." Then the properties of this not directly known or experienceable X are gradually filled in by postulates, one by one, as the indispensable requirements for a solution of the problem appear. Each property of X is determined exclusively by the necessary relation of X to the datum-to-be-explained, that is, by its function in the solution of the problem. If X did not possess something equivalent to such and such a property, with these minimum requirements, then it could be shown clearly that the problem would be insoluble in principle or the solution internally contradictory. Hence, one postulates all these minimum requirements in one's already postulated X, knowing or having to know in any determinate or determinable way just how they are present.

One can, of course, start off with a vague nominal definition of what one hopes to reach, drawn not from the problem itself but from some outside pre-existing religious or philosophical belief held by men. But it is clearly impossible and unreasonable to ask for a clear detailing of the properties of the X that solves a problem before actually working out the solution to the problem![17]

The Development of Positive Meaning. With these preliminary roadblocks out of the way, one is left with the central, but now more manageable problem of how one actually does attribute positive meaning to one's language about God in terms of the above process. Here the analysts have the right to demand a much more precise, complete, and especially more concrete and experiential analysis of just what procedure religious people and theistic philosophers actually follow when they speak of God as good, or loving, or Father, or ultimate cause, or Creator.

One is accustomed to propound technical theories of analogy in all kinds of learned discussions. But as for myself, I will honestly admit that it was only recently that I awoke, to my embarrassment and under the challenge of linguistic analysis, to the following situation. For years I had been teaching a doctrine of Thomistic analogy, and many of my students could repeat it and explain it quite accurately. Nevertheless, I had never really asked either myself or them pointblank, "Come now, forget all your abstract theories of predication and analogy, what do you yourself actually do, what do you in the concrete actually mean, and what concrete psychological process do you go through, when you call God 'good,' or 'loving,' or 'infinitely wise,' or 'ultimate cause'?" Without this phenomenological analysis of the actual meaning-giving process at work in religious and philosophical language about God not much progress will be made in contacting and satisfying most modern thinkers. On the other hand a surprising amount of light would emerge for all concerned, including traditional theists, from such an analysis.

In the space remaining this process obviously could not be worked out in detail. In fact, a great deal more comparative work in religious psychology will undoubtedly have to be done before the full phenomenological process can be adequately analyzed. What follows is a general sketch of the main lines of the philosophical process. The above contains enough suggestions as to how the basic notion of ultimate cause would be given meaning. 'Cause' would be given the deliberately vague and general heuristic meaning of whatever it is that is ultimately (that is, with no further relevant questions remaining to be asked) and adequately *responsible* for the actual existence and nature of the datum-to-be-explained: the finite, changing, material universe of our experience. Presuming the basic causal relation established, without which no attributes could be predicated of God from our experience, it is now possible to develop in a little more detail how some of the standard attributes can be given meaning.

First, one discovers some property of things of one's experience which are judged to be a "perfection," that is, better had than not had at all. This is then subjected to the traditional process of "purification," that is, examined as to whether in its very meaning it necessarily implies some limitation, imperfection, or negation of further positive perfection. When one has gone through this process of sifting and testing for intrinsic imperfection the various positive properties of the things known, one concludes with basic values (or attributes of which one can approve) :

(a) which are purely positive (containing no negations) ;

(b) to which one finds that he can and must give unqualified or unconditioned approval, so that one finds himself rationally constrained to judge that it is absolutely better to have them in the highest degree ;

(c) which one finds susceptible of degrees of intensity or perfection which cannot be closed off or limited at the top short of an unrestricted plenitude (whatever this might be) ; and, finally,

(d) which one very much desires to possess oneself in the highest degree possible.

All these "pure" perfections turn out to be reducible to the following: existence, knowledge, love or loving will, and power. These, in fact, are the basic values or standards in terms of which one evaluates everything else. One calls 'good' anyone or all together of these considered in relation to the will as approving. To deny any one of these as an unconditionally affirmed value would be to go against one's human nature, rendering impossible one of the characteristically human modes of evaluation and hence of reasonable action.

Application to God. The next crucial step is to apply to God those basic value-attributes which have been sifted out and purified. Here, it is essential to introduce the dynamism of the intellect and will towards the infinite in order to ground the meaning-giving process. This is also rarely done in elucidating analogous predications of God. Reflecting on the above-mentioned basic value-attributes, one notices two things about one's relation to them. First, one tends strongly toward them or, if you wish, towards one's fulfillment through them. There is such a deep natural desire of one's whole intellectual-willing being, that one cannot not desire them without renouncing one's own deeper self. Secondly, one discovers that their degree of presence both in oneself and in all the finite things one has experienced or can conceive is radically incomplete, defective, and disproportionate to one's deepest inner longing. In a word, a person experiences their limited realization in the things around him, their falling short of the ideal realization which alone would satisfy his yearning.

Every experience or realization of a limit immediately implies a movement of transcendence beyond the limit, a transcending intention towards a beyond by that which is aware of the limit. The existence of an ultimate X which is the ultimate responsible 'cause' of this world and of oneself, and thus the final goal of all one's dynamisms, has already been postulated. Hence, one now makes the crucial act of projection of one's basic values beyond the present limited and unsatisfying degree in which one finds them and onto the Ultimate, removing all limits and deficiencies as one does so. In this act of projection one does not at all attain any act of perception, intellectual grasp, representation, or comprehension of what this state or perfect realization in the ultimate X at the other end is like in itself, distinctly, and positively. One points to it off in the darkness, so to speak.

This very transcending dynamism which enables one to point meaningfully beyond one's experience and all finitude, as not coming up to the demands of one's innate and ineradicable desire for fulfillment, enables one to sketch out dimly, in silhouette, or reverse image so to speak (through negations but not aiming at negations), the hidden positive state of plenitude in what one calls 'God.' Above all, and here is the crucial point, it permits one to affirm positively that these values must be realized beyond limitation in God, even though one can get no conception of how.

This is not a mere blind leap into the dark, though it is indeed a leap into the conceptual darkness of the "cloud of unknowing." The positive element which grounds one's projection of meaning onto an entity beyond one's experience, is drawn from one's own experience. It is percisely the unique experience of dynamically transcending the limited, deficient realization of basic values around and in one, understood explicitly or implicitly as limited, deficient, and falling short of one's deep and ineluctable expectations. The very awareness of the gap between the unlimited scope of the intellectual and voluntary desire and the deficient realizations it encounters enables one in some mysterious and indirect way, which can only be experienced rather than abstractly argued about, to know what it is one is looking for, what must be hidden in that ultimate Beyond.

In a word, this is a process of knowing what one is looking for by knowing what one is not yet satisfied with; of knowing what one does want by knowing what one does not want; and of knowing what one means and affirming it by knowing what does not yet exhaust the richness of the meaning that one intends dynamically and obscurely, but positively. As Pascal put it, "Lord, I could not have sought you unless I had already in some way found you." One has no right to neglect such a profound and authentically human experience in one's analysis of the process of human meaning-giving.

The concepts used in this process must all be open-ended ones, with floors or lower limits but no ceilings or upper limits and hence adjusting flexibly to fit the level of whatever the subject of which they are predicated. The predications made by means of them do not pretend to represent how God possesses the perfections signified at His own level. They merely point through these predicates, as though down a series of corridors without limits at the farther end. The predications affirm that God is somewhere along the line or in the direction indicated by these unqualified perfections or values. They serve not as portraits but as windows or doors opening out from within the limited walls of this human habitation onto unlimited perspectives where one's vision finally fails in a blur of light and mist.

Though one does not know just what lies out there waiting for one, he does know unerringly by his judgment of imperfection on all the degrees of realization of these values around him that along this line lies one's fulfillment. It is an unqualifiedly better-than-here, the unqualifiedly best, that in whose presence and communion I want to be with the deepest longing of my nature. This is indeed a positive knowledge of God, but of a very special, mysterious, and trans-conceptual kind. It is a knowledge not through representation but through what is implicit in an innate dynamic tendency which cannot be contained within any given or conceivable limits recognized as limits. The above notion of predications or affirmations which point through open-ended concepts is to my mind the indispensable key to one's legitimate development of meaning for human language about God.[18]

Analogy. It will surely not have escaped the reader's notice that the doctrine of analogy was nowhere mentioned in the preceding analysis. Yet those who know the technical doctrine will certainly realize that its basic content was present implicitly or equivalently throughout. The reason for not appealing explicitly to the traditional Thomistic theory as the answer to the analysts' difficulties is the painful but undeniable fact that this so-called traditional Thomistic doctrine has singularly failed to impress analysts, both theists and otherwise, as shedding any really helpful light on their problems. There are several reasons for this. One is that the theory is enveloped in such unfamiliar technical terms that access to it by most is rendered very difficult. Another is that for many it seems to be inextricably tied up with further characteristically Thomistic metaphysical doctrines, such as the real distinction between essence and existence, participation, and causality, which they find it impossible to either understand or be committed to.

However, there is also another and stronger reason which must be faced. That is the serious deficiency in the till recently most widely accepted "traditional" interpretation of Thomistic analogy according to the proper proportionality theory of Cajetan. As mentioned briefly in an earlier section of this paper, if taken by itself, this theory leaves one in almost total agnosticism as to the positive content of the analogous term as applied to God. It offers no rule justifying the actual application of an analogous term to God or giving some positive content to its meaning in this case. Granted that the above two have already been established, it then gives a formal rule-governing the proportional variability of the meaning-content according to the various subjects of which it is predicated. Given that God is good and that this has some legitimate meaning as applied to God then, since one has explained this meaning as a relational proportional one, he knows that the degree and mode of the divine goodness or other attributes will be proportional to His essence. But it is the first two steps that the analysts consider crucial. Hence they consider the proper proportionality doctrine as perhaps true, but trivial as regards the solution of what they deem the really important problems of elucidating the meaningfulness of language about God. There is a good deal of truth in their contention.

This last remark may seem hardly loyal to the Thomistic tradition. But it should by now be no secret to a professional Catholic philosopher that a striking coincidence—since there seems to have been no direct influence—took place at the time that the analysts for their own reasons were finding wanting what they took to be the traditional Thomistic doctrine. At that same time contemporary Thomistic scholars, in one of the most rapid and profound shifts of interpretation in the history of modern Thomism, were coming to the conclusion, on both historical systematic grounds, that the so-called "traditional" doctrine of Cajetan was both seriously defective in itself and not actually the mature position of St. Thomas himself.

Leading scholars, such as Lyttkens, Klubertanz, and most recently and decisively Montagnes, have now drawn massive support behind the thesis that St. Thomas, after making use of the structure of proper proportionality in only two or three places in his earliest works, quietly abandoned it thereafter as too agnostic to adequately justify one's predications about God. He substituted for it the much richer and more soundly metaphysically grounded doctrine of the analogy of participation, or of causal participation as it is now commonly called. This is built on the explicit reference to a single causal source that possesses a given perfection in plenitude and communicates it by causation to many different recipients according to varying degrees of intensive participation.[19]

Most analysts do not seem aware of this recent highly significant development in Thomistic thought. Further, the subject is still so clouded in intra-school technical disputes and metaphysical terminology that one could hardly expect outsiders at present to find their way easily through this technical tangle.

Even if they did, however, in addition to this general doctrine of analogous predication based on causal participation, they would legitimately demand a much more concrete and detailed psychological, phenomenological, and logical-semantic analysis of just what goes on in the process of giving meaning to terms predicated analogously of God. They would want to know just how the users of this language actually understand and concretely carry out the process from within.

The full analysis of the above process in its concrete totality would use all the resources, not only of metaphysics, but of modern semantics, phenomenological analysis, and symbolism theory. This seems to me one of the most worthwhile and urgent tasks now facing Thomistic and all theistic philosophers if they wish to make vital contact with contemporary needs and solve the problems in their own right. This constitutes a strong invitation to participate in this task of collaboration.

1. See Thomas Aquinas, **Summa Theologica** (New York: Benziger, 1947), I, q. 3, a. 4, ad 2m; Thomas Aquinas, **Summa contra Gentiles** (London: Burns, Oast & Washbourne, 1923), I, c. 30, and III, c. 49.

2. See Maxwell Charlesworth, **Philosophy and Linguistic Analysis** (Pittsburgh: Duquesne Univ. Press, 1959); Maxwell Charlesworth, **Logical Positivism** (Glencoe: Free Press, 1959); A. J. Ayer, **The Revolution in Philosophy** (New York: Macmillan, 1956).

3. H. Feigl, "The Power of Positivistic Thinking," **Proceedings of the American Philosophical Association,** XXXVI (1962-63), 21-42.

4. See Maxwell Charlesworth, **Philosophy and Linguistic Analysis** (Pittsburgh: Duquesne Univ. Press, 1959); Logic and Language, ed. A. Flew (New York: Philosophical Library, 1951); "Symposium: What is Philosophy?" **Proceedings of the Aristotelian Society, Supplement,** XI (1932), 23-67; "Symposium: Is Analysis a Useful Method in Philosophy?" **ibid.,** XIII (1934), 53-118.

5. See R. Rorty, "Realism, Categories, and the 'Linguistic Turn,' " **International Philosophical Quarterly,** II (1962), 307-22, for a challenging account of how closely the results of constructive analysis parallel the conclusions of metaphysicians like Aristotle, though in different terminology.

6. See Maxwell Charlesworth, **Philosophy and Linguistic Analysis** (Pitts-

burgh: Duquesne Univ. Press, 1959); Fred Ferré, **Language, Logic and God** (New York: Harper, 1961). As samples of negative critique, see A. Flew and A. MacIntyre, **New Essays in Philosophical Theology** (London: SCM Press, 1955); Ronald Hepburn, **Christianity and Paradox** (London: Watts, 1958); R. Braithwaite, **An Empiricist's View of the Nature of Religious Belief** (Cambridge: Cambridge Univ. Press, 1955).

7. See M. Charlesworth, "Linguistic Analysis and Language about God," **International Philosophical Quarterly**, I (1961), 139-67; J. Collins, "Analytic Theism and Demonstrative Inference," ibid., 235-63; **Faith and Logic**, ed, Basil Mitchell (London: Allen and Unwin, 1957).

8. See C. Martin, **Religious Belief** (Ithaca, N.Y.: Cornell Univ. Press, 1961) where this objection occupies a large part of the book; also the essay of Paul Ziff, "About 'God,' " in **Religious Experience and Truth**, ed. Sidney Hook (New York: New York Univ. Press, 1961), pp. 195-202.

9. I. Bochenski, "Some Problems for a Philosophy of Religion," ibid., pp. 48-54, and my own brief comment on Ziff's paper, pp. 224-25.

10. Several essays in **New Essays in Philosophical Theology** take up this point, pro and con. In "God and Necessary Being," **Journal of Philosophy**, LVIII (1961), 725-34, John Hick defends the use of the term to indicate necessity of fact only. Cf. also W. N. Clarke, "Linguistic Analysis and Natural Theology," **Proceedings of the American Catholic Philosophical Association**, XXXIV (1960), 110-26.

11. See J. Hick, "God and Necessary Being."

12. For St. Thomas, 'contingent' and 'necessary' have quite different meanings from their now traditional use in modern philosophy, including modern scholasticism. For him, 'contingent' meant simply any composite of matter and form, any generable and corruptible, whose prime matter could be or not be according to the substantial form it now has. 'Necessary' means just the opposite: any pure form that is not subject to substantial change. Both angels and God are such, God having his necessary being **a se**, not **ab alio**. See T. B. Wright, "Necessary and Contingent Being in St, Thomas," **New Scholasticism**, XXV (1951), 439-66; also T. C. Pater, "The Question of the Validity of the Tertia Via," in **Studies in Philosophy and the History of Philosophy**, ed. J. Ryan (Washington: Catholic Univ. of America Press, 1963), II, 137-77; T. K. Connolly, "The Basis for the Third Proof of the Existence of God," **Thomist**, XVII (1954), 282-379.

13. See my own article on "Aseity," the history of the term **ens a se**, in the **New Catholic Encyclopedia** (New York: McGraw-Hill, 1967).

14. See especially Flew's essay in **New Essays in Philosophical Theology** and the answer to it.

15. John Hick has attempted to defend a verification in the next life: John Hick, **Faith and Knowledge** (Ithaca, N.Y.: Cornell Univ. Press, 1957), and "Theology and Verification," **Theology Today**, XVII (1960), 12-31. See the answer of Kai Nielsen, "Eschatological Verification," **Canadian Journal of Theology**, IX (1963), 271-81, and his acidly critical attack on the meaningfulness of language about God in general, "On Speaking of God," **Theoria**, XXVIII (1962), 110-37.

16. See R. Braithwaite, **An Empiricist's View of the Nature of Religious**

Belief (Cambridge: Cambridge Univ. Press, 1955).

17. The notion and role of heuristic concepts are given central importance by B. Lonergan throughout his **Insight** (New York: Philosophical Library, 1956), and elsewhere in his writings.

18. A similar use of pointing concepts to refer to the self or subjectivity as such of myself and other persons is made by R. Johann, "Subjectivity," **Review of Metaphysics,** XII (1958), 200-234. It should be obvious that in the analysis I have made above I am strongly indebted to the notion of dynamism of intellect and will toward the infinite as developed by E. Coreth, **Metaphysik** (Innsbruck: Tyrolia, 1961); J. Lotz, **Metaphysica operationis humanae** (Romae: Univ. Gregorianae, 1958); J. Maréchal, **Point de départ de la métaphysique, V** (Paris: Desclée de Brouwer, 1949); and K. Rahner, **Geist in Welt** (München: Kosel-Verlag, 1957). How one can obscurely know the good by one's very tendency toward it is brought out well in the profound article of J. de Finance, "La motion du bien," **Gregorianum,** XXXIX (1958), 5-42.

19. See the key works: G. Klubertanz, **St. Thomas Aquinas on Analogy** (Chicago: Loyola Univ. Press, 1960), with its copious bibliography, and the recent widely praised B. Montagnes, **L'analogie de l'être d'après S. Thomas d'Aquin** (Louvain: Nauwelaerts, 1964).

Christian Talk of God

◊

by
Peter Slater

The topic of this paper is language concerning God, with special reference to recent analyses of "religious language."[1] In order to discuss this it is necessary to range further afield to consider how we may talk of our ways of life in this world. As linguistic analysts have increasingly stressed, we must look not simply into the meanings of words but into our uses of sentences and the contexts in which their meaning and truth are found. The totality of such contexts is our world. Thus if we ask whether talk of God is still meaningful, we are asking in effect what makes such talk possible in the world today.

In order to try to answer such a question, or to show in what directions to look for answers, we must ask not only what we mean by the word 'God' but also how we are able to talk of "the world." We have to consider what kinds of questions we are asking and what kind of language is appropriate to their answering. Accordingly, in the first two sections of this paper, I will deal generally with the place of a concept of God in thoughts on life in this world and then offer some arguments concerning the nature of the language appropriate to this context. Such arguments apply generally, I think, to any traditionally religious use of terms.

Not everyone who says "Oh God!" is pious, nor need his utterance be the beginnings of prayer. We cannot simply collect sentences with the word 'God' as their subject and assure that we thus have a fair sample of "religious language." We have rather to see how such language is used in particular religious traditions. In the third section, therefore, I will turn more explicitly than before to consider the Christian connotations of terms and how a Christian may justify his use of them in parables and analogues.

Notice that we should not speak of "religious language" but of the religious uses of such languages as English, Arabic, Hebrew, Greek and Sanskrit. I assume that Christian usage is a type of religious usage on the grounds that, traditionally at least, Christianity is a religion or complex of religions, that is, a way or ways of life relying on some transcendent reference which determines our priorities in life. In the fourth and final section, however, I shall acknowledge the challenge of the so-called Christian atheists and discuss, not only what use the word 'God' has had, but also what use it may continue to have amongst thoughtful Christians today.

Talk of God is presupposed in any traditionally Christian use of language. But in traditional usage, God is more often invoked than talked about. The primary forms of religious usage include prayers, commands and contemplative texts, rather than abstract comments upon these. Statements about God, such as we find in systematic theologies and metaphysical theories, are secondary. They pertain to the criticism and appreciation of first-order language in religion. Nevertheless, such criticism is vital. Without it, first-order utterances may become indistinguishable from magical incantations, injunctions to superstition, and sermons of the heterodox. In this paper, I shall mainly be concerned with the status of second-order statements, though I shall have to refer to primary usage when discussing the context in which such statements are ordinarily made.

Most studies of religious usage have tended to concentrate on but one type, the assertive, and the issue of its verification or falsification. Much that has been written on this topic constitutes the background for what I have to say and I refer readers unfamiliar with the literature to some of the works mentioned in the footnotes.[2] Rather than review the most important of these, I will try to consider what can be said positively on my subject, particularly with regard to Christian usage.

In doing so, I assume that any religious way of life is informed by the set of aims and intentions expressed by its leading exponents. This use of the concept of intention is one which I hope, in another paper to consider more systematically than is possible here. For the present, I use it as a far from perfected tool for opening up our understanding of the spirit in which we seek to lead our lives. This spirit is so central to Christian thought and action that we must use whatever aids we have, however rudimentary, in exploring its meaning for our lives.

Failure to consider the contexts in which theological assertions are made has led many critics to demand more clarity and precision from theologians than their language properly allows. In this, theologians have been at fault for tying talk of God to outmoded ontologies in ways which have made such phrases as 'necessary being' seem essential to the theological task. They have so constructed their theories that philosophers have been encouraged to treat theological assertions as being of the same kind as those of cosmologists. Thus the demand has been made that we show 1) how one is to identify the referent of theological assertions from outside the so-called circle of faith; 2) how this referent may be described in supposedly neutral terms; and 3) how such descriptions may be tested for meaningfulness and truth.[3] In the course of what follows, I shall try to suggest not only the extent to which this demand may be met but also how the non-assertive uses govern what theologians have to say.

GOD AND WORLD: THE PROBLEM OF THE REFERENT

The primary reference in any religious use of language is to a life lived in relation to that which transcends our immediate physical environment. In Christianity, what is primarily symbolized is a way of life in this world, not the nature of God or man taken in isolation. This is reflected in the fact that the central analogies in religious thought are analogies drawn from relationships—of father to son, judge to judged, redeemer to redeemed—rather than from discrete entities. Theological discussions of the nature of God are abstractions from the religious uses of language in which the fundamental relationship between God and man is celebrated and reaffirmed. Our concept of one pole of this relationship is informed by our concept of the other; and this fact is crucial for our choice of language. If, in Christian thought, we have but a dim idea of what God may be like in himself, we nonetheless have a very lively idea of what it might mean for us to live as his sons, slaves, and heirs. The practical significance of such thought provides us with criteria in adopting one set of terms rather than another. Thus, for example, in this "world come of age," we tend to reject paternalistic talk of God because we would no longer live as sons. We seek other symbols for that which informs our most meaningful relationships in life.

Although the practical significance of our terms makes their selection less arbitrary than has been supposed, it is not enough to establish the validity of our metaphysical presuppositions. It may provide us with a reason for beginning to use some symbols rather than others, but it is not sufficient to justify their continued use. Only our experience in using them can enable us to judge their validity as symbols of reality.

In this connection, however, we should remember that our experience in leading a particular way of life is not a wholly subjective affair. We should recognize that, although we speak of choosing our ways of life, there is a limit to the live options before us. One of the limiting factors is the nature of the world. Living out sheer fantasies is no more lastingly successful in religion than in love and it is no accident that the number of viable symbol-systems offered us by the world's philosophies and religions is relatively small.[4] The realism of our symbolism gives it power to survive, as we see whenever a technologically superior culture confronts one in which witchcraft and necromancy still play a central role. From the strengths and weaknesses of our ways of life we learn not only about ourselves but also about the world.

What hampers discussion at this point is the ambiguity of our concept of the world.[5] When our concern is with what it means to be fully human, we cannot rest content with any metaphysical system which sees the physical world as the whole of reality. We have also to know the world as the arena in which some ways of life prove more viable than others. We have to recognize that this "Lebenswelt" allows for the structure of intentions which constitutes a way of life as such. We have to recognize that the precise structure of intentions informing some ways of life differs from that of others. We are all aware of such differences, of course. But too often we simply assume that, because we share the same physical environment, we must share the same intentional nexus of events. We are led to conclude that we occupy the same world, of which only one possible or current view can be the right one. That there are still so many differing world-views has to be explained away wholly in terms of the subjective biases of the viewers.

Differences amongst world-views may be token differences amongst the real worlds in which we actually live. The plurality of faiths may be made possible by the variegated structure of reality. Their differences could perhaps be explained at least as much by differences in the facts as by differences in our feelings about the facts. When we speak of "the world of Plato" or "the world of music," for example, we are not just referring to how Plato felt or to the sentiments of musicians. We have in mind historical, factual differences between these "worlds" and others.

The thought of several worlds is so intolerable in our post-polytheistic age that we are moved to retain the concept of *the* world for the single spatio-temporal situation that we share and to find some other concept for that which empowers us to realize a variety of ways of life. Such a concept is that of God, or Brahman, or Purusha, or the Dharmakaya. In religious life, the reality of God is so basic that it is assumed to be logically and temporally prior to that of man. Thus in the biblical tradition, as Donald Evans reminds us, the initial creative "word" is said to come from God and the subsequent word of man is regarded as a self-committing word in response.[6] Accordingly, the chosen way of life and view of the world is said to be revealed by God to man rather than projected by man onto the blank screen of passing events. The theologically realistic man is called a "muslim" or a submitter to the will of God, who adds nothing to the concept given him of his life.

Unfortunately, theology tends to become dangerously one-sided. Its recent emphasis on the "objective" pole of our relationship in isolation from references to human experiences, for example, has had an effect contrary to that intended. It has made it possible to assert the unreality of the objective pole altogether while trying to retain the basic aims of Christian living. Such a rejection represents an equally one-sided emphasis on the subjective side which we should avoid. In our analyses of religious life we must do justice to the sense of relationship on which this life is based.

Symbolizing the Transcendent Spirit

In order to articulate their sense of this transcendent relationship, religious people use a wide assortment of myths, symbols, allegories, and abstract metaphysical terms. It is important to notice that what is so depicted does not entirely transcend all experience; nor is it reducible to reports of sensations in strictly physical-object language. What is meant is of the order of our own intentions and aspirations, which far outrun the limitations of place and time imposed upon our bodies. What is referred to is the spirit in which we recall the past and reshape the present. This "spirit," according to religious people, is not limited in an ordinary human way. Rather the human religious experience is alleged to be of a source of creativity and strength which meets the human spirit and enables it to overcome its individual limitations. The dialectical progression of thought here is from the relatively less limited achievements of the human mind, as contrasted with the body, to achievements which seem to transcend even the limitations of purely human thought and action.

If I am right about the way in which the concept of divinity functions in our thought, it is a concept of that which is a precondition of our being human, rather than of an extension of our collective humanity. However conceived in detail, it is conceived as having "objective" reality over against our subjectivity (or, if one prefers to avoid the subject-object dichotomy, then as having "inter-" or "trans-subjective" status). We do not directly observe the divine being as we do a physical object, however. It is not nonsensical or proof of our misunderstanding the meaning of words to call in question its objectivity, as it would be to question that of the earth. The divine mode of being is in a quite different category from that of physical objects. It would not be what it is thought to be if its objectivity could be established as that of such an object.

Rather we are led to think of its independent being on the analogy of our establishing our own independence of will against the will of another. (It is, after all, a comparatively recent assumption that such independence need not be established and that different bodies must be motivated by different wills, viz. the Buddha-Nature and the multitude of Buddha-bodies.) We establish and exhibit our independence of will by our independent actions (*not* 'movements'), as in the familiar rebellion of child against parent. So, in biblical thought, whether rightly or wrongly, the independence of "the divine will" is established by contrast with the rebellious wills of God's people. This suggests that we should receive considerable insight from our ordinary talk of human thought and action into what is meant in talk of God.

When analysing the relationships between God and the world, metaphysicians have tended to rely on some version of the "mind-body dualism."[7] But there has always been room for disagreement and suspended judgment concerning particular metaphysical analyses of theological assertions. One need not have completed one's metaphysical system before one can judge whether or nor a particular way of life is viable. At this point I agree with Plantinga against Nielsen in saying that we can expect as little agreement from all philosophers concerning the nature of the divine being as we find among them concerning the status of minds other than our own.[8]

Nielsen rejects this analogy on the grounds that first-order talk of mental acts is conceptually in order regardless of the outcome of second-order analyses of it; whereas first-order religious usage is impossible without some coherent account being given of the reality of God. I think that the analogy does hold.

I submit that our first-order talk of thinking and intending would not be congruent with the conviction, for instance, that our minds are nothing but S-R machines. Given such a conviction, the translation of such first-order talk would be at least as radical as Bultmann's program of "demythologizing." As it is, we may indeed learn how to use the language of prayer and believe that we thereby invoke that which transcends us spiritually, without agreeing as to the nature of the object (or subject) of worship. Such a belief is beside the point only if it can be shown that all possible talk of God is self-refuting.

Nielsen, it seems to me, fails to distinguish sufficiently between religious and theological usage. Moreover, he makes an unwarranted assumption in supposing that questions of meaning and truth can be kept completely separate when the method of verification is being used as the criterion of meaning. In general, he fails to appreciate that metaphysical-theological talk is symbolical, gaining in precision only as it is acted on by individuals, i.e. only in the process of its testing. Nevertheless, he is rightly concerned to seek conceptual clarification of claims concerning the reality of God. As we shall remark below, failure to provide at least the beginnings of an analysis of our major concepts on this topic can only lead to confusion concerning the issues and the manner of their resolution.

If it is to be true to religious insights, language about God must capture something of the spirit in which God is said to have acted toward men. Here the sense of the word 'spirit' is supplied by the Hebraic idiom of the Bible rather than by the context of Greek philosophical systems. Its source is a system of thought less tied to traditional versions of "mind-body dualism" than some philosophers and theologians have realized. Any account of Christian usage must acknowledge this source if it is fairly to convey the sense in which the divine is said to transcend the human and to allow for the freedom and sovereignty traditionally ascribed to divine action. In pointing to this source, I do not at all mean to suggest that if only we attend to Hebraic usage instead of Greek all our metaphysical problems will disappear. But I do think it important for us to remember that the biblical imagery portrays the divine spirit as a creating, directing, moral power in the life of a people rather than as the immutable substance of the schoolmen. How the biblical imagery is used is something that we must consider further when inquiring into the Christian connotations of terms.

THE SYMBOLIC NATURE OF ALL METAPHYSICAL LANGUAGE

Speculation concerning the reality of God and of man's relationship to God in the world is metaphysical. It has to do with the being of God and man, and one's doctrine of being or ontology is a function of one's tacit or avowed metaphysical position. In order to consider the question concerning the reality of God, therefore, we have to look briefly at the status of metaphysical assertions. In particular, we have to appreciate the symbolical nature of such assertions if we are not to misconstrue the status of our theological terms.

Any description of "reality" or "being" as a whole is necessarily symbolic because we can only describe such a whole in terms of its parts. We cannot get outside our skins to appraise our entire situation. We cannot abserve the world *in toto*, but only some of its parts. We assume that some processes within it are typical of all processes, some incidents symbolic of the significance of many incidents. Thus we come to think in terms of preferred analogies concerning the relations of the parts to the whole and to exclude as inappropriate those analogies which conflict with our preferred ones. This is true also for talk of ourselves and of what transcends the physical dimensions of existence. We understand ourselves in terms of some of the major roles we play and we understand our purposes in life by reference to particular patterns of events in history. In all such cases, we not only observe certain features of ourselves and our world but we see these as symbolic of more transcendent relationships. This sense of "seeing ... as ...," coupled with our earlier stress on relationships, is fundamental for any discussion of the possibility of metaphysical thought.[9]

I used the term 'symbol' in this paper for the whole range of verbal images and analogues which may be regarded as significant of the nature of some aspect of reality, such as the "spiritual" side of life, or of the nature of the whole of reality. Strictly speaking, symbols are concrete objects such as a flag or cross which have historic significance for a particular people. In a related sense, certain ideas and images may become symbolic of the aspirations and intentions of a political party or religious community.[10] What is symbolized is the intention to live in certain ways. Thus in accepting the designation Christian, for instance, one embarks upon a specific way of life. At baptism, the sign of the cross is made to symbolize the reality of this intention.

The contrast between concrete symbols and verbal images approximates Tillich's well-known distinction between signs and symbols. Tillich thought in a Platonic way that the latter somehow "participate" in the reality which they symbolize. I would stress rather that symbols are "open-ended" in the sense that they are used to suggest several possibilities in life which have been or may be realized by an individual or group. They are not so much talismans of essences as foci for the continuing intentions of historical communities. Such continuity of spirit, as discerned by the religious leaders, is the key to the unity which undergirds the diversity of religious expressions in particular traditions.

In passing we should notice a further distinction that Tillich was compelled to make between what he called primary and secondary symbols.[11] This distinction corresponds to one we may draw between preferred analogies and analogies that happen to serve the purpose of the moment or, in another idiom, to that between "root" metaphors and ordinary metaphors.[12] What is noteworthy is that a theologian like Tillich would willingly give up secondary symbols which proved unhelpful in debate. To give up any of his primary symbols would have required a basic change in his ontology and theology. This fact tells us much about the structure of religious theories and we shall return to it later.

The symbolical nature of much metaphysical thinking has long been recognized and I shall not labor the point. What has not been so clearly recognized is that we are far from having a metaphysical system which encompasses all our experience. Rather we are in the era of meta-ethics, meta-logic, meta-history and, if you will pardon the jargon, meta-theology. The relevance of this fact is that it forces us to look for different types of justifi-cation for different types of metaphysical thinking. We cannot assume that there is a single problem of analogy for all ontological contexts or that a single solution will serve all occasions equally well. My interest is in solutions that serve the theologian and student of religions.

Theological Assertions

The task of the systematic theologian is traditionally understood to be the explication of the "nature" and "work" of God. To it belong the doctrines of the Trinity and of Creation and Redemption. The function of such doctrines is primarily normative and regulative, having to do with what the Christian says and thinks. This cannot be divorced from what the Christian does, for the core of Christianity is a set of intentions, a will to live in a certain way, which continually reasserts the links between thought and action. There is thus a pragmatic thrust to systematic theology which marks it off from more speculative metaphysical works. While there is a purely metaphysical element lurking in theological assertions which cannot be ignored, there is also the pragmatic element, without which we could not hope to understand a theologian's choice of terms or his willingness to try to mean more than he can literally say in using them. In brief, religion is an affair of the spirit symbolized in word and deed, and the theologian is the censor of the life of the spirit.

I assume that "the life of the spirit" is or should be controlled by certain broad intentions—traditionally, faith, hope and love— and that the important symbols in religion are those which enable us to articulate and refine these intentions. By 'intention' here I generally mean the structure of aims and aspirations informing our lives rather than specific intentions to do this or that. Instead of intentions, we might speak of attitudes or emotions, perhaps, but to me the concept of intentionality, despite our incomplete analyses of it, best suggests the "intersubjective" character of the truly religious spirit.[13]

The familiar difficulties about the preferred analogies or primary symbols of metaphysicians and theologians is that their preferences seem arbitrary and the putative connections with reality highly problematical. To talk of reality in a way applicable to all contexts seems no better than to talk of reality out of all contexts; and this, in Wittgensteinian terms, is to let language "go on holiday." Yet when we move from the level of vague truisms about order in the universe to slightly less general topics, we find little consensus among scholars concerning the status of their key terms. Thus, in the philosophy of science, we have considerable discussion of the status of models and, in the philosophy of religion, much argument about myths and symbols. If we are to advance the discussion, we have to appreciate the different interests served in the different contexts. More especially, we have to show that theological symbols do indeed have a use in thinking about our ways of life.

In order to appreciate the sense in which theological language is symbolical, I find it helpful to compare the theories of scientists about the world with the doctrinal schemes of theologians about God and to point up some parallels between the latter and political thought.[14] I turn briefly to such comparisons and contrasts in the next section. They are especially relevant to our topic because of the lingering positivism still found among critics of the religious use of language.[15]

SOME CONTRASTS WITH SCIENTIFIC ASSERTIONS

Generally speaking, the aim of scientific theorizing is to adduce laws by which to explain regular natural processes. In this context, models are aids to inquiry and their structural correspondences with observed phenomena are their major virtue. These models have symbolic significance for many scientists. By contrast, in religion the concern is with truths to live by and these are elicited by the use of parables and analogues. These provide the symbols for theologians, who formalise and criticise them. They have to do with actions, both ordinary and extra-ordinary, and the aim of thought is to produce policies governing such actions. Policies rather than cosmological laws are the products of theological thinking; actions requiring teleological explanations rather than natural processes are the object of this thinking.[16] In this context, parables and analogues are valued as aids in reaching decisions and help in making wise decisions is what is most prized.[17]

The contrast between the natural sciences and theology is not simply one of methodology. Rather, differences in method are dictated by differences in purpose. In the sciences, we have relatively clearly defined and agreed upon objectives, in view of which we may set aside much data as irrelevant. Here pre-diction and experiment are the order of the day. But in religion, as in politics, even our objectives are in process of definition. True, tradition sets our objectives in a ritualistic sort of way, with much recourse to slogans and ancestral norms.[18] But such ritual is in constant need of renewal and reform. In these con-texts, we need and value symbols which are both vague and evoc-ative—vague so that they allow many interpretations of their significance, and evocative so that they engage the emotions and direct the intentions of whole communities of people. The consequence is that, whereas in the sciences the purposes served by models can generally and in principle be achieved even with the substitution of literal, alternative descriptions of the pro-cesses to be explained, in politics and religion the symbolical uses of terms are irreplaceable.

In one sense, all words are symbols which must be supplied with some context for their precise use. The extent to which a statement is or is not to be taken literally is a matter of degree. However, most contexts are so established by convention that we are scarcely aware of our need of them in talking meaningfully. In the sciences, the conventions governing the uses of key terms are fixed at their introduction into the professional literature.

In politics and religion, meaningfulness still depends upon conventional usage, but now the conventions must take account of situations which are not entirely repeatable. This is because the basic symbols are taken over from previous generations who used them in contexts historically different from our own. Consequently, our canons of meaning in politics and religion must leave room for improvisation in the application of the key terms. The use of these is not literally the same as it was before and any who take them so misunderstand their nature.

Accordingly, in political theory and theology, we have to do less with symbols for precisely describable segments of recurring experiences than with those for the spirit in which we reorganize all experience to help us meet hitherto undescribed situations. We need symbol-systems which are suggestive of how we are to proceed, rather than legislative prose telling us exactly what to do next. At least this is true in our egalitarian age, when every man is to some extent his own improviser and no ward-boss or bishop may tell him what to think. It follows that the aim of political and religious theories is to enable us to go on using our symbols in the right way. Such rightness consists not just in fitting our ideas to how things are or have been, but in imagining how new things may be brought about in civic and religious life.

Consider, by way of example, the intention of being a citizen in a democracy. We have some idea of what good citizenship requires and some illustrations to help us from the past. But the notion includes within it the ideal that the citizens themselves may modify the institutions which they have inherited. Indeed, the value of democracy is diminished if citizens do not participate actively in the processes of government and their further development. Thus what it means to be a good democrat in a certain time and place is not wholly determined by those who train future citizens. The intention to be a good democrat is not wholly translatable into a series of previously specifiable acts. Rather, being a citizen requires one to act and react in concert with other persons. Certainly there has to be institutional stibility if society is not to dissolve in chaos. But political order is not achieved simply by ritual re-enactment of some eternal archetype of political being. There are ritual occasions to remind citizens of their ongoing aspirations and loyalities, but there must also be now policies and programs to realize such aspirations in the present. Any theory of democracy which fails to reckon with these facts will prove inadequate.

Likewise, in "the City of God," what it is to be a member of the covenantal community has to be variously realized and expressed through the ages. The controlling intention here is of a love which cannot be calculated in advance.[19] Thus to be a Christian requires a kind of creativity in the life of every person which is not matched in the relation of the average observer to the findings of modern science. Whether or not it has always succeeded, theology must try to defend its symbols against a constant pressure to conform them to the characteristics of more uniform and less religious terminologies. Thus the Church Fathers, confronted with the psychology of their day, asserted the creative novelty of Christ's historical existence and the unity of his being with the divine spirit. Today we may not accept their assertions or their own choice of terminology. But we must surely recognize that the symbols of their faith were quite different in kind from the formulae of modern scientific theory. Again, any theory of religion which fails to take account of these facts will prove inadequate to its task.

RELIGIOUS LIFE AS THE CONTEXT OF MEANING

The problem of meaning in "religious language" posed by such philosophers as Antony Flew, pertains primarily to the metaphysical implications of theological assertions rather than to the religious uses of language as such. What is called in question finally is the reality of God and this is simply assumed in most religious and theological contexts. Theologians have presupposed the "existence" of God, leaving it to metaphysicians to sort out what kind of existence has been meant. Yet the question is crucial. If the assertion of God's existence turns out to have no basis in fact as well as feeling, if the metaphysical positions assumed in theology have no basis in our experience of the world, then religious commands and theological critiques may all be beside the point. As has often been said, in the absence of fire it is pernicious to yell "Fire!" in a warning tone of voice. Similarly, if one were sure of the unreality of God and the incoherence of all possible conceptions of the divine, it would be mischievous to go on using language in traditional, theistic ways.

My own contention is that religious assertions get their meaning from the context of decisions concerning our priorities and programs in life and that the relationship between God and man must be symbolized accordingly. Since it is the function of theology to scrutinize the faithfulness of religious usage to the ongoing spirit of a way of life, we cannot consider the truth of theological assertions apart from the existential concerns which prompt us to make them. We have to consider questions concerning their meaning and truth by referring these to the declarations of intention that inform our way of life, rather than by construing them as straightforward descriptions of matters of fact. The difference here is in the relation of meaning to fact. For whereas descriptive statements set forth what are now the facts, declarations of intention state rather what may become the facts.

No doubt, when forming particular intentions, we refer to existing matters of fact. Equally important are references to previously formed intentions and possible future actions. If, for example, I intend to catch the morning train to Washington, there must be such a train scheduled. Why I want to catch it will depend on what I want to do in the afternoon, and whether I catch it will depend both on the reliability of the rail service and the firmness of my resolution.

No amount of outside observation will establish the facticity of all these factors. Until I actually catch the train, no observer can be sure that I will really do so. Likewise, in theological parlance (whether that of "realized" or "proleptic" eschatology), whereas the road to Hell may be paved with good intentions, the path to Heaven is lined with solid achievements which can only be contemplated in retrospect. Since no man can "go" to either "place" for another, the achievements of others in religion can only serve as symbols for what we may ourselves achieve. Thus, in the religious context, historical facts are transformed into testimonies of the spirit and explanations of the past are traded in for future expectations, so that questions of meaning and truth have to be resolved in terms of these expectations.

In religion, most "facts" are only adumbrated in the symbolic talk. What is described is not something like the presence or absence of fire in a particular place but the reality or unreality of the divine spirit which is said to enliven our world. When speaking symbolically of such "metaphysical facts," our interest is not in whether the facts are as stated (since this is generally assumed) but in what we propose to do about them.[20] Given that we seek peace and happiness and personal fulfillment, and given that the world is as it is, how shall we go on living in it? Such are the religious questions to which theological answers are directed. They have to do with the style and aim of life rather than with circumscribable matters of fact.

As noted earlier, we decided upon our style of life and the priority of our goals by using parables and analogues. The point of such language is to specify for us the roles entailed by and the policies determinative of a proposed way of life. Our intention to achieve the proposed end-state directs our choice of imagery and serves as our criterion in the adoption of one policy rather than another. For example, the New Testament parables are typically stories drawn from everyday life and formulated to foster the twofold intention of loving God and our fellow-men. The community of this love is what talk of Heaven is all about, as we learn from the parables. To what shall we liken life under God's rule? Who is my neighbor? The parables challenge us to decide the answers for ourselves. Moreover, as the Form Critics have taught us, the earliest parables have but a single prescriptive point to make rather than a series of allegorical descriptions to sustain. Those who understand the parables understand the basic intention of life "on earth as it is in heaven." What is revealed to them is not a set of predictions about future events, but the sort of spirit in which to face whatever the future may bring. Accordingly, it is the manner rather than the matter of our expectations that is of most concern.

The fact that religious usage belongs in a context of decision, however, does not in any way remove the need to justify the particular decisions proposed. For, as Flew has argued with regard to parables and analogues, we may know very well what a parable means and yet question the validity of its suggested conclusion.[21] For instance, we may understand the Parable of the Unjust Judge (Luke 18) and still challenge the assumed analogy between God and the judge (verse 7). While we know human agents well enough to be able to judge their actions or inaction, we do not know the divine nature well enough to be able to tell whether the parable applies or not. How then can we know whether the policy proposed will lead to the desired results?

JUSTIFYING CHRISTIAN USAGE

Flew's challenge reminds us that the justification for the use of a parable depends upon that of the central analogue which it develops. This in turn depends upon the primary symbol which it has been used to explicate. For religious thought concerning the divine is brought into focus by reference to specific symbols of the divine-human relationship. It is these which turn the vague theism mentioned in our first section into the particular religious traditions that we know. By taking certain historic figures or incidents as symbolic of our actual, spiritual situation we become involved in our own particular way of life. Indeed, so dependent is religious thought on such symbols that some begin their accounts of it by dwelling on these entirely. In fact, the process of thought is a dialectical one between "figure" and "ground," never a straightforwardly deductive move, say, from theism to Christianity or *vice versa*. Nevertheless, in justifying our use of particular parables and analogues in a given tradition, we generally fall back on its primary symbols as the touchstone of its distinctive brand of religious experience.

For Christians, the primary symbol of the spirit in which this world is conceived, renewed and judged, is the life of Jesus. Where other traditions have focused on a legal corpus or an enlightened mind, Christians have looked to a particular human life in history. That Jesus is the primary symbol is what is meant by the traditional confession that he is the Christ. It is this confession, moreover, rather than the Bible as such, which we must keep in mind when considering the context of "ordinary" Christian usage. The Bible remains the *locus classicus* for statements of this confession.

At the outset of this paper we noted that the religious use of language is part of one's religion. It is not language about life but part of living. Accordingly, as Donald Evans has shown, the ordinary Christian use of parables and analogues is performative and expressive rather than neutrally descriptive. The Christian does not generally speculate about God's creative work, for instance. Rather he acknowledges God's lordship over nature and sees himself as God's creature. When he calls on God as father he commits himself to living as God's son. When he regards God as judge he puts himself under God's jurisdiction. Of course, others may talk of God's creation in dispassionate, speculative terms. The intention governing Christian usage is confessional and self-involving and it has to be justified through such involvement. Even such descriptive statements as are found in the biblical context are meant to serve some commissive or expressive purpose.[22] To mean what a Christian means by his use of language is to commit oneself to a Christian way of life. What finally has to be justified is the making of such a commitment.

Since it makes a real difference to one's way of life whether or not one gives words their customary Christian connotations, Christians have always been careful to refer their usage to the life of Christ. Thus they have preferred analogies which elucidated the manner of his existence and secondary symbols from it which provided them with a way of life to emulate. Thus they have stressed the analogies of father to son and lord to servant and symbols of Jesus' obedience and freedom for others. The personal analogues have been especially helpful in suggesting that spiritual and moral power is what is meant in talk of the divine (a cardinal point in classical conceptions of the divine "substance").[23]

Moreover, as an outgrowth of the Hebrew tradition and heir to many of its symbols, Christianity modifies these quite radically by referring them to God through Christ. Thus we see the symbol of the Kingdom of God, which formed the attitudes and goals of many Jewish generations, receive new meaning with the identification of Christ as King. What we find in this transition is not a fully developed conception of Christhood from which a doctrine of the Kingdom was deduced, but rather an interaction between concepts of kingship and kingdom modified by reference to what Jesus actually said and did. As the situation of the Church changed, we find Hellenistic Christians replacing the symbol of the Kingdom with that of Eternal Life. At the same time, we know that non-Christian Jews de-emphasized talk of the Kingdom and re-emphasized the Torah as their primary symbol of God's relationship with men.

We learn from such examples how religious thought operates with primary and secondary symbols. We learn how secondary symbols are used to specify the relevance of basic policies for a new age and the conception of what is primarily symbolized is gradually changed. In the period of the Church Fathers, for example, we see how Hellenistic connotations of lordship fostered attribution of divinity to Christ, with ramifications in the liturgy and a heightening of the division between clergy and laity. Generally, we should not classify symbols as either primary or secondary, but recognize that we have to do with a range of symbols, some of which prove more important than others according to the time and theologian involved. As we learn from the example of the Kingdom, we are not bound always to prefer the same symbols and analogies as our fathers in the faith. What is important in religion, once again, is the dominant intention which such symbols enable us to share, not the repetition of the symbols as such.

THE VALIDATION OF CHRISTIAN CLAIMS

If assertions about God are tied to declarations of intention rather than predictions of physical processes, then the validation of these assertions must come from the vindication of those policies. Such vindication rather than verification is all that we can expect from those who assert truth in religion, given the symbolic nature of their assertions. Their vindication, moreover, must come from the lives of those who live by the truths proclaimed. Accordingly, witnessing to historical truth has always been central to Christianity. The lives of the saints are important to it not just for their entertainment or moral value but for their testimony to the feasibility and worth of their chosen ways of life. As witnesses to historic truth, they become part of the truth and not just symbols of eternal verities. In history, at least to some extent, the facts are what we make them. Thus the lives of the saints are among the facts to be accounted for in any theory of religion. In this connection we agree with Marcel in saying, not that Christianity is true, but that it becomes true.[24]

The vindication of intentions by certain actions is a topic which I hope to consider more fully in another paper. It involves us not only in the so-called problem of evil but also in the less familiar problem of the false witness.[25] Briefly, with regard to the former we may note that what is called in question is the wisdom of the policies ascribed to God. The New Testament witness is that the wisdom and power of God are revealed in the mission of Jesus and here is found the conviction of strength and goodness to carry us through the vicissitudes of life. With regard to false witness, the standard is again the witness to the life of Christ. Here we must remember that such a standard is not some external rule or law but the guiding spirit in which men face the boundary situations in this world. Such boundary situations, whether they be the martyrs' meeting of premature death or the theologians' wrestling with the raw edges of human thought and experience, tell us more about the feasibility of the way of life proposed than any number of untried believers attending suburban churches. In short, the quality of witnesses varies tremendously; the witnesses that count are those whom we trust. At this point, the basis of the Christian way of life has always been that of faith.

Whether the life of Christ is really symbolic of some divine life which transcends the human is a question of truth rather than of meaning. One has to have experience of living in terms of such a symbol before one is in a position to judge. Even then, no single moment of experience should serve in the manner of a crucial experiment. In each new situation, rather, we have experiences which may or may not be ordered by reference to our primary symbols. Whether Christ is to remain such a symbol is the ever recurring question in the life of a Christian. Thus, for instance, when we are confronted with the fact of evil, we have to decide anew which event is more symptomatic of God's action or inaction—our present hurt or the pain of the Cross. To remain a Christian, one does not have to be able to make sense of every intolerable situation. But one does have to be able to continue to formulate one's policies in terms of those revealed in Christ (in this case, of achieving victory through suffering rather than of escaping from suffering). Faithfulness is thus a matter of giving his history priority over ours in the quest for meaningful symbols in life.

A primary symbol in religious theory is like a concept of Nature in scientific theory. Generally we touch on it only indirectly as we formulate policies or laws. When articulating these, we use preferred analogies or models which become so central to our thinking that, rather than give them up, we jettison or suspend judgment on any experience which puts their use in doubt. Thus in theology we tend to redefine or "demythologize" our concept of God rather than abandon it entirely. The reality of God is as central to theology as is the order of Nature to the sciences. We give up particular conceptions of these more readily than we relinquish belief in the reality that is symbolized in our conceptual schemes. In scientific research, general laws lead to more specific laws which may be tested by reference to specific phenomena within the world. In theology, by contrast, reflection on the basic symbols leads to policies which govern specific actions expressive of our whole way of life and these policies are justified by reference to a paradigmatic way of life already led in history. Here the difference between "scientific" and "metaphysical" facts is such that to revise our conception of what is true of the latter requires a major change in our whole way of living.

Our argument has been that the Christian choice of parables and analogues is justified by reference to Christ as the primary symbol of the realities they express. It is the task of theology to make systematic sense of what such parables presuppose concerning the relationship between God and men. If we deny the reality of God, of course, we need no longer do theology. But then we need no longer do Christian anthropology and ethics either, for these are intrinsically related to theological assertions concerning creation and redemption. Traditionally, we cannot as Christians separate how we talk of God from how we think of ourselves, any more than we can separate how we think of God from how we articulate our own position in the world. This is the central lesson of Evans' analysis of Christian usage. Its corollary is that to adopt or give up such usage is a matter of conversion or deconversion to or from the faith which regulates it.[26] What justifies such a change is our sharing or no longer sharing the intentions informing the Christian way of life. As we do so, we find that we are led into quite different expectations and practices from those we knew before. The result is that the way in which we interpret our common general observations on life is also quite different. Conversion or deconversion leads to a change in the historical facts in a way that is not matched, for instance, when we revise our opinion of a work of art.[27] Any account of the justification of religious beliefs will have to analyse and further explain these differences.

Sharing the intentionality of a religious symbol-system is not a matter of having mystic or apocalyptic visions. We do not peek behind the clouds to see what formulae may have been programmed into some heavenly computer, as if intentions were little coded previews of what is to come. Rather, sharing intentions is a matter of seeing things as others see them. In Christianity, it is a matter of seeing a particular human life as revelatory of the spirit whose intentions these are thought to be. The more we share such religious intentions, the less able we are to distinguish from the outside between what is revealed and what is invented. What is distinguishable from without is physical rather than spiritual presence. Yet when asked about our intentions, we do not rummage about in our minds to see what "ideas" may be tucked away in there. Rather we declare our intentions and show by our actions that we mean what we say. So, as Christians, we take Jesus to be "the declaration of God's intentions" and regard his actions in history as their revelation. It follows, incidentally, that "the quest for the historical Jesus" is a perennial prerequisite to renewal in theology.[28]

Once again, to share someone's intentions is to approach things in the same spirit as he does. It is not a matter of slavish imitation. Even when the dominant intentions are attributed initially to God, there is still room in religion for developing the meaning that we bring to life. We can and should introduce new symbols in specifying the roles that we should play and the policies that we should adopt. Today, for example, we should perhaps no longer speak of the Kingdom of Heaven but of the Free Society and think impersonally of God as that power which makes true freedom possible rather than as an oriental despot multiplied a thousandfold. No doubt some biblical writers had the latter image in mind in talk of God, but the power that inspires us is rather that suggested by the story of the concerned parent awaiting the return of his prodigal son. When we assess such images, what is important theologically is not the reiteration of biblical phrases but faithfulness to the biblical witness. What constitutes such faithfulness and what language this requires, however, are problems raised for us once more by the Christian atheists. For their suggestion is that divinity itself is a secondary symbol with which we must dispense in this secular age.

CHRISTIAN ATHEISM AND FUTURE CHRISTIAN USAGE

We remarked earlier that the presupposition of Christian usage has been that talk of the divine is as irreducible to talk of the human as is talk of persons to talk of things.[29] This is now challenged, for just as philosophers of science disagree amongst themselves as to whether scientific models correspond to "the way things are" or are nothing but useful devices for generating formulae, so philosophers of religion now disagree as to whether talk of God as personal is true to life or simply an effective way of promoting policies conducive to neighborly love.[30] Since we are not in the position of "ideal observers" who can tell what corresponds to all the facts, we cannot judge between these views with certainty. We simply have to act as if certain beliefs are factual and discover what follows from such action. In the case of theological beliefs, their symbolic content is such that their precise meaning depends partly upon our decisions in a given situation. What it means for me to live as one redeemed by Christ, for instance, depends upon my conception of redemption, my conception of myself, and my willingness to live in the way entailed by my conceptions. Knowing about intentions here is no substitute for action on them, since only in the moment of action are the intentions precisely formed.

In Christianity, we seek to make God's "intentions" our own. We use the word 'God' in this context as the name or conventional term of reference for the "objective" pole of a relationship which is depicted by the whole complex of our parables and analogues. In every religious tradition we find terms such as 'the Tao' and 'Nirvana' which serve such a purpose. They seem to have developed into names from previous analogical or anagogical uses. They signify the major presupposition of a whole way of life, i.e. that pole of the relationship which is regarded as fundamental in thinking of man's highest aspirations. As befits their relational contexts, these terms generally go in pairs—God and Nature, Heaven and Earth, Nirvana and Samsara, Brahman and Atman.

In their developed use, their sense is more abstract than before, but they retain many of their historical connotations for those who use them through the ages. In this fact lies the source of much confusion, for the name means different things to many who yet give it the same liturgical use.

Outside investigators, who fasten on one set of meanings for a given term, are constantly baffled by the resiliency with which a name is used in religion even after many of its connotations have died away or been discredited. Thus atheistic philosophers hark back to the meaning of 'God' for the great theologians such as Augustine, Aquinas, and Calvin.[31] They know better how the name was used than how it may be used in the world today. They are tempted to conclude that it no longer has a "proper" use at all. In the process, however, they tend to gloss over the fact that a word may have a proper use which can be learned, even though we remain unable to give everyone a satisfying analysis of its use.

A person continues to bear his name when not being called and even while changing quite radically from child to adolescent and from adult to ancestor. The reference is to a continuing personal identity even though the one identified means different things to different people. Thus one may seem a hero to his nation but a fraud to his valet. Just who a person is may be more fully revealed, not only on some occasions rather than others, but also to some persons rather than others, depending on their relationship to him and their perspicacity. Nor need we decide which set of characteristics defines the "real" person, since the relevant characteristics may vary according to context. For instance, your eloquence and wit may be of vital interest to me if I am choosing a companion for a long journey, but not if I am going on a retreat and intend to keep my vow of silence. Moreover, as Wittgenstein has taught us, the criteria for the use of a word may change so that no single criterion is always a member of the set. Metaphorically speaking, no single strand runs right through the rope of discourse.[32] This may not be true of the words for strictly defined figures in geometry, for instance, but it does seem true of the names of individuals in history.

In the mythological language of the Bible, God is referred

to as a quasi-historical agent. Certainly in some passages he is portrayed as one person amongst others. However, the Christian tradition has generally precluded thinking of God as one personal being amongst others by insisting that, if God is known anywhere, he must be knowable everywhere. Since we identify persons by reference to physical objects (their bodies), we cannot identify God as such a person. Though particular incidents may be thought to be especially revelatory of his "intentions," the perspective given in revelation leads to acknowledgement of his lordship over all incidents. He cannot be one object among others for this presence or absence is shown in any and every object. In this respect, the word 'God' is like 'the world' in the scope of its reference. Epistemologically speaking, especially in reply to critics like Hepburn, we might even say that the world *is* "God's body."[33] Ontologically speaking, however, God is no more like an individual person than the world is like a solitary thing.

Nevertheless, we may yet continue to regard God as personal rather than impersonal in his mode of being, on the assumption that he is more adequately addressed as personal rather than as impersonal in distinctively religious discourse. Of course, we do not always address God as such. If we mention him at all, for instance, when investigating the orderly processes of nature— and we need not mention him here—then our conception may be of a power which sustains the existing order in being. In the context of the natural sciences, one might refer to such a power quite impersonally or ignore it altogether.

By contrast, in the context of worship, the sense of personal relationship is so strong that even overtly atheistic traditions such as Theravada Buddhism can scarcely suppress the language of "I and Thou" (considering here the actual practice of *puja* rather than what apologists sometimes say of it). In the modern world, personal references to God are still found in most liturgical contexts but in few secular ones. Consequently, part of the issue raised by the Christian atheists is whether the context normative for religion is to be the liturgical or the mundane. Insofar as theological thinking is systematic in a way that religious devotions are not, any such discrepancy between contexts constitutes a problem to be solved. In passing we may note that when a comparable problem was posed by popular polytheism in the Roman world, theologians solved it not by denying the existence of such gods but by demoting them to the status of demons. What was denied was not so much their reality as their common characterizations.

What makes continuing talk of God as personally difficult today is a general uncertainty over metaphysical identifications and a decline in the practice of prayer.[34] In the Bible, God is familiarly identified as "the God of Abraham, Isaac and Jacob," that is, through association with historical figures. In Israel, there were prophets who understood "God's will" and declared it to others. When the voice of prophecy was no longer heard in the land, the people concluded, not that God was dead, but that men were dead. In any case, what counted with them was not the recurrence of visions but the constancy of the covenantal relationship.

When John and Jesus broke the silence, they discerned God's intentions in terms of the coming kingdom and saw their mission as the fulfillment of the covenantal promise. Throughout, the relevant continuity for their way of life was that of the spirit, not the body, though the body of witnesses bore testimony to the activity of the spirit. The criterion of identity was the constancy of intentions—God's and man's—judged to be such by the consensus of the community. This constancy in the structure of intentions on which we premise our understanding of life is more important to religion than the question whether or not to regard God as one being amongst others. It symbolizes the positive thrust of references to God in relation to the world. It is what is meant in differentiating his spirit from ours in the context of covenant-keeping.

Until we consider the contexts supplied by specific ways of life, we can only refer to God and describe him very generally. At such an abstract level, our language is used least literally. Even talk of "divine intentions" and "the spirit" is highly symbolical. We have to abandon the abstraction of metaphysical speculation and look further into the practical situations of primary usage, if we wish to know why we speak of God precisely in one way rather than another. All that we can say generally is that Christians have learned over the centuries to focus their thoughts concerning the spiritual aspects of human living by referring to "God."[35] We cannot even rule out reductionist interpretations of such thought as conceptually confused. The word 'God' is the name for that universal spiritual power which makes Christian living possible. But what the divine nature is like and whether it is as some theologians and metaphysicians have thought it must be are matters of continuing debate amongst religious people. In such a debate, the non-believer is at a real disadvantage, however, because he does not share the ongoing intentions by reference to which what is to count as Christian or non-Christian will be decided. He may understand what Christians mean and might mean by continuing to speak of God, but he will not share their vantage-point in assessing the truth of what they say. This fact may seem unimportant to him; but it becomes important if he used his tests for truth as a way or deciding what kind of meaning is being given to the traditional terminology. Then questions of meaning and truth can no longer be kept in neatly separated compartments.

Whatever the ontological status of the divine spirit may be, we can and do speak in religion of the spirit in which we live our lives. We need symbols in order to evoke that spirit and focus our thought on it. I have tried in this paper to suggest that the reason for this is not so much the mystifying nature of spiritual realities as the importance of creativity and novelty in "spirited" existence. On this view, symbols are not second-best substitutes for some ideal map of the "eternal forms" of things, which can only be viewed when we get to "Heaven." Rather symbols are precisely what is needed to enable each individual to participate as an individual in our distinctively human structures of being.

If I am right in discussing statements of faith in terms of fundamental declarations of intention, then the one presupposition with which theologians cannot dispense is that intentionality is a structure of being in the world and not just the subjective

wishing of our egos. Where others deny this, we need not con-
vert them to calling on the name of God. We should examine
their talk of Freedom or Humanity to see whether it implies,
avowedly or not, some such transcendent reference as is involved in
"God-talk." The assumption is that reality is such as to make
some intentions more feasible than others and that these will
appear in the history of mankind. It is the task of Christians,
amongst others, to declare what these intentions are. In doing so,
some will cling to outmoded mythologies, some will find the traditional analogues powerful and some, like myself, will be more
mystical. My conclusion is that talk of God gives us very little
information outside of the context of commitment.[36] It suggests
that if one lives in the way symbolized, then one will discover for
oneself whether the source of spiritual strength is onself or not.
What it tells us about is life led in a world regarded as the
product of creative activity. It tells us little or nothing about
God "in himself."

If we would still talk of God as personal we must do so
because we continue to be members of a community which sees
itself as founded on the covenantal relationship of life in "Israel."
We shall use the word 'God' as the name for the transcendent
pole of that relationship. If we do so, we must continually distinguish, for ourselves and others, between concepts central to
reflection on our way of life, such as that of spiritual power, and
secondary analogues which no longer serve to articulate our
common intention. On the other hand, those who no longer talk
of God will have to clarify whether or not this is because they
find no such "pole" to be part of their "religious experience" (in
which case, they might still use the name in saying that "God is
dead"). Also, they will have to show how the symbols which we
regard as indicative of divine activity are to be interpreted in
some other way.[37] In any case, we should distinguish between
the reality of God and our conception of God and, if we still believe in God, we should be prepared to point to signs of that
reality in what non-believers have positively to say about their
relation to the world.[38]

Since what is primarily symbolized in religion is a way of

life and only secondarily what is supposed to make such a way of life possible, we may understand how it is that some can seriously call themselves Christians and yet proclaim the death of God. Indeed, among the former pupils of Karl Barth we may detect a move to redress the balance which the master weighted so heavily on the paternalistic side. Even Barth would surely agree that one who uses language concerning God as part of his metaphysics, without letting it affect his ethics at all, might wrongly be thought to be more Christian than one who rejects all talk of God and yet leads an "agapeistic" way of life. In saying this I do not mean to confer "verbal baptism" on my atheistic colleagues (my language is descriptive, not performative!). I do wish to conclude that the real issue is not whether we speak explicitly or traditionally of God but whether we experience, as the basis of our way of life, that which is traditionally referred to as divine "grace."

The difficulty which writers like Barth and Evans evade but with which others like Bultmann and van Buren confront us is that traditional Christian usage is not the idiom of secular modern man. We have tacitly acknowledged this in suggesting the need for new parables and analogues. If we would speak in the accents of our own age at the same time as we would be faithful to the biblical witness, then we have continually to run the risk of losing the Gospel in the process of translation. Indeed, one of the contributions of the Christian atheists is to run this risk for us, thereby enabling us to articulate our own convictions in reply. The dilemma of choosing between the demands of tradition and the need for contemporary expression is not peculiar to Christianity. Nor is it new in the history of Christian thought. What is new, as mentioned before, is the suggestion that the term 'God' be relegated to the status of a secondary symbol which we should do without in our interpretations of the Gospel. My own preference has been to keep the word as a name and to revise our symbolism for that which is so named. In this connection, it is worth recalling that the part of wisdom in religion has always been to recognize that too much knowledge of the divine would overpower our intellects.[39] What must be believed in is that which is necessary for spiritual growth, and no more. What has always been believed by Christians and cannot lightly be ignored is that conditions of such growth are found not only in ourselves but also in the situation in which we find ourselves.

CONCLUSION

In summary, the burden of the philosophers' demand is that Christian talk of God be shown to have an identifiable referent which may be meaningfully described in non-religious terms. My contention has been that the referent really only becomes known through historic witness and theological reflection on what makes human living possible according to a particular tradition. Talk of God is necessarily symbolical and its precise meaning becomes clear to us only as we use it in the context of a specific way of life. Outside of such a context, we cannot tell whether or not the reference truly transcends the human being who talks of God. What is at issue here is an affair of the spirit, a way of adopting policies and going on sharing intentions, which is not subject to scientific testing. Such factual claims and descriptions as we find in the tradition are supplied incidentally by parables and analogues and are very general in nature. What is specified is a way of life, so that in the final analysis religious claims are vindicated only to the extent that a particular religion permeates one's whole existence and enables one to establish valid priorities amongst one's goals. Yet there has always been a "reality-interest" in Hebraic thought, motivated by the fight against idolatry. Without the moral urgency of this fight there would be little difference between the Christian religion and magic. Were there no such difference, we should no longer defend our right to go on talking of God but should rather let it die.

1. This is a completely revised version of a paper on "Language Con-

cerning God," read at the June, 1967, Philosophy Workshop at The Catholic University of America, Washington, D.C. I wish to thank Prof. Kai Nielsen and my father for their criticism of that paper.

2. See e.g. J. A. Martin, Jr., **The New Dialogue Between Philosophy and Theology** (New York: Seabury, 1966), and Malcolm Diamond, "Contemporary Analysis: The Metaphysical Target and the Theological Victim," **Journal of Religion,** XLVII (1967), 210-32.

3. See Kai Nielsen, "On Fixing the Reference Range of 'God,' " **Religious Studies,** II (1966), 13-36.

4. Consider the concept of "reality-interest" developed by H. H. Farmer, e.g. in The World and God (London: Nisbet, 1935), Chap. II.

5. See W. H. Poteat, "Birth, Suicide and the Doctrine of Creation: An Exploration of Analogies," reprinted in **Religion and Understanding, ed.** D. Z. Phillips (New York: Macmillan, 1967), Chap. VI, p. 127-40.

6. In **The Logic of Self-Involvement** (London: SCM Press, 1963), Part II. Part I is based on the work of J. L. Austin posthumously published in **How To Do Things With Words** (Oxford: Clarendon Press, 1962).

7. On which see H. D. Lewis, e.g. in **Philosophy of Religion** (London: English Universities Press, 1965), Chap. XXIV.

8. See **Faith and the Philosophers,** ed. J. Hick (New York: St. Martin's. 1964), pp. 226-27 and 229-31. See also George Mavrodes, "God and Verification," **Canadian Journal of Theology,** X (1964), 187-91, and Kai Nielsen, "God and Verification Again," **Canadian Journal of Theology,** XI (1965), 135-42.

9. See V. C. Aldrich, "The Outsider," in **Religious Experience and Truth,** ed. Sidney Hook (New York: New York Univ. Press, 1961), pp. 27-38; and Virgil C. Aldrich, "Chess Not Without the Queen," **Proceedings and Addresses of the American Philosophical Association,** XXXI (1958), 23-43. For symbols in non-Western traditions and more on "seeing as" see my paper "Parables, Analogues and Symbols," in a forthcoming issue of **Religious Studies.**

10. On religious symbols see especially Clifford Geertz, "Religion as a Cultural System," abridged and reprinted in **Reader in Comparative Religion,** ed. W. A. Lessa and E. Z. Vogt (New York: Harper, 1965), 204-16.

11. See the papers by P. Tillich and W. P. Alston in **Religious Experience and Truth,** Chaps. I and II, esp. p. 8.

12. On analogy see Dorothy Emmet, **The Nature of Metaphysical Thinking** (London: Macmillan, 1945), and on "root metaphors" see S. Pepper, **World Hypotheses** (Berkeley, Calif.: Univ. of Calif. Press, 1942).

13. On intersubjectivity see G. Marcel, **The Mystery of Being,** 2 vols., trans. G. S. Frazer (London: Harvil Press, 1951).

14. On the former see I. T. Ramsey, **Models and Mystery** (London: Oxford Univ. Press, 1964). I prefer to use the terms 'symbol' and 'analogue' rather than 'model' in order to underline the differences between science and theology.

15. On which see J. A. Passmore, "Christianity and Positivism," Review Article, **Australasian Journal of Philosophy,** XXXV (1957), 125-36.

16. For discussion of actions and teleological explanations see R. S. Peters, **The Concept of Motivation** (New York: Humanities Press, 1958),

and Charles Taylor, **The Explanation of Behaviour** (New York: Humanities Press, 1964). Probably neither would be happy with my use of 'action' and 'intention' but they show that the door to such use is not as firmly closed as some suppose.

17. See further my article, "Parables, Analogues and Symbols," **Religious Studies**, IV (1968), 25-36.

18. On ritual in politics see R. N. Bellah, "Civil Religion in America," **Daedalus: Proceedings of the American Academy of Arts and Sciences,** XCVI (1967), 1-21.

19. See the discussion of love by R. W. Sleeper, "On Believing," **Religious Studies**, II (1966), 75-94. The bridge between Sleeper's "relations" and Price's "attitudes" is, I suggest, the concept of intention. Professions of love are not only expressions of feeling but also declarations of intention (as in the wedding ceremony's "Will you love her? . . .").

20. On "metaphysical facts" see F. P. Ferré, **Language, Logic and God** (New York: Harper, 1961), p. 159-61.

21. See **New Essays in Philosophical Theology,** ed. A. G. N. Flew and A. C. MacIntyre (London: SCM Press, 1955), Chap. VIII.

22. See Evans, op. cit. concerning the biblical context, esp. Introduction and pp. 160-65.

23. See Augustine's **Confessions,** ed. Roger Huddleston (New York: Regnery, 1956), Bk. VII.

24. I heard this from him in a lecture; see **The Mystery of Being,** II, 178 ff on "the metaphysical status of hope."

25. On the latter see Karl Barth, **Church Dogmatics** (New York: Scribner, 1958), Vol. 2.2, para. 35.4.

26. See the discussion of evil in this connection by H. D. Aiken, "God and Evil: A Study of Some Relations Between Faith and Morales," pp. 77-97, and Nelson Pike, "God and Evil: A Reconsideration," pp. 116-24, in **Ethics,** LXVIII (1958).

27. On which see J. Wisdom, "Gods," reprinted in **Philosophy and Psycho-analysis** (New York: Philosophical Library, 1953), pp. 149-68.

28. See Van Harvey, **The Historian and the Believer** (New York: Macmillan, 1966).

29. On the latter see P. F. Strawson, **Individuals** (Garden City, N.Y.: Doubleday, 1963), Chap. III.

30. See R. B. Braithwaite, "An Empiricist's View of the Nature of Religious Belief," reprinted with rebuttals and reply in **Christian Ethics and Contemporary Philosophy,** ed. I. T. Ramsey (New York: Macmillan, 1966), Chaps. III and IV.

31. Compare C. B. Martin, **Religious Belief** (Ithica, N.Y.: Cornell Univ. Press, 1959), p. 40-57.

32. See L. Wittgenstein, **Philosophical Investigations,** trans. G. E. M. Anscombe (New York: Macmillan, 1953), and the article on this subject by Roger Albritton, "On Wittgenstein's Use of the Term 'Criterion,' " **Journal of Philosophy,** LVI (1959), 845-57. For application of the rope metaphor to religious discourse see Ninian Smart, **Reasons and Faiths** (London: Routledge & Paul, 1958).

33. See R. W. Hepburn, "From World to God," **Mind,** LXXII (1963),

40-50, and **Christianity and Paradox** (London: Watts, 1958). The Christian does not infer "God" from "World" but rather sees the world as God's creation (cf. Donald Evans, **op. cit.**). We modify "the world" to see it so as we act on our parabolic insights. Hepburn does not tell us how he got "to" the world or what he means by "world."

34. See D. Z. Phillips, **The Concept of Prayer** (New York: Schocken, 1966).

35. On various ways of referring to God, see W. A. Christian, **Meaning and Truth in Religion** (Princeton: Princeton Univ. Press, 1964), Chap. X.

36. On which see also I. T. Ramsey, **Religious Language** (London: SCM Press, 1957).

37. See e.g. Paul van Buren, **The Secular Meaning of the Gospel** (New York: Macmillan, 1963).

38. See Illtyd Trethowan, "In Defense of Theism—A Reply to Kai Nielsen," **Religious Studies**, II (1966), 46.

39. On this see the **Bhagavad Gita** and the discussion of it by R. L. Slater in **Can Christians Learn From Other Religions?** (New York: Seabury, 1963) Chap. II.

Sense and Nonsense in Theological Myths:
An Essay on the Limits of Demythologization

◊

by
R. W. Sleeper

"THE MYTHICAL VIEW of the world must be accepted or rejected in its entirety," says Rudolph Bultmann in his classic essay on the subject.[1] In his own rejection of the first century world-view which he finds in the New Testament, there can be no doubt that he set in motion the train of 'demythologizing' which resulted in the radical theology of the "death of God." "Indeed," writes Altizer, "it should be emphasized that the very word 'myth' indicates a loss of the meaning—or reality—to which myth points . . . The mythical appears as mythical only when the reality to which it refers can no longer be immediately grasped."[2] In the following, I will ask how far 'demythologizing' can go and still be justified by the rationale provided for it by Bultmann. Are there limits to the extent that New Testament religion can dispense with the matrix of myths with which it began? In posing this question, it will be necessary to explore the logical relation of myth to religion. Thus, a large part of what I shall have to say consists merely of logical analysis and has no particular theological significance. In the end, however, my analysis leads to metaphysics, for it is there, if at all, that the theological import of myth may be discerned.

DEMYTHOLOGIZING AND KERYGMA

Baldly stated, Bultmann's purpose in "New Testament and

[381]

Mythology" is to distinguish the "Kerygma" of Christianity from the mythic language and perspective of the authors of the Gospels and Epistles. Only if we are able to make this distinction can we up-grade Christian belief to the point where it can be accepted by modern man. The rationale for demythologizing is simple and straightforward. If the Kerygma is found incredible because of the obsolete mythical view of the world in which it is embedded, then to that extent theology must "undertake the task of stripping the Kerygma from its mythical framework."[3] It is a presupposition of this rationale that the Kerygma itself is true, that it is a proclamation and a message.

It is not, however, entirely clear what sort of thing Bultmann believes the Kerygma to proclaim or what sort of message is embedded in the mythical framework of the New Testament. Moreover, it is not certain just what Bultmann means by the word 'myth.' On the one hand, he speaks of myth as the "use of imagery to express the other worldly in terms of this world."[4] On the other hand, he holds that myth expresses "man's understanding of himself in the world in which he lives."[5] It will be necessary to seek the roots of both of these confusions before we address ourselves to the question of how far the Kerygma can be made intelligible apart from its mythical matrix. I shall examine first the range of reference which Bultmann supplies for the word 'Kerygma' in the hope that some of our doubts as to his meaning can be removed.

It might at first appear that Bultmann's use of the word 'Kerygma' is perfectly consistent with the concise definition which he himself accepts, i.e., ". . . the proclamation of the decisive act of God in Christ."[6] Unfortunately, it is not at all clear whether Bultmann always uses the word as defined or whether he supplies any other consistent meaning based upon the way in which it is used. At least five distinct uses are readily discerned, each of which is sometimes combined with one or more of the others. Thus the Kerygma can (1) describe particular historical events, (2) describe an eschatological event which occurs at every historical moment, (3) describe a present personal encounter, (4) prescribe a way of life in social and/or personal terms, and

(5) be directly performative in accomplishing a change of history and/or of my personal life. Although Bultmann accepts all five of these meanings, he argues that the first should be regarded as subordinate to the others. There is no consistent ranking of the remainder; first one sense appears dominant and then another. It is evidently part of Bultmann's rationale that Kerygma in sense (1) is both less significant and more dangerous[7] than the others. It is less significant because straight historical description fails to reach the transcendent God and is capable only of giving us an historical picture. It is more dangerous because it presents us with the temptation of thinking that the 'Kerygma' might be proved or verified by purely historical facts. Each of the other senses of 'Kerygma' preserves the essential element of paradox, 'skandalon,' or mystery. This element is essential, Bultmann argues, because it is what protects the 'Kerygma' from being interpeted as wholly mythical. "It is precisely its immunity from proof which secures the Christian proclamation against the charge of being mythological."[8]

From this it may be readily concluded that Bultmann views the language of the Kerygma as multi-functional, that the words taken on faith as comprising the Word of God serve not one purpose, but several. Thus the proclamation cannot be grasped by any one method or interpreted by any one principle. Its meaning cannot be merely historical, ethical, or concerned with our existential situation; but it can be a message about all of these at once. The connecting link between the different functions of the language which unites and gives them a common range of reference is the essential element of 'skandalon' in each. The 'skandalon' itself is comprised by the presence of God in history, at a particular point in time, and, subsequently, to every, point in time. It is primarily this latter eschatological feature of the 'Kerygma' that constitutes an offence against philosophy and which requires faith and obedience.[9] The mystery is not that the New Testament gives a sober and factual account of the human life of Jesus, but that this account has reference to what transcends that life. Only by virtue of the reference to what transcends does that life come to have what Bultmann calls "saving efficacy for man."[10] The notion of transcendence, then, plays a central role in Bultmann's understanding of the "Kerygma." It is so central, in fact, that New Testament theology becomes meaningless without it. To reduce that theology to its non-transcendent elements is to reduce it to theological nonsense.[11]

From this it may fairly be concluded that Bultmann's understanding of the Kerygma plays a decisive role in determining his interpretation both of the function of theological myths and of the need for 'demythologizing' theology. It is clear that Bultmann accepts the fact that God's transcendence is originally understood and expressed in essentially mythical terms. Bultmann considers it possible to express that same transcendence in non-mythical language. From these two controlling facts, much of what appears to be confused vacillation between two different conceptions of myth in Bultmann's position may be clarified. From the fact that God's transcendence is originally grasped in terms of Jewish apocalyptic and Gnostic redemption myths,[12] it follows that at least one of the functions of theological myths is to express the grasp of that transcendence. From the fact that the meaning of that transcendence for man is independent of the pre-scientific cosmological concepts implicated in the framework of the myths themselves, it follows that the meaning can be expressed in terms other than those in which it was originally received. The notion of transcendence and its meaning for man is thus presumed by Bultmann to be logically independent though not anthropologically or psychologically independent, of the historical conditions which gave rise to it.

The difficulty or confusion which Bultmann faces arises from the fact he does not clearly distinguish what is logically independent from what is not. Thus, for example, he defines mythical thought as comprising a way of representing the other worldly in terms of this world and the 'divine' in terms of human life. Although this definition serves quite adequately to express his own contention that the purpose of the mythology surrounding the Kerygma is to show (in a revealing way) the transcendent background of the Christ event, it is open to some serious misunderstandings. Both Henderson and Macquarrie have objected to the definition on the ground that it arbitrarily excludes all purely secular myths such as the Nazi myth of the master-race or the Marxist myth of the classical paradise.[13] It is, moreover, a definition which excludes much of the Babylonian cosmology that was presupposed in the New Testament world-picture, and whose remnants Bultmann intends to expunge from the Christian faith. On the premise that the sole function of myth is to express the fact that there is a "transcendent power which controls the world and man,"[14] it is certainly not at all obvious that purely secular myths such as those cited cannot accomplish this. What bothers Bultmann about mythology as such is its tendency to obscure the message of transcendence which it was originally designed to express.

A more serious objection arises from the fact that Bultmann's definition itself is at least partly mythological.[15] On this view, Bultmann is trapped in an inevitable contradiction because the definition is wide enough in scope to include all pictorial, analogical, and symbolical language whatever. This would mean that Bultmann's apparent concession that all talk of acts of God and the like are analogical[16] is tantamount to the admission that theological language is irreducibly mythological. An admission of that sort is in direct contradiction to the enterprise of demythologizing and makes it a logically impossible task. Surely Bultmann's endeavor is not easily reduced to theological nonsense, for if it is correct that the message is logically independent of the specific linguistic and pictorial imagery in which it may happen to be couched—which is Bultmann's main contention—then it is also logically independent of analogy. The objection rests upon the admission which is implicit in Bultmann's definition of mythical thought, that analogy is a species of mythological language. But even if that is admitted, the objection still would fail[17] because there remains the possibility of demythologizing even analogical language—or does there?

Bultmann himself admits that behind the theologian's objection to demythologizing "there lurks the fear if it were carried to its logical conclusion it would make it impossible for us to speak of an act of God, or if we did it would only be the symbolical description of a subjective experience."[18] This is the fear that the 'Kerygma'—the message that worldly happenings are related to transcendent purposes and powers in ways obscure to ordinary observation—may be rejected along with the medium in which that message was historically received.[19] It is the fear that the message is inextricably bound up with the medium, that it is not only historically, anthropologically, and psychologically dependent on the mythology which reveals it, but that it is logically dependent as well. So the question of the logical independence of the notion of transcendence is, indeed, a crucial one. Unless it can be affirmed, the limits of demythologization have been reached; 'Kerygma' and myth stand or fall together.

THE NEW HERMENEUTICS AND PHENOMENOLOGY

Bultman's move at this point is well known. In order to preserve the original meaning of the 'Kerygma,' its truth as an account of a life that has meaning only by virtue of an essential reference to what transcends that life, Bultmann sets himself the task of a 'New Hermeneutic.' Traditionally, heremenutics set forth the interpretation of the Biblical Word by means of the received dogmas of theology as defined by the Church. With the rise of Protestantism, and later with the advent of historical criticism of the Biblical literature, the interpretive principles of hermeneutics underwent a number of changes. In Bultmann's case there are no received dogmas to serve as interpretive principles; hermeneutics must depend solely upon the phenomenology of faith.

Theology is understood as the task of clarifying the content of faith and bringing it to conscious recognition. Thus for Bultmann, hermeneutics, in the form of an existentialist interpretation of the Bible, comprises the whole of theology.[20] In bringing to light the understanding of human existence expressed in the scriptures, we find our own self-understanding transformed. We become more authentic beings. In Bultmann's view, it is axiomatic that a change in our self-understanding of our existence is a change of our existence itself. It is also axiomatic that true self-understanding cannot be achieved apart from the personal encounter with the transcendent and hidden God of the 'Kerygma.' Thus the pheomenology of faith elicits an authentic existence in response "only when Scripture is heard as a word addressed personally to ourselves, as kerygma—i.e. when the experience consists in encounter and response to the address."[21]

The significant fact about this move, which is often mistakenly thought to be a capitulation on Bultmann's part to Heidegger's philosophy, is that it places the key features of the 'Kerygma' in an almost totally different linguistic context from that of Jewish apocalyptic and Babylonian cosmological myths. The notion of transcendence is stripped from its original context and recast in the matrix of existentialist phenomenology. Is this meaning of the notion now the same as it was? If not, it might be objected that we have achieved a new understanding of the 'Kerygma' only at the cost of losing the old and true meaning.

It is a feature of Bultmann's theology that the meaning of the 'Kerygma' is constantly changing. The true meaning cannot be fixed at any particular moment in time, but must continually be re-experienced at every moment.[22] Only when the Word of God is understood as an "address which encounters us ever and again" does it lead to authentic self-understanding. Thus, Bultmann contends not that the Biblical 'Kerygma' is the guarantee of authentic faith, but that authentic faith, as the authentic self-understanding of existence, is the guarantee of the 'Kerygma.' "That Scripture is the Word of God is something which happens only in the here and now of encounter; it is not a fact susceptible to objective proof. The Word of God is hidden in Scripture, just like any other act of his."[23]

No doubt the compressed description which we have given of Bultmann's move to reinstate a theology of transcendence within the matrix of existentialist phenomenology distorts, perhaps to point of caricature, what Bultmann intends to say. The judgment must be left to the reader as to whether any serious injustice has been done. There is something to be said about the thesis which Bultmann seems to have been maintaining all along; i.e. that the notion of transcendence is logically independent of any particular language. Not only is this thesis essential to the task of demythologization, it is equally essential to the reinterpretation of the 'Kerygma' in terms of the new hermeneutic.

THE EXPERIENCE OF TRANSCENDENCE

There remains a crucial question: what of the notion of transcendence itself? What does it mean? If awareness of transcendence marks off the authentic in existence from the inauthentic, what are the signs by which we can recognize that awareness?

Bultmann's contention that "true faith is not demonstrable in relation to its object"[24] is not the question here, for even if it were agreed that there are no objective proofs of God the question would still remain. How can I recognize what Bultmann calls the 'here and now of encounter,' or, as Kieth Gunderson has put it in his commentary on a paper by H. H. Price, "Are there criteria for encountering God?"[25] Bultmann's response is not that there are none, but that we recognize the activity of God when it "vouchsafes to us a new understanding of self." He goes on to cite his agreement with Luther's view of the matter.[26] This new understanding is what, in the end, justifies not only the possibility but the necessity of demythologization. This is not, as William James would want it, a 'justification *of* faith' but, rather, a 'faith *in* justification'; "Security can be found only by abandoning all security, by being ready, as Luther put it, to plunge into the inner darkness."[27]

The response is a familiar one. From Tillich and Maritain to Clarke and Trethowan similar if not identical answers are given: experiences of God are self-authenticating, self-verifying and self-justifying. For Tillich there is no way of getting inside the theological circle unless one is first 'grasped by the power of Being Itself' or, more dramatically, encountered by the 'God above the God of theism.' For Maritain it appeared necessary and not just 'useful' to add a sixth way to the traditional five of St. Thomas. Thus, in *Approaches to God*,[28] he argues from the experience the self-insufficiency of the operations of the human intellect to the experience of their self-sufficient source. Father Clarke, in response to Gunderson's request of criteria, states that there are indeed reliable signs whereby we can be sure that we have been encountered by God. They are found in the experience of being acted upon by another. Like Bultmann, he stresses the gratuitous awareness of being affected.[29] Trethowan's response to a similar challenge by Kai Nielsen is much the same. Stating that he sees no ground for Nielsen's or Flew's contention that the believer is not logically entitled to regard his beliefs as meaningful unless he can make them appear meaningful to an unbeliever, Trethowan argues that the believer who knows his business will insist that his awareness of God is his ground for affirming God—that this is a state of affairs that has distinct empirical content. Moreover, he tries further to determine that content by saying that: "The believer's belief in God does not just rely on certain characteristics of the world itself, which are guaranteed to reveal or imply God's activity. It relies on God himself, because it springs from an awareness of him not as making this or that difference to the world but as being the source or cause of the world. It is insofar as the believer's experience takes him 'outside' the world that he has this awareness." Again: "We are aware of God because we are aware of the world as related to him."[30] Thus, in his own words, Trethowan seconds Bultmann's thesis that the notion of transcendence is logically independent of particular myths; we do not infer it from anything, we are directly made aware of it by experiencing what is transcendent.

Bultmann is not alone in accepting this sort of argument. For those who accept it all statements of faith and theology depend for their meaning upon the possibility of apprehending the transcendent, usually expressed in terms of a personal encounter, in experience. The experience itself, indeed, is said to be religious because of this distinguishing feature. Now the importance of the argument derives not just from the fact that so many of our contemporary theologians have resorted to it as a defense against philosophical skepticism. The argument, as Martin Buber and others have pointed out, has roots in the most important ancient Biblical tradition; that is, the tradition in which God chooses

Abraham and Abraham believes, God acts and man re-acts by turning and trusting.

This tradition speaks of loving God because he first loves us, and of faith as a type of grace granted by God whereby he draws near to men. It is the tradition in which the prayer to God to "help my unbelief" makes sense; it is the tradition in which it is reasonable to speak of faith *(fides)* as the condition of understanding. It is, finally, the tradition of which Karl Rahner speaks when he says, in *Theological Investigations,* that ". . . the actual support given to faith under the grace of the Holy Spirit is not merely ontological modality of the act of faith beyond conscious apprehension, but also a specific effect in consciousness (which is not necessarily to say that it is reflexively distinguishable)."[31]

As a defense of theological meaning against skeptical attack this argument has a certain glaring weakness, for it is precisely because the unbeliever denies that he is possessed, either consciously or unconsciously, of such an experience of encounter with the transcendent that he is an unbeliever. The sincere religious apologist, not wishing to confess the weakness to be fatal to his position, therefore resorts to a variety of gambits in order to win over his skeptical adversary. In doing so he seeks to establish grounds for faith. He does not need these grounds for himself but he thinks they may cônvince the unbeliever that believers are not just talking nonsense when they speak of a God who is transcendent but nevertheless encounters the believer in discernible ways. One effect of this search, an effect which is patently observed in the various ill-fated philosophical proofs of the existence of God, is that God himself is endowed with a status that he does not have in faith; he is given the status of an existing object or of a being.

ANAGOGY VS ANALOGY

Following Martin Buber, we could refer to this reifying tendency of theologians as the 'Hellenization' of our Western Theology.[32] Much of our traditional talk about God is conditioned by the Greek habit of thinking of reality as a hierarchical structure of a more or less static type. In this structure God, the creator, pre-exists at the top and presides in a designing and often despotic, though always benevolent, fashion.

However, it should also be clear, though this may not be beyond question, that this Hellenized theology has always been counter-balanced by a theology which takes the mystical experience of grace as its foundation. The views of Tillich, Clarke, Maritain and Trethowan might be said to constitute a revival of this tradition. Its central theme in the epistemology of faith is empiricist in contrast to the dominating rationalism of Hellenized thought. To distinguish my meaning of religious empiricism, I have space only to identify it briefly by relating it to such men as Plotinus and Augustine, Bonaventure and Meister Eckhardt, Jacob Boehme and Martin Luther, Immanuel Kant and Friedrich Schliermacher. I also associate Bultmann with this list and point out that it is an association which is independent of otherwise important philosophical alliances and differences. Despite Bultmann's apparent lapse into the jargon of analogy,[33] I would stress the fact that each of these thinkers employs both a distinct emphasis on experience as the ground of theological statements and a remarkably consistent theological logic. Reviving an ancient but neglected nomenclature, I call this logic anagogy; I contrast it with the logic of analogy which is employed by their opposite and more rationalistic theological counterparts.

It should be conceded at once that not every theologian is clearly in one camp or the other. Great numbers of theologians— St. Thomas not the least among them—have employed both anagogical and analogical discourse at different times, and it is not easy to know which is which. It is a general feature of the analogists' case that the grounds of theological discourse rest upon certain fairly well defined metaphysical doctrines, among which the idea of necessary cause is perhaps preeminent. That, with the proper qualifications, we are able to justify the truth of a large number of theological predicates is closely allied with the thesis of the rational predicables and with the claim that being is sufficiently rational and intelligible in a uniform distribution. It is a basic presupposition of analogy that the universe would be perfectly intelligible to any rational being such as God, in whom the rational capacity is itself capable of unrestricted development. Man, due to his finitude or fallen state, is deprived of this capacity; in the end, analogy is not enough for the ultimate knowledge required for salvation. So it happens that the logic of analogy, adequate for some purposes, is yet not adequate for all. Even the staunchest defenders of analogy—Cajetan, Penido, Garrigou-Lagrange among them—resort at last to what the mystics hold to all along.

If the logic of analogy needs metaphysical support, it would seem equally to be the case that the logic of anagogy, despite its claim of direct encounter with the transcendent, requires at least some defense by metaphysics, for how else can the charge of psychologism be turned aside? As a first approximation to an answer to these questions we might observe that all those who dismiss the language of the mystics on the ground that it is merely the description of the interiority of the mystic himself and a grand illusion presuppose a metaphysics closed to the transcendent. The proper approach to anagogy, they say, is from the point of view of literary criticism or psychoanalysis, for if there is knowledge conveyed by the reports of the mystics, it will be exclusively (by metaphysical fiat) a knowledge about the discoursing subject himself. In any case, it will not be about the alleged transcendent object—God, the One, Ultimate Reality, Ground of Being, or Wholly Other. These reductive arguments are far from convincing. Not only do they clamp a quite arbitrary lid on the top of experience, they seem to commit the fallacy of taking the part for the whole. It must be admitted that there is a great deal of subjectivity in anagogy: emotion, feeling, concern, and attitude are all genuine and essential parts of what the experience of divine-human encounter contains. But for all its moodiness and obscurity, anagogical discourse strives to present to our minds something about reality that is true, something that is real, perhaps above all else that is true and real. As William James observed, it is characterized in an unmistakable way by its noetic quality. For this reason we can insist that if mysticism tells us only of the soul of the mystic and nothing of the rest of reality, then it is, as Findlay has recently said: ". . . in a deep sense, very false indeed, since it certainly professes to tell us something about it."[34]

EXPERIENCING THE DIVINE

What demands our attention, at this point, is the simple claim of the believer that he has encountered, or been encountered by, either God or whatever (as James put it) he considers to be the divine. What comprises the content of this experience, the nature of the transcendent for example, is a later question to be approached only when we are satisfied that there is indeed a possibility of the experience itself. Here we want to know what it is that might enable us to distinguish such an experience from mere illusion, delusion, hallucination, and the like. In this respect, C. I. Lewis had a good point when he stated that the 'givens' of immediate experience, which he called the awareness of the directly presented, can neither be true nor false. They are what we 'have' in John Dewey's language. Only statements about what the experience is of or about, together with descriptions of the experience itself, can be true or false.

Bultmann's report is, then, that he has seen with the eye of faith an act of God in Christ and that this act recurs in the here and now of encounter. Someone like Tillich would say 'I was grasped by the power of being itself.' Another, like Dom Trethowan, says 'I am aware of God.' These are not reports that we can confirm like checking the accuracy of reports received from scientific laboratories or read in the daily newspaper. In these later cases one can understand, even if he had only the most casual experience of the laboratory and had never visited the scenes the newspaper describes, what it would be like to confirm these reports by actually doing lab work oneself or travelling to the scene of the crime. In the cases of anagogical reportage, however, we may not have the faintest notion of what it would be like to have undergone the experiences alleged to have occurred. So Bultmann[35] and others, such as Bishop Ramsey and D. J. Evans, like to point out that being aware of

God is more like being aware of the presence of another person, with whom we become 'self-involved' as he disclosed himself to us. The well known claim that God loves us as a father loves his children—the paradigm case which Flew challenges by the principle of falsifiability—is clearly an attempt to express the apprehension of God as more like the discovery of the creative power that we find in our relationships with persons than that which we have with the naked and impersonal forces of nature.

Even this language is not immune to criticism. There is no basis for the analogy between the relationship of persons with each other and the relationship persons feel that they have with God if there is no God. Predicates in the personal mood may require as profound a treatment of deanthropomorphization as mythic speech requires of demythologizing. As Ramsey has insisted, such concepts as 'loving father,' as predicates of God, need as much qualification as those which seem free of anthropomorphism like 'Rock of Ages.' Yet the very qualifiers that we add, such as 'infinite,' 'eternal,' 'perfect' and the like, are lacking in the empirical referability which they require if we are to claim for them the lucidity for which we strive. If, as believers like to claim, God is just 'there' in a nearly, but not quite, matter-of-fact way, it is also claimed that he is, like no other matter-of-fact, also transcendent—a predicate that we can attribute to nothing else in quite the same way. If he acts upon us, it is in some wholly unique and unprecedented manner. The mystics themselves, noticing this, give in to the temptation to call their experience wholly ineffable, while expressing them, as Findlay puts it, "so richly and so eloquently as to demonstrate their extraordinary effability."[36]

EMPIRICAL WARRANTS AND RELIGION

At this point we seem to have reached the limits of demythologization. The dilemma of Bultmann and any demythologizer stems from the fact that the reports of the mystics are so often made effable by couching them in the language of myth. On the one hand the truth of Kerygma must not be made logically dependent upon mythic thought and language lest the meaning of transcendence be lost when mythic thought collapses. On the other hand there seems to be no way of expressing the meaning of transcendence except in terms of myths or analogies of which the metaphysical grounds are open to serious question. It is because predicates ascribed to God, such as transcendent, infinite, and eternal, have no non-mythical or empirically established meaning in discourse that skeptics draw the conclusion that believers are only deceiving themselves when they say that God is not only transcendent but acts in history. Such claims, the unbeliever says, 'die the death of a thousand qualifications.' And yet, the claims may live beyond the grave prepared for them by the skeptics, for the way between the horns of the dilemma has already been prepared. It consists in the claim that notions such as transcendence are logically independent of specific myths.

In this move I am not at all suggesting that transcendence is logically independent of any or all linguistic frames of reference, but simply that it is not tied by any logical bonds to any particular myth or body of myths such as that of Jewish apocalyptic or Babylonian cosmology.[37] What I do want to suggest is that the great variety of myths of transcendence, the very diversity of the predicates ascribed to the gods, may partially disclose a coherent center around which they cluster, unifying them in their diversity. Attending to the logic of these myths we may be able to discern the warrant for these predicates which are supplied by the most diverse experiences. I will give a brief explanation of what is both a central characteristic of that logic and the chief empirical warrant for anagogically ascribing predicates to the divine.

Our first step must be very Bultmannian, for it is to concede at once that there is no way of speaking about God which is not at the same time a reference to man. As anthropologists never tire of telling us, myths arise from human needs and refer to human aims. It is for this reason that we are tempted to ascribe to them purely utilitarian meanings. The reports of the mystics are not always or as easily reducible. Though there may indeed be some universal and deep-seated need that finds expression in the believer's claim to be aware of God's presence, it is not obvious just what that need is. Nor would it be thought reasonable to argue from the universality of a need to the reality of what is required to meet that need. Nevertheless, the fact is that reference to a transcendent source of both man and the cosmos, as well as to a transcendent presence of that source to the mystic and to many ordinary believers, unites both anthropological myths of origin and personal reports of mystical experiences. This suggests that transcendence in presence is a common logical denominator of both. I shall accept this as being the case and as the central characteristic of the logic of anagogy.

Take a typical anagogical utterance like 'I am aware of God's presence' and seek its grounds. Clearly remarks like this can and must be readily differentiated from ordinary factual reporting, for it is not like saying "I am aware of this table" or even like "I am aware of Smith's presence in this room." This difference lies in the fact that it will be only the most stubborn solipsist who will fail to grant me the warrant to inferences about the real presence of the table and Smith; it does not take solipsism, however, to withdraw the warrant in the case of the real presence of God even though I claim it as something of which I am aware. Plainly, the logic of God is not the same as that of material objects or persons.

However, it is worth noticing that, in our examples, the logical warrant for ascribing predicates to material objects is not always sufficient to justify ascribing them to persons. In my remark about Smith, I might have meant that "I am aware of Smith's presence in this room although I know perfectly well that he is not here but in Los Angeles." This sort of remark, allowing the substitution of remoteness in time for remoteness in space, is often made in ways that suggest ways of talking about the sacramental presence of Christ in the Eucharist.

I now wish to turn to yet another sort of predicate ascribed to persons.[38] Take a person who says of himself 'I am depressed' and another who says of him 'He is depressed.' The logical warrant for the latter, as Strawson's analysis established, is that both speakers are self-ascribers and other-ascribers. That is, there is a type of predicate which we apply to persons not merely on grounds of the sort of observation that we employ with respect to material objects, but which is unambiguously ascribable both on the basis of observation of another and not on such observation. When we ascribe such states as that of depression to ourselves our position as observers is surely not the same as when we ascribe such states to others. It should be noted, moreover, that there is not only this logical warrant for ascribing such states to others as well as to ourselves; there is an ample empirical warrant as well, though, to be sure, it will be a different sort of evidence (facial expressions, general behavior responses, etc.) than would count in self-ascription. Now one might be ready, after considering a wide range of such cases, to view the remark 'I am aware of God' as logically parallel to 'I am aware of being depressed.' Still the question arises concerning the validity of the believer's claim that this state of awareness is not just self-consciousness but consciousness of another, and the question is crucial to the argument to transcendence.

It is obvious that when a person says 'I am aware of God's presence' we should have not only an ample logical warrant but also a good empirical basis for understanding his remark provided we ourselves are aware of God's presence. That is a Janus-faced argument, however, and can be used by the skeptics to fully as great an advantage as by the believer. There are believers who press on nevertheless and, while admitting that the unbeliever may have no awareness of God's presence at all, still insists that the unbeliever must have some notion of what awareness of God is like. They point out, for example, that a person who has never been struck by the experience of ineffable beauty or excruciating pain has at least some idea of what the experience of these things would be like. They argue that the difference is one of degree and not of kind. But even if it be admitted that cases like ineffable beauty and excruciating pain are acceptable, though limiting, cases of experiences that we can understand although we don't have them ourselves, there are still some formidable obstacles in the way of suggesting that experiences of God are likewise intelligible even to one who lacks them. The presupposition here that at least some experience of beauty and pain is universal among men might readily be granted by an unbeliever while he denies, without contradiction, a similar presupposition in the case of encounters by God or awareness of the transcendent. Moreover, though it may be inspired by some material object or person, beauty may be in the eye of the beholder and not at all logically independent of the awareness of it. Pain, likewise, seems to be something that exists only for an experience—real enough, and yet not real apart from any experience of it.[39]

No doubt it is considerations like these that drive such theologians as Bultmann to speak of the "objects of faith" and the "facts of salvation" as if they are not only immune from proof but also "ascertainable and visable to faith alone."[40] Yet, at the same time, such theologians are reluctant to concede that their talk of God must necessarily seem to be just so much meaningless nonsense apart from faith. Emphasizing on the one hand, that the fruits of salvation are not to be won without the considerable risk of accepting the 'skandalon,' they never tire, on the other hand, of insisting that faith is not just blind acceptance of authority and unreasoning conformity to norms and ideas uncritically embraced in fear and trembling. The sense of ambivalence here is crucial. It compels the theologians to strain against the bounds of the very concepts they employ, to stretch their chosen language to the breaking point—and perhaps beyond. Thus, Bultmann argues that the impossibility of seeing God apart from faith does not imply that God does not exist apart from it. In the same context, though, he suggests that the explanation of unbelief can legitimately be understood only from the standpoint of faith: ". . . unbelief is a token of God's judgment."[41] As if to cushion the impact of such pious smugness, he adds a footnote in which he says: "This does not of course imply that the idea of God is properly inconceivable apart from faith. The idea of God is an expression of man's search for him, a search which motivates all human existence."[42]

What can one make of this? Only, it would seem, that the sole logical ground on which it can be maintained that statements about God are meaningful is that awareness of God is, in some sense at least, universal. But what is this sense? One is made uncomfortable, for example, by Tillich's famous contention that what he calls 'ultimate concern' is universal and present, though often disguised, to all men without exception. One may be equally and rightfully suspicious of Dom Trethowan's claim that all men who are aware of any categorical obligations are, in some dim and indirect way, aware of God's presence who is the origin of those obligations. What causes discomfort about these claims and arouses our suspicions is the thought that this line of argument seems to purchase its invulnerability at too great a cost, for, if the argument is consistently maintained, there must be in the world no hopeless cases of unbelief. What will the unbeliever make of such an admission? It seems an almost unbearably smug and condescending move on the believer's part!

The case of Tillich is an instance. He argues that every person has some concern which he puts ahead of all others; this is called his 'ultimate concern.' However distorted and demonic this concern may be, Tillich thinks that it is, in the end, a concern with God who, by definition, is the object of ultimate concern. There can be, therefore, no unbelievers in Tillich's world. In another mood, Tillich is willing to say that awareness of literally anything is the awareness of the unconditional power of being-itself to transcend non-being, or, in other words, is awareness of God. This seems to be victory by mere definition. It certainly runs the risk of failing to take the unbeliever seriously, of saying to the fool who says in his heart that there is no God, "Thou art a fool indeed and have no right to judge, for in saying that there is no God you are really affirming him without knowing it."

On the other hand—and in this fact I find my own misgivings and suspicions at least partially allayed—there certainly are innumerable cases in which we are aware of something and do not know what it is, or cases in which we are deceived or deceive ourselves about what we are aware of and what encounters us. Feelings, emotions, intuitions that we experience, even our most direct sensations, may not always report accurately what they seem to do.[43] The fact of illusion on which the skeptic likes to base his case is also Janus-faced and can look with favor upon the situation of the believer. The noise that I think is in my head may turn out to be an insect buzzing around my room, an imagined pain may turn out to signal a genuine hurt, the tuft of grass that I see may suddenly take to its heels and hop away for all the world like a rabbit. In like fashion it may be that what I take to be merely the awareness of objects, persons, and values may turn out to be embedded in the larger context of the divine presence. It may be that an inextricable part of becoming aware of them is also my becoming aware of what is transcendent to them and, though I may fail to acknowledge it, of God.

If we credit the reports of the mystics and heed the logic of their anagogy, that is just what happens. For what they say is that beyond all experienced objects and persons there is yet a background of activity by means of which all these are unified. This background is at once one and necessary, beyond contingency, and yet unifying in itself all diverse contingencies. They report that it is present to all things and to all persons while yet transcending them. In a logic strange to analogy Plotinus says: "All there is heaven and earth is heaven, and so are animals, plants and men."[44] And Meister Eckhardt: "Here all blades of grass, wood and stone, all things are one."[45] Even Wittgenstein, who had his own way of arriving at the transcendent one: "The world and life are one."[46]

To credit these reports it is necessary to concede that transcendence is a viable notion apart from this or that mythology, and that there are many linguistic frames in which it can be pictured. That is not to say that it is itself empty of meaning or that the anagogical language in which our expressions of the way in which the transcendent relates to us, to our world, and to all that that is in it tells us nothing that is true. Those who have suggested that it is in no way necessary that religious claims about the transcendent be understood as saying anything true have no doubt thought of the meaning of these claims as inextricable from various bits of obsolete mythology. It will stand to Bultmann's credit that he has shown this not to be the case even though, in his enthusiasm for particular theological contentions, his logical point is sometimes obscured by his rhetoric.

Those who have spoken of their experiences of the transcendent God have not always made their meaning clear. Perhaps the most successful of them have used quite ordinary words to tell us what is so. When Jesus said, "Except a man be born again he cannot see the kingdom of God,"[47] Nicodemus asked "How can a man be born when he is old?"[48] Jesus at first replied with an interpretation, but then said, "We speak that we do know and testify that we have seen."[49]

◇

1. Rudolf Bultmann, "New Testament and Mythology," **Kerygma and Myth**, ed. Hans Bartsch (New York: Harper, 1961), p. 9.

2. Thomas J. J. Altizer, "The Religious Meaning of Myth and Symbol," **Truth, Myth and Symbol**, eds. Thomas J. J. Altizer, W. Beardslee, and J. H. Young (Englewood Cliffs, N.J.: Prentice-Hall, 1962), p. 91.

3. Bultmann, "New Testament and Mythology," p. 3.

4. **Ibid.**, p. 10.

5. **Ibid.**

6. **Ibid.**, p. 13.

7. **Ibid.**, cf. pp. 13 and 118.

8. **Ibid.**, p. 44.

9. **Ibid.**

10. **Ibid.**

11. Bultmann's argument against both Harnack and the 'History of Religions' School" in "New Testament and Mythology," pp. 12-15. turns essentially on this point. It is also easy to see why Bultmann's insistence upon the key role of a reference for 'transcendence' would bring him into sharp opposition to P. Van Buren's **Secular Meaning of the Gospel** (New York: Macmillan, 1963). The case of Harvey Cox's **Secular City** (New York: Macmillan, 1965) is not as easily decided. Since the publication of that book, Cox seems to have moved to a more open position on 'transcendence' than was there implied. Cf. W. R. Comstock, "Theology After the 'Death of God' " in **The Meaning of the Death of God**, ed. B. Murchland (New York: Random House, 1967), passim.

12. Bultmann, "New Testament and Mythology," p. 15.

13. John Macquarrie, **An Existentialist Theology** (New York: Harper, 1965), p. 167. Macquarrie's complaint that Bultmann is "still obsessed with the pseudo-scientific view of a closed universe that was popular half a century ago" (p. 168) is perhaps justified. But this does not mean, as

Macquarrie seems to imply, that modern Christians are not bothered by miracle stories involving the intervention of supernatural forces into the natural order. There seems to be no more openness to miracles in contemporary cosmological theory than there was half a century ago, though there have, indeed, been many other changes.

14. Bultmann, "New Testament and Mythology," p. 11.

15. This objection has been carefully formulated by R. W. Hepburn in "Demythologizing and the Problem of Validity," **New Essays in Philosophical Theology,** eds. A. Flew and A. MacIntyre (New York: Macmillan, 1964), p. 227ff. That it fails as an objection may, hopefully, be seen from my subsequent argument.

16. Bultmann, "Bultmann Replies to His Critics," **Kerygma and Myth,** p. 197.

17. Bultmann tries to avoid the admission by redefining 'mythology' as the representation of "divine activity, whether in nature or in history, as in interference with the course of nature, history, or the life of the soul, a tearing of it asunder—a miracle in fact." (**Ibid.,** p. 197) He contrasts this with analogy which describes the divine activity as hidden from objective observation. While miracles are supposedly objective, their real meaning is said to be observable only to the 'eye of faith.' Inasmuch as Bultmann continues to employ such phrases as 'the eye of faith,' it would seem that his analogical language is at least metaphorical if no longer mythological.

18. Bultmann, "Bultmann Replies to His Critics," p. 196.

19. The contention of Karl Barth is that, at least in the case of the 'Kerygma,' the medium is the message (**pace** McLuhan). This, I take it, is the reason why Barth is so deeply opposed to philosophical theology, for if the message can be received apart from the medium (of the Bible) one might reasonably ask why revelation is necessary at all.

20. Cf. Bultmann's essay, "The Problem of Hermaneutics," in **Essays Philosophical and Theological,** trans. J. C. G. Greig (London: SCM, 1955). The discussion of "Hermeneutic Since Barth," in **New Frontiers in Theology,** eds. J. M. Robinson and J. B. Cobb, Jr. (New York: Harper and Row, 1964), Vol. II, pp. 1-77, is valuable as background for this problem.

21. Bultmann, "Bultmann Replies to His Critics," p. 201.

22. **Ibid.,** p. 207.

23. **Ibid.,** p. 201.

24. **Ibid.**

25. Both papers are printed in **Faith and the Philosophers,** ed. J. Hick (New York: St. Martins, 1964). Cf. also my own discussion of this problem as raised by H. Price, "On Believing," **Religious Studies,** II (1966), 75-93.

26. Bultmann, "Bultmann Replies to His Critics," p. 202.

27. **Ibid.,** p. 211.

28. J. Maritain, **Approaches to God** (New York: Harper, 1954).

29. Father Clarke's paper is also printed in Hick's **Faith and the Philosophers.**

30. Illyd Trethowan, "In Defence of Theism—A Reply to Professor Nielsen," **Religious Studies,** II (1966), 40.

31. Karl Rahner, **Theological Investigations** (Baltimore: Helicon, 1965),

Vol. I, p. 51. As I understand this difficult passage, Rahner is making much the same-point as Bultmann in the following: "It goes without saying that this existential self-understanding (faith) need not be conscious. It permeates and controls imperceptibly all anxiety and resolve . . . It is something which sustains us even in childhood . . . there is an understanding not only of self but also of the object of encounter . . ." (Bultmann, "Bultmann Replies to His Critics," p. 203).

32. Buber's thesis is developed in **Two Types of Faith,** trans. N. P. Goldhawk (New York: Harper, 1951). It is, in somewhat modified form, also the main contention in Leslie Dewart's controversial book, **The Future of Belief** (New York: Herder & Herder, 1966).

33. Bultmann, "Bultmann Replies to His Critics," p. 197ff.

34. J. N. Findlay, "The Logic of Mysticism," **Religious Studies, II** (1967), 148.

35. Bultmann, "Bultmann Replies to His Critics," p. 203.

36. Findlay, "The Logic of Mysticism," p. 146.

37. Nor is it tied in any way (**pace** Bultmann) to any specific system of metaphysics or ontology—not even that of existentialism.

38. In this, as in what follows, I rely heavily on the arguments of Peter Strawson in **Individuals** (Garden City, N.Y.: Doubleday, 1963).

39. Here I might just raise the question as to whether the attempt on the part of many believers to discuss God with unbelievers as if they were talking about beauty in a painting is, on the one hand, based on the assumption that the unbeliever already has an awareness of God but has failed to identify it as such, or whether, on the other hand, it is based upon the hope that the unbeliever can come to an awareness of God that he does not already have by having certain facts of history and nature pointed out to him. Analogical arguments seem, on the whole, to be based on the latter assumption while anagogical discourse seems to presuppose the former. The case of the ontological argument seems to be unique in that it now appears to be predicated on the former and now the latter. Newman's 'illative sense' and Kant's 'moral argument' seem to require both the implicit awareness of the transcendent which needs to be identified and made explicit and the use of references to nature and historical facts as means to that end, even though there is an undeniable moral sense ascribed to these facts.

40. Bultmann, "Bultmann Replies to His Critics," p. 201.

41. **Ibid.**

42. **Ibid.**

43. Sensations, of course, are what they are. The point is that what any given sensation reports is conditional upon, among many other things, the way we interpret it according to habit and imagination.

44. Plontinus, **Ennead V,** Treatise viii, n. 3 and 4.

45. Quoted by J. N. Findlay, "The Logic of Mysticism," 149.

46. **Tractatus Logico-Philosophicus,** 5.621.

47. John 3:3.

48. John 3:4.

49. John 3:11.

INDEX OF NAMES